Technology and Public Management

DI009250

At last, here is a textbook that covers the field of Technology and Public Management in an informative and engaging style. Ever since the National Association of Schools of Public Affairs and Administration required greater infusion of technology into the curriculum, faculty and administrators have struggled with finding the right course materials designed specifically for the public administration environment.

Technology is no longer the sole domain of an information technology office, as it has evolved into a growing set of complex tools that influences every area of government. To be effective, every public manager needs to be actively engaged in technology decisions. This textbook is designed for students of public administration at every level who need to know and understand how technology can be applied in today's public management workplace.

The book explores the latest trends in public management, policy, and technology and focuses on best practices on governance issues. Finally, this book provides real-life examples about the need for policies and procedures to safeguard our technology infrastructure while providing greater openness, participation, and transparency.

Technology and Public Management covers:

- how information system design relates to democratic theory;
- how and where public policy and technology intersect;
- skills and tools that are useful in information management, information technology, and systems dedicated for the effective flow of information within organizations;
- understanding the role of e-government, m-government, and social media in today's society and in public organizations;
- possibilities and challenges associated with technology applications within public organizations;
- how technology can be managed through various governance models;
- the latest technology trends and their potential impact on public administration.

Alan R. Shark is the executive director/CEO of the Public Technology Institute. He also serves as Associate Professor of Practice in the School of Public Affairs and Administration at Rutgers University–Newark, USA. As an author, lecturer, and speaker on technology developments and applications for most of his distinguished career, Dr. Shark's experience both balances and embraces the business, government, education, and technology sectors. He is a Fellow of the National Academy of Public Administration (NAPA), where he is the chair of the Academy's Standing Panel on Technology Leadership. He is also a Fellow of the Radio Club of America (RCA), and Fellow of the American Society for Association Executives (ASAE). He is the recipient of the prestigious National Technology Champion Award from the National Association of State Chief Information Officers. The award is in recognition for his outstanding contributions promoting government performance excellence through sound information technology solutions, policies, and practice. Dr. Shark holds a doctorate in Public Administration from the University of Southern California, USA.

A range of further resources for this book are also available on the companion website: www.publictechbook.com

"There is perhaps no greater area of expertise for governments to grasp than information technology. Alan Sharks' ground breaking book Technology and Public Management is required reading for most government officials and students who want to make a career in government. Shark reviews all the major areas of technology impacting government today as well as the cross-cutting issues of project management, human resources, and privacy and ethics. This is a true IT bible for public sector officials."

Robert D. Atkinson, President of The Information
Technology and Innovation Foundation

"Dr. Shark has compiled the seminal book on technology and public management, and students of public administration at all levels can learn lessons from the multiple case studies and historical background presented. The book provides a valuable tool for practitioners and students in better understanding how public administration and information technology intersect – and offers a one-stop shop for context and application of these two important fields."

Dan G. Blair, President and CEO of the National
Academy of Public Administration

Technology and Public Management

Alan R. Shark

Routledge
Taylor & Francis Group

NEW YORK AND LONDON

First published 2015
by Routledge
711 Third Avenue, New York, NY 10017

and by Routledge
2 Park Square, Milton Park, Abingdon, Oxon OX14 4RN

Routledge is an imprint of the Taylor & Francis Group, an informa business

© 2015 Taylor & Francis

The right of Alan R. Shark to be identified as author of this work has been asserted by him in accordance with sections 77 and 78 of the Copyright, Designs and Patents Act 1988.

All rights reserved. No part of this book may be reprinted or reproduced or utilised in any form or by any electronic, mechanical, or other means, now known or hereafter invented, including photocopying and recording, or in any information storage or retrieval system, without permission in writing from the publishers.

Trademark notice: Product or corporate names may be trademarks or registered trademarks, and are used only for identification and explanation without intent to infringe.

Library of Congress Cataloging-in-Publication Data

1. Public administration—Technological innovations.   2. Internet in public administration.   3. Electronic government information.   I. Title.
   JF1525.A8S53 2015
   352.3'80285—dc23
   2014037277

ISBN: 978-1-138-85265-5 (hbk)
ISBN: 978-1-138-85266-2 (pbk)
ISBN: 978-1-315-72337-2 (ebk)

Typeset in Bembo
by Apex CoVantage, LLC

Contents

Figures

Foreword

"Technology" is a concept with great import. In the 1950s, Isaac Asimov's *I Robot* collection of short stories suggested an increasingly interdependent future between humans and their creations, with substantial moral implications. From the 1970s onward, *Star Wars* reinforced that vision. And concurrent with those movies, the Internet, to which we are linked by any number of high-tech devices, famously "changed everything."

For two decades Alan Shark has been a keen observer of that momentum within the public and nonprofit sectors, and his observations, insights, and thoughtful recommendations in *Technology and Public Management* map out a most promising future. Governments and their nonprofit partners are very much dependent on a broad range of technologies, and as citizens we are all dependent on those organizations. Our collective purposes—security, education, public health and personal health care, transit and transportation, culture and commerce, etc.—are very much a function of the capacities of our public services to improve the quality of our private lives. We have been inventing and refining those relationships for millennia, and perhaps the skepticism—or declining trust—that government has encountered in the last fifty years is a crisis that can best be addressed by promising technologies applied to the dozen or so critical issues and areas that Shark highlights.

As Shark argues, the public sector has been starved for technological resources. This text will equip students with the critical insights and management skills to argue for such investments as necessary priorities for our public organizations, as essential to making much better use of public resources and improving all public services at much higher growth rates. Shark also sets out a vision as to how new technologies can empower both citizens and their public agents in terms of e-government, m-government, and future, yet unimagined, technologies. As a society we have learned that transparency is critical to public trust and that all data is eventually public data, and Shark addresses the opportunities and conundrums inherent in the relationship between data, privacy, and personal rights.

Shark addresses technology's issues with the clarity that we expect in a textbook. Many authors writing about technology are guilty of too much arcane language, too many acronyms, and too many assumptions as to the expertise of their intended audience. But Shark has not written this textbook as a "techie" addressing others in a narrowly defined community. Rather, his language is explicit rather than arcane, his examples are presented at a level that is salient to both managers and policy makers, and his overall presentation is frank and engaging.

This text is not simply a schematic for applying technology, but implicitly an argument for doubling or tripling government's investments in technology as opportunities for high payoffs, as the means to improving the delivery of necessary services to all segments of our citizenry. The nonprofit community needs to attend to the same issues as does government, and Shark addresses those concerns just as well as he does government's technological responsibilities and opportunities.

Shark modestly frames this text as intended for students of public and nonprofit management. But it would be just as valuable as a text for MBA, social work, education, and other degree programs that produce graduates who will work with and within those organizations that deliver public services.

Marc Holzer, Ph.D.
Dean and Distinguished Board of Governors
Professor of Public Affairs and Administration
Rutgers University-Newark, USA

Preface

It used to be that a subject focused textbook could be expected to provide a rather comprehensive treatment of the subject matter within its covers; however, the subject of government and information technology is in a state of constant flux. Indeed, all fifteen chapters of this book are changing faster than the ink can dry on any given page. And it is not only the pace of change it is also the speed of change that makes this book all the more challenging.

The aim of this book is to inform, engage, and direct students to various digital destinations for more information and to stimulate thinking towards research and, perhaps, employment opportunities. So, this text is designed to be more like the beginning of a journey leading to further exploration and inquiry as opposed to serving as a final destination. Consider each chapter as a lecture begging for questions, discussion, collaboration, and further research.

Recognizing the fast-moving changes in the government information technology environment, I have created a way for students and faculty to stay on top of things with the creation of www.publictechbook.com. This companion website includes subject tabs that correspond to each of the book's fifteen chapters, and will be updated with new sources—books, reports, and websites worth visiting. The site also provides for a discussion board where the community of interest can share in their ideas, sources, research, and other publications that might be useful.

In today's world it would be unimaginable for a student of public administration *not* to have at least a basic understanding of the role technology plays in governing. Many schools of public policy and administration are now providing related stand-alone courses, incorporating technology and public administration throughout the entire curriculum. Though I have taught a masters level course entitled "Technology and Public Administration" in both synchronous and asynchronous environments for more than twelve semesters, it's been a struggle to find any one textbook that could provide a reasonably contemporary overview. This textbook is based on more than nineteen years of lectures plus over 500 presentations, keynotes, and panel discussions on information technology that may help explain why this book may be viewed differently than more traditional textbooks. It is also based on information gathered over the past two decades, working directly with hundreds of government employees and technology executives.

One of the great casualties in the new digital age is the seeming loss of public trust and privacy. Today, open government initiatives are trying to address the issue of trust through providing greater opportunities for citizen participation, transparency, and the improved delivery of services—all through enhanced technology.

Each branch of government has found itself trying to stay ahead of all the technological change. The Commissioner of the IRS, speaking before a Congressional committee, likened their information technology systems to that of an old Model T Ford car. On the judicial side, the US Supreme Court entered the digital age by a 9–0 decision (that in itself is newsworthy) where the Court decided that cell phones cannot be searched without a proper warrant. In Europe, the European Union requires companies like Google to allow citizens to actually delete data and information that Google normally might save forever. So on one hand governments are trying to keep up with systems that they use to provide critical services, safeguarding citizen information, and ensuring our nation's infrastructure is protected against attacks. However, governments also struggle with maintaining the balance between privacy and security.

For those who have an inherent mistrust of technology, your healthy skepticism is welcomed and you are not alone as we must always remember that technology in all its forms is nothing but a set of sophisticated tools. Being aware of the pros and cons of technology and applying critical thinking to how it is applied is always required—especially when it involves public management and maintaining the public trust.

Forgiveness is requested—as I'm sure I will be made aware of resources that should have been included. As I come across such obvious or hidden treasures, I will be sure to include them in the next updated version as well as add them to the companion website. Meanwhile, I hope you find this resource helpful in your exploration of public technology in government today and tomorrow.

Dr. Alan R. Shark
July 2014
Alexandria, VA

Acknowledgments

Books of this scope are years in the making well before one begins the actual writing process, thus many people along the way deserve recognition for their direct and indirect contributions to the development of this text. First and foremost I must recognize Kyle Psaty who played a significant role in researching and helping with the writing of some of the chapters. Without Kyle's assistance this project would have taken much longer to complete. Kyle has been writing about technology, with a focus on new products, emerging markets, and best practices. He was the founding editor-in-chief of *BostInno*, an award-winning publication, a New England regional web publication covering new technologies and startups impacting both the public and private sectors.

Kyle is an active member of the technology and startup communities in both Boston, Mass., and Rochester, NY and regularly hosts events to catalyze those economies and to educate young entrepreneurs on technology product development best practices. Today, Kyle works as a senior product marketer for Brand Networks, a technology company providing software solutions that help Fortune 100 companies reach their customers and prospects on social channels and the open web. A great thank you to Andrew Rice and Katrina Busch of Roberts Communications in Rochester for their help and expertise with this book project.

I must also recognize Dr. Marc Holzer, Dean of Rutgers University School for Public Policy and Administration who was instrumental in encouraging me to teach and work on many technology-related studies and projects, and has been a great mentor and friend. I also need to recognize the help of Rutgers doctoral student, Yueping Zheng who provided some background research.

My profound gratitude to Sally Hoffmaster, who painstakingly took the initial raw copy and converted it into a readable format, recreated some of the illustrations, added new ones, and checked each insertion along the way. Perfectionist that she is, she couldn't help but edit text when she saw the need and opportunity.

I also have to acknowledge my spouse, Nancy, for her unwavering support and understanding in having to put up with my crazy hours and, sometimes, grumpy disposition while in the midst of this project.

Thanks also to the Public Technology Institute Board of Directors, and in particular to the Chairman, Honorable Brian O'Neill, for their encouragement and understanding. PTI staff members Dale Bowen and Emily Gaines were forever patient, supportive and a great help too.

Finally thanks to Harry Briggs for his interest and encouragement well before M.E. Sharpe, was purchased by Taylor and Francis. For that matters, I am grateful to the entire publishing team at Taylor and Francis for their professionalism, understanding, and enthusiastic support for the project.

1 Contemporary Trends in Public Administration and Technology

Technology can mean many things to different people. It is a process of inquiry; it involves methods, often science, often machines, and usually one way or another—computers. Many equate technology as a set of tools that serve us in everyday life, the work environment, and most certainly all levels of government. In the 21st century, it is inconceivable for anyone studying public management not to have a healthy appreciation and understanding of the role technology currently plays and will play in the future. This is especially true as public managers consider the collecting, storing, and indexing of information, vital records, pictures, video, and maps that lead to the analysis of reports, studies, and the newly forming fields of big data and predictive analytics required for improved data-based decision-making.

Technology tools in public management are essential to service delivery—both internal requirements as well as external efficiencies. Just as auto mechanics would find it impossible to work on a car without a good set of tools, public managers are facing similar challenges in today's contemporary office and mobile field environment, and they must also possess a mastery of modern tools. While a car mechanic must possess the skills needed to use wrenches and drivers, they now need to know even more about sophisticated onboard computers and sensors. Similarly, public managers must be able to look up records and forms, many still located in file cabinets, but they also need to know about hardware and software programs and systems in order to meet their public mission. As importantly, they also need to keep up to date on the latest technologies along with an appreciation of what they can do, how they are applied, and how they are aligned with the agency or department goals. Finally there is an ongoing challenge to ensure that any technology used is therefore, deployed for the right reason and cost-justified.

Public managers have the added challenge of staying on top of their specialty as well as keeping up on the tools and the rules governing them, which are constantly changing. In the past, technology was often left to an information technology (IT) or management information systems (MIS) department. Today, public managers can no longer rely entirely on someone else to

Figure 1.1 Three young women at work in an office circa 1930
Source: Library of Congress #LC-USZ62-111333

be the go-to-technology person. So not only is technology changing, so too is the way technology is governed.

With modern technological tools we can perform tasks faster, easier, more effectively, efficiently, and almost always—*if* carried out correctly—with less overall cost. The federal government spends approximately eighty billion annually on technology (Welsh 2013), and that number does not count defense or national security expenditures. State and local governments spend a combined $60+ billion dollars per year (Nunziata 2010). Governments at all levels play a significant role in using technology and, at the same time, perform a leading role in research and development aimed at improving it.

> The federal government spends approximately eighty billion annually on technology, and that number does not count defense or national security expenditures. State and local governments spend a combined $60+ billion dollars per year.

Any discussion about technology and government must also include the role of private enterprise. Companies such as IBM, Microsoft, Google, Apple, and Amazon, Lockheed Martin, Textron, and Xerox all invest heavily in developing government technology solutions. There is hardly a technology company that does not sell to at least one level of government. Furthermore, there are thousands of companies that are directly and indirectly employed by government agencies, often as subcontractors, which depend on the private sector to assist in carrying out their public missions. Such companies either contract out work for special projects or simply supplement government staff.

This text is about public management and information technology—how technology and public policy often intersect at nearly every turn. Public mangers may find themselves working with the private sector in various roles as to the procurement of technology services, managing government contracts or contractors, or perhaps developing the rationale as to how technology programs should be regulated or possibly funded through grants or contracts. Public managers, many of whom may never have studied the growth and use of technology, may find themselves developing new rules and regulations that govern technology. Those in the nonprofit management field will need to understand and manage technology as a means of survival as these organizations are forced to do more with less, which is especially true when economic conditions and behaviors have sifted and resources have become scarcer than ever before.

Technology and Science

The terms science and technology are often used interchangeably; however, in practice they are both as complementary as they are different. Science is usually associated with knowledge and the active quest for inquiry into various subject areas. Most noticeably science focuses on the study of biology, microbiology, chemistry, physics, psychology, and astronomy as a few solid examples. Technology is more likened to applied science where the focus is on outcomes based on science. Science focuses on the pursuit of knowledge and analysis, where a scientist would be more interested in creating and/ or proving theories. Science has a passion for explaining something, while technology usually aims towards creating or developing a useful purpose for something. As science may be the guiding force behind the advances in wind and solar energy, technology builds upon the science with actual adaptations for everyday use. Both science and technology are somewhat different yet inseparable. Science is the foundation of technology, as it drives innovation and new possibilities that wind up as technological advances.

The federal government plays a leading role in both science and technology supporting over 300 federal laboratories and centers. Mostly housed in the US Department of Energy, there are twenty-one labs and technology centers. The US Department of Homeland Security maintains no less than eight Homeland Security Centers and Labs including the National Urban Security Technology Laboratory. Every federal agency supports some form of technology information program. For example, the Environmental

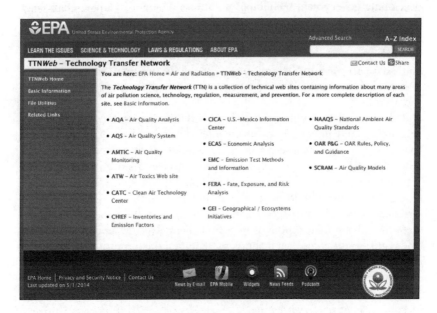

Figure 1.2 United States Environmental Protection Agency

Source: Environmental Protection Agency website

Protection Agency has many IT programs such as the "Technology Transfer Network." For more information see the Environmental Protection Agency website. Every department or agency has many hundreds of employees in charge of technology in all its forms and applications.

In an attempt to help keep information and coordination flowing between such massive undertakings, the Federal Laboratory Consortium (FLC) was created in 1974. The FLC is chartered by the Federal Technology Transfer Act of 1986 designed to promote and strengthen technology transfer nationwide. The mission of the FLC is to add value to the federal agencies, laboratories, and their partners to accomplish the rapid integration of research and development resources within the mainstream of the US economy. Aside from its stated goals many critics have weighed in stating the FLC has for various reasons not lived up to its mission. Most who study government have not even heard of the FLC. See the Federal Laboratory Consortium website for more information.

When considering the use of technology in government one cannot ignore the impact of the US military. The largest agency known for its technology advancement is the Defense Advanced Research Projects Agency (DARPA). Their stated mission is "Creating & Preventing Strategic Surprise." DARPA was established in 1958 with the goal of preventing strategic surprises from negatively impacting US national security and create strategic surprise for US adversaries by maintaining the technological superiority of the US military. The term *surprise* might sound somewhat unusual but the US was completely taken by surprise when the Russians launched a basketball-sized satellite called Sputnik in 1957 that flew over the United States. Having a satellite orbiting the Earth and over the US was a surprise and caused great concern among its citizens and, of course, the military. Thus was the compelling reason to create DARPA. See the Defense Advanced Research Projects Agency website for more information.

The Army maintains many technology labs of its own as does the Navy and Air Force. The military and its vast network of defense contractors have achieved many notable advances that have found their way into the civilian mainstream; an indirect benefit to military research and development.

The federal government has many levers it can pull and tools it can deploy to further technology advances that better serve the public good. The following is a list of methods that the government uses in one form or another and which encourage the use of technology adoption and are carried out in some form or fashion in just about every federal agency and commission.

Main Consumer and User

We know that the federal government spends over eighty billion a year throughout all its civilian agencies, commissions, and institutions. Similarly, state governments spend over sixty billion dollars a year in technology systems and infrastructure. Some applications are rather unique such as maintaining a safe and reliable air traffic control or a weather monitoring system. The Federal Bureau of Investigation requires many centralized databases such as fingerprint storage and retrieval, crime profiles, etc. States have the unique responsibility of maintaining driver license systems that keep track of licensed drivers, license plates, and must be accessible to law enforcement authorities throughout the state. Another example is the Veterans Administration that claims to have one of the finest online health record systems in the world. Cities maintain birth records, geographic information systems, and transportation systems that all depend on technology systems. At the heart of every agency one will always find some form of computer system, and hopefully, people trained to use it. To sum up, even the smallest local government units have no less than 200 lines of business, and each application is dependent on one or more technology systems.

Prime Promoter

(Think car safety information systems, like back-up beepers and cameras, accident avoidance systems online banking and commerce transactions, paying federal taxes online, etc.) Governments have the political and administrative capacity to promote certain technologies that support special policies, behaviors, and adoption. For example, it is not uncommon to find government agencies promoting technologies aimed at safety such as rear-view cameras or accident avoidance systems. Other examples include outbound emergency call alerts to cellular devices, or the ability for customers to use wireless devices to report crimes or suspicious activities. In the case of car safety, the federal government mandates special high-tech safety systems to be installed in every new car sold.

Agencies routinely promote the use of online services wherever they can to drive more citizens towards online transactions as opposed to having them personally travel to and appear at a government office, thus wasting time and money filling out and mailing paper forms. The federal government has taken the lead in both promoting and requiring telework programs and policies using the latest technologies as a means of achieving greater flexibility in managing the federal workforce.

Collector of Data and Statistics

The federal government spends a lot of time and resources collecting data and turning it around into key statistical measures for business, education, and public consumption. The most popular statistical service is that administered by the US Census Bureau. Mandated by the US Constitution, census data is used to determine the distribution of Congressional seats to states and used to apportion seats in the US House of Representatives. Census data is also used to define legislature districts, school district assignment areas, and other important functional areas of government.

The Census Department is but one agency that collects data distributes statistics. The Labor Department issues employment data, the National Oceanic and Atmospheric Administration, better known as the US Weather Service, issues weather forecasts—both current and extended. This data is invaluable to all forms of business; including aviation, maritime, and surface transportation. The US Agriculture Department keeps statistics on crop yields, commodities and market pricing indicators, local and world trends, and more. Crime is reported by the Federal Bureau of Investigation (FBI) and the Centers for Disease Control reports on health statistics. There

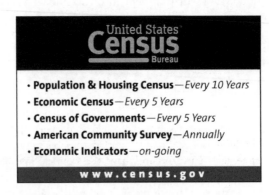

Figure 1.3 Census Bureau data collection cycles

Source: Census Bureau website

are of course many more agencies that collect and disseminate data. The point here is that information technology systems and management play a key role in collecting, analyzing, and disseminating both data and statistics.

More recently the federal government created Data.gov for the sole purpose of releasing government information from among all its agencies to the public. For more information see Data.gov.

Department of Veterans Affairs	Cabinet
• National Center for Health Statistics	Centers for Disease Control and Prevention
• Agricultural Research Service	Dept of Agriculture
• Economic Research Service	Dept of Agriculture
• Food and Nutrition Service	Dept of Agriculture
• Foreign Agricultural Service	Dept of Agriculture
• Forest Service	Dept of Agriculture
• National Agricultural Statistics Service	Dept of Agriculture
• Natural Resources Conservation Service	Dept of Agriculture
• Bureau of Economic Analysis	Dept of Commerce
• Census Bureau	Dept of Commerce
• Economics and Statistics Administration	Dept of Commerce
• International Trade Administration	Dept of Commerce
• National Oceanic and Atmospheric Administration	Dept of Commerce
• Army Corps of Engineers	Dept of Defense
• Defense Manpower Data Center, Statistical Information Analysis Division	Dept of Defense
• National Center for Education Statistics	Dept of Education
• National Institute on Disability and Rehabilitation Research	Dept of Education
• National Center for Education Evaluation and Regional Assistance	Dept of Education Institute of Education Sciences
• Energy Information Administration	Dept of Energy
• Office of Health, Safety, and Security	Dept of Energy
• Administration for Children and Families	Dept of Health and Human Services
• Administration on Aging	Dept of Health and Human Services
• Agency for Healthcare Research and Quality	Dept of Health and Human Services

Figure 1.4 Federal agencies with statistical responsibilities

Source: FEDSTATS website

• Agency for Toxic Substances and Disease Registry	Dept of Health and Human Services
• Centers for Medicare and Medicaid Services	Dept of Health and Human Services
• Health Resources and Services Administration	Dept of Health and Human Services
• Indian Health Service	Dept of Health and Human Services
• Bureau of Customs and Border Protection	Dept of Homeland Security
• Federal Emergency Management Agency	Dept of Homeland Security
• Office of Immigration Statistics	Dept of Homeland Security
• Office of Federal Housing Enterprise Oversight	Dept of Housing and Urban Development
• Bureau of Reclamation	Dept of Interior
• Fish and Wildlife Service	Dept of Interior
• Minerals Management Service	Dept of Interior
• National Park Service	Dept of Interior
• Bureau of Justice Statistics	Dept of Justice
• Bureau of Prisons	Dept of Justice
• Drug Enforcement Administration	Dept of Justice
• Federal Bureau of Investigation	Dept of Justice
• Bureau of Labor Statistics	Dept of Labor
• Employment and Training Administration	Dept of Labor
• Employment Standards Administration	Dept of Labor
• Mine Safety and Health Administration	Dept of Labor
• Occupational Safety and Health Administration	Dept of Labor
• Federal Aviation Administration	Dept of Transportation
• Federal Highway Administration	Dept of Transportation
• Federal Motor Carrier Safety Administration	Dept of Transportation
• Federal Railroad Administration	Dept of Transportation
• Federal Transit Administration	Dept of Transportation
• Maritime Administration	Dept of Transportation
• National Highway Traffic Safety Administration	Dept of Transportation
• Bureau of Transportation Statistics	Dept of Transportation Research and Innovative Technology Administration

Figure 1.4 (Continued)

• Agency for International Development	Independent agency
• Broadcasting Board of Governors	Independent agency
• Consumer Product Safety Commission	Independent agency
• Environmental Protection Agency	Independent agency
• Equal Employment Opportunity Commission	Independent agency
• Institute of Museum and Library Services	Independent agency
• National Aeronautics and Space Administration	Independent agency
• Interagency Forum on Child and Family Statistics	Interagency forum
• National Cancer Institute	National Institutes of Health
• National Center for Complementary and Alternative Medicine	National Institutes of Health
• National Eye Institute	National Institutes of Health
• National Heart, Lung, and Blood Institute	National Institutes of Health
• National Institute of Allergy and Infectious Disease	National Institutes of Health
• National Institute of Arthritis and Musculoskeletal and Skin Disease	National Institutes of Health
• National Institute of Biomedical Imaging and Bioengineering	National Institutes of Health
• National Institute of Child Health and Human Development	National Institutes of Health
• National Institute of Dental and Craniofacial Research	National Institutes of Health
• National Institute of Diabetes and Digestive and Kidney Diseases	National Institutes of Health
• National Institute of Mental Health	National Institutes of Health
• National Institute on Aging	National Institutes of Health
• National Institute on Alcohol Abuse and Alcoholism	National Institutes of Health
• National Institute on Deafness and Other Communication Disorders	National Institutes of Health
• National Institute on Drug Abuse	National Institutes of Health
• National Institutes of Health, Office of the Director	National Institutes of Health
• National Marine Fisheries Service	National Oceanic and Atmospheric Administration
• National Science Foundation, Science Resources Statistics	National Science Foundation

Figure 1.4 (Continued)

Applied Research, Sponsorship, and Funding (NASA, NSF)

Every federal agency sponsors and supports some form of research that encourages the scientific method as well as the experimentation into the appropriate use of technology. The federal government maintains dozens of its own research institutions and supports hundreds of special programs throughout the US. Subject areas include: education, agriculture, telecommunications, health care systems, public safety, transportation, aviation, law enforcement, and space exploration, to name just a few. The National Science Foundation, while focused mainly in science, also has programs that fund action research projects in applied technologies. Of course the National Aeronautical Space Administration sponsors applied research in technology. These are but two examples, there are many more that can be found in just about every federal agency.

Grants and Contracts (To Companies, Research Universities, and Nonprofit Institutions)

Many agencies support competitive grant and contract programs that are aimed at encouraging the use of, and implementation of, technological tools methods, and systems. Grants and contracts are usually developed with a specific goal in mind allowing the institutions to develop the best solutions. While some federal agencies maintain their own staff capabilities, most turn to the private or nonprofit sectors to perform the actual research or work through grants and contracts.

Tax Treatments (Incentives)

Congress provides special tax treatments and incentives to companies as a means of further stimulating innovation with the goal of bringing certain technologies to the commercial marketplace. One example of this is the call for greater energy efficiencies found in solar and wind power as well as other alternative energy systems. Another example is the encouragement to further develop alternative energy technologies and/or transportation systems. Without tax incentives or direct payments for research and development many new technologies may never be able to come to market as the expense and risk is too great for any one company.

Legislation (Policies and Regulatory Environment, "Rules of the Road")

Congress routinely passes legislative acts that outline policies, regulations, and rules for technology. Examples include the use of safety features in cars, the allocation of radio magnetic spectrum for cell phones and other mobile devices, or the limits on government's ability to eavesdrop on citizens.

Legislative action may be enacted in order to protect intellectual property rights and patents, as well as shielding certain companies from certain legal liabilities. Some companies or even other governmental bodies may receive federal support for a particular technology or service using technology—such as a state government agency that processes unemployment benefits and Medicaid payments.

Regulation (HD TV, Cell phones)

Regulations, similar to legislative actions, are usually promulgated by federal agencies. The Federal Communications Commission (FCC) is responsible for the allocation of spectrum for HD TV, cell phones and satellite broadcasts, as well as public safety communications throughout the nation. Other federal agencies issue rules and regulations that state types of information that citizens have a right to know and in many cases comment on. The Federal Communications Commission regulates which radio frequencies (airwaves) can be used and the terms of their usage. The Environmental Protection Agency (EPA) develops regulations aimed at promoting cleaner air and water and supports the technology to test the various environmental factors.

Standards

The issuance and acceptance of standards play a critical role in technology systems. The Internet Protocol (IP) is the accepted language of the Internet and was initially created under the auspices of government support. Without standards regulating the "rules of the road," of what some have referred to as the "Information Highway," there would be chaos and interference of different protocols colliding with one another canceling each other out. The federal government sets standards for geographic information systems (GIS) that determine the usage of fleets of navigation satellites that enable use of GPS systems in cars and mobile devices. Other examples of standards include the EPA's "Energy Star" Program where the federal government rates electronic devices such as laptops and other types of computers for not only energy usage but also the types of environmental-friendly components found inside the various devices. The US Department of Energy has minimum standards for electrical appliances such as furnaces, air conditioners, and water heaters. The federal government is promoting health efficiency standards and technologies. The National Oceanic and Atmospheric Administration, better known as NOAA, is charged with naming and tracking hurricanes, weather balloons, and buoys, and maintains a national network for All Hazards Radio. It also designs and maintains a network of weather satellites and monitors oceans. The Communications Assistance for Law Enforcement Act (CALEA) is another example where all public safety agencies, state and local government, as well as commercial broadband carriers must comply with various standards in regard to all forms of telecommunications and allow for law enforcement to undertake authorized surveillance activities. For more information see the Federal Communications Commission (2013).

One of the oldest agencies that has focused on technology standards is the National Institute of Standards and Technology (NIST). NIST was created in 1901 and is now a part of the US Commerce Department. For more information see the National Institute of Standards and Technology website.

Subsidies

When deemed to be in the national interest, the federal government may decide to provide direct financial support for a particular technology or application as a means of "investment" for future use and adoption and the possibility of use and adoption on a commercial scale. Subsidies, however, are generally looked upon as a last resort when no other remedy appears to be working. The federal government provides for student loans and sometimes provides a special subsidy or scholarship if the student is enrolling in a subject area that is in high demand such as math, science, and technology.

Training

The federal government spends a good deal of resources on training programs, many of which provide training and capacity building among its workforce. On average, over the past twenty years the federal government has spent between seven and eight billion a year on job training and this number does not take into account the amount each agency and commission sets aside for employee training.

Support of National Labs

The federal government operates and supports no less than thirty-nine national laboratories. These national labs include Ames, Argonne, Brookhaven, Jet Propulsion Laboratory, Lawrence Livermore, National Center for Atmospheric Research, Oak Ridge, Los Alamos, Sandia, plus many more. Given the sensitive and classified nature of the types of studies and projects, the federal government maintains its own institutions. These labs fall under the auspices of the US Department of Energy.

Military Research and Development (Think, DARPA, All Military Facilities and Contractors)

As mentioned earlier, DARPA (Defense Advanced Research Projects Agency) remains the best-known research and development arm of the military and enjoys a solid reputation for defense innovation. It should be pointed out, however, that each branch of the military conducts its own research either through its own internal organizations, or through the support of private and public research institutions around the country.

Certifications and Ratings (Cars, Airplanes, Trains, Appliances, Institutions, etc.)

The federal government rates cars regarding emission requirements as well as consumer information. All aircraft must receive an air worthiness certification for safety before a plane can fly. The Office of Management and Budget requires budget certifications and sets standards as well. The EPA sets air and water quality certifications and standards. There is hardly a federal agency that in some way or another does not have a standards-setting responsibility. Even the Federal CIO (Chief Information Officer) Council provides for a Federal CIO Certification.

Collaborator

Government has often turned to public and private enterprise as a collaborator to help reach certain goals or objectives. In recent years the White House has collaborated with state and local governments in recognizing innovation in citizen engagement strategies and technologies. Most recently, the White House Office of Science and Technology called for a National Day of Civic Hacking where citizens throughout the country were invited to share in an opportunity for software developers, technologists, and entrepreneurs to unleash their can-do American spirit by collaboratively harnessing publicly released data and code to create innovative solutions for problems that affect Americans. In times of emergencies, the federal government collaborates with the states and local governments as well as organizations like the United Nations, The Red Crescent, or the Red Cross to share technology and information in order to reach mutual goals.

Thought Leader

Helped by technology, the federal government can play the role of thought leader. It can set health goals and standards, as well as education goals and standards, as guidelines and not necessarily punitive laws and regulations. The US Department of Health sets what it believes to be a healthy diet for most Americans and can illustrate the importance of getting immunized in order to prevent certain diseases. Government can attempt to sway people towards online communications and today even the White House has a Facebook page as well as a Twitter account.

Demonstration Projects, Programs, and Services

Government agencies are often able to demonstrate the use of new technologies such as alternative fuel vehicles, whereby they purchase large fleets to show how well they can work. The National Science Foundation provides funding for innovative practices at utilizing technology to better engage with citizens through improved communication and shared information. Many federal telework programs serve as examples in local communities for other agencies including state and local governments to emulate as a best practice.

Infrastructure Investment (Think, Electricity, the Internet, Broadband, GPS Systems)

The federal government has spent billions of dollars over the past 60+ years on technology infrastructure. In the 1920s the federal government actively sought to provide electricity and basic telephone service to rural areas across the country. The Rural Utility Service (RUS) was housed in the US Department of Agriculture that invested in electric transmission lines as well as telephone lines and more. In 2004 the Rural Development Agency began to encourage and fund rural broadband systems throughout rural America. The federal government has built and supports a number of comprehensive satellite systems that support location-based devices such as GPS systems in cars and mobile devices, weather satellites, and even spy satellites run by the military.

Cybersecurity

As technology has become increasingly complex as it is interconnected, protecting technology infrastructure and critical systems, such as our nation's defense, business and banking communities, transportation, and utilities such as electricity and water requires a federal coordinated approach. The Department of Energy, the Federal Bureau of Investigation, the US Secret Service, the Department of Homeland Security are just some of the non-military agencies that are taking a leadership role in protecting and defending the nation's technology infrastructure.

State and Local Government

Certainly closer to the average citizen, state and local governments play a significant role in utilizing information technology too. Local governments are in a unique position that allows them to foster and develop better public-private partnerships for programs such as broadband deployments, smart transportation systems, and even electronic signage are but a few examples. It is important to note that states often serve as an administrative agent for various federal programs and therefore it is critical that state systems be in sync with federal systems. Likewise, many local governments who depend on state assistance for various programs need to stay in sync with their state governments. The takeaway here is that federal, state, and local governments are becoming increasingly interconnected and interdependent on one another.

State government functions requiring information technology systems

- Budget and Administration
- Community Affairs
- Corrections (prisons)
- Education (state systems)
- Environmental Protection
- Employment Services
- Health Systems and Human Services
- Highways and Maintenance
- Insurance Administration
- Licensing (vehicles, registration, titles)
- Justice and Courts Systems
- Lottery
- Parks and Recreation
- Pension Systems
- Prisons
- Public Safety (police and emergency)
- Social Services
- State Judicial Systems
- Taxation
- Transportation
- Vital Health Records
- Voter Registration

Figure 1.5 Sample of state government functions all requiring information technology systems and applications

IT vs. ICT

There can be little doubt about the role that the federal government plays when it comes to technology support. Today's public manager will be using and dependent on many forms of technology in order to carry out their work. Many public employees may find themselves involved with technology as a science or applied science. This textbook will mostly focus on the role of information technology when applied to public management. Going a step further in setting the stage it should be pointed out that most of the world continues to refer to information technology as "Information Communication Technology" or ICT. In the US it is commonly referred to as "Information Technology" or simply "IT." Regardless of term, they are essentially one and the same.

The Information Age

In the 20th century we migrated from an industrial economy to an information economy that spills well into the 21st century. Information is exploding everywhere and those who found themselves buried in piles of paper before are now besieged by tons of information and data. According to those who study knowledge management, a topic that will be covered later in the text, 90 percent of the world's data has been generated since 2010 and every day we create 2.5 quintillion bytes of data. We are just now beginning to fathom the challenges of information and data growth. According to Cisco (2014), the Internet will be four times as large in four years and those worldwide devices and connections will grow to nearly nineteen billion, thus doubling from 2011 to 2016. By 2016, global Internet Protocol (IP) traffic is forecast to grow to be 1.3 zettabytes. It should be pointed out here that a zettabyte is equal to a sextillion bytes or a trillion gigabytes. Moreover, by 2016, 1.2 million video minutes, which is the equivalent of 833 days or over two years, would travel the Internet every second of every day. These numbers are difficult to explain, let alone imagine.

Ninety percent of the world's data has been generated since 2010 and every day we create 2.5 quintillion bytes of data.

The public manager will need to adapt to and learn many new terms and meaning. They will need to develop the ability to become more creative in determining how government can better function with a growing and aging population at home in the US. At the same time they will need to better understand how to interact with the rest of the world where technology has the ability to level the playing field.

The Pace of Change

It is important to understand the pace of change because of rapid advances in all fields, which require public managers to not merely respond to change—but to anticipate it too. With every advance in technology comes compounded growth. An analysis of the history of technology shows that technological change is exponential, contrary to the common sense "intuitive linear" view. So we won't experience 100 years of progress in the 21st century—it will be more like 20,000 years of progress at today's rate. For more information on accelerating intelligence see the website of Dr. Ray Kurzweil. Governmental institutions are desperately trying to keep up with the shift in citizen needs regarding the Internet and mobile devices. The federal government used to print and mail over 76,000 checks per month until recently when it switched to a mandatory direct deposit policy. Those who don't have checking accounts or wish not to receive payments through banking can choose to receive payments via a special debit card that can be remotely recharged with what would have been a monthly payment. One could imagine how the policies were formed with technology playing a very key role. The Internal Revenue Service (IRS) used to mail out tax forms to millions of citizens but no longer does this because of time and expense. Today, forms are available online to be downloaded or can be obtained at public places like libraries and other agencies that will print out copies on demand.

What stands out in this intersection of technology and policy is that public administration's justification, which has usually been is it "effective," and is it "efficient" now has a third "e"– is it "equitable." There is a growing number of the US population that is online but there still remains a significant number of the population that is not. This is often referred to as the digital divide or the "gap." It is wrong for the "digitally unconnected" citizen to be ignored by public managers as their rights can easily be eclipsed by the digitally connected. As will be pointed out later, as the gap widens, a significant portion of the population will be disenfranchised in terms of critical communications, economic and health, as well as education, programs.

Convergence

Convergence is the term used to describe the combining of traditional voice, data, and video into ways but essentially it all converts back to what we refer to as the Internet Protocol (IP), the common language for the digital age.

Figure 1.6 Data is nothing more than a complicated series of 'ones' and 'zeroes'

For example, can be likened to the purchase of a top-of-the line digital music player and perhaps adding to that an expensive pair of digital headphones. Despite the quality of the purchase, the fact remains that the human ear can only receive sound as analog sound waves—not digital sound waves.

Likewise, the human eye can appreciate higher definition displays but are limited to the five senses—not technology. Convergence, then, is the digitation of various data feeds that can be consisting of one or all of voice, data, and video information that has been placed into a common feed or data path that is extracted or separated out at a later time and destination. This transition occurs in microseconds.

Interdependence of Technologies and Systems

As our information technologies continue to evolve and converge, we must recognize the interdependence of technologies and their corresponding systems. The state, local, and federal workforce is rapidly changing and new skills are required. Information technology once began in the form of individual desktops that initially were not connected to any central source. It was not uncommon for a typical workstation to have an electric outlet, a telephone outlet, a modem outlet (for dial-up computer communications), and a dedicated printer. The electrical outlet supported a PC, a monitor, and often an external modem. Today we have built-in desktop systems that have the monitor and computer as one device, with one electrical connection and one (hopefully) high-speed network connection. Some workstations get their high-speed network connectivity wirelessly. With today's workstation one can view documents stored elsewhere, look up information across the globe in an instant, listen to music, watch videos, and perhaps engage in video and audio-video teleconferencing without having to leave one's seat. Your telephone is connected to the network and most likely is digital or a voice over Internet Protocol system called VoIP. In today's government office, workers routinely print to remote printers located in various locations and they share and store information. They are all part of a vastly growing complex system with what technologists refer to as "endpoints." With more endpoints such as laptops, external storage devices, USB thumb drives, tablets and cell phones come greater complexities and the need to manage by way of system rules and policies. One careless worker can unwittingly undermine an entire agency. In recent years, desktop computers have been replaced by laptops given the latter's versatility and portability. It is predicted that tablets will begin to overtake laptops as they provide even greater portability and functionality such as instant on and off, superior battery life, light weight, and dramatically improved touchscreens and displays. The possibilities are endless, making it difficult to predict future trends and usage of technology. It is important to remember that Microsoft co-founder Bill Gates once commented that he saw no reason why a person would want a computer in their *home*. The recent past is littered with many fine examples of highly successful people making some unbelievably wrong predictions. The final chapter in this book will explore future trends and possibilities.

The Power of Power (Energy)

Modern society has never been more dependent on power and energy for its very survival. Civil society has always depended on some rather basic necessities, which include air, water, food, and shelter. Electricity is a relatively recent addition (regardless of energy source) to the modern building blocks of life. Our increasing dependence on the Internet and all it connects has made society vulnerable to attacks and technology failures. Today's society depends on a working Internet for banking, communications, commerce, education, information, news, entertainment, etc. The more society becomes dependent on power and the Internet, the more risk it faces—what happens when the power goes off? During the blackout in 2011, four million people across Southern California and the western half of Arizona lost power—some for

Figure 1.7 In a digital world it's always good to have a back-up

over two and a half days. The cause was a maintenance worker in Arizona who accidentally started an unexpected chain reaction shutdown. There were two major blackouts in the northeast, one in 1965 and one in 2003. In 1965 over thirty million people were affected and, for many citizens, for as much as twelve hours. It should be pointed out that in 1965 there was no Internet. In 2003, forty-five million Americans were affected along with another ten million people in Ontario, Canada for up to two days. The initial cause was an overheated transmission line. The worst blackout to date occurred in 2012 in India, where roughly 10 percent of the world population live and as many as 670 million people were without power for as long as fifteen hours.

The Government Office for Tomorrow

The concept of the office is changing due to technology. The concept of office and place is being rethought based on advances of technology where more workers are mobile and have less or no need to travel to an office. When public safety is taken into account, many local governments find that over half their staff are mobile. Many can now work out of the house, submit reports electronically, or meet with customers or citizens or even staff colleagues via video conference. With reliable broadband and the right software, productivity can be measured regardless of office location. Advantages of the new mobile workforce include greater employee satisfaction, improved productivity, reduction in office overhead costs, less wasted time on over-crowded roads, better energy savings through less vehicle use, and reduced need for traditional office space.

Innovations in the workplace involve not only more energy efficient lighting, but also more comfortable lighting for employees. The concept of space is being re-imagined to include more light, more glass, fewer walls, and more open space for collaborations and meetings. The office for tomorrow will include more high definition displays and shared offices used by multiple employees with flexible schedules. Finally, the future office will deal with less paper and physical storage—more information will be found online and stored in the Cloud.

The Power of Information

Technology has its roots in financial management where the earliest applications involved accounting, budgeting, payments, taxes, checks, time sheets, and human resources. Today there appears to be paradigm shift from keeping information private and confidential towards a far more transparent environment where information is shared, a shift from the traditional means of gaining or maintaining power by withholding information to the sharing of information. Certainly there will always be a continued need for keeping certain proceedings and rulemaking confidential—especially in the defense and justice areas of government.

Policy and information technology have evolved in ways few could have anticipated just twenty years ago when office automation was still the major focus of technology. Advances in computer technology, such as miniaturization, greater and reliable broadband, plus the wide adoption of broadband usage among citizens have increased the way government at all levels collects, communicates, and uses data for making sounder policy and better informed decision-making. Public administrators have new tools that require an entirely new appreciation for what these tools can do and how they can be constantly improved as new situations and opportunities arise.

The law of the land that protects intellectual property, better known as copyright, has attempted to keep pace with the changes in technology over the years. Since the passage of the Copyright Act of 1790 there has been dramatic change that no one in the day could have foreseen. As technology has grown and improved, copyright—initially aimed at protecting publishing and protecting the rights of maps, charts, and books—has changed to reflect the times. In 1998, Congress passed the Digital Millennium Copyright Act. The Internet, which went online commercially in 1993, was to be an open conduit for exchanging raw data between researchers. The commercial vision began with simple chat, discussions and mail, and quickly evolved into sharing text, images, sounds, videos, and the creation of content.

The US Constitution was signed in 1786 and went into effect with the passage of ten amendments known as the Bill of Rights in 1789. At the turn of the 19th century just as copyright law could not foresee the change ahead, electricity would not be available to power lights until 1890. Initially electricity was viewed as nothing more than something that could power light bulbs. The origins of information technology have many on-ramps, all of which contribute to a fast-moving evolution of progress. Here is a brief list of some of the major contributions that helped set the stage for information technology to grow and ultimately empower both citizens and governments alike.

The Internet, which went online commercially in 1993, was to be an open conduit for exchanging raw data between researchers. The commercial vision began with simple chat, discussions and mail, and quickly evolved into sharing text, images, sounds, videos, and the creation of content.

They are:

1794   First nonelectric telegraph—using flags and signs
1844   Samuel Morse sends first telegraph
1876   First telephone call

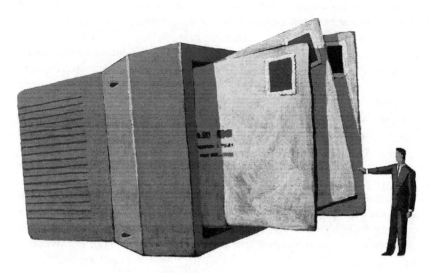

Figure 1.8 Email has replaced paper mail many years ago

1880   Electricity used for lights
1969   ARPANET network was created which was the beginning of the Internet
1971   First email sent
1974   Ethernet protocol was established
1976   First commercial email service called "Comet"
1982   TCP/IP was adopted
1983   MCI advances commercial email
1989   AOL is formed and sent out disks allowing "members" to communicate with one another, referred to as a "walled garden," there were thirty million users at its zenith
1991   Military uses what we now call Wi-Fi
1993   World Wide Web is started
1996   Clinger-Cohen Act (CCA) formerly known as the Information Technology Management Reform Act of 1996
1996   Electronic Communications Privacy Act of 1986 (ECPA)
1998   Government Paperwork Elimination Act 1998 (GPEA)
1999   Wi-Fi is commercially available
2002   The E-Government Act of 2002

While the Internet wasn't made commercially available until 1993, this was a significant application–perhaps as dramatic as the first application of the light bulb. Both innovations changed American society in many significant ways.

This text will provide the student with a useful framework for understanding the latest technologies in a non-technical way to better prepare public managers for the challenges ahead. This goal will be accomplished with the following objectives:

1. Understand how information system design relates to democratic theory.
2. Understand the skills and tools that are useful in information management, information technology, and systems dedicated for the effective flow of information within organizations.
3. Develop an understanding of the role of e-government, e-governance, m-government, and social media in today's society and in other public settings.
4. Develop an understanding of the possibilities and challenges of technology applications within public organizations.
5. Understand how technology can be managed through various governance models.
6. Understand the changing nature of the concept of "office."
7. Appreciate the role of public policy and technology.

Beyond E-government

By 1996 the Clinger–Cohen Act was passed by Congress and signed into law leading to the creation of the Office of E-Government and Information Technology within the Office of Management and Budget (OMB). This office is headed by the Federal Government's Chief Information Officer (CIO) who is tasked with developing and providing direction in the use of Internet-based technologies and to make it easier for citizens and business to interact with the federal government, with the goal of saving taxpayer dollars, and streamlining citizen participation. The CIO heads the Federal CIO Council that comprises the CIO's of each of the federal agencies. Through its own words the Federal CIO Council "aspires to promote a bright and prosperous future for the United States through the strategic use of federal information technology. It seeks to drive efficiency and effectiveness across government, spurring innovation, protecting and defending our resources and more effectually bringing government services to Americans." To learn more about the Office of E-Government and Information Technology, see the White House website.

The CIO Council is the principal interagency forum on federal agency practices for IT management. Originally established by Executive Order 1301 (Federal Information Technology) and later codified by the E-Government Act of 2002, the CIO Council's mission is to improve practices related to design, acquisition, development, modernization, use, sharing, and performance of federal government information resources. For more information see the US Chief Information Officer and the Federal CIO Council website.

The White House's Office of Management and Budget is but one of many offices within the executive branch of the administration. By contrast, the US Government Accountability Office is an independent, nonpartisan agency that works with Congress. It is often referred to as the Congressional watch-dog, as the GAO investigates how the federal government spends taxpayer dollars. Its overall mission is to support the Congress in meeting its constitutional responsibilities and to help improve the performance and ensure accountability of the federal government for the benefit of the American people.

The GAO has authored thousands of reports that focus on some aspect of information technology. Report titles include "information technology" with an emphasis that agencies need to fully implement major initiatives to save billions of dollars. Other reports focus on digital technologies, opportunities to improve transparency, oversight of investment risk of select agencies, and the need for agencies to strengthen oversight of billions of dollars in operations and maintenance assessments. As of this writing there are 2230 reports under the category information technology along with seventy reports that focus on information management. For more information see the GAO website.

Suffice it to say that every federal department, agency and commission has some form of information technology infrastructure component. Indeed, this is also true for states, cities, and counties. City and counties, regardless of size, all utilize information technology in one form or another. Even the smallest local government has at least 200 lines of business. Lines of business can be defined as a specific business area where forms, fees, or taxes are collected and accounted for regarding some form of government service such as parking tickets, licenses, permits, parks and recreation usage, public works, and public safety information systems to name a few.

The primary goal of this chapter is to set the stage for understanding information technology and how federal, state, and local governments in general utilize and or encourage it. A secondary goal is to embark upon a deeper understanding of how policies drive technology and more recently, how technologies drive policy. The battle over citizen rights, privacy, and surveillance is an ongoing subject as it becomes apparent that the nation's laws are still very much rooted in an analog world and not yet well suited for the digital environment. This text will further explore the role of technology regarding citizen engagement, transparency, digital ethics, and technology-related tools that can either make for a better standard of living for all or—if misused—can work against society in ways that can lead to civil disobedience and anarchy. Today's technologies are still being conceived and carried out by humans. Tomorrow's technologies may not only be built by robots, but conceived by robots as well. Some seek comfort and legal standing in referring back to the US Constitution and the Bill of Rights in seeking guidance as to what the Founding Fathers' intentions might have been when applied to today's challenges. Recall, however, that there was no electricity, data storage, radio or TVs, cell phones, computers, or cameras, let alone automobiles, during the late 1700s. Collectively, today's society is setting a new course one advancement at a time, with each advancement rapidly building upon the other. Only time will tell as to how well society fares in the future in terms of whether it harnesses the power of technology or will the power of technology harness it?

Discussion Questions

1. Analyze and discuss where most IT spending is occurring in the federal government.
2. Which Congressional committees have oversight on technology spending at the federal level?
3. Which government agencies seem to do the best job in utilizing information technologies?
4. Can you identify key improvements in information technology at the federal, state, and or local levels? Cite examples, and explain why.
5. How can government do a better job in funding and managing IT projects?
6. Find three websites that do a very good job in reporting the cost of information technology projects and or how they are being used. Choose one website from each of the three major categories: a federal agency, a state or state agency, a city or county.
7. Can you identify the ten most important types of data collected by government?
8. How is technology best utilized in your agency or department? What could be improved, how and why?
9. Can you identify the main causes as to why some technology projects seem to fail or to live up to their stated goals?
10. How do state and local governments manage technology? What are the advantages and disadvantages when compared to the federal government?
11. What is your favorite government-sponsored technology application that you appreciate the most? Describe and state why?

References

CISCO. 2014. *The Zettabyte Era—Trends and Analysis*. Accessed October 17, 2014. http://www.cisco.com/c/en/us/solutions/collateral/service-provider/visual-networking-index-vni/VNI_Hyperconnectivity_WP.html.

Federal Communications Commission. 2013. "Communications Assistance for Law Enforcement Act." Accessed October 17, 2014. http://www.fcc.gov/encyclopedia/communications-assistance-law-enforcement-act.

Nunziata, Susan. 2010. "Government IT Spending: $61.5 Billion by 2015." *CIO Insight*. Accessed October 17, 2014. http://www.cioinsight.com/c/a/Research/Government-IT-Spending-615-Billion-by-2015-465251/.

Welsh, William. 2013. "Federal IT Spending To Grow Slightly In 2014." *Information-Week*. Accessed October 17, 2014. http://www.informationweek.com/enterprise/federal-it-spending-to-grow-slightly-in-2014/d/d-id/1112204.

Digital Destinations

Census Bureau. http://www.census.gov
Data.gov. http://www.data.gov
Defense Advanced Research Projects Agency. http://www.darpa.mil

Deltek. http://www.deltek.com
Environmental Protection Agency. http://www.epa.gov/ttn
FCW. http://www.FCW.com
Federal Laboratory Consortium. http://www.fererallabs.org
FEDSTATS. http://fedstats.gov/agencies/
GAO. http://www.gao.gov
Gartner. http://www.gartner.com
GCN. http://www.GCN.com
Government Technology. http://www.govtech.com
International Data Corporation. http://www.IDC.com
IT Dashboard. https://www.itdashboard.gov/
Kurzweil, Dr. Ray. http://www.kurzweilai.net/
National Institute of Standards and Technology. http://nist.gov
National Oceanic and Atmospheric Administration. http://www.noaa.gov
NextGov. http://www.nextgov.com
USA Spending. http://www.usaspending.gov/
US Chief Information Officer and the Federal CIO Council. http://www.cio.gov
White House. http://www.whitehouse.gov

Further Reading

Greisler, David and Ronald J. Stupak. 2007. *Handbook of Technology Management in Public Administration.* CRC Press, Bocba Raton, FL.
Mayer-Schönberger, Viktor and David Lazer (eds.). 2007. *Governance and Information Technology: From Electronic Government to Information Government.* MIT Press, Cambridge, MA.

2 Governance and Leading Innovation

Who Decides?

This chapter will cover, review, and describe the various roles and models regarding technology governance, with the overarching theme—who decides. It will also describe why this continues to be a critically important issue despite the vast improvements in automated systems and information technology. In one way or another, as a public manager you will work with someone in charge of technology, hire and or manage someone who is the top technology manager, therefore it is very important to understand who is making technology decisions, and as important, why. In today's environment there is simply no escaping technology's impact.

The pendulum of information technology has shifted back and forth between centralized systems and decentralized systems with a growing middle ground. Many professionals can still recall having large monitors on their desks that were largely considered "dumb terminals." This referred to the fact that the intelligence was coming from the network via wires and the desktop terminals served mostly as a viewing screen and meant that most functionality was loaded and stored on a mainframe. Until recently, this is much like how a television works, it provides news and entertainment but does not store any programs and does not contain much more than the ability to process video and audio signals through the air or through a cable.

The earliest of terminals (later called screens) had a black background display with green type and the so-called "intelligence" was housed in a large mainframe, centrally located computer. Today's screens have become incredibly thin, contain dazzling colors; some with HD quality and stereo sound, and are often attached to smaller boxes called PCs (Personal Computers) or desktop computers. PCs have intelligence built in via software programs, internal storage devices, modems for telecommunications, and more. Today the pendulum may be swinging again where those dazzling terminals may be transforming back into what we once called "dumb" as was the case in the 1970s and 1980s. This trend is the result of new technologies that rely on desktop provisioning and virtualization, whereby software that would traditionally reside inside a PC could more cost-effectively be loaded and summoned from a central computer system without the user being aware. This of course can only happen with reliable high-speed networks and connectivity.

"Whomever pulls the sword from the stone shall lead this project."

Figure 2.1 Technology is not about magic—it's about applied proven technologies

Of course one thing that hasn't changed quite yet is the need for a keyboard and pointing device, yet even this is beginning to change with the vast improvements with touch screens and speech recognition technologies.

Unfortunately, judging how government has managed or, better, *mismanaged* technology in the recent past, government can be expected to be dead last in adopting new timesaving technologies. The reasons for the *mismanagement* of information technologies have much more to do with leadership than the technology itself. Whether a system is centralized or decentralized, someone had to make a decision as to why, what, and how. This chapter will provide a framework for how technology is managed or governed in a government setting.

IT Governance

While information technology moves like a giant and invisible pendulum swinging over time between centralized and decentralized computing systems, there is also a corresponding force that swings between centralized and decentralized information technology management. Indeed someone has to make decisions and plan for maintaining the system for today as well as look ahead to the system needs and requirements for tomorrow. Given today's rapidly moving technological pace regarding change and innovation, the concept of planning for tomorrow is being realized in much faster cycles of change. This explains, in part, why there is a rapid move to support new forms of devices that may take the form or shape of a desktop PC, laptop, tablet, or other mobile offering. Technology leaders, hoping to save money, are moving into what is referred to as a "thin client" environment where the software and user profiles that once were loaded onto each individual PC or workstation can now be summoned and utilized by the end-user without regard to where the software physically resides. This task is automatic and is seamless and raises a question—who is making these types of decisions? Who decides who gets what type of equipment, how often, and how will it "fit" into the current system and how will it be supported over time? Should each department shop for the best deals in printer, laptops or tablets, or should purchasing be done in a more coordinated and centralized way? The same thought process applies to purchasing software packages and programs, or to deciding to move an operation into what is now commonly referred to as the Cloud. Moreover, what are the other considerations that one must take into account besides functionality, quality, and price?

> Technology leaders, hoping to save money, are moving into what is referred to as a "thin client" environment where the software and user profiles that once were loaded onto each individual PC or workstation can now be summoned and utilized by the end-user without regard to where the software physically resides.

The federal government has very specific rules for the purchase of hardware and software. In fact every government be it federal, state, or local operates under a number of procurement rules and regulations. It should be remembered that there are many steps that must come first before ever getting to the procurement process. The first step is usually to assess or articulate a need.

When computer networks were largely centralized, the answer to who decides was relatively simple—there was always a network administrator in charge, usually headed by a director of management information systems or simply referred to as MIS. Since the first general usage of large computers in public organizations was performed by accounting and finance departments, many MIS departments were attached in some form or fashion to the finance department. Many state and local governments continue to maintain the same governance systems by reporting to the chief financial officer. For example the State Chief Information Officer (CIO) of New Jersey reports to the State Treasurer. Advances in technology have been growing exponentially over the past decade and the governance of technology has struggled to keep up with the balance between what is necessary (critical) and what is possible (desired), and finally what can be looked upon as being sustainable (affordable).

With all the advances in technology and its applications, there are a variety of governance models that range from localized decision-making, a federated approach, or centralized decision-making—with many variations in between. Regardless of the type of governance model, someone or some group has to make many important decisions regarding what types of hardware and or software systems need to be purchased, supported, utilized, and implemented. Someone or some group must also decide under what conditions and circumstances equipment should be retired or disposed of and how it will be discarded or replaced.

The Rise of the CIO and the CTO

Information technology was handled throughout the federal state and local governments with each department and agency doing its own thing and to some extent there were many attempts to coordinate polices by the federal government's Office of Management and Budget (OMB). It wasn't until 1996 that the first Federal CIO position was created. Meanwhile, borrowing from private sector best practices, local and state governments and referred to the lead director as the Chief Information Officer (CIO) or Chief Technology Officer (CTO), with many using such labels interchangeably; perhaps given its size, the federal government has both. Changes in titles have been more than a relabeling or name change as they reflected a shift in required or desired skill sets. This also made it a bit easier for public managers to recruit technology leadership from among the private sector. The early MIS directors were generally technically-oriented problem-solvers and usually found themselves swallowed up by the demands of "putting out the fires" and "keeping the lights on" as they would say. They were the ones who made sure the mainframe computers were optimized and serviced, and they were the ones who would troubleshoot a frozen program or screen, or recapture a lost or forgotten password, etc. While many today still operate in a similar fashion there is a growing recognition for technology leaders to be as strong in strategic planning and managing people as they are in understanding, implementing, and maintaining technology. They are also expected to be a master at managing expectations from the technical staff to department managers—as well as elected leaders too.

It was not that long ago, every departmental function had its own technology staff expertise, be it someone who would buy equipment, add print cartridges to printers, and even buy and load software. In some instances this might be performed by a single person or even a few—in any event these were people who simply expressed an interest or who were recruited to perform technology-related tasks and rose to the occasion. Many smaller government entities still use this type of governance scheme by default. Application-specific tasks were left to each department or division. However when data systems became more centralized, mostly for reasons of greater overall efficiency, the question of who supports what and who pays for what became a growing concern. Every day stories are told about a senior manager, who should have known better, deciding to purchase a particular device or application for his or her operations without any realistic comprehension of how and who would support it. Who provides the immediate and ongoing training? Who does the updating? Who is responsible for securing the system? Who does one call when there is a problem? If there is a service or software agreement how long will it last? Once it expires what might the cost be in order to keep it running? What will the replacement cost be? How well does this system or application integrate with other systems? How secure is the system? To what extent is there duplication elsewhere? Might the new service or application also serve other departments thus spreading the cost and benefit amongst a larger group—either short or long term?

Some problems can be traced back to over-eager commercial vendors who at times have been known to overstate what they could provide, in what time frame or, cost, or underestimated the government's true internal capabilities and capacity. All too often, purchases are made because someone received a grant that simply had to be spent—and quickly—or they would lose the money and thus the "opportunity." Other examples of system failures have

Figure 2.2 The need for tools has never changed—but now we have digital toolboxes

stemmed from over-zealous staff that became blinded by their overwhelming enthusiasm thus failing to recognize any inherent risks and potential conflicts. In any event, purchasing equipment and new software-based systems requires a great deal of objectivity and planning, integration, and training. Ideally, in our ever-evolving technology-dependent world, systems need to be purchased with an eye towards spreading the cost over a larger number of government entities whenever and wherever possible (Shark 2012).

Government officials certainly are not without blame as they have had their share in technology management missteps. They have been known to make last minute pre- and post-contract modifications, poorly timed changes in requirements, and changes that greatly impact the outcome of contract and systems development.

In government, with everyone believing their "mission-critical" application is the most important application in the universe, tension arises when they don't receive immediate action from the technology support group—they get very frustrated at best. As a case-in-point, a medium-sized city was beset with the challenge of dealing with five separately operated and maintained geospatial information systems (GIS). Each department having their own system recognized both the advantage and need to integrate all the databases and informational layers into one solid robust system. At the same time, each "owner" voiced the need for the others to integrate the other systems in *theirs*. In this case, the tragedy was that no one with authority, including the city manager, wanted to intervene because they felt less than qualified to make such a decision among the "experts." This is where high-level IT leadership and trust is required (ibid.).

Traditionally, the CIO is the one responsible for keeping the information systems operating on a 24/7 basis.

What Does a CIO Do?

Traditionally, the CIO is the one responsible for keeping the information systems operating on a 24/7 basis. This usually includes the computer centers— in larger organizations there can be multiple data centers each with a separate location and manager. The CIO is the one that plans for and hires, maintains, and makes sure he or she has the right staff with the right training and qualifications. Many have argued that current civil service requirements (or union negotiated labor agreements) often prevent the CIO from making timely staffing decisions because of rules that are too cumbersome or complicated. In today's technology environment one must be able to be flexible and agile in order to keep pace with new demands and technologies. Technology is changing faster than many staff can keep up with—which often results in having staff that have been trained on equipment that is no longer supported or needed and as often, resist learning new skills well or easily. Of course this can work both ways. It is well known that in the federal space the Social Security Administration has for years tried to develop a new, more modern system. Yet despite millions, if not billions, of dollars already spent, the core computer system components still rely on COBOL programmers. The programming language, COBOL, has not been commonly used in systems in a few dozen years. While legacy systems still remain in service, it is the programming language that still requires staff with skills of yesterday, and many computer replacement components are scarce or unavailable.

> The CIO is the one who makes sure that technology supports the various business functions of the department or agency. The term used to describe this is *business alignment*, where the CIO is always assessing how well the technology is aligned with the various business operations any given department or agency may have.

The CIO is the one who makes sure that technology supports the various business functions of the department or agency. The term used to describe this is *business alignment*, where the CIO is always assessing how well the technology is aligned with the various business operations any given department or agency may have.

The Role of the Chief Information Officer

- **Plans:** Prioritizing projects, consolidation, infrastructure.
- **Coordinates:** With other functional departments and agencies.
- **Hires:** Recruits, ensures performance, training, and provides motivation.
- **Communicates:** Communicates to and among all levels of government status of systems and projects.
- **Purchases:** Plans, budgets, and purchases new equipment which includes hardware and or software and also helps decide when it is best to buy or turn to a managed service and or the cloud. Today contractors are often brought in to fill employment gaps and help address the need for greater flexibility with changing technologies.
- **Recommends:** Different types of technology solutions aimed at improving business processes.
- **Technology Infrastructure:** Making sure the basic and specialized technology infrastructure is operating as it should.
- **Budgets:** Plans for current and future technology needs and how they might be financed.
- **Permissions, Access, and Usage Policies:** Who can have access to which systems and how such systems can be used and by whom.
- **Security:** Develops strategies, policies, and systems to best protect the technology infrastructure from internal as well as external threats.

Figure 2.3 The role of the Chief Information Officer

The CIO as Technology Leader

Before the CIO came into favor, the head of a technology department was called something like "director of information technology," or "director of management information systems" (MIS). These departments generally played a support role in making certain that the main network computers were operating and supporting the enterprise. Some local governments still operate with this type of governance (the federal government has its own unique history and set of issues that will be covered later in this chapter). However, as the job requirements have changed and evolved—so too have position descriptions and titles. There has been an evolutionary trend towards the type and qualifications of the person leading today's technology enterprise. This is occurring on at least two levels. The first level is the qualification for what best constitutes a technology executive regardless of title. The second is where should this person be positioned within an organization–and why? After all, technology governance (a term often used to describe technology management) is all about decision rights—or simply, who decides?

There is no one model that will solve or address all problems and situations—it depends on the locality, history, current needs and resources, and what it is they are trying to achieve. At the local government level, cities and counties continue to upgrade the top technology position when the opportunity presents itself. In fact, many larger jurisdictions frequently have recruited executives from the private sector—often with great success, and yet there are as many stories to the contrary. When one examines the critical responsibilities that are required to manage today's technology, how can local governments expect anything less? In the end it is the public who hold governments accountable, and technology is playing a larger role in helping to provide better and faster services.

The successful Chief Information Officer (CIO) or Chief Technology Officer (CTO), each with their own classic definitions, have become almost interchangeable in daily use. To be clear, a CIO is not the same as being a CTO. Both positions are normally charged with looking at all aspects of the enterprise from not only the technology infrastructure but they must also take into account the proper alignment of business processes to the needs of government. By comparison the Chief Technology Officer is the one who usually focuses on the technology part of the enterprise as well as the system or various systems architecture. Smaller organizations simply have one person playing both roles in varying degrees.

From here on out the term CIO will be used to symbolize the *chief technology strategist*. From the CIO perspective, he or she must wear a number of hats, be more people-oriented yet technically grounded, and speak many "languages," to different stakeholders—almost simultaneously.

To be successful, CIOs today must be leaders first—not simply managers. They must be technologists—not technicians; business-minded—not closed-minded; financiers—not accountants; proactive–not reactive; and finally, diplomats—not politicians. These distinctions can be significant. Without prejudice, there is nothing wrong with acting as an accountant but in the technology setting, their role is generally that of a historian. By comparison, a finance-oriented person looks at the many options that exist for funding—moving forward—where decisions are made with skill and acknowledged risk. Being proactive suggests that the CIO must develop a vision for the future, and not merely sit around and wait for the phone to ring or an email or text message to arrive. On the political side, one cannot be a politician that successfully tells people want they want to hear as opposed to a diplomat skilled at telling people, however delicately, what they need to know.

Leadership requires a variety of skills; especially people skills that necessitate developing trusted relationships inside as well as outside of the IT area. Entirely too many technology managers spend a huge amount of time putting out fires, or what they refer to as "break-fix" activities and acknowledge not enough time developing strategic planning and enterprise visioning, or building and maintaining relationships among the internal client base.

> Leadership requires a variety of skills; especially people skills that necessitate developing trusted relationships inside as well as outside of the IT area.

Possessing strong leadership skills that encompass both the technical side as well as the people side is essential. The new CIO must be as adept at how technology can work best, as having the people skills to better understand the business processes that can benefit from innovative IT support. When it comes to the business side, one cannot solely focus on budgets and reports, but must be active in continuously assessing how well the various systems are working from a technology standpoint, as well as an operational business perspective. What good is a computer network that is operating perfectly but no one is using the system because it doesn't perform as was expected, or because an application might be perceived as being too complicated?

The successful chief technology strategist needs to be able to speak interchangeably on different levels of communications depending on the audience. Deeper and more detailed communications skills are required for technology managers, perhaps offering a little less in-depth information—but nonetheless convincing information needs to be communicated among senior managers, and the so-called "5-minute elevator" speech is reserved for the political side. Each group has different needs for information and how it is processed.

Being a CIO today is perhaps similar to that of being a symphony conductor where you come to the podium with your own specialty yet, behind the scenes, recruit, place, train, mentor, and orchestrate a sense of human and technological harmony throughout the enterprise. Recognizing the need for

Figure 2.4 The contemporary CIO is much like a symphony conductor

more training and development for the next generation of technology, no less than three universities offer a CIO certification program to help in building and promoting the profession just as has been done for city attorneys, city managers, chief financial officers, and purchasing officers (Stone 2012).

The Federal CIO

The Clinger-Cohen Act of 1996—which was formerly known as the Information Technology Management Reform Act of 1996—required each federal agency to establish effective information technology leadership. The E-Government Act of 2002 created the Federal CIO position which is appointed by the President and located within the OMB and serves as the most senior management office within the administrative branch of government. While the Act has been around for some eighteen years, many of its key provisions have still not been implemented. The thrust of the Act was to have the CIO viewed as a business partner and not just act as a support fix-it type technologist. The Act also mandated that each Federal CIO have direct reporting relationships with their respective Cabinet Secretary—one of the Acts key failings.

The Federal CIO essentially oversees federal technology spending, federal IT policy, and strategic planning of all federal IT investments. The Federal CIO is charged with establishing a government-wide enterprise architecture that ensures system interoperability, information sharing, and maintains effective information security and privacy controls across the main federal government departments and agencies.

The Clinger-Cohen Act of 1996, which created the Federal CIO position, outlined the following responsibilities for the CIO:

1. Provide advice and assistance to senior managers on IT acquisition and management
2. Develop, maintain, and facilitate implementation of a sound and integrated IT architecture
3. Promote effective and efficient design and operation of all major IRM processes for the agency, including improvements to work processes

In addition, this position has primary duties annually, as part of the strategic planning process.

The Federal CIO Council was established in 2002 and was designed to serve as the principal interagency forum on federal agency practices for IT management. The mission of the CIO Council has been to the design, acquisition, development, modernization, use, sharing, and performance of the current federal government information resources.

The Act also called for the creation of the Federal CIO Council. Each department and agency has its own lead CIO with many others reporting to them. The Federal CIO Council represents the CIOs from among the major federal agencies and defined ten competency areas. Though simply a list, the areas in Figure 2.5 are commonly illustrated in the form of the "CIO Wheel."

Figure 2.5 CIO wheel

Source: Clinger-Cohen Act of 1996

1. Develop recommendations for the Office of Management and Budget (OMB) on federal government IT management policies and requirements.
2. Establish government-wide priorities on information technology policy and monitor their implementation.
3. Share lessons learned, ideas, best practices, and innovative approaches related to IT management.
4. Assist the Federal Chief Information Officer (Federal CIO) in the identification, development, and coordination of multi-agency projects and other innovative initiatives to improve federal government performance through the use of IT.
5. Promote collaboration and community building among federal agency CIOs for purposes of sharing best practices, transferring knowledge, and developing a unified approach for addressing federal IT challenges.
6. Promote the development and use by agencies of common IT management performance measures under Chapter 36 and Title II of the E-Government Act of 2002.
7. Serve as a forum for collaboration on intra-agency IT portfolio management to reduce duplicative IT investments and drive the efficient use of IT resources across agencies within the federal government.
8. Partner, as appropriate, with the National Institute of Standards and Technology (NIST) and the Office of the Federal CIO (OMB) to develop recommendations on IT standards. Work with the Office of Personnel Management (OPM) to assess and address the hiring, training, classification, and professional development needs of federal employees in areas related to IT management.
9. Work with the Archivist of the United States to assess how the Federal Records Act can be addressed effectively by federal IT initiatives and activities.
10. Solicit perspectives from the Chief Financial Officers Council, Federal Acquisition Officers Council, Chief Human Capital Officers Council, Budget Officers Advisory Council, and other key groups in the federal government, as well as industry, academia, and other federal, tribal, and state and local governments, on matters of concern to the Council as appropriate.

Each cabinet-level department has many agencies. For example the US Department of Transportation (DOT) has thirteen major agencies and there are dozens of departments within each agency. Using DOT as an example, there is one central CIO, thirteen department CIOs, and perhaps another ten or so at the department level too. This leads to a total of no less than 30+ CIOs in one federal agency. Given the size of most federal agencies and commissions, working among CIOs within different sub-organizations and often in physical different locations can be a leadership challenge all unto itself.

> Given the size of most federal agencies and commissions, working among CIOs within different sub-organizations and often in physical different locations can be a leadership challenge all unto itself.

The Federal CIO and the CIO Council have been charged with establishing a Federal Enterprise Architecture (FEA). This provides a common approach for the integration of strategic, business, and technology management as part of organization design and performance improvement.

Federal CIO Priorities

Under the leadership of the Federal CIO, the CIO Council has identified four major areas of focus for 2013 and beyond:

1. **Innovate**—innovating for the American people; which includes the future-ready workforce, digital government strategy and open data policy, Cloud, and transition to the latest generation of the Internet Protocol.
2. **Deliver**—maximizing the value of federal IT; which includes data center consolidation, IT shared services, *TechStat, PortfolioStat,* and the IT Dashboard.
3. **Protect**—advancing our nation's cybersecurity; which includes FedRAMP, Identity Management, Continuous Monitoring, and Trusted Internet connectivity.
4. **National Initiatives**—which includes *BusinessUSA*, and the Permitting Dashboard (the Permitting Dashboard is a webpage that allows the public to track the federal permitting and environmental review process for expedited high priority infrastructure projects) (CIO website).

At the federal level there are a number of degree and certificate programs offered by numerous institutions of higher learning. The CIO university coordinates various programs that are offered by participating institutions of higher learning where a student can earn either a certificate or diploma, or both. Currently there are seven universities that participate in the Federal CIO program offering either, or both, degree programs or certificates. For more information see the CIO University website.

At the state and local level there are presently four universities that offer certificate or certification programs. One thing is clear, there is a growing need for a new professional class of CIOs. Moreover, with the record number of retirements that is expected to occur over the next several years, the need for new, highly skilled CIOs will only become more critical.

Chief Information Officer
Job Description

SUMMARY
- Responsible for the technological direction of a "Agency" of "company." Proposes budgets for programs and projects, purchases and upgrades equipment, supervises computer specialists and IT workers, and presides over IT-related projects.

PRIMARY RESPONSIBILITIES
- Provide technological guidance within an organization.
- Supervise information system and communications network.
- Develop and implement a customer service platform to serve the organization in every aspect.
- Design, establish, and maintain a network infrastructure for local and wide area connectivity and remote access.
- Consult with administration, department managers, and manufacturing representatives to exchange information, present new approaches, and to discuss equipment/system changes.
- Participate in vendor contract negotiations for all new computer equipment and software purchased for the corporation.
- Create a cost-benefit analysis as well as supporting a detailed definition of data requirements and departmental workflows.
- Oversee Internet and computer operations.
- Manage the day-to-day operations of the information technology department including directing staff, who support administrative computing, networking, user services, telecommunications, and other information technology functions.
- Assess and anticipate technology projects and recommend appropriate action and resources.
- Establish and direct the strategic and tactical goals, policies, and procedures for the information technology department.
- Propose hardware/software solutions to accomplish the company's business objectives.
- Identify user needs and resolve problems.

Note: Whether these qualities are found within one individual or not, the person in charge has to oversea such criteria and if that person doesn't possess the necessary expertise than it is incumbent on that individual to hire someone who can.

Figure 2.6 Chief Information Officer job description (generic sample)

The State CIO

Nearly every state has a CIO with some reporting directly to the Governor, with others reporting to the State Treasurer or other senior executive. State CIOs are well represented by the National Association of State Chief Information Officers (NASCIO), a nonprofit association whose mission is to foster government excellence through quality business practices, information management, and technology policy.

CIOs indicated different reporting structures, including reporting to the Heads of Finance, Administration, Budget, or the Governor. Of the CIOs

State officials/staff	Percent responding
Executive branch heads	92%
State budget officer	90%
Chief of staff/COO	79%
Governor	75%
Legislators	71%
Legislative staff	69%
General counsel	50%

Figure 2.7 NASCIO 2012 state survey

Source: NASCIO 2013b

interviewed, approximately 50 percent are considered a Cabinet-level position, yet only 30 percent report directly to the Governor. Responsibility for setting IT and IT security policies for agencies under the Governor is consistent. The majority of states either have an informal oversight relationship or no reporting relationship with agency CIOs. As a result, most CIOs have policy setting authority and executive authority, but not managerial authority (NASCIO 2013a). Figure 2.7 illustrates the results of a 2012 survey by NASCIO in which state CIOs were asked which of the following state functions sought their input or opinion on policy or operational decisions.

While most CIOs do not have direct authority over agency CIOs, the result is different when examining their influence on agency IT plans. An estimated 50 percent of state CIOs indicated they have direct approval authority over agency technology plans. The other 50 percent indicated an indirect review or approval authority, typically through an advisory relationship with the budget director (NASCIO 2013c).

Typically each state maintains departments that have administrative responsibilities for issuing drivers' licenses, licensing of motor vehicles, health and human services, education, employment and unemployment, state police, state parks, department of health, economic development, transportation, state highways, and cybersecurity to name a few. Each of these areas has its own top CIO in addition to numerous others within each of the agencies.

Given the political climate in which most state CIOs operate, especially since most serve at the pleasure of the Governor, the average state CIO's tenure is between eighteen and twenty-four months. This makes it particularly challenging for state CIOs to see and manage many key initiatives from start to finish.

NASCIO Priority Strategies, Management Processes and Solutions, Top 10 Final Ranking

1. **Security:** risk assessment, governance, budget and resource requirements, security frameworks, data protection, training and awareness, insider threats, third party security practices as outsourcing increases, determining what constitutes "due care" or "reasonable"
2. **Consolidation/Optimization:** centralizing, consolidating services, operations, resources, infrastructure, data centers, communications and marketing "enterprise" thinking, identifying and dealing with barriers
3. **Cloud Services:** scalable and elastic IT-enabled capabilities provided "as a service" using internet technologies, governance, service management, service catalogs, platform, infrastructure, security, privacy, data ownership, vendor management, indemnification, service portfolio management
4. **Project and Portfolio Management:** project management discipline, enterprise portfolio management, oversight, portfolio review, IT investment management, training/certification of staff, traceability to mission and strategy, scope management, execution
5. **Strategic IT Planning:** vision and roadmap for IT, recognition by administration that IT is a strategic capability; integrating and influencing strategic planning and visioning with consideration of future IT innovations; aligning with Governor's policy agenda
6. **Budget and Cost Control:** managing budget reduction, strategies for savings, reducing or avoiding costs, dealing with inadequate funding and budget constraints
7. **Mobile Services/Mobility:** devices, applications, workforce, security, policy issues, support, ownership, communications, wireless infrastructure, BYOD
8. **Shared Services:** business models, sharing resources, services, infrastructure, independent of organizational structure, service portfolio management, service catalog, marketing and communications related to organizational transformation, transparent charge back rates, utility based service on demand
9. **Interoperable Nationwide Public Safety Broadband Network (FirstNet):** planning, governance, collaboration, defining roles, asset determination
10. **Health Care:** the Affordable Care Act, health information and insurance marketplaces, health enterprise architecture, assessment, partnering, implementation, technology

Figure 2.8 NASCIO priority strategies, management processes and solutions, top 10 final ranking

Source: NASCIO 2012, p. 4

City and County CIOs

There are approximately 89,000 local units of government when taking into account cities, counties, towns, schools, and special districts. Each unit of government has someone who is in charge of technology. Today there are over 3,000 counties and 36,000 cities and townships and over 13,500 K-12 school districts. The CIO in the local government setting has become one of the newer professionals to be considered as part of the senior management team. Local governments provide numerous citizen-sensitive services in order to satisfy both current and future needs. The technology component

TRADITIONAL	EMERGING
Government's mission and role are well defined	Government's mission and role are changing, constantly being redefined
Leadership is mostly directing, managing	Leadership is more about vision, mission, empowering and guiding
Change is relatively slow, linear, predictable, managed	Change is relatively rapid, organic, guided rather than managed
Change is a source of apprehension	Change is seen as natural, inevitable
Programs are relatively static	Programs are more adaptable, agile, fluid
Multi-levels, more hierarchy, more supervision	Fewer levels, less hierarchy, more empowerment
Decision making is mostly centralized	Decision making is mostly decentralized
Individual achievement is valued	Value of collaboration, team-based work is on the rise
Information and knowledge often hoarded	Information and knowledge more shared, distributed

Figure 2.9 Change in technology governance

Source: Dearstyne 2009

of most localities is growing faster than most other departmental functions—yet they struggle to keep up with the fast-pace of technological change and a growing educated citizenry. While still the CIO of Washington, DC before becoming the nation's first Federal CIO, Vivek Kundra said "I was sitting having a cup of coffee and observed that the people walking by all had more power in their hands with their mobile devices than the overwhelming majority of government workers."

Enormous change in technology governance is taking place at the local level as illustrated in Figure 2.9.

Need for High-level Champions

Those studying the needs and challenges of today's CIOs over the past decade tend to agree that the most successful CIOs are the ones who, one way or another, have the strong and active support of a champion. This champion might be a governor, mayor, county administrator, state treasurer, or even the President of the United States. They recognize the importance of having supportive champions involved in technology decision making and help to seek broader support as well as financial resources. Most successful CIOs usually enjoy the support from a higher authority. Of course, the opposite can occur when a city manager takes little interest in technology and innovation. Some city managers who have experienced difficulties in the past regarding the purchase and implementation of new technologies have become "technology adverse" and are in no hurry to seek out new technology applications. This can make it difficult to take advantage of the tried and proven technologies. Perhaps one of the most unfortunate outcomes is the negative impact such lack of support has on staff at all levels.

Despite the enormous sums of money governments spend on technology, it appears that just about every level of government continues to play catch-up in regard to the adoption of new technology solutions. Today departments and agencies still struggle with legacy equipment that is costly to maintain, outdated software, and difficulties finding people to keep things operating as they should. Elected leaders as well as high-level administrators often lack the vision or fail to recognize the need to invest more in both technology leadership and technology systems. The speed of technology growth—fueled largely by the corporate sector and followed by the consumerization of technology—has left government lagging far behind.

> The speed of technology growth—fueled largely by the corporate sector and followed by the consumerization of technology—has left government lagging far behind.

CIOs have traditionally focused their attention inward making sure the day-to-day operations are performing as they should. Many claim they have little time to develop and maintain relationships and at the same time they acknowledge they need to work more at developing and maintaining external relationships. External relationships are with their "customers" or department heads where they provide technology support services. While this is evolving into a key performance indicator for successful CIOs, many overlook the citizen community that relies on a government's ability to supply and support vital citizen-facing services.

Many local and state governments have begun to experiment with public-facing governance structures that might include a Technology Committee, City Council Technology Committee, or even a Citizen Information Technology Advisory Committee. A key question always seems to surface when discussing the need for champions, whether it is an elected official or public manager— should a government entity create a more formal relationship with the community it serves? For example, should a city or county establish a technology advisory committee? If yes, then who might head such a technology committee? Should it be a mayor, or a senior public administrator? Having an active technology committee can provide a forum that is more inclusive rather than exclusive. Since technology systems cut across so many traditional department and division boundaries, having a group that meets regularly can help in the strategic planning and visioning process. The group can assist in setting priorities and look for opportunities leading to greater collaboration. Projects are more likely to be successful when there is strong and visible support from the top.

NASCIO	PTI
1. Security	1. Security
2. Consolidation/Optimization	2. Budget & Cost Control
3. Cloud Services	3. Strategic IT Planning Management
4. Project & Portfolio Management	4. Consolidation/Optimization
5. Strategic IT Planning Management	5. Project & Portfolio Management
6. Budget & Cost Control	6. Cloud Services
7. Mobile Services/Mobility	7. Mobile Services/Mobility
8. Shared Services	8. Shared Services
9. FirstNet	9. FirstNet
10. Health Care	10. Health Care (N/A)

Figure 2.10 2014 CIO priority strategies, management processes and solutions survey data

Source: PTI website

The Trend Towards "Chiefs"

Government agencies began using the CIO title only within the past decade or so and more recently state and local governments have begun using new corporate-borrowed titles such as Chief Data Officer, Chief Innovation Officer, Chief Knowledge Officer, and last, Chief Information Security Officer. Perhaps the thinking behind this trend is to elevate a function to a level where it fits more prominently within an organization. This of course raises some interesting questions regarding who reports to whom?

Strategic Planning

Strategic planning is a critical element in the information technology enterprise. When asked how many IT departments have a written strategic plan—an overwhelming majority answered that while they would like to, they lacked the time to do so. This goes back to the argument that CIOs are frustrated in spending too much time in crisis mode and not enough time for planning and building relationships. There are essentially two types of strategic plans. The first might be a plan that is internal to the IT department or division. An internal plan can be helpful when it comes to ensuring how the department operates and provides a clear picture of the levels of reporting relationships and authority as well as department priorities. The second type of strategic plan usually focuses on the needs and requirements of the entire governmental enterprise. It is here where the technology department seeks alignment with overall city or county requirements and needs.

> When asked how many IT departments have a written strategic plan, an overwhelming majority answered that while they would like to, they lacked the time to do so. This goes back to the argument that CIOs are frustrated in spending too much time in crisis mode and not enough time for planning and building relationships.

Perhaps in the end, the most important planning document is the budget plan itself. It is here that priorities have already been addressed, and it is here where the city and county is committed to spending its resources. The most successful strategic plans, in one way or another, link to an annual budget document.

Leading Innovation

Ideally, the CIO is often the one to lead the innovation challenge as long as that person is well connected to all the business lines of a governmental enterprise. Surely, things have changed since the days when the IT department was not much more than a support shop. Of course, due to historical issues or limited skill sets, many local governments continue to operate the way they did twenty years ago. Someone has to be the one to contemplate the possibilities and match business needs and requirements with the availability of technology solutions. This innovator must be well connected to the various departments and must always be scanning for newer solutions and learn from others' best practices. One of the top three complaints from CIOs is the lack of time or resources that enable them to serve as an innovator as opposed to being merely a fixer. CIOs also complain about the lack of travel monies for training and development for themselves and their staff. After all, lawyers, accountants, network engineers, public safety officials, as well as city managers, each require continuing education credits to maintain their certifications and competencies. CIOs rarely come to the job complete with all the skills necessary to be truly effective and this of course means much on-the-job training which can be problematic for all. So the question must be asked—why shouldn't the CIO who is part of the fastest growing field (technology) expect much the same when it comes to professional development programs?

> One of the top three complaints from CIOs is the lack of time or resources that enable them to serve as an innovator as opposed to being merely a fixer. CIOs also complain about the lack of travel monies for training and development for themselves and their staff.

The Case for CIO at the Table

Far more controversial than a title is the level of responsibilities of the CIO and his or her reporting relationships. Many observers of technology governance argue that given the complexity and what's at stake with today's rather complicated and interdependent technology, the CIO should be an integral part of the management team at the "cabinet level." This means that when the mayor and city council, or the county commissioners meet, the CIO should be present too. The more the CIO knows about what is being discussed and planned, the more effective the CIO will be. This will also provide a greater opportunity to become better acquainted with other high-level decision-makers and thus provide the opportunity to form strategic relationships that can lead to better teamwork, communication, and improved productivity.

Centralization, Decentralization, Consolidation

The terms centralization, decentralization, and consolidation can have varying definitions depending upon how they are applied. Given today's severe economic realities, many governmental jurisdictions are centralizing and consolidating their operations at the same time. There is an irony here, in that many of the newer technologies cater to more specific program or service-based applications so that, while it probably makes sense to consolidate network and storage systems, IT departments may want to push back from supporting just about everything considered "technology." Many of the newer government workers are quite familiar with today's workforce-related technologies. Public mangers along with IT leaders must look at their respective organizations from a holistic point of view. There is a need today as never before to reduce waste, unwanted redundancy, and inefficiency (Shark 2009).

> Despite the recognition and need for highly skilled CIOs, many senior managers take great pains to avoid having to deal with the CIO. Some view the CIO as the "officer of 'no'"—or the one who will cause delay in certain projects.

In an overly simplistic view, technology began as a centralized function and evolved into a more distributed set of systems. Over the years the pendulum has swayed towards centralization to decentralization and now back again. The goal here is maintain a sense of balance. Like any governance system, technology systems require periodic reviews and tune-ups. There is no universal solution as every jurisdiction has different cultures and needs.

However, what is a universal principal is the increased need for business level decision-making and leadership.

Today's technology leader must view their mission as not only supporting the enterprise where they can, but to seek out ways to get more out of less. Such expectations must be met with the appropriate decision-making authority, which includes titles and positions that give them the undisputed power to actually lead.

Technology Enterprise

Just as those who kid about the initials of CIO standing for "career is over," the term enterprise resource planning (ERP) has been joked about too, referring ERP to "enhanced retirement program." Both share a common thread, which is increased leadership, responsibility, and visibility, plus added risk that goes along with added responsibilities. At a training class for new CIOs, one of the facilitators who was a seasoned CIO nearing retirement said his success was due to him never being found. He loved working in the background and bragged about often hiding and not being located. That might have worked in the past, but in today's environment, it is quite the opposite. Today ERP undertakings carry greater weight, as the expectations are so much higher than ever before. ERP is something that everyone appears to look forward to and most are supportive of the goals and objectives—at least in the beginning of the planning process—of looking at the entire enterprise and seeking system-wide solutions. Unfortunately, there are many devils buried in the details. Agencies, divisions, and departments who start out supporting ERP often find themselves arguing for exceptions to the plans down the road. Arguments may include wanting to preserve current business practices, resisting any changes to existing processes or reporting requirements. Rather than take a bold hard look at how to live with a new system and the changes it will bring, managers often fight to preserve the status quo. Such behavior will lead not only to serious delays—but is also likely to cost more money due to writing exception code. In the end the more deviations to the new system norm, the more it will depart from what ERP is trying to achieve.

The main purpose for mentioning ERP here is to once again restate the need for high-level technology leadership and champions. When it comes to ERP, this is no place for "lone rangers" or weak leaders—regardless of intentions. ERP requires strong leadership and commitment and must engage staff at all levels with technology, business process mapping, and change management solutions. Finally, public administrators all too often ignore or pay too little attention to supporting the process of project management (Shark 2011).

In the Real World

Despite the recognition and need for highly skilled CIOs, many senior managers take great pains to avoid having to deal with the CIO. Some view the CIO as the "officer of 'no'"—or the one who will cause delay in certain projects.

Figure 2.11 There has never been a greater need for high-level technology leadership

Many don't appreciate the CIOs project management approach, feeling that their project is more important than others and believe they have to move more quickly. Moreover, with the advent of bring your own device (BYOD) and the consumerization of technology, many have come to believe that the CIO is becoming irrelevant or a hindrance. Unrealistic demands and expectations have often been placed on today's CIO, making the position difficult and hard for the CIO to actually lead. Failure to understand and appreciate the role of the technology leader could lead to some rather serious consequences.

HealthCare.gov: A Failure in Technology Leadership?

Like the sinking of the Titanic in 1912, those who study government will be re-examining the causes of the colossal failure of the initial rollout of Health-Care.gov on October 1, 2013 for some time to come. What was to be the enduring legacy of President Obama's presidency, the Healthcare.gov website was slated to be the main gateway and highly visible centerpiece of this initiative. Instead, by every standard, the initial rollout was a huge failure, frustrating millions of Americans as well as further eroding confidence in government's ability to build and maintain complex systems. Critics of large government will use this example for years to come as just another example of government's inability to design and manage complex information systems.

While it may be too early to understand all that went wrong and why, initial accounts reveal that at the very least, there was a catastrophic failure

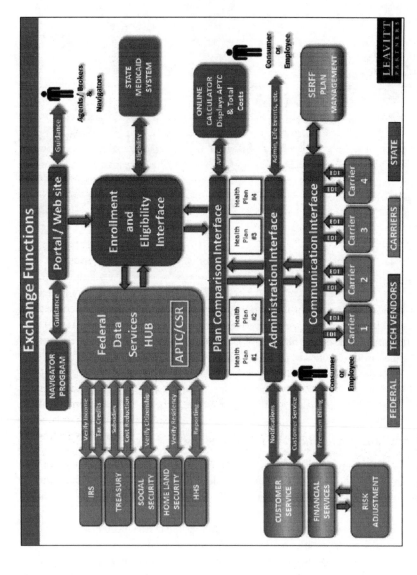

Figure 2.12 Exchange functions

Source: Leavitt Partners website

of leadership across all levels of the program and beyond. While it may not have made much difference, the Federal CIO was not involved. Instead, a relatively unknown agency was assigned the leadership responsibility for the entire project. There are many angles of the story to be studied which include such factors as the political environment (politics), administrative oversight, procurement, policy oversight, project management and oversight, policy versus administration, untimely changes in system requirements, and failure to communicate and test each component of a very complex system before any rollout.

Even at this early stage of criticism, it appears that the greatest problems had more to do with leadership discrepancies as opposed to acknowledged glitches and shortcomings with the software. Even with the best of leadership, the law with all its nuances was extremely complicated and required various databases to be queried and records authenticated from among no less than five federal and state agencies including the IRS, Social Security, Treasury, Homeland Security and HHS, as well as private insurance companies. What the public saw on the sign-up screen was a simple and rather straight forward website. However, no one could imagine all that went on behind the scenes except those closest to the project. By any measure, this had to be the greatest failure in a public-facing program to date.

Public administrators at all levels of government need to be keenly aware of the role that leadership plays in managing technology and must do a better job towards understanding the various roles involved in any project involving technology. Perhaps the most important role one can play is that of creating and maintaining an open and innovative environment. The ideal environment would be one that encourages ongoing communication and to encourage various ideas and informed opinions without fear of retribution or retaliation. The ideal environment has to encourage the testing of every application, link, and data stream continuously. Perhaps on a larger scale, politicians need to recognize that the signing of an Act or Bill does not in itself signify the end of a battle, or the instant beginning of a remedy. Instead, all must recognize that technology is only a set of tools that at times has its own limitations. One cannot simply pass an Act or Bill, and walk away expecting it to be carried out to the letter of the law. When technology is expected to play a significant role, it is critical to have the right leadership in place and to constantly monitor the process at all levels in order to realize a successful launch of any legislative or administrative mandate.

Discussion Questions

1. What are the various pros and cons of specific reporting relationships regarding the CIO? Why might this be important?
2. Taking into account an organization you work for or are familiar with, which person has the most influence in making technology decisions? How well are they performing this duty, and what might be improved?

3. What types of opportunities exist in your area for technology leadership?
4. How might technology leadership be improved in your organization?
5. What are the best arguments for making the case for the CIO to be an essential participant within the government enterprise?
6. If you became the CIO of your department or agency what would be your five most important objectives? In what time frame?
7. Can you list at least five references and or resources where one could learn more about the role of the CIO?
8. With all the changes in technology, do you believe the role of the CIO will remain relevant in the years to come? If not, why, and what forces might cause this?
9. Can you name the CIO of your city, county, or state? Do you know what the technology priorities are? Can you find how much is spent on technology in your city, county, or state?
10. Can you describe a technology related failure that can be attributed to a failure of leadership? Please explain.

References

Dearstyne, Bruce. 2009. "Chief Information Officers: Leading Change Through Challenges and Change," in *CIO Leadership for Cities and Counties—Emerging Trends and Practices*. PTI, Washington, DC.

National Association of State Chief Information Officers. 2012. *The 2012 State CIO Survey*. NASCIO, Lexington, KY. Accessed October 17, 2014. http://www.nascio.org/publications/documents/NASCIO-2012StateCIOSurvey.pdf.

National Association of State Chief Information Officers. 2013a. *The Enterprise Imperative: Leading Through Governance, Portfolio Management, and Collaboration*. NASCIO, Lexington, KY. Accessed October 17, 2014. http://www.nascio.org/publications/documents/2013_State_CIO_Survey_FINAL.pdf.

National Association of State Chief Information Officers. 2013b. *State CIO Leadership in Government Innovation and Transformation*. NASCIO, Lexington, KY. Accessed October 17, 2014. http://www.nascio.org/publications/documents/State-CIO-Leadership-Final.pdf.

National Association of State Chief Information Officers. 2013c. *State CIO Priorities for 2014*. NASCIO, Lexington, KY. Accessed October 17, 2014. http://www.nascio.org/publications/documents/NASCIO_StateCIOTop10For2014.pdf.

Shark, Alan R. ed. 2009. *CIO Leadership for State Governments–Emerging Trends & Practices*. PTI, Washington, DC.

Shark, Alan R. ed. 2011. *CIO Leadership for Cities and Counties–Emerging Trends and Practices*. PTI, Washington, DC.

Shark, Alan R. 2012. *Seven Trends That Will Transform Local Government Through Technology*. PTI, Alexandria, VA.

Digital Destinations

CIO University. https://cio.gov/
———. http:// www.cio.gov/agenda
———. https://cio.gov/innovate/future-ready-workforce/cio-university-faq/

————. https://cio.gov/wp-content/uploads/downloads/2013/02/2012-Learning-Objectives-Final.pdf

Clinger-Cohen Act of 1996. http://en.wikipedia.org/wiki/Clinger%E2%80%93Cohen_Act

————. http://ocio.os.doc.gov/ITPolicyandPrograms/Capital_Planning/DEV01_003758

Leavitt Partners. http://leavittpartners.com/

PTI. http://www.pti.org

White House. http://www.whitehouse.gov/omb/circulars_a130_a130trans4

Further Reading

McKinney, Richard. 2009. "IT Consolidation: Tearing Down the Silos," in *CIO Leadership for Cities and Counties—Emerging Trends and Practices*. PTI, Washington, DC.

3 E-government and M-government

The Rise of the New Civic Media

The Birth of Electronic Government

This chapter will delve into what e-government is and is not, as well as its many expanding dimensions. E-government in its simplest form is a shortcut for the term *electronic government*. It has been used to describe the relationship between government and citizen services, and more recently it describes the business or administrative processes between government to government as well as government to businesses and all the relationships that transpire among each other. The common connection is that of communicating "electronically" or "digitally" between computer systems. Of course to move data and communications between computer systems, one needs reliable broadband connectivity, and it needs to be able to connect via the Internet. Broadband, be it wired or wireless, goes hand in hand with Internet data traffic in order to complete the circuit. But how information is addressed, formatted, and sent via an agreed-upon standard lies with the greatness of the Internet.

The first application-based use of computers in government began during World War II and the first digital computer began in the late 1940s with a computer so large it filled a large room. Today, by comparison, a typical handheld smart device has many times more computing power than its ancestors and in a fraction of the space. E-government didn't just happen, it evolved from the growth of technologies beginning with the migration from manual typewriters to electric typewriters, and then to word processing systems. With each advance in technology a new baseline for innovation and improvement is built upon—layer by layer, which in turn brings further advances. Technology responds to opportunity and there was plenty of opportunity and need to automate office systems such as records management. Before the office computer, government was inundated with slow-moving record management systems. They lacked a common approach to system design and architecture. Here too advances in computing technology as well as network protocols were evolving to the point that they began to offer the promise of greater things to come. Take Ethernet for example. It became standardized in 1985 and has replaced what was once competing wired local area networks (LAN) such as token ring and ARCNET. Ethernet is the standard of choice for moving information

Figure 3.1 What used to fill a room now fits inside the space of a bottle cap

Source: National Archives photo no. 111-B-4246 (Brady Collection)

from one computer to another computer or network, or to and from the Internet.

Ethernet is the standard of choice for moving information from one computer to another computer or network, or to and from the Internet.

Like so many great inventions, the Internet began as a concept with a relatively limited goal and no one in their day could have foreseen what the Internet would ultimately become. By the end of 1969 after a series of discussions and research papers, hundreds of meetings and on-going collaboration, four host computers connected together to form what was then called the Advanced Research Projects Agency Network, or better known as ARPANET. This was the first packet-switching network that would make it possible to transfer huge amounts of data from one computer to another and at great distances too. Originally funded by the Advanced Research Projects Agency, it was later adopted by the Defense Advanced

Research Projects Agency (DARPA) that is housed within the US Department of Defense. Its main purpose was initially to link universities and research laboratories working together on special projects. This network would become the foundation of what was to become the Internet as we know it today. Aside from having great talent, shared vision, and perseverance, had it not been for the federal government's initial support, the Internet, as we know it today, would not have been built. As it was, the Internet would not be commercialized until 1995. For a brief history of the Internet see Internet Society (2013).

Government computers were already in use during World War II, well before the Internet, but pre-Internet systems were largely localized and housed within specific geographic limitations. In today's business and government environment, a computer system or network is by itself quite limited if not totally ineffective when not connected to the Internet. It is the Internet that makes it possible to transmit and receive voice, data, and video communications which, if need be, can travel the globe within milliseconds. The term electronic government or e-government emerged in the early 1990s and has continued to evolve through a confluence of complimentary but separate pathways, electricity, broadband, Internet, and computer devices.

The Clinger–Cohen Act of 1996

Congress passed the Information Technology Management Reform Act of 1996 commonly referred to as the Clinger–Cohen Act of 1996 in recognition of the Bill's champion sponsors; Rep. William Clinger, R-PA, and Senator William Cohen, R-Maine. This new federal law was a groundbreaking legislation aimed at improving the way the federal government acquires, uses, and disposes of information technology. Up until this period there were many fragmented approaches, which largely mirrored the way information technology had been managed and deployed. Until the passage of the Act, each agency had its own standard operating procedures—but what was lacking was a unified approach common to all when it came to policies and procedures.

The Clinger–Cohen Act was groundbreaking legislation aimed at improving the way the federal government acquires, uses, and disposes of information technology.

The Act called for effective IT leadership in each agency, and for each agency to establish clear accountability for IT management activities. Towards this end the Act called for the creation of the position Chief Information Officer (CIO) for each agency, with "the visibility and management responsibilities necessary to carry out the specific provisions of the Act." Among the agency CIO's responsibilities were:

- help to control system development risks;
- better manage technology spending; and
- succeed in achieving real, measureable improvements in agency performance.

The Act also called for a CIO Council to be headed by the OMB and required overall efficiencies and accountability when it came to managing IT in all its forms. For example, it called for the acquisition, planning, and management of information technology, which was to be treated as a "capital investment" and operated just as an efficient and profitable business would operate.

The Act was quite broad in scope and assigned the Director of the Office of Management and Budget (OMB) the responsibility for improving the businesses processes of government through the better use of information technology as well as to reduce the burdens of information gathering to the public. The Act supplemented the information resources of the Federal Paperwork Reduction Act by establishing a competitive approach to improving the acquisition and management of agency information systems through work process redesign, and by linking planning and investment strategies to the budget process.

The Director of the OMB was given considerable responsibilities which not only carried specific tasks regarding the Executive Branch of Government but to assess, on a continuing basis, the experiences of executive agencies, state and local governments, international organizations, as well as the private sector in managing information technology.

When it came to standards and guidelines that pertained to federal computer systems, the OMB Director was to be responsible for overseeing the management and coordination through the Secretary of Commerce via its National Institute of Standards and Technology (NIST).

To help standardize IT purchases, the Act required executive agencies to:

- establish an IT capital planning and investment review process;
- utilize performance measurement measures to better assess just how well IT supports programs;
- justify the continuation of systems that deviate from cost, performance, or schedule.

The Chief Information Officer's responsibilities for each federal agency included:

- reporting directly to the agency head;
- having information resources management referred to as ERM (Electronic Records Information) as their primary duty;

- providing advice and assistance to the agency head on IT and information resources management;
- promoting efficient and effective design and operation of IRM processes;
- using performance measures to monitor IT programs;
- assessing the knowledge skills of IRM personnel;
- sharing with the CFO responsibility for the provision of financial and performance data for financial statements;
- assuming the responsibility of the Designated Senior Official defined in the Paperwork Reduction Act;
- serving on the CIO Council.

All this may not sound significant today, yet going back to 1965 the General Services Administration (GSA) had exclusive authority to buy all information technology goods and services on behalf of the federal government. This came about with the passage of the Brooks Act, which provided for a centralized purchasing policy that allowed for contractor selection based on technical knowledge and competency, and not by price alone. Over time however, things began to bog down and the process itself, which sounded great on paper, had become a burden in both efficiency and timeliness. Until the passage of the Clinger-Cohen Act, federal agencies had to go to the GSA with a business case that laid out the rationale for what it was that they were trying to procure, and why. They could not purchase hardware or software without going through this approval process. The Clinger-Cohen Act introduced the use of government-wide acquisition contracting which allowed agencies, once they articulated their needs, to be able to place orders against their contracts—thus streamlining the process.

The E-Government Act of 2002

Building on the foundational framework of the Clinger-Cohen Act, the E-Government Act expanded upon the federal IT framework and began to address citizen interests and involvement too. The E-Government Act of 2002 was signed into law in December 2002. Title II of the Act focused on accessibility, usability, and the preservation of government information. The stated purpose was to improve the methods by which Government information, including information on the Internet, is organized, preserved, and made accessible to the public. Clearly, Congress was becoming aware that computers and the Internet had a growing and significant impact on the way government was using information technology to provide various programs and services to other government agencies and, departments as well as the business community, and in some cases to the general public. Congress viewed the use of advancing information technology as being applied unevenly and not necessarily taking advantage of IT's potential.

Congress passed the Act in hopes of making the federal government more "transparent and accountable" as well as "provide enhanced access to

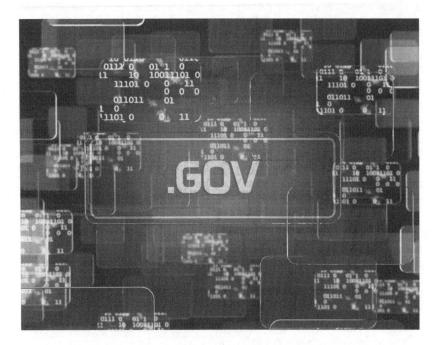

Figure 3.2 ".gov" is considered a first tier domain introduced in 1986

Government information and services in a manner that was consistent with laws and regulations regarding the protection of personal privacy, national security, and records retention, access for persons with disabilities, and other relevant laws."

OMB issued its implementation guidance for the E-Government Act of 2002 in August 2003. The administration stated that it saw this Act as a significant step forward in the way the federal agencies should consider using information technology to transform agency business into a more citizen-oriented and user-friendly process. The E-Government Act:

- advocated a greater citizen focused approach to current IT polices and programs;
- established an Office of Electronic Government in the Office of Management and Budget to coordinate IT policy;
- formalized the establishment of a Chief Information Officers (CIO) Council;
- permanently reauthorized and amended agency information security requirements through the Federal Information Security Management Act (FISMA);
- protected the confidentiality of certain types of data across the government and allowed key statistical agencies to share business data through the Confidential Information Protection and Statistical Efficiency Act (CIPSEA);

• supported activities that OMB and the executive branch were already pursuing under the President's Management Agenda's Expanding Electronic Government initiative.

The Office of Electronic Government was headed by the Administrator for E-Government and Information Technology. The Office was housed within OMB, and in 2009 the title of *Administrator* was replaced with that of the title, *Chief Information Officer*. In August 2009, Vivek Kundra was appointed by President Obama to become the nation's first Chief Information Officer (CIO), or at least the first to carry such a title. The President also appointed a Chief Performance Officer as well as a Chief Technology Officer to help round out the President's objectives of making government more effective and efficient through better adoption and usage of information technology. The Act called for a comprehensive approach to managing information technology and to better interact with citizens. Under guidance from OMB, the agency issued a number of implementation of responsibilities under the Act. In section II.A, the following requirements pertain to all federal agencies:

1. Agencies are expected to make their public regulatory dockets electronically accessible and searchable using Regulations.gov, the President's rulemaking e-government initiative. Agencies are also expected to accept electronic submissions to the online dockets.
2. Agencies must conduct privacy impact assessments for new IT investments and online information collections, consistent with OMB's forthcoming guidance on the privacy provisions of the key government act.
3. Agency heads must establish and operate IT training programs, taking advantage of learning partnerships, such as the GoLearn.gov, the online training portal for federal government employees.

The OMB Guidance directive also detailed specific responsibilities to certain agencies. These special responsibilities included a provision for the training of federal employees, calling for a study on best practices for Community Technology Centers and to develop an online tutorial for assessing government information and services thus furthering the federal government's understanding of citizen use of public facilities for Internet access. The Department of Homeland Security was charged with conducting a study on the use of IT for crisis management. The Department of the Interior through its Federal Geographic Data Group was charged with developing common protocols for geographic information sharing. The Archivist of the United States was charged with issuing guidance to agencies regarding record-keeping policies and procedures for federal government information on the Internet and other electronic records. Finally, the General Services Administration was charged with issuing rules on state and local government use of Federal Supply Schedules for purchasing IT.

The E-Government Act also required the OMB Director to issue guidelines in several sections of the Act, including:

- electronic signatures, so that citizens can interact electronically with the federal government in a secure manner;
- categorizing and indexing standards for government information;
- standards for agency websites;
- agency reporting dissemination of federally funded research and development (R&D);
- privacy issues, including privacy impact assessments, privacy notices on what government uses today websites, and privacy policies in machine-readable formats.

The Act addressed the role of the agency's CIO, as well as reporting to Congress annually on the status of the implementation of the Act. While much of the Act has been fully implemented, there are number of stated requirements that have yet to been fully realized, or for that matter, implemented at all. For example, the Act made clear that each agency CIO would report directly to the agency administrator or top director. Today, many agency CIOs are far removed from the agency director and instead report through a complicated maize of public managers. While not everything has been implemented as originally required, the overall impact of the E-Government Act has nonetheless been both substantial and enduring.

One question remains, with all the advances in information technology, has information technology brought citizens closer to the federal government and all its citizen-facing initiatives, or has technology, regardless of intent, further alienated them?

> One question remains, with all the advances in information technology, has information technology brought citizens closer to the federal government and all its citizen-facing initiatives, or has technology, regardless of intent, further alienated them?

E-government at the State and Local Level

Other then filing taxes and looking to the federal government to issue and enforce rules that protect us—let alone defend the nation—most citizens view state and local government as being more relevant to them on a day-to-day basis. Citizen interaction with local governments such as with cities and counties essentially starts at birth with the issuance of a birth certificate. Local governments issue licenses and permits such as marriage licenses, building permits, recreational permits, health certificates to name a few.

Before office automation took hold in government, all of these functions were once handled entirely through paper forms. State government's main interaction with citizens traditionally has been with the state department of motor vehicles (DMV) where one must go through the process of applying and receiving a driver's license, or the registration of a vehicle. States also administer unemployment and often health benefits as administrative agents of the federal government. Going to the local DMV has often been looked upon as a dreaded experience because of long lines and antiquated systems. Today, most DMVs have streamlined their business processes and dozens of transactions can now be handled entirely online.

The impact of e-governments appears to have taken hold at the local level faster than that of the federal government for several key reasons. First, despite local bureaucratic challenges, when compared to the federal government, they are by comparison often more agile and are able to move more diligently, usually with less layers of management to navigate. Second, local governments operate on a much smaller scale as compared to the federal government. Third, the public is closer in every respect, thus able to exert greater political pressure, which in turn makes local government public administrators more accountable. Of course e-government, when it comes to citizen involvement, could not have taken hold without the growing trust and usage

Figure 3.3 Protecting public information is at least as important as obtaining it

of the Internet. Many citizens were initially distrustful of using credit cards for all kinds of online transactions but Congress came along to help with the passage of the Fair Credit Billing Act (FCBA) which was enacted in 1975 as an amendment to the Truth in Lending Act. Among a host of protections to consumers was the protection against loss or stolen credit cards where any liability was capped to fifty dollars—regardless of any unauthorized or fraudulent charges made. This protection of credit cards did not extend to ATM cards as for the most part they did not exist during this time. Of course today, even with such protections, credit card theft continues to be an issue, Congress is considering extending protections to debit cards, and identity theft has grown to become an even greater national problem.

Privacy and Security Implications

The E-Government Act of 2002 was both groundbreaking and far-reaching in scope. In contemporary life, the issue of *privacy* has moved to the forefront of policy debates. Contemplating the impact of technology and privacy, Section 208 of the Act required all federal agencies conduct a "privacy impact assessment" (PIA) for all new or substantially changed technology that collects, maintains, or disseminates personally identifiable information (PII) or for new aggregation of information that is collected, maintained, or disseminated using information technology.

The Federal Information Security Management Act, referred to simply as FISMA, was also enacted as part of the E-Government Act of 2002. FISMA was designed to provide a comprehensive framework for ensuring effective security controls regarding federal government information resources. In addition, FISMA required all federal agencies to:

- designate a Chief Information Officer (CIO);
- delegate to the CIO authority to ensure compliance with the requirements imposed by FISMA;
- implement an information security program;
- report on the adequacy and effectiveness of its information security policies, procedures, and practices;
- participate in an annual independent evaluation of the information security program and practices;
- develop and maintain an inventory of the agency's major information systems.

FISMA also required the Director of the OMB to ensure the operation of a central federal information security incident center. While FISMA establishes a framework implementing information security programs for federal information systems, it does not apply to systems used for routine administrative and business applications. This would include administrative and business applications systems that are related to personnel management that could likely contain personally identifiable information. While honest attempts at protecting privacy continue, recent disclosures by the nation's top intelligence gathering agencies has prompted a renewed effort to better safeguard citizen's privacy. More on security and privacy will be covered in Chapter 10.

The Town Hall

The town hall has always served as a symbol of where people come to learn about government actions as well as participating in debates and other government affairs. IT is also the place where people come to pay bills, fill out applications and forms, etc. It has been often been said, in politics all things are local. When it comes to e-government, cities and counties have followed information technology from a different perspective—mostly starting with a more citizen-centric direction. For many local governments, information technology adoption has basically mirrored the private sector in terms of automating standard business practices along with customer services. Local governments have always had an ongoing requirement to collect data, have citizens complete various forms, fill out applications, collect revenues, and disburse payments. Like any business, local governments have done a remarkable job in embracing technology as both a necessity in better serving citizens and saving scarce resources; mainly staff, time, and money.

Regardless of advances in IT, the overwhelming majority appreciates the option of completing online transactions from wherever they may be, or whatever time of day or night. It should be pointed out there are citizens who actually enjoy coming to a city hall to conduct business because they feel transactions are more personal, they lack the computer skills, or value face-to-face human assistance. As a result, a fissure exists between the digitally enabled verses the digital opt-outs. As government continues to drive more citizens towards online transactions there is growing concern as to what do about those who are not online or unable to be online. These digital "outcasts" will face greater isolation and economic disadvantages (this topic will be covered in greater details in Chapter 13).

Here are but a few examples:

1. The Internal Revenue Service (IRS) used to mail out blank tax returns to just about every taxpaying citizen on record. Paper forms were also available in most post offices. In 2010 the IRS in a cost-saving move stopped mailing out forms automatically and began actively promoting downloadable forms and direct online tax form submissions. The IRS claims that it will save taxpayers approximately ten million per month.
2. The federal government used to mail out over seventy million checks per month to those on social security and federal entitlement programs. In 2011 the Treasury Department began a policy that stopped the practice of mailing out checks and provided instead two options; direct deposit to an authorized bank account, or receive a government-issued debit card that

Main Attraction of E-Government At The Local Level
• Always Open (24 hour city hall)
• Locality Neutral
• Faster Transactions
• No Lines
• Saves Government Money
• Citizen Satisfaction
• Business Satisfaction
• Improved Security Applications
• Accessibility (can be almost anywhere)
• Language Options
• Greater Citizen Participation Possibilities

Figure 3.4 Key features of e-government

would be recharged electronically. In March 2013 this practice would include all citizens receiving federal benefit payments. The Treasury Department claims that they will save taxpayers one billion dollars over a ten year period.

3. The State of Virginia Department of Motor Vehicles (DMV) charges a five dollar "fee" for anyone physically coming to a DMV office if that transaction could have been accomplished by going online.

In each of these examples, there is a group within the US population that is either inconvenienced by the changes in policy, or they are directly disenfranchised. What other examples can you think of?

At the local level there are essentially four modes of citizen-centered e-government. The first three are essentially web-based; whether accessed by a PC, tablet, or other mobile device.

Static/Informational E-government

The first mode can be termed *static/informational*. This is the most basic form in terms of options and functionality. To this day there are still many communities that still operate in this mode of limited functionality. Reasons for not progressing to greater functionality are usually attributed to a lack of financial resources and or lack of staff talent. However, as we shall see in Chapter 7 there are now companies in the private sector that offer local governments website design, hosting, and more, for a monthly fee and off premise.

Some local government websites might contain spectacular pictures and artwork, but lack the ability to complete online forms, and accept

Main Features of Static/Informational E-Government
• Citizen Access to Information
• Government Functions and Services
• Directory & Directions to Parks and Community Centers
• Calendar of City-Sponsored Events & Activities
• Property Information
• Citizen Services
• Job Postings
• Phone & Staff Directories
• Meeting Notices
• Statistics of City
• Tourist Information
• Maps of Key Locations

Figure 3.5 E-government—features of static/informational model

credit card payments. These systems provide citizens with directories of whom to call, office hours, maps and directions of government run facilities, names and contact information for key administrative staff as well as elected leaders.

Transactional E-government

The second mode usually contains all of the items found in the first with the addition of interactive administrative functionality, which can be called *transactional e-government*.

As one can see by Figure 3.6, this second mode contains far greater functionality. Here citizens can pay fees, taxes, and other types of online payments as well as fill out and have forms, permits, and some types of other applications—all processed online. Citizens can save time by not having to travel to a government facility as well as save on transportation costs. One could also make the argument that fewer people traveling to a government facility translates into energy savings and cleaner air and a reduction in car traffic. Local governments can realize savings by having citizens complete time-consuming transactions online without staff time and help. When someone does require help, it is usually easier to start with looking up a record online.

Participatory or E-democracy E-government

The third mode of e-government is called participatory or e-democracy.

Main Features of Transactional E-Government
• License Renewal & Payment
• Payment of Parking Tickets, Fines
• Registration for Functions
• Interactive Job Applications
• Online Permits, Business Licenses, Court Documents
• Online Purchase Orders, Bid Documents
• Sales Tax Collection
• Distance Learning
• Webcasting of City/County Meetings
• Communications with Local Leaders
• Links to Other Key Sites (airport, transportation, hotels)
• Interactive Maps of Key Locations—often with from here to there directions

Figure 3.6 E-government—features of transactional model

Main Examples of Participatory or E-Democracy
• Digital Democracy—citizen two-way interaction
• Respond to Proposed Rules & Regulations
• View & Comment on Other's Comments/Pleadings
• Vote on Certain Issues (see results)
• View & Participate in Live Meetings
• View Streaming Video of Past Meetings
• Online Voting—in the future

Figure 3.7 E-government—features of e-democracy model

An App for That/E-government

The fourth mode bypasses a government website completely and uses, in addition to a website, social media and smart device *applications*, simply referred to as *apps*. Today there are hundreds of government-related apps that can be found at the respective Apple, Android, and Microsoft app stores.

Many of the more popular and useful apps are the ones that carry the name of a particular city, county, or government agency. At the local level, one can send confirming pictures and forms regarding a particular no-emergency problem such as a pothole or water main break. Most have the ability to

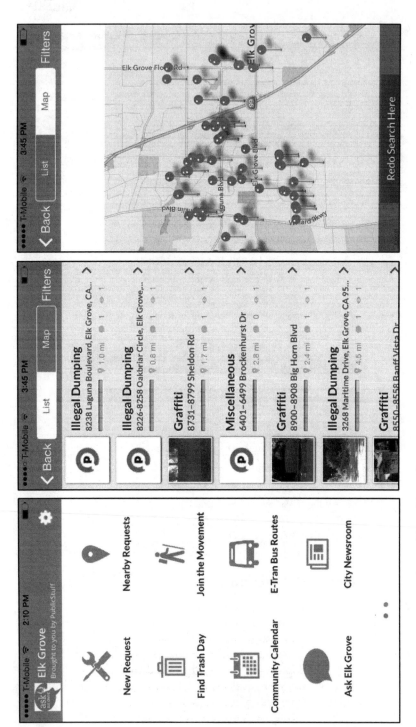

Figure 3.8 Elk Grove, CA app designed by PublicStuff

Figure 3.9 Miami-Dade Transit Tracker iPhone and Android apps

Source: Miamidade.gov

Figure 3.10 IRS2Go mobile app

map it and receive feedback and in some cases, progress reports. Still others provide comprehensive and interactive transit information (Shark 2012).

Social and Civic Media

E-government had its roots well planted before social media became such the phenomenon that it has become today. In fact prior to 2004 social media did not even exist. Since then, advances in website technologies, and the increase of Internet and broadband penetration, have served as the digital fertilizer that provided the necessary ingredients for social media to emerge and evolve. Just five years ago, few could imagine that millions of people worldwide would be heavily involved in sending messages limited to just 140 characters as in Twitter. Studies have consistently shown of those who use text messaging, they prefer texting to voice conversations. Each new platform and improvement creates new opportunities for innovation in social media. The term Web 2.0 is still in use and the meaning has been interpreted in many different ways. Perhaps the most significant factor lies in an individual's ability not simply to receive content, but to create it. Some common characteristics of Web 2.0 include:

- interactive
- web-based
- browser-based
- intuitive
- content sharing
- content development by users
- collaboration tools
- interactive games
- applications
- mobile applications

Web 2.0 also includes elements such as searching, linking, authoring, podcasting, blogging and social networking, creating content, as well as sharing. All of that is wholly dependent on a vibrant and open information data system called the Internet. Unfortunately, when it comes to technology, for every advantage there appears to be some form of disadvantage. On one hand citizens enjoy the speed of information flowing around from place to place within milliseconds but on the other hand there are plenty of examples of the speed of ignorance or worse. False and baseless accusations can travel as fast and could further add to civil discord and uncivil behavior; digital mobs causing havoc. Social media then holds the promise of instant intelligence, but at the same time governments need to safeguard against instant ignorance.

While social networking is only a derivative of Web 2.0, the two terms are most often used synonymously. Social media goes far beyond the traditional website, and instead of providing mostly one-way information, it provides a way to connect emotionally, where content can be created by just about anyone and shared. Over 73 percent of the US population uses social media and collectively, people spend more than 700 billion minutes per month on social media—and that is just for Facebook.

State and local governments have evolved along with their citizens from e-government to m-government and have moved away from a web-centric model to a more multi-channel approach. While websites continue to serve an invaluable purpose of providing key information and offering online services and payments, governments are now moving to mobile devices—be it a smartphone, a laptop, or a tablet—as another way to reach and engage citizens.

State and local governments have evolved along with their citizens from e-government to m-government and have moved away from a web-centric model to a more multi-channel approach. While websites continue to serve an invaluable purpose of providing key information and offering online services and payments, governments are now moving to mobile devices—be it a smartphone, a laptop, or a tablet—as another way to reach and engage citizens.

Mobile applications (apps) are a relatively new channel of communication. They may exist and operate entirely outside a local government operation and website. They might take the form of a stand-alone application or one that is fully integrated into a local government's communications center.

State and local government leaders and managers are challenged as never before to seek out new and better ways to engage and interact with the publics they serve. With a greater than 97 percent penetration rate of mobile devices, which are becoming smarter with each new model, government leaders must understand and adequately address how the citizens they serve prefer to be engaged. At the same time, these same managers must always be aware of those in the population who either cannot afford or choose to opt out of communication technology and thus are as happy not to be engaged.

Social Media Policies

Public administrators have learned that there is a price to be paid for what appears on the front end as being *free* social media outlets. Within hours, any agency can create a Facebook or Twitter presence for *free* but there are many associated costs that are not at first obvious. First and foremost, there needs to be a social media policy that sets forth the mission, goals, and objectives of a social media strategy using social media tools. Second, there needs to be dedicated staff to make sure content is up to date and, to the best extent possible, relevant from the eye of the intended customer/citizen. Third, the social media sites (and apps, if used) need to be monitored 24/7 to make sure that the sites are not being abused, misused, or in a worst case—hijacked. Fourth, there are federal regulations that must be adhered to that carry stiff penalties for non-compliance. For example, in 1988 Congress amended the Rehabilitation Act of 1973 so that federal agencies would be required to make their electronic and information technology accessible to people with disabilities. Section 508 was enacted to eliminate barriers in information technology, to make available new opportunities for people with disabilities, and to encourage development of technologies that will help achieve these goals. In particular Section 508 contains guidelines that agencies must follow that makes their website accessible to anyone with disabilities. Section 505 applies to all form of federal electronic documents, including websites, and it would also apply to any government app too.

Civic Media and News Reporting

Among governments many challenges in the information age is the issue of finding the best means of providing information to the public. Most citizens receive news about government largely from the print media; however, there is a diminishing role for "print" newspapers, as we have known them. Today the trend continues away from traditional printed newspapers where circulation continues its inevitable downward spiral while at the same time online readership continues to grow.

Not surprisingly perhaps, the study also found that the Internet has become the third most popular news source. Local television has become less local and more regional and national with even less time devoted to government, except in the cases that involve scandals, budget cost overruns, and outright crime.

It appears the daily *news* has transformed into daily *views*, which can become particularly worrisome for government managers. Citizens are not just reading news online—they are contributing to it too. According to the Pew Internet & Family Study "Understanding the Participatory News Consumer" (Purcell et al. 2010), 37 percent of Internet users have contributed to the creation of news, commented about it, or disseminated it via postings on social media sites like Facebook or Twitter. Also, according to a study by the Pew Internet & Family Life Project called *Civic Engagement in the Digital Age,* (Pew Research Internet Project 2013), the well-educated and the well-off are more likely than others to participate in civic life online—just as those groups have always been more likely to be active in politics and community affairs offline.

> The well-educated and the well-off are more likely than others to participate in civic life online—just as those groups have always been more likely to be active in politics and community affairs offline (Pew Internet & Family Life Project, 2013).

Public administrators realize they can no longer rely on traditional media to reach the public. They have little choice but to experiment with and develop programs leading to innovative channels where they can attempt to broadcast their messages through various digital media applications. Many government jurisdictions offer citizens the choice of having specific news and information feeds sent directly to them in the form of alerts, weather and traffic bulletins, or meeting notices.

While slow to adopt social media that some refer to as civic media, governments of all sizes have a social (civic) media presence through Facebook, Twitter, YouTube, and more. The Federal Office of Management and Budget has issued guidelines for all federal agencies to embrace social media. Cities such as New York, Philadelphia, Boston, Chicago, San Francisco, as well as counties like Montgomery County (MD) and Miami-Dade County, have embraced social media as a means of better service delivery and more direct citizen communication and interaction. But social media is not limited to large jurisdictions alone, and it need not be expensive. Today, thousands of small local governments have turned to social media in one form or fashion. Apps generally provide scalability where they can be easily replicated from one jurisdiction to another as well as being designed to be highly customizable. With smart devices growing faster than any other form of mobile device technology, it makes sense for citizens to shop online or

Figure 3.11 Over 125 billion apps have been downloaded through 2014

"chat" with friends and family, and when need be, take care of government business with the press of an (app) button. People don't download websites for information, but they do download apps.

M-government

M-government is a term used more frequently outside of the US. It refers to mobile technologies that connect citizens to government. The Organization for Economic Cooperation and Development (OECD) along with the International Telecommunication Union (ITU) issued a report in 2011 that essentially catalogs best practices in mobile government technologies with most applications centered on regular cell phones or to some extent smartphones (Shark 2011). The data points out that there is an impressive increase in the use of and access to mobile technology in both developed and developing countries. It may be hard to imagine that many innovative approaches simply using SMS messaging technologies enable citizens in developing countries to receive administrative information or support farmers with weather forecast information and market price alerts.

Figure 3.12 Standard website using responsive design

Source: http://www.miamidade.gov/transit/transit-tracker-app.asp

Figure 3.13 Same webpage on a cell phone screen using responsive design

M-government is enabling developing countries to provide better government services especially when the local government infrastructure is weak, inefficient, or non-existent.

In developing countries e-government and m-government initiatives are treated as one. Today, "responsive design" technology is being adopted that allows a website's content to be displayed on any screen size and with any operating system. If one is viewing a page on a small screen the information will be stacked making for a better user experience and saving governments from having to offer numerous outputs to meet this type of challenge (Shark 2011).

E-government: Measuring Performance

There are many approaches in measuring how well e-government is performing. One can measure visitors, page views, actual completed online transactions, citizen surveys provided at the end of an online transaction, as well as internal savings in staff time on task and other resource measurement techniques. There is also a need to measure overall progress from a comparative point of view. How well is "City A" performing from one year to another or measured against a set of evenly applied standards? Towards this end the E-Governance Institute at Rutgers University School of Public Affairs and Administration has developed a global rating system and has published its findings beginning with its first report in 2003 (2014). The E-Governance Institute's mission is to explore how the Internet and other information and communication technologies have and will continue to impact productivity and performance in the public sector and how e-governance fosters new and deeper citizen involvement within the governing process. The instrument modified and expanded over the years asks 103 questions divided into five main categories, which are: Security/Privacy, Usability, Content, Service, and Citizen & Social Engagement. Each of the five areas rates each of the cities thus creating five sub-ratings.

> The E-Governance Institute's mission is to explore how the Internet and other information and communication technologies have and will continue to impact productivity and performance in the public sector and how e-governance fosters new and deeper citizen involvement within the governing process.

	2007		**2009**		**2011**	
Rank	City	Score	City	Score	City	Score
1	Seoul	87.74	Seoul	84.74	Seoul	82.23
2	Hong Kong	71.24	Prague	72.84	Toronto	64.31
3	Helsinki	71.01	Hong Kong	62.83	Madrid	63.63
4	Singapore	68.56	New York	61.10	Prague	61.72
5	Madrid	67.98	Singapore	58.81	Hong Kong	60.81
6	London	65.79	Shanghai	57.41	New York	60.49
7	Tokyo	59.89	Madrid	55.59	Stockholm	60.26
8	Bangkok	59.01	Vienna	55.48	Bratislava	56.74
9	New York	56.54	Auckland	55.28	London	56.19
10	Vienna	53.99	Toronto	52.87	Shanghai	55.49
11	Dublin	53.38	Paris	52.65	Vilnius	55.35
12	Toronto	51.99	Bratislava	52.51	Vienna	54.79
13	Berlin	51.36	London	51.96	Helsinki	54.22
14	Zurich	51.02	Jerusalem	50.64	Auckland	53.19
15	Prague	50.34	Tokyo	50.59	Dubai	53.18
16	Buenos Aires	49.89	Zagreb	50.16	Singapore	52.21
17	Bratislava	49.82	Ljubljana	49.39	Moscow	51.77
18	Sydney	48.60	Lisbon	48.82	Copenhagen	50.06
19	Amsterdam	47.72	Brussels	48.01	Yerevan	49.97
20	Rome	46.98	Johannesburg	47.68	Paris	48.65

Figure 3.14 Rutgers University e-governance summary

Source: Pew Research Internet Project 2013

The United Nations publishes an annual e-governance index where it rates countries—not cities. The *United Nations E-government Survey 2012: E-government for the People* is the latest survey that presents a systematic assessment of the use and potential of information and communication technologies to transform the public sector by enhancing efficiency, effectiveness, transparency, accountability, access to public services, and citizen participation within the 193 Member States of the United Nations. It is based on what they call their *e-Readiness Index*. The findings of the study point out that many have put in place e-government initiatives and information and communication technologies applications for the people to further enhance public sector efficiencies and streamline governance systems to support sustainable development. Among the e-government leaders, innovative technology solutions have gained special recognition as the means to revitalize lagging economic and social sectors.

Rank	Country	E-government development index
1	Republic of Korea	0.9283
2	Netherlands	0.9215
3	United Kingdom	0.8960
4	Denmark	0.8889
5	United States	0.8687
6	France	0.8635
7	Sweden	0.8599
8	Norway	0.8593
9	Finland	0.8505
10	Singapore	0.8474
11	Canada	0.8430
12	Australia	0.8390
13	New Zealand	0.8381
14	Liechtenstein	0.8264
15	Switzerland	0.8134
16	Israel	0.8100
17	Germany	0.8079
18	Japan	0.8019
19	Luxembourg	0.8014
20	Estonia	0.7987

Figure 3.15 UN world e-government development leaders 2012

Source: United Nations Public Adminsitration Network 2012

The UN survey and index is derived from a number of sources which like any international survey have to take into account language, interpretation of terminology, culture, as well as geographic considerations.

Finally, Waseda University, a private university located in Japan, has released its 2013 international e-government ranking report. The Waseda international e-government ranking report uses seven main indicators to rank the e-government development of countries in the world (Waseda University 2013). These indicators are network preparedness/infrastructure,

No.	Final Rankings	Score	No.	Final Rankings	Score
1	Singapore	94.00	29	UAE	63.34
2	Finland	93.18	30	India	62.77
3	USA	93.12	31	Brunei	60.89
4	Korea	92.29	32	Israel	60.25
5	UK	88.76	33	Brazil	59.88
6	Japan	88.30	34	Russia	59.32
7	Sweden	87.80	35	Macau	58.65
8	Denmark	83.52	36	South Africa	57.77
9	Taiwan	83.52	37	Vietnam	55.42
10	Netherlands	82.54	38	Czech Rep.	55.06
11	Australia	82.10	39	Chile	54.87
12	Canada	81.78	40	Indonesia	53.05
13	Switzerland	81.33	41	Philippines	50.88
14	Germany	80.08	42	Romania	49.72
15	Italy	79.11	43	Argentina	49.23
16	New Zealand	77.29	44	Pakistan	47.25
17	Norway	75.53	45	Venezuela	47.20
18	Belgium	72.01	46	Peru	46.56
19	Estonia	71.76	47	Nigeria	45.20
20	France	69.49	48	Egypt	44.11
21	Thailand	69.49	49	Kazakhstan	37.27
22	Portugal	69.11	50	Georgia	34.98
23	Turkey	67.10	51	Cambodia	33.52
24	Malaysia	66.26	52	Fuji	32.65
25	Hong Kong	66.12	53	Tunisia	31.33
26	Spain	65.89	54	Iran	30.77
27	China	65.69	55	Uzbekistan	30.35
28	Mexico	64.24			

Figure 3.16 Waseda University international e-government ratings

Source: Waseda University 2013

management optimization/efficiency, required interface-functioning applications, national portal/homepage, CIO in government, e-government promotion, and e-participation/digital inclusion. There are also thirty subcategories.

There are some obvious discrepancies between the Rutgers University E-Governance Institute survey, the United Nations e-governance readiness index and Waseda University international e-government ratings. This can best be explained by differing variables such as timing and using similar but different survey and measurement criteria. More importantly than any pronounced differences, the surveys provide a clear picture that demonstrates that the trend continues to move towards greater adoption of e-government and e-governance practices throughout the world. The surveys also point to the fact that being number one in one particular year does not necessarily mean that one can expect to be number one in another, there is much change and innovation going on.

The Significance of 311

Once upon a time citizens had limited options when contacting government agencies. If local they could simply walk or drive to the nearest government building such as a city hall. They might try and write or respond to a letter, or they might try and find a phone number and place a call. Before websites, finding the right government telephone number extension was quite a challenge. Most phone books, referred to as the *Yellow Pages* once large, plentiful, and printed by one company, usually contained a special section with key agencies and telephone contact numbers. All too often a citizen would be met with a busy signal, a pre-recorded away message, or a number that has been reassigned or no longer working. With the growing adoption of the Internet it didn't take long for the large yellow books to become much smaller, with limited circulation, specialized, and published by different companies. The newer phone books had one thing in common however, they mostly no longer contained any government page listings.

E-government initiatives are by no means limited to government websites or apps as they still include telephone/cell calls. Most practitioners, when focusing on citizen to government interaction of any kind, refer to the process as "multi-channel" approaches. After all, citizens have different needs and requirements at different times. The challenge for any citizen has always been "who do I contact when I have a problem, need an answer, or want to file a complaint, who do I contact, and how?" As a response, many local governments today have turned to 311 systems. Like its counterpart, 911, 311 systems were designated by the Federal Communications Commission to be used nationally for non-emergency citizen support systems. Such systems are enjoying a good deal of success in that a citizen has one simple-to-remember number and once a call is made it goes directly to the 311 contact center for further action and follow-up. As an example, though not necessarily representative, New York City's 311 system handles anywhere from 35,000 to 50,000 calls per day and claims that they can respond to citizen requests with over 150 languages if requested. Calls may vary from a request for having missed trash removed, to report a broken streetlight, water main break, or other non-emergency issue. The 311 systems have evolved along with technology to go beyond fielding telephone calls to include webpage interfaces, smartphone apps, and SMS messaging.

Once considered simply a call-taking center, 311 contact centers have evolved from taking and directing calls to tracking work orders and reporting the types of issues, frequency, and location thus providing critical data that can assist in planning and the proper deployment of resources.

> Once considered simply a call-taking center, 311 contact centers have evolved from taking and directing calls to tracking work orders and reporting the types of issues, frequency, and location thus providing critical data that can assist in planning and the proper deployment of resources.

Open Government and Citizen Engagement

Enlightened politicians and public administrators have promoted in concept and practice a more open government that includes greater citizen empowerment, transparency, and engagement. It appears there has been a paradigm shift between power through withholding information to power through sharing information. Much of the shift has to do with the fact that citizens have become increasingly distrustful of government and many believe that there is much more to be gained by greater citizen involvement and transparency than not. After all, a democratic society cannot function well if the citizens are held in the dark and or they are mostly distrustful. There is another element that has been working in the background, and that is the rise of information technology applications as well as public adoption of being easily connected to the Internet.

On January 21, 2009, one day after taking the Oath of Office, President Obama said, "My Administration is committed to creating an unprecedented level of openness in Government. We will work together to ensure the public trust and establish a system of transparency, public participation, and collaboration. Openness will strengthen our democracy and promote efficiency and effectiveness in Government" (White House 2009).

While critics complained that this became a largely unfulfilled promise, few, if any, can argue how the federal government has made finding useful information from among federal agency websites, has been extraordinary. Today website addresses have been greatly simplified and Data.gov,

USA Jobs.gov, USASpending.gov, USA.gov, Whitehouse.gov/open, are but a few examples.

The White House issued an Open Government Directive in 2009 that had four central categories, which were:

1. Publish Government Information Online.
2. Improve the Quality of Government Information.
3. Create and Institutionalize a Culture of Open Government.
4. Create an Enabling Policy Framework for Open Government.

In September 2011, the United States released its first Open Government National Action Plan, setting a series of ambitious goals to create a more open government. The United States has continued to implement and improve upon the open government commitments set forth in the first plan, along with many more efforts underway across government, including implementing individual federal agency Open Government Plans.

On a grander and global scale, the Open Government Partnership (OGP) was created. It was formally launched on September 20, 2011, with eight founding governments (Brazil, Indonesia, Mexico, Norway, the Philippines, South Africa, the United Kingdom, and the US). The Open Government Partnership is a multilateral initiative that aims to secure concrete commitments from governments to promote transparency, empower citizens, fight corruption, and harness new technologies to strengthen governance. The number of members has grown significantly since its launch (Open Government Partnership 2014).

In October 2013, in conjunction with the Open Government Partnership Annual Summit in London, the White House released its *Second Open Government National Action Plan*. This newer plan built upon the foundation of the first and added both new and enhanced initiatives. Among the highlights of the second National Action Plan:

- **"We the People"**: The White House will introduce new improvements to the *We the People* online petitions platform aimed at making it easier to collect and submit signatures and increase public participation in using this platform. Improvements will enable the public to perform data analysis on the signatures and petitions submitted to *We the People*, as well as include a more streamlined process for signing petitions.
- **Freedom of Information Act (FOIA) Modernization:** The FOIA encourages accountability through transparency and represents an unwavering national commitment to open government principles. Improving FOIA administration is one of the most effective ways to make the US government more open and accountable.
- **The Global Initiative on Fiscal Transparency (GIFT):** The United States will join GIFT, an international network of governments

and non-government organizations aimed at enhancing financial transparency, accountability, and stakeholder engagement.

- **Open Data to the Public:** Over the past few years, government data has been used by journalists to uncover variations in hospital billings, by citizens to learn more about the social services provided by charities in their communities, and by entrepreneurs building new software tools to help farmers plan and manage their crops. Building on the US government's ongoing open data efforts, new commitments will make government data even more accessible and useful for the public, including by reforming how federal agencies manage government data as a strategic asset, launching a new version of Data.gov to make it even easier to discover, understand, and use open government data, and expanding access to agriculture and nutrition data to help farmers and communities.

- **Participatory Budgeting:** The United States will promote community-led participatory budgeting as a tool for enabling citizens to play a role in identifying, discussing, and prioritizing certain local public spending projects, and for giving citizens a voice in how taxpayer dollars are spent in their communities. This commitment will include steps by the US government to help raise awareness of the fact that participatory budgeting may be used for certain eligible federal community development grant programs (White House 2013).

We the People is an intriguing social media experiment that attempts to replicate the process whereby citizens have the right to petition their government with new ideas, policies, and even grievances. In the past this would be accomplished through town hall meetings and signed petitions. Attempting what has been largely an in-person and paper-based process to an online process is a challenge. The first attempt to do so failed as certain groups learning about the new system were able to overwhelm the system with followers that ultimately not only "gamed the system" to their advantage, but exposed some fatal flaws in the process. In 2013 the site was redesigned and stronger safeguards were put in place aimed at reducing or eliminating the possibility of a well-organized group with limited overall popular support from overwhelming and thus distorting the process.

It is too early to tell how well citizen engagement will work in the digital world. Many initiatives have been developed to better engage the citizen in ways that are meaningful to all parties. When it comes to government agencies, citizen engagement is about restoring and building trust in addition to developing a better understanding of how governments share information in today's contemporary world. Citizen engagement is also about making government more transparent and, accessible, providing greater forms of meaningful information, submitting forms, paying taxes online, and finally downloading maps and other forms of data, and of course, providing for online transactions such as credit card payments. E-government has moved a long way since

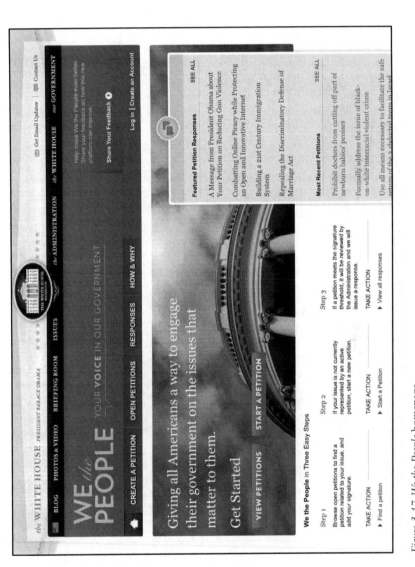

Figure 3.17 We the People homepage

Source: https://petitions.whitehouse.gov/

Figure 3.18 Citizen engagement: White House initiatives

Source: http://www.whitehouse.gov/engage

2002 and with the amazing growth of smart mobile devices and highly functional lightweight tablets, there is much more to be discovered and experimented with.

Citizen engagement *is not* about:

- *Not* about online credit card transactions
- *Not* about using cool mobile device apps
- *Not* about public safety broadcast alerts
- *Not* about filling out online forms
- *Not* about stunningly attractive websites
- *Not* about "tweeting" or being a "fan."

Citizen engagement is about:

- Creating meaningful dialog
- Two-way communications
- Focusing on process
- Informing and seeking comment
- Articulating values
- Meaningful participation
- Building trust through transparency
- Voting.

Discussion Questions

1. In your opinion, is citizen engagement a slogan or is it real, please explain?
2. What further improvements would you like to see regarding citizen engagement?
3. What government apps have you used, why or why not?
4. Have you ever used 311? If so what was your experience?
5. How can government better communicate with citizens?
6. What types of government data have you used and where did you obtain it?
7. Will online voting ever happen? Would you like to have the option of voting online? Describe the obstacles when it comes to online voting.
8. Using information technology, how can citizens better communicate with government at the various federal, state, and local levels?
9. Considering a community with which you are familiar, how well would you rate the overall effectiveness of their main website? What needs to be improved?

10. Do you think government agencies should accept video chat with citizens? Might this be a good thing, or bad, explain why?

References

Internet Society. 2013. "Brief History of the Internet." Accessed October 17, 2014. http://www.internetsociety.org/internet/what-internet/history-internet/brief-history-internet.

Pew Research Internet Project. 2013. "Civic Engagement in the Digital Age." Accessed October 17, 2014. http://www.pewinternet.org/2013/04/25/civic-engagement-in-the-digital-age-2/.

Purcell, Kristen, Lee Rainie, Amy Mitchell, Tom Rosenstiel and Kenny Olmstead. 2010. "Understanding the Participatory News Consumer." Pew Internet & Family Study. Accessed October 17, 2014. http://www.pewinternet.org/2010/03/01/understanding-the-participatory-news-consumer/.

Rutgers University School of Public Affairs & Administration. 2014. "E-Government Institute at Rutgers SPAA." Accessed October 17, 2014. http://spaa.newark.rutgers.edu/egov; http://spaa.newark.rutgers.edu/egov-publications.

Shark, Alan R. (ed.). 2011. *M-Government—Mobile Technologies For Responsive Governments and Connected Societies.* OECD Publishing, Paris, France.

Shark, Alan R. 2012. *Seven Trends that Will Transform Local Government Through Technology.* PTI, Alexandria, VA.

United Nations Public Administration Network. 2012. "UN E-Government Surveys." Accessed October 17, 2014. http://www.unpan.org/egovkb/global_reports/08report.htm.

Waseda University. 2013. "International E-Governance Rankings 2013." Accessed October 17, 2014. http://www.e-gov.waseda.ac.jp/pdf/Press_Released_on_e-Gov_ranking_2013.pdf.

White House. 2009. "Transparency and Open Government." Accessed October 17, 2014. http://www.whitehouse.gov/the_press_office/TransparencyandOpenGovernment.

White House. 2013. "Open Government Initiative." Accessed October 17, 2014. http://www.whitehouse.gov/blog/2013/12/06/united-states-releases-its-second-open-government-national-action-plan/.

Digital Destinations

Center for Technology in Government. http://www.ctg.albany.edu
———. http://www.ctg.albany.edu/publications/guides/social_media_policy
City of Boston Citizen's Connect. http://www.cityofboston.gov/doit/apps/citizensconnect.asp
City of Denver 311 Help Center. http://www.denvergov.org/311helpcenter/Denver-311HelpCenter/tabid/442045/Default.aspx
City of Philadelphia—Philly 311 Mobile App. http://www.phila.gov/311/mobileapp.html.
City of New York 311 Service Request. http://www1.nyc.gov/311/
GSA and Section 508. http://www.section508.gov/about-us
Health & Human Service Section 508 Example. http://www.hhs.gov/web/508/accessiblefiles/checklists.html

IBM Center for the Business of Government. http://www.businessofgovernment.org/content/about-center-business-government-connecting-research-practice

NASCIO A National Survey of Social Media Use in State Government—Friends, Follower, Feeds. http://www.nascio.org/publications/documents/NASCIO-SocialMedia.pdf

Open Government Partnership 2014. http://www.opengovpartnership.org/

Open Montgomery–Montgomery County MD. http://montgomerycountymd.gov/open/

We The People. https://petitions.whitehouse.gov/, last accessed October 17, 2014.

White House Initiatives. http://www.whitehouse.gov/engage

4 The Data Factor

Transparency, Reform, and Improved
Data: Driven Decisions

In the early 20th century, philosopher and essayist George Santayana wrote, "Those who cannot remember the past are condemned to repeat it" (Santayana 1905–06). This idea, that societies must maintain their own histories for the sake of their citizens and their futures, took some time to gain favor among our nation's leaders, at least in practical application. Finally, in 1934 Congress established the National Archives building in Washington, DC, where the US Constitution and other pieces of critical historical information are kept. Today, the National Archives has over 40 facilities around the country to record and document the nation's history regionally as it unfolds. The National Archives plays a central role in preserving our history; the nation's city, state, local and federal governments, along with many government agencies. The National Archives plays a significant role in documenting the collective histories of their organizations and the citizens they serve. To be sure, these entities themselves are also chronicling societal histories. Today, public sector organizations gather birth records and marriage licenses as well as record other historic moments of the people they serve. They collect reams of information that might seem much less meaningful too, for example, permits, applications, tax records, and licenses to drive, fish, or to practice professionally. The information the public sector collects can be even less complex and nuanced, too. A local government might collect and record the dates on which town meetings took place, or the hours each member of the town police force worked. As this kind of information becomes more and more basic—times, dates, addresses, occurrences—we often begin to think of these pieces of history as individual datum in collections of data. *Data* is a set of basic information, which together can be interpreted to supply knowledge, insight, and wisdom. All together, the data gathered by contemporary government can deliver a very cohesive, unified history.

Figure 4.1 The National Archives homepage

Source: http://www.archives.gov

The History in Our Data

The federal government began keeping regular, national birth records in 1942. After World War II ended in 1945, it became qualitatively clear that a baby boom was happening—thousands of soldiers returned home, and started new families. But without accurate birth records, the quantitative scope of the baby boom might have gone undocumented. Sure, historian Landon Jones might still have written that "the cry of the baby was heard across the land," but we might not have known what that really meant— that the number of births in the United States jumped almost 20 percent between 1945 and 1946, from 2.86 million births to 3.41 million births. Perhaps more importantly, the correlated societal impacts of the baby boom might have been immeasurable, unpredictable, and unwieldy. Without data, this important story about the history of the United States would have been told in a very different way. The ability of the government to serve its rapidly multiplying citizens, a generation with new complex needs, would have certainly suffered.

Further back in US history, Congress passed the Immigration Act of 1790 that formalized the process and criteria to apply for US citizenship. The Act required the standardization of collecting data. This data is in use, for example, at Ancestry.com where a family tree can be looked up dating back hundreds of years with data collected by ports of entry beginning in the early 1880s. In the early days, census data of entering immigrants was somewhat haphazard and inconsistent. Many important records that were stored in the late 1800s and early 1900s were damaged or lost due to poor storage methods

Figure 4.2 Millenniums will be the majority in the workforce by 2025

and flooding or fire such as the loss in June 1897 when the Ellis Island Immigration Center burned to the ground and along with it, hundreds of thousands of immigration records dating back to 1855.

In 1973 the National Personnel Records Center (NPRC) in St. Louis caught fire and raged for five days destroying approximately 73 to 80 percent of the approximately twenty-two million individual official military personnel files (National Archives 2013). While better policies and procedures are now in effect that are designed to better protect paper and digital records, many legacy systems are still at risk for possible loss. Today having digital copies and back-ups makes it easier to recreate official records in case of a catastrophic disaster. At the same time, there are many digital tools available that can help restore damaged records or equipment.

With today's modern handheld devices it is difficult to imagine that most data collected by government was once collected and stored by hand. This data consisted of birth and marriage records, land ownership, and of course taxes. The first US census took place in August 1790 and while there have been numerous attempts to further automate the door-to-door of the regular census, it relies heavily on census takers.

Figure 4.3 Enumerator is about to knock on the door of a home for the 1980 census

Source: United States Census Bureau #counting_1980_03

Today we almost always turn to the computer for data. Small amounts of data can be stored on a single computer's hard drive. An Excel spreadsheet, for example, might be enough to record the names, addresses, places of business, phone numbers, and email addresses of a city council, or even of a city's entire workforce. The document could be updated over time to preserve accuracy, and distributed again after updates were made. Simple. Useful. Effective. But what if a city needed to store all of this information for all the voters in town? What if the city had an even bigger dataset—one that detailed the locations of all the road signs, storm drains, and benches public works is responsible for maintaining? What if the dataset included all the public works projects for the last ten years? When one considers the amount of data even a small town's government could create about its citizens and its day-to-day operations, it's clear that data can really add up. For this reason, organizations in the public sector have witnessed an increased demand for data storage. For these types of datasets, public sector organizations require massive and multiple databases.

A *database*, defined as a collection of data, can come in a wide range of types and formats. Likewise, there exist a wide range of *database management systems* (DBMs) that organize and deliver subsets of data, and respectively cater to each type of database. Beyond DBMs, there are hardware systems that suit the needs of the DBM and the size of the database in terms of total storage. There are local databases—dedicated computers held in close proximity (often within the same building) to the terminals that are used to interface with the data inside. Because Internet connectivity is now very fast, a database and the terminals used to access the data no longer need to be in close proximity. For this reason, and because incrementally more storage in remote databases often costs less and less as the demand for a database's size increases, many public sector organizations have begun sharing databases with one another. Some of these databases are *cloud databases*, because they exist on a large array of disparately located computers connected in real-time in what has come to be called a "cloud" environment.

Because Internet connectivity is now very fast, a database and the terminals used to access the data no longer need to be in close proximity. For this reason, and because incrementally more storage in remote databases often costs less and less as the demand for a database's size increases, many public sector organizations have begun sharing databases with one another. Some of these databases are *cloud databases*, because they exist on a large array of disparately located computers connected in real-time in what has come to be called a "cloud" environment.

The Evolution of Federal Data

No matter how a database is structured or where the data is stored, public sector organizations that make use of digital data storage are positioned to extract more value from them than those still functioning through antiquated paper systems. Databases can be searched in minutes or seconds to construct very specific datasets that would take an individual days or even weeks to extract manually by combing through paper file systems. The Paperwork Reduction Act of 1980, amended in 1995, was primarily designed to reduce the paperwork burden the federal government places on private citizens and organizations (Public Law 104-13 1995). But lawmakers included a second purpose in the amendment, which was to, "ensure the greatest possible public benefit from and maximize the utility of information created, collected, maintained, used, shared, and disseminated by or for the Federal Government" (ibid.). This law, its significant amendment in 1995, and a number of subsequent executive orders pertaining to both paperwork reduction and regulatory reduction, including Executive Order 13610 *Identifying and Reducing Regulatory Burdens*, have pushed federal agencies away from paper databases and towards digital ones (White House 2012b). The federal government is moving towards further adoption of digital databases and the streamlining of that data because these priorities ease the burden on citizens and because they help the federal government operate more efficiently. These are lessons that state and local governments have already learned from and will continue to learn from in coming years.

Big Data and Big Problems

It is easy to assume that all government data can be found on computers and is completely searchable—if only one knew where to look and had appropriate authorization. Those in government know that while most data collected in the last dozen years is automated, many critical datasets are still kept on paper, microfiche, or in databases that are ancient by today's standards. Before government officials attempted to coordinate record keeping (data), every department and agency was left largely to itself regarding programming languages and alphanumeric assignment of records. Some databases might contain an alphanumeric string while others might simply be numbers only. Another issue was different agencies required different lengths of characters. For example, social security numbers contain nine numerals and always in the same sequence. Trying to merge and compare different datasets from among legacy systems requires a lot of programming workarounds.

In May 2012, the Office of the Inspector General of the Social Security Administration issued an Audit Report that focused on the problems associated with progress to date in modernizing its data processing capabilities. The report found:

> Our review determined that SSA does not have a strategic plan to convert its legacy COBOL application programs to a more modernized

programming language. Nonetheless, the Agency has developed an approach to gradually reduce its reliance on COBOL for its core processing of program transactions, such as retirement and disability claims. Although there is no specific federal requirement for agencies to modernize their legacy applications, there is federal guidance that requires that agencies include IT modernization as part of their enterprise architecture process.

Office of the Inspector General of the Social
Security Administration 2012

The report went on to urge that at a minimum, SSA should address the following factors in its modernization roadmap: (1) projected future service delivery demands; (2) growth of IT and maintenance costs; (3) loss of institutional legacy programming knowledge; (4) lack of integrated business processes; and (5) outdated user interfaces. Although these factors are not unique to COBOL, SSA relies on COBOL applications to deliver its core services. The SSA is not the only agency that continues to struggle to bring its legacy systems into compliance with the best practices in data management.

Data for the People

As awareness of the power of digital data has grown, the federal government has taken steps to deliver more data and the benefits it can bring to citizens. In a way, this has been a push to deliver the history of the people back to the people. Much of this work has been done by the Obama Administration in the form of dialogues and new requirements to support an idea the administration has widely referred to as "open government." In May of 2009, the administration released a new website, Data.gov, which includes a massive collection of government-generated open datasets as well as tools to help citizens analyze them (Center for Effective Government 2009).

In December of 2009, the Office of Management and Budget issued the Open Government Directive, which mandated that each federal agency develop an Open Government Plan and ordered the agencies to make at least three new datasets available to the public through the Data.gov portal (ibid.). Some criticized this first step as being invaluable, because the data were posted in nonstandard formats and the agencies were not required to keep the data current; some saw the data as obsolete the moment the datasets were posted. By May of 2012, the Obama Administration updated its definition of the word "open," issuing an executive order that required federal agencies to offer open application programming interfaces (APIs), which give software developers access to the live datasets kept by the agencies, a markedly different ask than had been made before (Gallagher 2012). Armed with this ostensibly well-maintained and updated data, developers could now develop mobile and web applications using the people's data. A year later, President Obama issued another executive order, mandating that the new standard for

Figure 4.4 Data.gov homepage

Source: http://www.data.gov

federal data be "open and machine-readable," which again raised the bar for the agencies with regard to the public availability of digital federal data (Gallagher 2013). All of these efforts indicate an overall trajectory in the direction of making the people's data available to the people.

It seems likely that the momentum towards open digital data will continue into the future, and not just at the federal level. Over time, state and even local data will need to be available to the public in order for citizens to better collaborate with their governments. Many, including President Obama, have argued that open data is the path to improved trust between governments and their people, as well. The idea that information should be freely available is not novel, either. The Freedom of Information Act, signed into law by President Lyndon Johnson in 1966, gave American citizens the right to request and receive information, and mandated that all federal agencies release their information to the people, with nine exemptions (see FOIA website). The Act was amended multiple times since then, including in 1976, 1982, multiple times in the 1990s, in 2001, 2002, 2007, 2009, and 2010. The discussion about what information citizens can and should have access to has been going on for decades, but by and large, these decisions have increased the availability of information rather than decreasing it.

It seems likely that the momentum towards open digital data will continue into the future, and not just at the federal level. Over time, state and even local data will need to be available to the public in order for citizens to better collaborate with their governments.

Digital Accountability and Transparency Act of 2014

On May 9, President Barack Obama signed into law the first federal open data bill that requires all federal agencies to publish expenditures publicly online and in a standardized machine-readable format.

This Act contains both a wide scope and narrow guidelines that will require federal agencies to report spending to USASpending.gov, so expenditures can be compared across jurisdictions—a service previously unheard of digitally or otherwise at the federal level (Shueh 2014).

Data-Informed Decision-Making

With more data comes more information, which powers insights. This is true when it comes to serving citizens, but it is also true within government organizations. Data is not just a right of free citizens; data is a powerful tool for public servants, too. As such, the idea that public servants should be using digital data to provide better services and develop better public policies has also gained favor. Data-informed decision-making is more scientific and less reliant on so-called "gut instincts." Simply put, if the public sector is to make intelligent, well-informed decisions, it helps to have valuable information present in the meetings where decisions are being made. While this is certainly true, it's also true that data-informed decision-making requires more than just sound data; it requires sound data interpretation too.

In the private sector as well as academia, analysts and mathematicians love to remind their collaborators that correlation does not equal causation. For example, from 1936 through 2000, every time the Washington Redskins won their last home game before a presidential election, the incumbent party always won (Dewey 2012). For fun, journalists tied the two datasets together, prognosticating that if the Redskins won, then the presiding political party would remain in the White House. They pretended that the Redskins were causing the election results—that there was causation occurring between the datasets. In 2004, the Redskins lost their last home game and the Democrats lost the presidency as well as the White House, demonstrating the flaw in this so-called predictive measure. Of course, no NFL football game could truly cause the outcome of a presidential election. Causation was an illusion; this was nothing but correlation. The difference between correlation and causation is just one important distinction for those working with data to keep in mind. Good public administrators of tomorrow will need to understand this and other concepts when it comes to data.

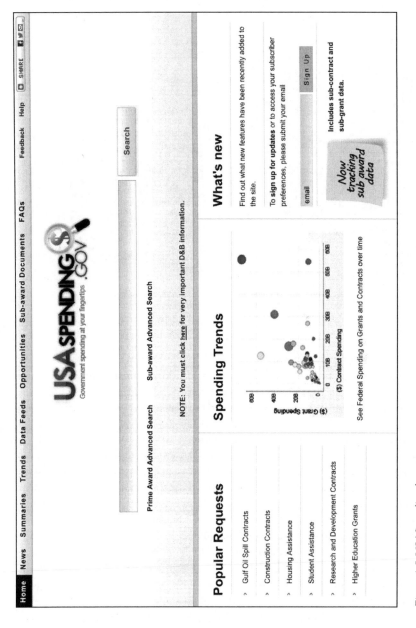

Figure 4.5 USASpending homepage

Source: http://usaspending.gov

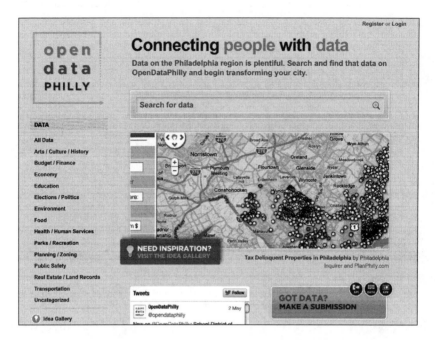

Figure 4.6 OpenDataPhilly homepage

Source: http://opendataphilly.org

Advanced computing technologies can provide extremely valuable short-cuts to the interpretation of datasets and information. Automated processes like regression analysis, which helps analysts uncover and understand correlations between datasets, or pattern recognition, and can sort datasets with multiple varieties of datum into groups, can streamline data analysis incredibly. New techniques and technologies are also enabling more accurate predictive analytics like statistical inference, which seeks to make predictions despite random variations in data. Of course, much of the academic field of algebraic mathematics is dedicated to describing the relationships between sets of dependent and independent variables; in practical application, this can mean very clearly describing causal relationships. With all the computing technologies now available and more to come, manual data interpretation work that might have once taken days or years will be performed in minutes or hours—timelines that are only shrinking as time passes. Suffice it to say that software is a powerful tool for data analysis and transforming reams of data into pages of information, paragraphs of knowledge, or even a single, succinct chart. This fact, combined with the general proliferation of digital data taking place in both the public and private sectors today, is resulting in the hoarding of more and more data by organizations in both sectors. With all the potential data represents, who would want to let any of it slip through the cracks? In the next section, attention will be paid to considering where this kind of thinking is good and where it is actually a detriment to many organizations. Nonetheless, data proliferation is happening. The age of big data is upon us. So what happens when an organization's data becomes so prolific that the sheer amount of it begins to become one of the problems technologists and IT professionals must solve?

> Advanced computing technologies can provide extremely valuable shortcuts to the interpretation of datasets and information. Automated processes like regression analysis, which helps analysts uncover and understand correlations between datasets, or pattern recognition, which can sort datasets with multiple varieties of datum in them into groups, can streamline data analysis in amazing ways.

Big Data: Volume, Velocity and Variety

In recent years, the concept of big data has received much attention—perhaps too much. This is not to say that there is not powerful information that can and will lead to the delivery of vastly improved public and private products and services hidden within the large and disparate datasets that these two sectors already maintain. Powerful information is most certainly present and waiting to be found in these datasets, which will absolutely lead to new invention and efficiency. The further accumulation of still more data will lead to even greater potential for humans to understand the current and future states of our societies.

Figure 4.7 Big data has become a major new tool leading to better data-driven decisions

Without a doubt, the analysis and interpretation of big data are already creating newfound efficiencies and whole new products and services. Google,
took a once bafflingly complex World Wide Web, indexed every single page
on it, and made it possible for anyone with Internet access to find, more or
less, exactly what they are looking for with just a few keystrokes—a powerful example of what big data analysis and interpretation can deliver. Finding
things on the Internet once required humans to take random guesses at web
addresses. In one of the more elegant and accurate discussions of what the
power and potential of big data really mean, authors Robert Scoble and Shel
Israel (2013) explain the following:

> In our opinion, the focus is on the wrong element: It's not the big data
> mountain that matters so much to people, it's those tiny little spoonfuls
> we extract whenever we search, chat, view, listen, buy—or do anything
> else online. The hugeness can intimidate, but the little pieces make us
> smarter and enable us to keep up with, and make sense of, an accelerat-
> ing world. We call this the miracle of little data.

Google simplified the web for humans by connecting it all together. It
offered us the right spoonfuls of "little data," as it were. It empowered us to
harness the web, compete on it, and spread information through it. In this
way, big data, as a concept, is very real and is already here.

But the idea of big data has also received somewhat sensational treatment from the press, from businesses hoping to capitalize on the demand
for advanced data analysis and interpretation and from the general public
in online forums. As with many things that are complex, abstract, and
difficult to adapt to, it's easy to misunderstand big data and presume it to
be much more than it is, or to panic about the idea of lost opportunity
within big data.

The concept of big data is not going to render humans obsolete, result in
an era of flying cars, nor deliver cold fusion—at least not in the near future.
There are many miles left to tread in the world of big data analysis. This is
the beginning of data-informed decision-making, not the end. Big data, as
an idea, is an extension of the power and flexibility of data that has already
been discussed in the first half of this chapter. And it constitutes a handful of
added complexities that IT professionals and public administrators can easily
understand as factors in analysis and interpretation. These challenges are at
once immensely daunting and a sign of the incredible promise big data holds,
and each of them will be discussed in the following pages.

In 2001, an IT research and advisory firm called META Group released
a research report titled "3D Data Management: Controlling Data Volume, Velocity, and Variety" (Laney 2001). In that report, the author, an
analyst at META Group named Doug Laney, described three factors generating newfound complexities in the datasets being amassed by many
organizations. Those complexities were data volume, data velocity, and

data variety. The same three complexities are still impacting organizations compiling large data sets today, and thus provide a concrete context for the discussion of the problems big data proliferation is creating for organizations both private and public.

Data Volume: The Growth of Datasets

As will be discussed further in Chapter 11, the sheer proliferation of data in recent decades is at once shocking and exciting. In 2007, the world's technological capacity to store information was about 295 exabytes, or about 29,500,000,000,000,000,000,000 bytes (Flatow 2011). But the world is proliferating data at a rate so massive that the total amount of digital data stored globally doubles roughly every three years and four months (*ibid.*). At the time of this publication that number was close to 1,200 exabytes, having doubled twice. For perspective, an exabyte of data has been estimated at roughly 100,000 times the text in the Library of Congress, which contained roughly twenty million books in 1997 when this calculation was originally performed (Johnston 2012). With these kinds of numbers in mind it's easy to see that the sheer volume of data being generated and stored by many organizations is unbelievably daunting.

These days, many organizations are literally gorging themselves with data storage, saving everything—they are creating their own data volume

Figure 4.8 State of Utah data portal

Source: http://www.utah.gov

problems. In the META Group report, Laney espouses a number of key pieces of advice, which still ring true in today's high-volume scenarios. He advises that organizations limit their data retention "to that which will be leveraged by current or imminent business processes" (Laney 2001). Laney also suggests "limiting certain analytic structures to a percentage of statistically valid sample data" (ibid.). In other words, save only what you can and will use, and remember that statistically significant analysis does not require an entire dataset, only a representative sample. These ideas will certainly still ring true, even after the world's data has double and re-doubled dozens of times again.

Data Velocity: The Fire Hose of Information

In some applications, even when the volume of data is not necessarily a problem—with more money, more storage can always be had—the problem of data velocity can be crushing. In these scenarios, new data are being collected at such a rate that the flood of data poses processing and identification problems. Take for example the Large Synoptic Survey Telescope, a project being undertaken in partnership between the National Science Foundation (NSF) and the Department of Energy (DOE) that will survey the entire night sky approximately twice per week (National Science Foundation 2012). This massive new telescope, when launched, will be able to gather an estimated 13 terabytes of information per night, the equivalent of over a half-million filing cabinets of text (Large Synoptic Survey Telescope 2014). This massive flood of information will need to be carefully catalogued and organized by the telescope's software systems. Without organization, it might be utterly useless. Perhaps more importantly, software systems will likely need to perform analyses in cycles that inform changes in the way the telescope is deployed—perhaps instructing operators to "check in that corner of the sky; something strange was happening there earlier this week." The same problems of data velocity are certainly making it difficult for technologists to deliver self-driving city buses. We have sensors that can detect the position of nearby vehicles, but doing so flawlessly in a split second and instructing robotic buses to apply the brakes is a problem of data velocity, not volume.

Of course, not all of the data being mined by the Large Synoptic Survey Telescope will need to be accessible immediately. Surely some of its analysis will require many days, weeks, months, or even years of compilation before hypotheses can be proven or disproven—say about the tilt of the Earth's axis or the annual orbit of the Earth around the Sun. This is why Laney suggests, "designing architectures that balance data latency with app data requirements and decision cycles, without assuming the entire information supply chain must be near real time" (Laney 2001). For tomorrow's public administrators, this means carefully considering which datasets will require rapid analysis, and which can wait.

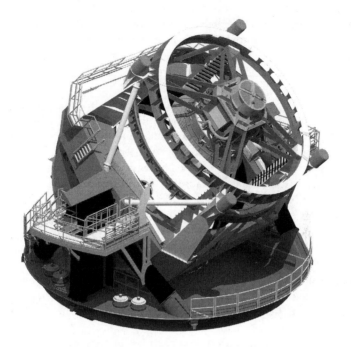

Figure 4.9 Large Synoptic Survey Telescope

Source: LSST Corporation 2013

Data Variety: The Complexity of Data Convergence

The third and final complexity creating greater challenges for data managers highlighted by Laney in the META Group report was data variety, which occurs whenever disparate datasets consisting of different structures, formats, or organizations are mixed into the same database. The results can be very hard to manage or even unusable. As an example, consider the spreadsheet of city employees mentioned earlier in this chapter. Viewing each row of that spreadsheet as its own unique piece of data, imagine what would happen if all of the rows in our hypothetical document were combined in the same spreadsheet with rows from a dozen or even a hundred other spreadsheets, each with a different formatting. The result would be such complexity that rendering any of the rows useful would require incredible work. This is a simplified example of the difficulty that can arise when different datasets are combined. To extend this simple example, one might *tag*, or label, each row with *metadata*, or information about a piece of data, to indicate what kind of document the row came from. Like rows could be re-combined quickly and interpreted in this scenario, so metadata tagging is one process database managers can undertake to ensure their data continues to make sense when placed in mixed datasets.

> Metadata tagging is one process database managers can undertake to ensure their data continues to make sense when placed in mixed datasets.

Of course Laney explains that there are other systems and approaches that make combining data together not just possible but simple, as well, highlighting the fact that mechanisms for interchange and translation of datasets will have been built into "most DBMSs" by 2003 or 2004 (ibid.). Laney advises that, "in selecting a technique or technology, enterprises should first perform an information audit assessing the status of their information supply chain to identify and prioritize particular data management systems," advice that still rings true today, when data complexities such as the myriad file types and structures make combining datasets quickly and seamlessly a tricky business (ibid.). The advice herein for public administrators of tomorrow is to remember that complexities can arise whenever datasets are combined; the extent of those complexities is often closely related to the variety of data converging. Automation through DBMs is possible but not a given. It's important to ask the right kinds of questions when selecting a DBM or a data-analysis software.

A subset of the data variety complexities analysts in both the public and private sectors are facing has come to be known as unstructured data. *Unstructured data* can be defined as a set of data where each piece of datum has its own unique structure or where the data are otherwise unorganized in a pre-defined manner. Unstructured data points are typically formatted as text files, but they can also include numbers or even facts. A common example of unstructured data can be found in a typical email inbox, which likely contains hundreds or even thousands of unique messages that might only make sense in the mind of the recipient. Each email is different, and might contain information of widely differing values. Email can be organized and examined, and sorted by date or sender. The words and phrases inside most email inboxes can be searched, quickly calling up every email in the inbox that includes them. But emails remain difficult to truly extract all of the information from, semantically or otherwise. This is what makes the problem of unstructured data so persistent. As humans, we have an innate ability to make sense of these kinds of datasets, and, of course, we have created millions of webpages and other stores of information on the Internet that are often viewed as unstructured.

> *Unstructured data* can be defined as a set of data where each piece of datum has its own unique structure or where the data are otherwise unorganized in a pre-defined manner.

Putting Data to Work for Government:
A Complex Task

Leading up to the publication of this book, a study performed by IT network-ing group MeriTalk and sponsored by EMC Corporation, a major provider of technologies and IT systems for governments, revealed some interesting thoughts about the potential of big data and the time it will take to make a large impact in the public sector, specifically within the federal government (MeriTalk 2013). A survey of 150 federal IT professionals was conducted to produce the study's report, titled, "Smarter Uncle Sam: The Big Data Fore-cast" (ibid.). Those federal IT professionals estimated that successful analysis of big data could yield in a saving of roughly 14 percent of the budgets allo-cated to federal agencies—or $500 billion. However, only 31 percent of those surveyed reported believing that their agency's big data strategy would be enough to deliver that kind of savings (Malykhina 2013). It follows that, while it's gaining momentum in the federal government, big data still has much maturing to do in order to realize its full potential. Again, the future holds much promise for big data analysis; we've only just scratched the surface. This is certainly true at local and state levels, where a focus on big data has been later to arrive than in the federal space. But beyond the challenges the public sector is facing in simply adopting truly game-changing data analytics tools and methods, some even more daunting challenges lie ahead.

Perhaps the best examples of practical applications utilizing big data can be found at the local government level. King County, Washington received a $1.2 million dollar grant from the Federal Highway Administration that led to the development of an app called *"Right Size Parking."* This project mashes up data representing relationships between population density, parking spaces, and public transportation availability. With this combined data residents and city planners alike can now access data on a neighborhood-by-neighborhood basis available for viewing on the web. This app also contains a great deal of regional data about land prices, average rents, and even the amount of annual greenhouse gases emitted by construction and maintenance of parking structures. Users can scan neighborhoods to see how well they are served by public transit and how many jobs are located within the selected neighborhood (GCN 2014).

Big Data's Threat to Privacy

Earlier in this chapter, the concept of data variety and the complexities it can create was examined in-depth. But some thinkers have posited that, when these complexities have all been conquered, and private and public entities can assemble all of their data into a single unified database, a much greater problem will emerge (Ohm 2012). If all of the information the government has on its citizens is combined into a single silo—if any individual's complete record can be called by any analyst with access to that silo—then all man-ners of personal information, including very private information, might be leveraged to do great harm. In Silicon Valley, many of the world's leading

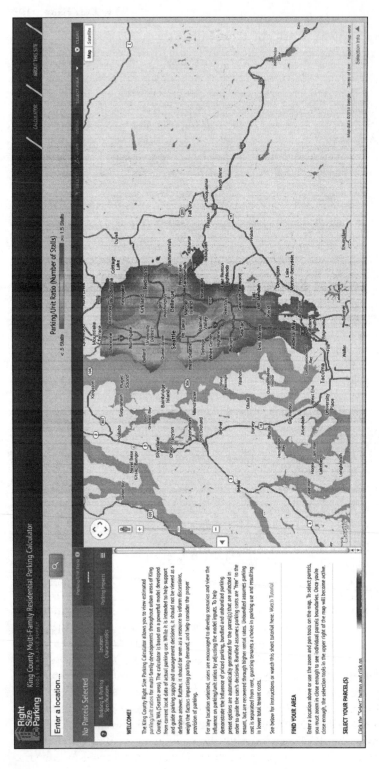

Figure 4.10 King County multi-family residential parking calculator

Source: King County/Rightsizeparking.org

technology companies are beginning to think very seriously about the same problem. Privacy has always been important to Americans, but today, it's being threatened by data analysis in previously unimaginable ways. The risk of personal invasion by the government seems to be a very real challenge for the government to tackle in the coming years.

> The risk of personal invasion by the government seems to be a very real challenge for the government to tackle in coming years.

For example, let's say a connected city of the future gains the ability to determine when a woman is pregnant, in much the same way the retailer Target has already been able to, based on subtle changes in purchasing behavior (Duhigg 2012). (Yes, this example of predictive analytics at its best and worst received national attention after *The New York Times* revealed the story of how Target discovered a teenage girl was pregnant before her father, whom she lived with, was even aware of the pregnancy.) In this scenario, the hypothetical connected city could provide women a service in notifying them of their rights or offering them lists of medical professionals willing to provide pro bono services to new mothers. The opportunity for improved services in this scenario is immense. But this scenario would also be a major invasion of privacy unless each individual female citizen in this hypothetical connected city willfully opted into this kind of monitoring and service. Unfortunately, where powerfully improved services exist thanks to big data analysis, the potential for equally powerful privacy invasion can often also be found.

> Unfortunately, where powerfully improved services exist thanks to big data analysis, the potential for equally powerful privacy invasion can often also be found.

Organizations in both the private and public sectors will need to engage their users and citizens in ongoing conversations about privacy, and much is yet to be determined in this space with regard to best practices. However, President Obama and the Federal Trade Commission (FTC) have both delivered recent privacy reports that public servants have begun to use as guides. In February of 2012, the Obama Administration released a "Consumer Privacy Bill of Rights," which encouraged organizations of all colors to engage in data-collection practices that protect the rights of individuals to "exercise control over what personal data companies collect from them," among other things (Office of the Press Secretary 2012). For more information, see *Consumer Data Privacy in a Networked World* by the Obama Administration (White House 2012a).

Likewise, the FTC has a long history of enforcing rules meant to protect the personal information of individuals, which is now being extended to

Figure 4.11 Fact Sheet: Plan to Protect Privacy in the Internet Age by Adopting a Consumer Privacy Bill of Rights on the White House website

Source: Office of the Press Secretary 2012.

Figure 4.12 FTC Bureau of Consumer Protection Business Center portal

Source: http://www.business.ftc.gov/privacy-and-security

the realm of digital data collection in an effort to educate and guide organizations about how to protect the right to privacy. To learn more see Federal Trade Commission (2013). Tomorrow's public administrators will need to continue to monitor developments in the world of digital privacy moving forward, using these and other new communications as the guideposts.

Personally Identifiable Information

One concept that has existed for a long time in the public sector of the United States, but which has only recently arrived at the forefront of the public sector's consciousness on the topic of privacy, is Personally Identifiable Information (PII). The federal government has defined *Personally Identifiable Information* since at least 2006 as,

> any information about an individual maintained by an agency, including, but not limited to, education, financial transactions, medical history, and criminal or employment history and information which can be used to distinguish or trace an individual's identity, such as their name, social security number, date and place of birth, mother's maiden name, biometric records, etc., including any other personal information which is linked or linkable to an individual.
>
> (Evans 2006).

Essentially, PII is, like its name implies, anything that can be used to distinguish an individual personally. In recent years, PII has come to stand as the definitive hallmark of scenarios where privacy should be considered carefully in the public sector. In large part, organizations have been encouraged to use *aggregate data*, information about a group of individuals, or condensed data such as means and medians, when describing or analyzing citizen activity, at least insofar as it makes sense. This helps prevent privacy from being a concern, because looking at the behavior of groups of people or the behavior of a typical person within that group helps keep the habits and behaviors of individuals out from under the microscope of personal scrutiny. In 2010, the National Institute of Standards and Technology, an agency of the US Department of Commerce, created a "Guide to Protecting the Confidentiality of Personally Identifiable Information," which specifically speaks to issues of computer security and is available online for download (NIST 2010). The biggest landmark in the conversation about PII dates back to 1996 when the Health Insurance Portability and Accountability Act was signed into law by President Bill Clinton (Public Law 104-91 1996). This law changed the way the medical community thought about PII forever by describing a series of regulatory must-dos with regard to the protection and dissemination of Protected Health Information (PHI), a type of PII.

Organizations have been encouraged to use *aggregate data*, information about a group of individuals, or condensed data such as means and medians, when describing or analyzing citizen activity, at least insofar as it makes sense. This helps prevent privacy from being a concern, because looking at the behavior of groups of people or the behavior of a typical person within that group helps keep the habits and behaviors of individuals out from under the microscope of personal scrutiny.

Making Use of Big Data to Improve Citizen Services

Big data still requires humans and human judgment to be valuable in many scenarios. We are nowhere near simply losing algorithms on data and letting computers do all the work of decision-making. Like many technologies discussed in this book, big data technologies are only as good as they are properly deployed and supported internally, and they are as powerful in changing the business of government as the core strategic goals to which they are aligned. It seems prudent, given the complex and abstract nature of big data, to directly address a few misconceptions about big data at this point.

Misconceptions About Big Data and Related Truths

Misconception 1. "Gathering data is a strategy."

Data can inform strategy or tactics. Gathering data can even be a tactic used to develop a clearer picture of a situation or the direction of an initiative. But gathering data for the sake of gathering it is not a business strategy.

Misconception 2. "Gathering more data is the answer."

While it may be true that an organization or initiative is lacking data that might help decision-making efforts, gathering the right or proper data to inform the team or initiative is unquestionably a better means to an end than simply gathering more data of any shape or form. Gathering the right data is critical.

Misconception 3. "Big data has all the answers."

While it's true that big data analysis and faster computing can yield powerful decision-making inputs today and in the future, humans will need to ask the right questions and carefully interpret analysis in order to truly yield powerful results from big data. This appears to be a truth that will hold true far into the foreseeable future.

**Misconception 4. "Big data technology is the answer
to all of our big data questions."**

As with many technologies discussed in this book, new technologies for big data analysis can only be the solution if they are fully adopted and if the right staff are put in place to operate the technology effectively. New technologies like these need to be carefully vetted and fully understood before they are purchased. And it often takes the full support of an organization to make sure they are properly implemented.

**Misconception 5. "We just need more time to get
answers from this big data."**

Although new technologies are making the analysis of big data much faster, analyzing and interpreting big data can, at times, constitute a trip down the proverbial rabbit hole. Smart public administrators of the future will be able to recognize dead-end pursuits sooner rather than later, even when those pursuits seem to involve scenarios where desired answers might be hidden around the next bend or within the next dataset.

**Misconception 6. "To be a data-informed organization,
we simply need to accrue more data."**

Being a data gatherer is not the same as being a data-informed decision-maker. While it's true that being truly data-informed about decision-making does require a core set of data to consider, true data-informed decision-making does not require big data or even large data sets. Instead, it requires rigor when it comes to tracking metrics and using them to determine the success or failure of efforts—to reveal the true strengths and weaknesses of initiatives and efforts. Rigorous data mining and analysis can be done by anyone; it's more about accountability than complex mathematics. Luckily, it's also baked into the cultures and histories of many government organizations. Rigor is what helps polling stations predict their foot traffic and what helps snow removal teams stay ahead of blizzards to keep whole cities open for business.

To Derive Value from Data, Demystify it

The best public administrators of tomorrow will ensure their teams know how and when the data could help. Engaging in dialogues about sample size, biases in datasets, the accuracy of data interpretation, and the quality of core datasets in general will help create a vocabulary across the organization that gives even non-data-oriented individuals common ground in understanding data and its application when analyzed and interpreted. These public administrators will be best served not when they treat data science as gospel but as any other science, which should be questioned or even refuted. Data-informed decision-making isn't about trusting data implicitly; it's about making sure data is part of the conversation. Good public administrators understand this critical distinction. The public sector organizations of the future that deploy sound data-informed decision-making as a whole will recognize the importance of rigor in their data and the true role it can play in informing decisions without letting it get in the way of the very human activity of public service.

The Future of Data-Powered Government

For governments, moving forward with data-informed decision-making means thinking about data, monitoring trends, finding causality, and forecasting in every department of the enterprise. Data-driven decision-making will help move the business of government away from gut instincts and knee-jerk reactions towards scientifically informed critical thinking. Instead of our police forces reacting to crime, they will be proactive about being where it is likely to happen in the same way the police force in Ft. Lauderdale, Fla., is trying to be with the help of IBM (Brinkman 2013). Rather than waiting for water mains to break, data analysis will help predict when they're likely to fail so they can be replaced beforehand. Instead of starting from scratch when natural disasters and emergencies happen, smart cities and states will be able to better prepare for them.

Moving forward, data won't just be leveraged to improve services externally. It will inform internal processes and drive savings, efficiency, and productivity across the government enterprise. This will free up resources to be reinvested back into citizen services. Citizens will play a role in gathering the data, too, like they are in Boston, Mass., where the mobile app Street Bump enables them to automatically report potholes and road damage much faster than they could be found through public works efforts alone. Boston has 800 miles of city streets to service, and public works fills about 19,000 potholes annually, so this reporting is streamlining that process and saving citizen dollars inside the government as well as outside, in the form of personal vehicle maintenance costs (Ngowi 2012). The new data gathered by governments will reveal new, valuable insights to improve services, too. For example, the Street Bump app revealed that metal utility caps are actually Boston's biggest source of bumpy roads (Moskowitz 2012). As a result, the city created an improved reporting system to notify utility companies of caps that are causing the most disruption to close the loop faster. Citizen data like this will still be powerful even when it is anonymous, and when it is not, those who gather and use it will be cognizant towards thoroughly protecting the privacy of citizens.

Moving forward, data won't just be leveraged to improve services externally. It will inform internal processes and drive savings, efficiency, and productivity across the government enterprise, as well. This will free up resources to be reinvested back into citizen services.

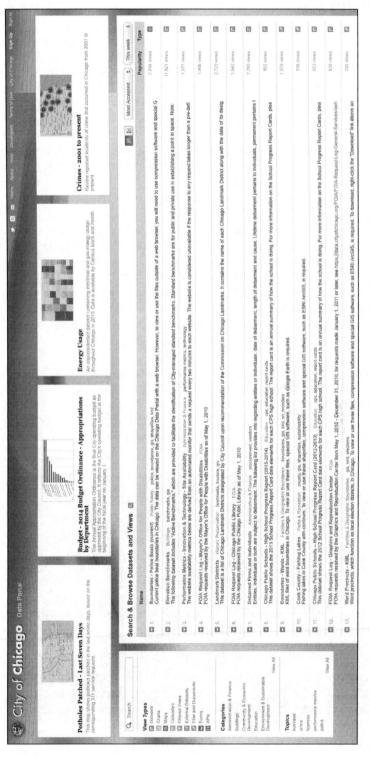

Figure 4.13 City of Chicago data portal

Source: https://data.cityofchicago.org

Smart Cities and Big Data

A further example of harnessing the power of data is what has been referred to as the "smart cities" movement. When one considers the amount of energy and natural resources cities consume, having better information will enable public managers to better manage city resources regarding transportation, urban planning, parks and recreation, infrastructure, telecommunications, and housing (Townsend 2013). As the population continues to grow, and for the first time more Americans are moving into cities as opposed to out of them, the pressure to manage resources wisely becomes much more critical (Shark, Toporkoff, Levy 2014).

The future of data-powered government will be more transparent. But that will take continued reform. Government will make better use of data, gather better data, and use it to better ends, but that will require more data-oriented workers across departments and functions—not just in the IT department. Big data will be put to use to improve all aspects of government, but it will still take great leaders to interpret the data and make the big decisions that big data can and will inform.

Big data has become a big deal. In May 2014, the White House issued the results of a comprehensive 90-day comprehensive study titled *Big Data: Seizing Opportunities, Preserving Values.* There is no better way to end this chapter than with the following from the White House study, which states:

> While big data unquestionably increases the potential of government power to accrue unchecked, it also holds within it solutions that can enhance accountability, privacy, and the rights of citizens. Properly implemented, big data will become an historic driver of progress, helping our nation perpetuate the civic and economic dynamism that has long been its hallmark.

Figure 4.14 Smart transportation is dependent on smart data

Big data technologies will be transformative in every sphere of life. The knowledge discovery they make possible raises considerable questions about how our framework for privacy protection applies in a big data ecosystem. Big data also raises other concerns. A significant finding of this report is that big data analytics have the potential to eclipse longstanding civil rights protections in how personal information is used in housing, credit, employment, health, education, and the marketplace. Americans' relationship with data should expand, not diminish, their opportunities and potential.

Discussion Questions

1. What role does government data play in recording the history of the American people?
2. Why are some public sector organizations now sharing databases?
3. What is "open data," and what power does it give to citizens?
4. What is "unstructured data" and why have humans created so much of it?
5. Why is big data creating a big threat to personal privacy?
6. What are a couple of public or private sector guidelines that can be used to help keep individuals safe when their information is being used?
7. What is Personally Identifiable Information?
8. What is one misconception about big data, and what is its corresponding truth?
9. As an individual or group project, take at least two different data sets and use them to describe a public policy issue. Articulate the data and discuss the pros and cons of public policy and administration issues.
10. Review and critique at least five state and or local data websites, i.e., City of Chicago Data Portal, see: https://data.cityofchicago.org/.

References

Brinkman, Paul. 2013. "IBM Chooses Fort Lauderdale for New Police Data Experiment." *South Florida Business Journal.* October 28. Accessed October 17, 2014. http://www.bizjournals.com/southflorida/news/2013/10/28/ibm-chooses-fort-lauderdale-for-new.html?page=all.

Center for Effective Government. 2009. "Administration Seeks Public Input on Open Government." June 2. Accessed October 17, 2014. http://www.foreffectivegov.org/node/10062.

Dewey, Caitlin. 2012. "Obama Victory Breaks 'Redskins Rule'." *The Washington Post.* November 7. Accessed October 17, 2014. http://www.washingtonpost.com/blogs/post-politics/wp/2012/11/07/obama-victory-breaks-redskins-rule/.

Duhigg, Charles. 2012. "How Companies Learn Your Secrets." *The New York Times.* February 16. Accessed October 17, 2014. http://www.nytimes.com/2012/02/19/magazine/shopping-habits.html?_r=0.

Evans, Karen S. 2006. "Reporting Incidents Involving Personally Identifiable Information and Incorporating the Cost for Security in Agency Information Technology Investments." *Executive Office of the President.* July 12. Accessed October 17, 2014. http://www.whitehouse.gov/sites/default/files/omb/memoranda/fy2006/m06-19.pdf.

Federal Trade Commission. 2013. "Privacy and Security." Accessed October 17, 2014. http://www.business.ftc.gov/privacy-and-security.

Flatow, Ira. 2011. "Defining a Data Deluge." National Public Radio. February 2. Accessed October 17, 2014. http://www.npr.org/2011/02/11/133686000/Defining-A-Data-Deluge.

Gallagher, Sean. 2012. "Open Government Reboot Focuses on APIs Instead of Data." *Ars Technica.* May 30. Accessed October 17, 2014. http://arstechnica.com/business/2012/05/open-government-reboot-focuses-on-apis-instead-of-data/.

———. 2013. "Obama Orders Agencies to Make Data Open, Machine-readable by Default." *Ars Technica.* May 9. Accessed October 17, 2014. http://arstechnica.com/tech-policy/2013/05/obama-orders-agencies-to-make-data-open-machine-readable-by-default/.

GCN. 2014. "How Parking Data Drives Urban Planning." Accessed October 17, 2014. http://gcn.com/blogs/emerging-tech/2014/04/parking-urban-development.aspx.

Johnston, Leslie. 2012. "How Many Libraries of Congress Does it Take?" *The Signal Digital Preservation Blog of The Library of Congress.* March 23. Accessed October 17, 2014. http://blogs.loc.gov/digitalpreservation/2012/03/how-many-libraries-of-congress-does-it-take/.

Jones, Landon. 1980. *Great Expectations: America & The Baby Boom Generation.* BookSurge Publishing, Charleston, SC. Page 11.

Laney, Doug. 2001. "3D Data Management: Controlling Data Volume, Velocity, and Variety." META Group. February 6. Accessed October 17, 2014. http://blogs.gartner.com/doug-laney/files/2012/01/ad949-3D-Data-Management-Controlling-Data-Volume-Velocity-and-Variety.pdf.

Large Synoptic Survey Telescope. 2014. "LSST: A New Telescope Concept." Accessed October 17, 2014. http://www.lsst.org/lsst/public/tour_software.

Malykhiana, Elena. 2013. "Big Data Analysis vs. Government Spending." *InformationWeek.* October 21. Accessed October 17, 2014. http://www.informationweek.com/software/information-management/big-data-analysis-vs-government-spending/d/d-id/1111252?

MeriTalk. 2013. "Smarter Uncle Sam: The Big Data Forecast." Accessed October 17, 2014. http://www.meritalk.com/smarteruncdesam.

Moskowitz, Andy. 2012. "App Shows Jarring Role of Cast-Metal Covers in Boston." *The Boston Globe.* December 16. Accessed October 17, 2014. http://www.bostonglobe.com/metro/2012/12/16/pothole/2iNCJ05M15vmr4aGHACNgP/story.html.

The National Archives. 2013. "Burnt in Memory: Looking Back at the 1973 St. Louis Fire." Accessed October 17, 2014. http://blogs.archives.gov/prologue/?p=12503.

National Institute of Standards and Technology. 2010. "Guide to Protecting the Confidentiality of Personally Identifiable Information." Accessed October 17, 2014. http://www.csrc.nist.gov/publications/nistpubs/800-122/sp800-122.pdf.

National Science Foundation. 2012. "National Science Foundation Will Advance the Large Synoptic Survey Telescope." Press release. July 18. Accessed October 17, 2014. http://www.nsf.gov/news/news_summ.jsp?cntn_id=124899.

Ngowi, Rodrique. 2012. "App Detects Potholes, Alerts Boston City Officials." *The Evening Sun* (Associated Press). July 20. Accessed October 17, 2014. http://www.eveningsun.com/localbiz/ci_21117645/app-detects-potholes-alerts-boston-city-officials.

Office of the Inspector General of the Social Security Administration. 2012. "Audit Report." Accessed October 17, 2014. http://oig.ssa.gov/sites/default/files/audit/full/pdf/A-14-11-11132_0.pdf.

Office of the Press Secretary. 2012. "Fact Sheet: Plan to Protect Privacy in the Internet Age by Adopting a Consumer Privacy Bill of Rights." February 23. Accessed October 17, 2014. http://www.whitehouse.gov/the-press-office/2012/02/23/fact-sheet-plan-protect-privacy-internet-age-adopting-consumer-privacy-b.

Ohm, Paul. 2012. "Don't Build a Database of Ruin." *Harvard Business Review.* August 23. Accessed October 17, 2014. http://blogs.hbr.org/2012/08/dont-build-a-database-of-ruin/.

Public Law 104-13. 1995. *Paperwork Reduction Act.* Accessed October 17, 2014. http://www.gpo.gov/fdsys/pkg/STATUTE-109/pdf/STATUTE-109-Pg163.pdf.

———. 104-91. 1996. "Health Insurance Portability and Accountability Act of 1996." August 21. Accessed October 17, 2014. http://www.gpo.gov/fdsys/pkg/PLAW-104publ191/pdf/PLAW-104publ191.pdf.

Santayana, George. 1905-06. *The Life of Reason. "Reason in Common Sense."* Page 284. Accessed October 17, 2014. https://archive.org/stream/thelifeofreasono00santuoft#page/284/mode/2up.

Scoble, Robert and Shel Israel. 2014. *Age of Context.* United States: Patrick Brewster Press. Page 6.

Shark, Alan R., Sylviane Toporkoff, and Sebastien Levy (eds.) 2014. *Smarter Cities for a Bright Sustainable Future: A Global Perspective.* PTI, Alexandria, VA.

Shueh, Jason. 2014. "The DATA Act Passes: 3 Takeaways and Interactive Timeline." Accessed October 17, 2014. http://www.govtech.com/pcio/articles/The-DATA-Act-Passes-3-Takeaways-and-Interactive-Timeline.html.

Townsend, Anthony M. 2013. *Smart Cities: Big Data, Civic Hackers, and the Quest for a New Utopia.* W.W. Norton & Company, New York.

White House. 2012a. "Consumer Data Privacy in a Networked World: A Framework for Protecting Privacy and Innovation in the Global Digital Economy." Accessed October 17, 2014. http://www.whitehouse.gov/sites/default/files/privacy-final.pdf.

White House. 2012b. "Memorandum on Reducing Reporting and Paperwork Burdens." Accessed October 17, 2014. http://www.whitehouse.gov/sites/default/files/omb/inforeg/memos/reducing-reporting-and-paperwork-burdens.pdf.

White House. 2014. "Big Data: Seizing Opportunities, Preserving Values." May. Accessed October 17, 2014. http://www.whitehouse.gov/sites/default/files/docs/big_data_privacy_report_may_1_2014.pdf.

Digital Destinations

City of Chicago Data Portal. https://data.cityofchicago.org

City of New York Data Portal. https://nycopendata.socrata.com/

City of Philadelphia Data Portal. http://www.opendataphilly.org/

Federal Government Data.gov. http://www.data.gov

Federal Government Spending.gov. http://usaspending.gov/

FOIA. http://www.foia.gov/about.html, last updated January 2011.

FTC Bureau of Consumer Protection Business Center. http://www.business.ftc.gov/privacy-and-security

King County Multi-Family Residential Parking Calculator. King County/Rightsizeparking.org

Montgomery County Data Portal. https://data.montgomerycountymd.gov/

The National Archives. http://www.archives.gov
State of Utah Data Portal. http://www.utah.gov/data/
The Statue of Liberty–Ellis Island Foundation, Inc. http://www.ellisisland.org/genealogy/
    ellis_island_history.asp

Other Resources

IBM. Big Data. http://www.ibmbigdatahub.com/whitepapers
————. http://www.ibm.com/big-data/us/en/
IDC. Big Data. http://www.idc.com/getdoc.jsp?containerId=IDC_P23177
————. http://www.idc.com/prodserv/FourPillars/bigData/index.jsp
McKinsey & Company. 2014. *Big Data: The Next Frontier for Innovation, Competition,
    and Productivity.* Accessed October 17, 2014. http://www.mckinsey.com/insights/
    business_technology/big_data_the_next_frontier_for_innovation
YouTube: IBM. http://www.youtube.com/watch?v=B27SpLOOhWw

5 Managing Technology through Project and Program Management

For years private sector companies have capitalized on advancements in information technology to improve their products and services and revolutionize the way they work. In a free market where those who lag behind are left behind, this ability to adapt alongside technology is practically a prerequisite for survival. At the same time, while government has been active in bringing new technology into its many operations—and, on occasion, in initiating revolutionary technological advancements—as a whole, the public sector has failed to reap the same benefits as the private sector. Driven by a multiplicity of factors, poor management of IT projects and programs has become a clear source of IT failure and government's inability to adapt, contributing to both minor inefficiencies and large-scale IT catastrophes (White House 2014). In a nutshell, many governments and government organizations need to get better at planning their work, and later, at working their plans.

To illustrate, imagine walking past the hypothetical construction of a large downtown high rise building in any major city in America. Beams, sheets of construction material, and panels of glass are all coming together on the busy worksite. At the top, a tower crane is putting large crossbeams into place, thanks to the gentle guidance of its operator, hundreds of feet away. On a lower floor, a team of plumbers is assembling pipefittings. Electricians are running massive lengths of wire into the infrastructure in direct paths to well-planned outlets. On the ground floor, the architect and the project director examine blueprints, discussing snags and delays that might be coming. Nearby, a handful of other managers and foremen are taking turns reporting on budgetary impacts and timelines to a project manager.

With a project of this magnitude and such a massive budget, nothing can be left to chance. This is not the first building to be created, so past successes and failures arrive on the worksite each day in the minds of everyone with experience. A formal process is followed for every component of the build, from laying the foundation to wiring the red flashing beacon at the tip of the spire on top. Months before ground had broken, a sizeable team of managers and stakeholders had already spent days planning, applying for permits, and discussing which contractors to partner with and how best to undertake the construction of the building.

Figure 5.1 System architecture is similar to planning for a new building structure

Now, in the throes of construction, specialists with a wide range of technical and managerial skills work in concert to make sure everything moves as quickly as possible. Some things can be done concurrently, on the same days or even at the same moments in time. Other pieces must be done in a series. The windows can't be put in before their frames are fully constructed, and that can't be done until the exterior walls are erected. Similarly, plumbers and electricians can't begin their work until the framing and roofing are completed.

This metaphor mimics the ideal way a major government IT project should be undertaken. It would be silly to leave all of the management of the project up to a single individual or the process up to chance. Though there's likely only one person who has oversight, he or she needs the support of many subordinate managers, each charged with keeping things on time and on budget. Some role players have highly technical specializations. Others do not. Everyone has a well-defined role and clear responsibilities.

But unlike in this metaphor, the odd passerby will have much more trouble noticing gaps and missing infrastructure when it comes to building new technology. It would be hard to move tenants into a building where a number of windows were missing and no bathrooms were plumbed. However, when it comes to major technology builds, critical missing pieces can easily go unnoticed. It is for this reason that planning, organization, and execution are even more difficult and require even more rigor in IT projects. And communication is paramount. If the boss cannot see at a quick glance that something is going sideways, it is up to the subordinates on the project with visibility into what might be wrong to speak truth to power. The consequences that can

Figure 5.2 Computer code is not easy to "see"

occur when such issues go unaddressed can be catastrophic. And catastrophic failure is unfortunately all too familiar for those involved with many of the major public sector IT undertakings of the recent past.

> When it comes to major technology builds, critical missing pieces can easily go unnoticed. It is for this reason that planning, organization, and execution are even more difficult and require even more rigor in IT projects.

As revealed by TechStat Accountability Sessions, an initiative launched by the Office of Management and Budget (OMB) to provide IT spending oversight, the government invests in over 6,000 IT projects every year yielding more than 75 billion in costs. The gravity of these numbers is amplified when you consider that an estimated 25 percent of the government's major IT programs are mismanaged (see ITdashboard.gov). Adding cause for concern, from 2003 to 2012 only around 6.4 percent of large-scale government IT projects were successful; the rest fell behind schedule, went over budget, failed to meet requirements, or flopped completely (Ditmore 2013).

Beyond these numbers, there are a handful of large-scale government failures worth noting to add real-world context around the need for improved project management.

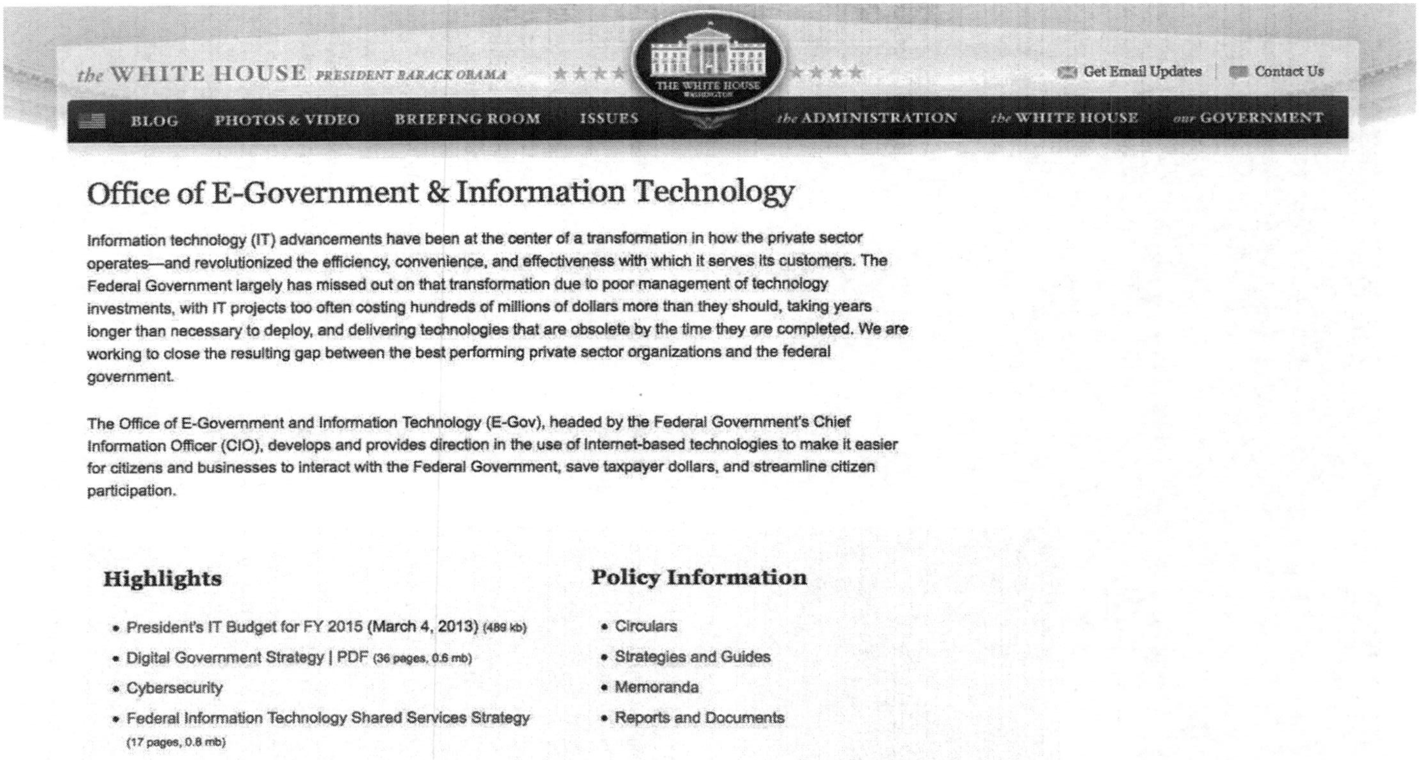
the WHITE HOUSE PRESIDENT BARACK OBAMA
THE WHITE HOUSE
Get Email Updates
Contact Us
BLOG
PHOTOS & VIDEO
BRIEFING ROOM
ISSUES
the ADMINISTRATION
the WHITE HOUSE
our GOVERNMENT
Office of E-Government & Information Technology
Information technology (IT) advancements have been at the center of a transformation in how the private sector operates—and revolutionized the efficiency, convenience, and effectiveness with which it serves its customers. The Federal Government largely has missed out on that transformation due to poor management of technology investments, with IT projects too often costing hundreds of millions of dollars more than they should, taking years longer than necessary to deploy, and delivering technologies that are obsolete by the time they are completed. We are working to close the resulting gap between the best performing private sector organizations and the federal government.
The Office of E-Government and Information Technology (E-Gov), headed by the Federal Government's Chief Information Officer (CIO), develops and provides direction in the use of Internet-based technologies to make it easier for citizens and businesses to interact with the Federal Government, save taxpayer dollars, and streamline citizen participation.
Highlights
• President's IT Budget for FY 2015 (March 4, 2013) (489 kb)
• Digital Government Strategy | PDF (36 pages, 0.6 mb)
• Cybersecurity
• Federal Information Technology Shared Services Strategy (17 pages, 0.8 mb)
Policy Information
• Circulars
• Strategies and Guides
• Memoranda
• Reports and Documents

Figure 5.3 At the time of this writing, the Office of Management and Budget was citing "poor management" as the reason government IT has failed to keep up with private sector IT innovation

Source: White House 2014

The FBI's Virtual Case Files Project

After costing more than $600 million and requiring several years worth of attempts to upgrade the FBI's paper-based filing system to a digital one, the final system many thought would revolutionize the FBI's work when it kicked off in 2000 was deemed unusable and eventually abandoned in 2004 (Eggen and Witte 2006).

Kinetic Energy Interceptor

In 2009, the Pentagon's Missile Defense Agency ended a multi-year, $1.2 billion project called the Kinetic Energy Interceptor program once it realized the system's capabilities would be too limited to achieve the desired missile protection goals (Wolf 2009).

IRS Business System Modernization

In the late 1990s, after a decade's worth of work, the $3.3 billion attempt by the IRS to develop a modernized database to house taxpayer information was regarded as a failure (Anderson 1998). Billions more have been reinvested into this ongoing program which has seen a combination of success and failure since that time.

FAA's En Route Automation Modernization System (ERAM)

ERAM was designed to replace the FAA's forty-year-old air traffic control system used at the twenty FAA Air Route Traffic Control Centers nationwide. The transition to ERAM is one of the most complex, challenging, and ambitious programs deployed by the FAA. In 2014, ERAM is years behind schedule and hundreds of millions of dollars over budget. In June 2014, the Los Angeles International Airport suffered a massive shutdown due to a failure of ERAM (Air Traffic Management website).

Perhaps the most noteworthy and recent in 2010 example of a government IT project failure is the case of Healthcare.gov. in accordance with the Patient Protection and Affordable Care Act, the government began the development of an online health exchange marketplace enabling citizens to shop for health insurance and compare coverage options. Hundreds of millions of dollars and more than three years later, thousands of Americans were left frustrated and unable to obtain new coverage when they encountered a technologically flawed website, ill-suited for handling high levels of traffic during the open enrollment period. In the days and weeks that followed, additional shortcomings were realized and brought under public scrutiny. Many of the website flaws were traced back to insufficient testing,

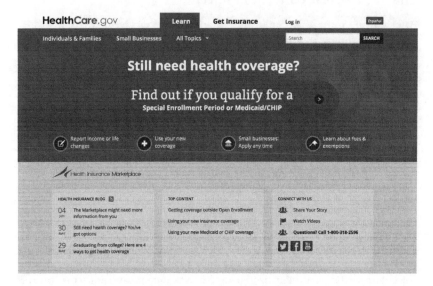

Figure 5.4 HealthCare.gov launched amid a cloud of criticism in the fall of 2013 raising
the buzz about public sector project management ineffectiveness from a quiet
hum to a loud roar

Source: White House 2014

a lack of communication, and unrealistic timelines—all signs of poor project
management.

While failures like these run rampant within government, improved project
management may very well hold the key to a brighter future for government
technology. Done right, this well-established field of management science has
the power to transform IT projects from top to bottom. Government project
managers must approach project management with integrity and be prepared
to weigh a wide range of competing demands. Ultimately, it is the responsibility of the project manager overseeing any large government undertaking to
use the funds provided by the taxpaying public to deliver on the goals set by
its elected officials. Doing so requires a truly well-rounded and disciplined
approach.

Ultimately, it is the responsibility of the project manager overseeing
any large government undertaking to use the funds provided by the
taxpaying public to deliver on the goals set by its elected officials.
Doing so requires a truly well-rounded and disciplined approach.

Project and Program Management: An Overview

Before an understanding of project management can be formed, a definition for a project must be established. The Project Management Institute defines a *project* as "a temporary endeavor undertaken to create a unique product or service" (Duncan 1996). Multiple projects typically fall under an overarching *program*, which is defined as "a group of related projects managed in a coordinated way" (Duncan 1996). Within federal and state governments, programs are more common than in local governments, as large organizations typically allocate resources to full-fledged programs rather than one-off projects (Project Management Institute 2002). While different, projects and programs both exist as part of the same continuum aimed at delivering new products, services, and technological tools for government workers and citizens.

So what is project management, really? It is the applied use of various techniques and expertise to achieve the desired project outcome as defined by the project stakeholders. More loosely, it's a process for setting and meeting expectations, which requires project managers to maintain balance despite diverse stakeholder demands regarding budgets, timelines, and the quality and specifics of the end product (PMI 2013a).

The Ten Project Management Knowledge Areas

The Project Management Institute breaks project management down into ten main knowledge areas (Project Management Institute website).

- **Project Scope Management**
  Ensuring the project contains all the work needed for a successful completion and no additional work
- **Time Management**
  Ensuring the project is completed on time
- **Cost Management**
  Ensuring the project is completed on budget
- **Quality Management**
  Ensuring the project satisfies initial objectives
- **Human Resource Management**
  Developing and managing the project team
- **Communication Management**
  Deciphering what information is needed, as well as how it will be managed and reported
- **Risk Management**
  Determining project risks and managing those risks
- **Procurement Management**
  Securing the resources needed for project completion
- **Project Stakeholders Management**
  Identifying, managing, and engaging project stakeholders

- **Project Integration Management**
  Unifying all project elements to drive the project forward as a single coordinated effort

The Public Management Institute offers many different project management certifications built around these ten knowledge areas. These include certifications such as the Certified Associate in Project Management certification (CAPM), an entry-level certification for individuals who are new to the project management discipline, the Project Management Professional certification (PMP), a globally recognized credential, and the PMI Risk Management Professional certification (PMI-RPM), a specialized certification for managing risk (PMI 2013b).

Process Improvement

Process improvement efforts can be deployed in conjunction with project management as a means of optimizing specific areas within individual projects, as well as maintaining and streamlining new systems created by the adoption of tools delivered through project management. While referred to by many different names, such as operational excellence and process engineering, the concept of process improvement remains consistent: it is a method of developing frameworks for success, fostering order, eliminating inefficiencies, and improving output. When addressing repeating processes created by a given project, it is important that a stakeholder with process expertise is involved in the development and management of the project in question.

While referred to by many different names, such as operational excellence and process engineering, the concept of process improvement remains consistent: it is a method of developing frameworks for success, fostering order, eliminating inefficiencies, and improving output.

There are numerous process improvement methodologies, all of which intend to improve processes within organizations to deliver more value and efficiency. Three of the most commonly cited include Business Process Management, which focuses on optimizing business processes; Lean, which focuses on eliminating waste; and Six Sigma, which focuses on reducing defects. All these methodologies involve a set of phases, look at current states, and aim for improvement using a particular set of tools and techniques. These process improvement efforts are never static. Processes must be constantly monitored and adjusted accordingly, evolving as organizations do.

Project and Program Management in Government

Forms of project and program management have indeed played a role in governments since the dawn of societies; however, throughout its existence in the governments of the United States, there has been no central body in charge of instituting project and program management standards across all of government (Weinstein and Jaques 2010). This has led to major project and program management inconsistencies across organizations and departments. In a recent study carried out by the Project Management Institute surveying both project managers and government project managers, only 11 percent of the government project manager respondents reported having a senior-level program manager in place, and less than 40 percent of respondents claimed to have a formal program management development process within their respective organizations (Project Management Institute 2013b).

> Research from the Project Management Institute shows that without strong project management, organizations risk nine times the amount of money on projects than organizations with strong project management.

Research from the Project Management Institute shows that without strong project management, organizations risk nine times the amount of money on projects than organizations with strong project management (Project Management Institute 2010). Establishing universal project management standards could greatly reduce discrepancies across governments, leading to overall improvement and reduced risk of failure. With formalized rules and procedures for hiring, accrediting, and assigning project managers to specific projects, as well as improved adherence to fundamental project management principals, greater reliability would be had—reliability that is in critical demand as evidenced by the major IT project failures detailed earlier in the chapter.

What Makes Government Projects Different?

Project management is in no way unique to government, but projects originating within government offices have qualities that are distinct from many of their private sector counterparts. The Public Management Institute identifies a number of key attributes of government projects (Weinstein and Jaques 2010).

- **A diverse set of stakeholders**
  Public sector projects impact Congress, voters, citizens, media, regulators, world leaders, and even other departments, just to name a few.

- **Significant consequences**
  Because they must serve large populations, projects can cost millions, if not billions, of dollars and affect many people over a long period of time.
- **Political change**
  Administration changeover given, its predictable cycles and unpredictable outcomes often results in the turnover in leadership, that can significantly influence management approaches.
- **Open to the public**
  As publicly funded projects, government projects are open to the public and therefore subject to high levels of public scrutiny.

Government IT Projects: Perils and Pitfalls

Public or private, IT projects are difficult to manage in general. According to a study by IBM, a quarter of US-based IT projects run over budget and 34 percent fall behind schedule (Poole 2012). Typical sources of critical failure are often rooted in the fact that whole new technologies are being invented from scratch, and that their invention requires adherence to very tight timelines; those cited frequently include high levels of risk involved with unfamiliar technology, hasty development to meet challenging schedule demands, and the short life of technology (Taylor 2004).

Public or private, IT projects are difficult to manage in general. According to a study by IBM, a quarter of US-based IT projects run over budget and 34 percent fall behind schedule.

Delivering revolutionary new IT solutions is challenging, but not just as a direct result of their technological complexity and timelines. Many sources of project failure relate more to the ways the projects are undertaken—reaching the summit of Mt. Everest was thought to be impossible until a better route was discovered. Likewise, delivering a new IT solution isn't a purely impossible task; most failures can likely be attributed most purely to flaws in the ways IT projects are undertaken. The good news is that project and program managers do not necessarily need to be well versed in IT to manage IT projects and programs, but rather they need to be well versed in project and program management. Successful technology departments are commonly comprised of a number of non-technical employees, and this will undoubtedly be true of tomorrow's government IT departments, as well.

Figure 5.5 Project management relies on communication, planning, and strong discipline

Program managers do not necessarily need to be well versed in IT to manage IT projects and programs, but rather they need to be well versed in project and program management.

The bad news is that the inherent difficulty of managing IT projects is compounded at the governmental level. Here, various factors make IT projects particularly difficult to manage at different stages throughout the project lifecycle.

Long, Complex Procurement Cycles

One major factor is the Acquisition Regulations system (FAR). FAR enforces regulation on government IT projects that impact government procurement processes. These regulations have been criticized as being too rigid to accommodate the wide range of technologies being developed (Gallagher 2013). And, as the CEO of a nonprofit government technology organization called Better Technology, Clay Johnson, and former CTO of Obama for America, Harper Reed, put it in a 2013 op-ed in *The New York Times*, the 1,800 pages of hard-to-understand legal documents generally guarantee that

Figure 5.6 RFPEZ.SBA.gov or "RFP-EZ" has helped make the RFP process easier for technology contractors, but there's still plenty of work to be done

Source: www.rfpez.sba

the company winning contracts "can navigate the regulations best, but not necessarily do the best job" (Johnson and Reed 2013). Contracts are almost always awarded to larger companies that beat out less expensive, more nimble firms with potentially greater expertise in unique verticals (Threadgill 2013). This type of contracting was present in the development of Healthcare.gov, in which larger vendors such as CGI won the contract, but ultimately delivered a below average product. The political environment exacerbates this issue, too, as constantly changing policy can result in new project requirements in the middle of the project lifecycle.

In recent years, the government has taken steps to tackle the problem of long, complex procurement cycles. Johnson, who co-authored the op-ed in *The New York Times* referenced earlier, was awarded a Presidential Innovation Fellowship in 2012 that resulted in the development of a website called RFP-EZ (RFPEZ.SPA.gov), which has been credited with improving the procurement experience for smaller technology firms and informing the government about ways to improve procurement.

Too Big to Fail. Too Massive to Succeed

Government IT projects are also commonly hampered by being too large in scope. Because IT projects are funded though the capital budget, governments are apt to tackle larger projects that take years to build and implement. In many cases, projects take so long, the technology becomes outdated before it is finished (Threadgill 2013). This was no more evident than in the case of the IRS Business System Modernization project, which spanned multiple decades and repeatedly saw more advanced solutions spring up during development. Moreover, the disastrous rollout of Healthcare.gov highlights another problem with large-scale IT projects: they can become so complex and have so many components, the project becomes virtually impossible to execute as initially planned and scoped.

> Because IT projects are funded though the capital budget, governments are apt to tackle larger projects that take years to build and implement. In many cases, projects take so long that the technology becomes outdated before it is finished. They can become so complex and have so many components, the project becomes virtually impossible to execute as initially planned and scoped.

Government IT project and program managers are often better suited to focus on smaller projects and minimum viable products (MVPs). Downscaling IT projects make them much easier to manage and simpler to implement, allowing the project team to react to fast-moving changes in technology or in the political and financial landscape. Additionally, shifting the focus to smaller projects opens the door for more specialized contractors that would be unable to bid for larger contracts.

The Big Bang Release and the Waterfall Approach

Governments also have a tendency to release large-scale IT projects all at once, rather than in small stages to allow for feedback, testing, and error correction. This stands in stark contrast to the ways many of the most innovative private organizations create new technologies. These "big bang" releases hamstring projects at the threshold of delivery. In fact, the most common project management methodology used in government management of IT projects is the waterfall approach, which tends to set projects up for all or nothing eventualities (Weinstein and Jaques 2010). Project stages under this approach are typically only completed once, leaving little room for iteration. After one stage is complete, the next stage is set in motion, similar to dominoes falling down a line. The downside, of course, is that any stage done poorly affects each stage following it. Ideally, projects leveraging the waterfall methodology should be completed twice to allow for quality assurance and testing (Royce 2010). After all, it is unclear how the product under development performs until it is fully tested. Project managers responsible for the rollout of Healthcare.gov learned this lesson firsthand, when the website launched after only minimal testing and countless glitches and bugs were revealed in short order.

. The waterfall approach stands in direct contrast to another common IT project methodology, the agile approach. This approach requires projects to be rolled out feature-by-feature, enabling continual feedback from users. Under this methodology, project managers and technologists are able to

Figure 5.7 A failure in one critical path can bring down an entire system

adapt to unanticipated user needs and catch problems early before they turn into insurmountable project roadblocks. Agile projects also benefit from the added dynamic of recurring end-user engagement that markedly increases the project's value to the individuals who will use the product or service upon project completion. Imagine the release of Healthcare.gov if an agile methodology had been implemented throughout. Website faults would have been detected and fixed as soon as they materialized. And the CGI Group, project managers from the Centers for Medicare and Medicaid Services, and President Obama would have received much more information and a much different reaction from the American public.

Evolution in Action: Government Project Improvement

Within the past decade, and especially as of late, the government has taken many steps to improve project and program management generally, with a specific focus on project and program management at the federal level, influencing state and local governments in the process.

In 2012 the Government Efficiency Caucus was launched to prompt government organizations to look at best practices in program and project management used in the private sector and adopt those practices in the public sector. A major objective of the caucus is to encourage members of Congress to consult with private sector project management experts to better understand how program and project management can save money and improve operations (PMI 2012). On a less comprehensive scope, in 2007 the Acquisition Certification for Program and Project Managers (FAC-P/PM) was put in place to institute requirements for program and project manager training and experience levels within civilian agencies. The primary objective is to provide a development program for program and project managers that are assigned to "major acquisitions" (Denett 2007).

IT-specific initiatives have been undertaken as well. After recognizing the increased reliance on IT within government, the IT Project Manager Guidance Matrix was developed to provide guidance in terms of experience and training levels for project managers of IT projects (Department of Defense 2014). The goal of the matrix is to ensure the efficient delivery of IT systems. All IT project managers at the federal level must meet the technical requirements of this matrix, which include stipulations such as needing increased experience for projects of higher complexity (Denett 2007). Additionally, in 2004 the CIO Council created the IT Project Manager Guidance, which calls for every major IT project to be managed by a qualified project manager as defined by requirements of the CIO Council (Energy.gov 2014).

The overall impact of these initiatives cannot be fully or accurately measured yet, but it is clear that there are isolated areas with government moving in the right direction. In 2010, a study from the Project Management Institute revealed a number of best practices exhibited by government organizations and agencies enjoying project and program management success (PMI 2010). Those best practices included the following:

- **Superior Stakeholder Engagement**
  Start with the end-user in mind by consulting with the customer to define the problem that needs to be solved and create a list of all stakeholder roles, responsibilities, and ways to address stakeholders if change occurs.
- **Culture of Communication**
  Open up lines of communication to connect the entire team, including outside stakeholders, in order to foster collaboration and keep everyone who is involved constantly in the loop.
- **Agile Program Thinking**
  Develop flexible project management processes that embrace risk and allow contractors to determine the best way to meet objectives, rather than holding them to rigid guidelines.
- **Active Executive Support**
  Demonstrate the program's connection to the overall organization goals to achieve executive support and leverage the support of executive sponsors.

State and local governments are also beginning to embrace project management as a critical and necessary skill set. For example, the City of Boston has its own Office of Project Management that serves as a resource to the city's operating departments. State and local governments are beginning to hire or train existing staff for the various project management certifications such as those offered by the Project Management Institute. In addition, many localities have purchased and are using off-the-shelve software programs aimed specifically at project management applications. Microsoft offers *Microsoft Project* as part of its Office Business Suite and well-known tax preparation software developer Intuit offers Quickbase. There are dozens of other project management offerings—some cloud-based-that are available to small and large organizations.

The Future of Project and Program Management in Government

Envision a future for government where project and program management has made governments much more nimble and useful to high-tech citizens. It's not just the government developing technologies more effectively; state and local governments are delivering better "products" and services, as well. Governments have adopted the characteristics of high performing organizations. Job classifications for project and program managers has been instituted at the federal level, and IT project and program management career paths have expanded government-wide. Training in project and program management has created a common vocabulary supporting newness and creative problem solving at all levels, both inside government organizations and in citizen-facing deliveries. Program management standards have been developed across the public sector, delivering common practices for the pursuit of strategic initiatives. This is all strengthened by leveraging process improvement to maintain technology tools longer, and streamline inefficiencies out of large-scale IT projects and programs.

Program management standards have been developed across the public sector, delivering common practices for the pursuit of strategic initiatives. This is all strengthened by leveraging process improvement to maintain technology tools longer, and streamline inefficiencies out of large-scale IT projects and programs.

This situation sounds idealistic, yet it is entirely achievable. With a laundry list of major IT failures as a constant reminder and motivator for change, tomorrow's public administrators have the power to continue strengthening program and project management within government, improving government's bottom line and mitigating both large-scale and small-scale IT project failure across the entire public sector, which is undoubtedly hurdling towards a more technical existence.

Discussion Questions

1. What are the similarities and differences between projects and programs?
2. Why is project stakeholder management particularly critical in government?
3. What makes government IT projects so different from those in the private sector?
4. Why are IT projects—public or private—inherently difficult to manage?
5. Why do government organizations typically award contracts to bigger companies, and what problems does this pose for government IT projects in general?
6. What can focusing on minimum viable products (MVPs) rather than "big bang" releases do for public sector IT project success?
7. What are some project management best practices recently demonstrated by high performing governments?
8. How could better project management have improved the rollout of Healthcare.gov?

References

Air Traffic Management. 2014. "ERAM Crash Sparked by Insufficient RAM." Accessed October 17, 2014. http://www.airtrafficmanagement.net/2014/05/eram-crash-sparked-by-insufficient-ram/.

Anderson, Curt. 1998. "IRS to Modernize Computer Systems." *AP News Archive*. Online, December 10. Accessed October 17, 2014. http://www.apnewsarchive.com/1998/IRS-To-Modernize-Computer-Systems/id-4bab6c1b4332a8b76edfba20dbe15ed1.

Denett, Paul. 2007. "Memorandum for Chief Acquisition Officers." *Office of Procurement Policy*. April 25. Accessed October 17, 2014. http://www.whitehouse.gov/sites/default/files/omb/assets/omb/procurement/workforce/fed_acq_cert_042507.pdf.

Department of Defense. 2014. "DOD IT Workforce." Accessed October 17, 2014. http://dodcio.defense.gov/dodit/dodit_specialty.aspx.

Ditmore, Jim. 2013. "Why do Big IT Projects Fail so Often?" *InformationWeek*. October 28. Accessed October 17, 2014. http://www.informationweek.com/strategic-cio/executive-insights-and-innovation/why-do-big-it-projects-fail-so-often/d/d-id/1112087?

Duncan, William. 1996. *A Guide to the Project Management Body of Knowledge*. PMI Communications, Sylva, NC. Pages 4 and 8.

Eggen, Dan and Griff Witte. 2006. "The FBI's Upgrade that Wasn't." *The Washington Post*. August 18. Accessed October 17, 2014. http://www.washingtonpost.com/wpdyn/content/article/2006/08/17/AR2006081701485.html.

Energy.gov. 2014. "IT Project Management Certification." *US Department of Energy*. Accessed October 17, 2014. http://energy.gov/cio/guidance/it-project-management/it-project-management-certification.

Gallagher, Sean. 2013. "Why US Government IT Fails so Hard, so Often." *Ars Technica*. October 10. Accessed October 17, 2014. http://arstechnica.com/information-technology/2013/10/why-us-government-it-fails-so-hard-so-often/.

Johnson, Clay and Harper Reed. 2013. "Why the Government Never Gets Tech Right." *The New York Times*. October 24. Accessed October 17, 2014. http://www.

nytimes.com/2013/10/25/opinion/getting-to-the-bottom-of-healthcaregovs-flop. html?_r=1&.

PMI 2010. "Program Management 2010: A Study of Program Management in the US Government 2010." Project Management Institute, Inc. June. Accessed October 17, 2014. http://www.pmi.org/Business-Solutions/~/media/PDF/Business-Solutions/ Government%20Program%20Management%20Study%20Report_FINAL.ashx.

PMI. 2012. "Project Management Institute Applauds Launch of Government Efficiency Caucus." Project Management Institute, Inc. April 18. Accessed October 17, 2014. http://www.pmi.org/en/About-Us/Press-Releases/Project-Management-Institute-Applauds-Launch-of-Government-Efficiency-Caucus.aspx.

PMI. 2013a. "What is Project Management?" Project Management Institute, Inc. Accessed October 17, 2014. http://www.pmi.org/About-Us/About-Us-What-is-Project-Management.aspx.

PMI. 2013b. "Which Certification is Right for You?" Project Management Institute, Inc. Accessed October 17, 2014. http://www.pmi.org/en/Certification/Which-PMI-Certification-is-Right-for-You.aspx.

Poole, Gina. 2012. "IBM PureSystems: Ushering in a New Era for Software and Systems Delivery." IBM.com. October 9. Accessed October 17, 2014. http://www.ibm.com/ ibm/puresystems/infographic/charts/budget-schedule.html.

Project Management Institute. 2002. *Government Extension to a Guide to the Project Management Body of Knowledge: 2000 Edition*. Newtown Square, PA. Page 4.

Project Management Institute. 2010. "Highlighting Key Trends in the Project Management Profession." Project Management Institute, Inc. Accessed October 17, 2014. http:// www.pmi.org/business-solutions/~/media/PDF/Business-Solutions/Pulse%20of% 20the%20Profession%20White%20Paper_FINAL.ashx.

Project Management Institute. 2013a. *A Guide to the Project Management Body of Knowledge (Fifth Edition)*. Newtown Square, PA.

Project Management Institute. 2013b. *The High Cost of Low Performance of the Government. PMI's Pulse of the Profession*. Project Management Institute, Inc. Accessed October 17, 2014. http://www.pmi.org/~/media/PDF/Business-Solutions/PMI-The-High-Cost-of-Low-Performance-of-the-Government.ashx.

Royce, Winston. 1970. "Managing the Development of Large Software Systems." The Institute of Electrical and Electronics Engineers, Inc. Pages 328–338.

Taylor, James. 2004. *Managing Information Technology Projects: Applying Project Management Strategies to Software, Hardware, and Integration Initiatives*. AMACOM, New York. Page 5.

Threadgill, Melissa. 2013. "Why Public Sector gets Technology Wrong." *The Boston Globe.* November 11. Accessed October 17, 2014. http://www.bostonglobe.com/opinion/ 2013/11/11/why-government-can-get-information-technology-right/SA7f2rL-6LxYZ1CCqXU4awJ/story.html.

Weinstein, Jonathan and Timothy Jaques. 2010. *Achieving Project Management Success in the Government*. Management Concepts, Vienna, VA.

White House. 2014. Office of E-Government & Information. *Office of Management and Budget*. Accessed October 17, 2014. http://www.whitehouse.gov/omb/e-gov.

Wolf, Jim. 2009. "UPDATE 2-US kills Northrop Grumman Missile-Defense Program." *Reuters.* June 11. Accessed October 17, 2014. http://www.reuters.com/article/2009/06/11/ missile-northrop-idINN1152256320090611.

Digital Destinations

DOE Project Management. https://www.directives.doe.gov/directives-documents/0413.1-APolicy

IT Dashboard. https://www.itdashboard.gov/

Government Accountability Office. http://www.gao.gov/about/strategic.html

GSA Project Management Services. http://www.gsa.gov/portal/content/115047

Intuit. http://quickbase.intuit.com/database-applications-for-business/project-management-software

Microsoft. http://office.microsoft.com/en-us/project/

Performance.gov. http://www.performance.gov/

Project Management Institute. http://www.pmi.org/business-solutions/pmi-us-government-relations.aspx

Project Management Institute (PMI) Certifications. http://www.pmi.org/Certification.aspx

RFPEZ.SBA. www.rfpez.sba

6 Broadband, Mobility, and the Internet

Policies and Technology

This chapter will focus on the roles both broadband and the Internet play in today's fixed and mobile government environment. While some have argued that broadband, along with Internet strategy and policy, should be left largely to the private sector, there is no escaping the fact that there is a definitive and necessary role for every branch of government to play. The real challenge is to recognize and deal with what is the right balance between a hands-off approach verses a hands-on regulatory approach at any given moment in time. Government cannot operate in today's highly connected society without reliable broadband service, as well as direct access to the Internet too. What are the key economic and policy issues regarding broadband, and what policies are currently being considered and debated regarding the Internet? This chapter is meant to be a general overview of a number of interrelated topics, each deserving its own entire book; mobile communications, the IT regulatory structure, a bit of history to provide the foundational underpinnings of the Internet and broadband technologies, and where to go for more in-depth information.

On any Sunday afternoon a person can place an order on Amazon.com and expect delivery as early as Monday morning. Likewise, an individual can send an email, compose and send a written report, or use a digital signature to sign a contract instantaneously—all at 36,000 feet aboard a commercial airliner. Local governments alone report that as many as 40–60 percent of their employees work in a mobile environment each and every day. This mobile workforce includes public safety, field inspectors, mass transit, social services, public works, which are just some of the categories. These are but a few examples of how the Internet and broadband are so well integrated in our work and daily life. Indeed so much of what we do every day completely depends on the Internet with broadband as the conduit for delivery. In today's world, it's difficult to imagine what it was like in the early part of the 20th century when electricity was first introduced for commercial purposes. In the early 1900s some argued whether electric power should be offered commercially or as a public utility—or both, especially since lighting was thought to serve the very wealthy exclusively. In either case electricity was originally viewed as limited to home and street lighting, as no one at the time imagined how electricity might also heat and cool homes or keep our food refrigerated or cook meals with electric ovens or microwaves.

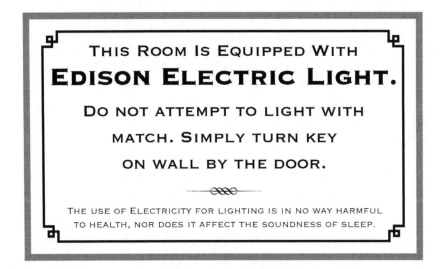

Figure 6.1 Electricity was once thought to power lights only

In the early 1900s some argued whether electric power should be offered commercially or as a public utility—or both, especially since lighting was thought to serve the very wealthy exclusively. In either case electricity was originally viewed as limited to home and street lighting, as no one at the time imagined how electricity might also heat and cool homes or keep our food refrigerated or cook meals with electric ovens or microwaves.

That of course would quickly change. The Internet however, would not arrive for another ninety-five years. Like so many great inventions, such as electricity, the Internet began as a concept with a relatively limited goal; to serve as a high-speed conduit to connect geographically separated research institution's computers. No one in the day could have foreseen what the Internet would ultimately become. By the end of 1969 after a series of discussions and research papers, hundreds of meetings and ongoing collaboration, four host computers were connected together to form what was then called the Advanced Research Projects Agency Network, or better known as ARPANET. This was the first packet-switching network that would make it possible to transfer huge amounts of data from one computer to another and at great distances. Originally funded by the Advanced Research Projects Agency, it was later adopted by the Defense Advanced Research Projects Agency (DARPA) that is housed within the US Department of Defense. Its main purpose was initially to link universities and research laboratories working together on special projects. This network would become the foundation of what was to become the Internet as we know it today. Aside from having great talent, shared steadfast vision, and perseverance, if it had not been for the federal government's initial support, the Internet as we know it today would not have been built. As it was, the Internet would not be commercialized until 1995. For a brief history of the Internet see Internet Society (2013).

So, Who "Owns" the Internet?

The answer is both no one and in a sense everyone. No single company or nation has single ownership—but to varying extents different entities can control or influence different parts of it. The Internet is a collection of inter-networked computer systems that spans the entire globe. It depends on several sets of rules called protocols, and depends on a network of routers and what once was originally four Network Access Points. Today, these components span across every corner of the globe. The original Network Access Points have long ago been replaced by Internet Exchange Points (IEPs). The Internet is highly connected and highly decentralized when it comes to networks access points. Today, Internet "traffic" travels via cable, wireless, microwave, fiber, and satellites. Internet Service Providers (ISPs) are the gatekeepers who charge fees to partners and end-users. The Internet is governed through the universal adoption of the common language called the *Internet Protocol* (IP). The addresses are distributed or sold through the Internet Corporation for Assigned Names and Numbers (ICANN). ICANN is the private sector nonprofit organization created in 1998 for the purpose of managing and coordinating the Internet Assigned Numbers Authority (IANA) functions, which are key technical services critical to the continued operations of the Internet's underlying address book, the Domain Name System (DNS). The IANA functions include: (1) the coordination of the assignment of technical protocol parameters including the management of the address and routing parameter area (ARPA) top-level domain; (2) the administration of certain responsibilities associated with Internet DNS root zone management; (3) the allocation of Internet numbering resources; and (4) other services. ICANN has performed the IANA functions under a US Government contract. ICANN is the nonprofit organization that has the responsibility for distributing (selling) Internet extensions, such as .com, org, net, us, eu, plus a vast array of newly released extensions. Since the Internet's inception, the US has controlled the oversight of Internet addresses through control of ICANN—it too has been under US control through a subcontract since 1998. The role of the US in its oversight of ICANN is scheduled to change in 2015 where it will turn over these responsibilities to an international group whose structure and administration is being worked out. Understandably there are those in the US that are quite concerned that the Internet addressing system might become politicized thus jeopardizing its neutrality. Of course, with public revelations that US intelligence agencies were "spying" on Internet traffic, the US government has lost a good deal of respect (Wyatt 2014a). This has hastened calls for ICANN to be turned over to an international body sooner than later, while at the same time international business leaders are concerned that proposed changes could lead to a "broken" Internet (CNET 2014).

Addressing the Address

Have you ever wondered how emails and text messages wind up where they are supposed to go regardless of location? Every device including computers, laptops, tablets, printers, and even cell phones, has an assigned IP address too. In order for one device to find and communicate with another there needs to be an established IP address. These addresses are characterized through numbers. Some addresses may be assigned to groups within organizations that in turn assign internal numbers within these groups for greater efficiencies. Today, most Internet users are working under Internet Protocol version 4, or simply IPv4. With each successive version, addresses become more versatile and take into account the millions of devices that are added every year. While by no means a crisis, there are no longer any new IPv4 addresses to be allocated. The good news is there remains a healthy inventory held by administering companies for the time being. Even better news is the fact Ipv6 has been adopted and contains new features that previous versions did not have. IPv6 is inherently more secure in several ways than previous versions, and has infinitely more room to grow with new numbers; 128 bit addresses vs. IPv4's 32 bit addresses. Without doing the math, the numbers speak for themselves. Holders or distributors of the remaining IPv4 addresses will find there are no new numbers to allocate. At this time, lacking any regulations or timetables to move away from IPv4, it will make the transition quite slow and force operators to build and maintain systems capable of handling both types of addresses.

Internet 2

While we enjoy the many benefits and features of the Internet we know of, there is another system called Internet 2. The Internet 2 was formed in 1996 by mostly educational institutions looking to collaborate and experiment with learning and information and high-end research activities that exceeded the bandwidth of the Internet most use today. The Internet 2 is built upon a much higher functioning network infrastructure with far greater bandwidth and now boasts over 500 members including mostly research institutions, plus companies and government agencies.

Figure 6.2 Broadband can be either wired or wireless – but the signal that is carried is always the same

What is Broadband?

The importance of broadband today is much like how society utilizes electricity. The Internet cannot function without broadband connectivity. Broadband is a rather odd term that tends to denote different meanings or connotations. The term broadband implies something broad, wide, fast, faster, faster than dial-up, DSL, 4G, 5G, Wi-Fi, HDTV, etc. When one looks at functional and comparative definitions, broadband is a relative term; compared to what? In 1996, the late Ted Steven (R-Alaska), the nation's senior policy maker who at the time headed the US Senate's lead telecommunications committee, once tried to describe the Internet as "a series of tubes." While he was ridiculed in the press for such a clumsy statement, it showed that even the most in-the-know policy makers found it difficult to describe and explain. Nonetheless, simply put, if the Internet is indeed a series of tubes, than broadband is the method in which information is carried through such tubes. However, the Internet is far more intricate than a series of tubes to say the least. Broadband has become a relative term when it comes to comparisons such as "faster than" which change over time with the rollout of new technologies. The Federal Telecommunications Commission (FCC) defines broadband as high-speed Internet access that is always on and faster than traditional dial-up access. Early definitions compared broadband to what was once the connection type of choice, dial-up. Dial-up was the original standard in which broadband was measured. Initially people could connect to the Internet using a home or office phone line that was connected via a telephone cord jack connected to a wall socket. One might expect typical speeds of up to 56 kbyts (kilobytes per second) under ideal conditions, but in reality this standard was never met under real-life conditions. By today's standards, dial-up was painfully slow and not only tied up ordinary home or office phone lines, connections could easily be broken with incoming calls or other forms of interference. As dial-up took hold most serious users simply installed a second or third telephone line—one for a standard telephone, another for a facsimile machine (Fax), and still another for Internet communications. In an office setting there was most likely a fourth connection— and that was to a computer network. In today's digital office environment, one network connection can do it all.

Broadband is not limited to fixed locations as it also applies to cell phones, laptops, tablets, wireless modems, and any other mobile device that is equipped with a built-in radio receiver. Many don't realize that today's modern cell phone is both a radio and a telephone combined. In fact today's smart devices contain many radios built into one, like wireless Bluetooth,

FCC Definition of Broadband When Compared to "Dial-Up"

How is broadband different from dial-up service?

- Broadband service provides higher-speed of data transmission. It allows more content to be carried through the transmission "pipeline."
- Broadband provides access to the highest quality Internet services—streaming media, VoIP (Internet phone), gaming, and interactive services. Many of these current and newly-developing services require the transfer of large amounts of data that may not be technically feasible with dial-up service. Therefore, broadband service may be increasingly necessary to access the full range of services and opportunities that the Internet can offer.
- Broadband is always on. It does not block phone lines and there is no need to reconnect to network after logging off.
- Less delay in transmission of content when using broadband.

Figure 6.3 FCC definition comparing broadband with dial-up connections

Source: www.broadband.gov

Definition of Broadband

The term broadband refers to the wide bandwidth characteristics of a transmission medium and its ability to transport multiple signals and traffic types simultaneously. The medium can be coax, optical fiber, twisted pair or wireless. In contrast, baseband describes a communication system in which information is transported across a single channel.

Figure 6.4 4 Broadband defined

Source: Glen Carty. *Broadband Networking.* McGraw Hill Osborne. p. 4.ISBN 007219510X

GPS, Infrared, plus multi cellular frequency bands. Taking it a step further, a smartphone is a radio, telephone, and computer combined into one device. Similar to the days when electricity was first being adopted, some now argue that broadband is so necessary to the economic welfare of contemporary society it should at least be regulated—if not operated as a utility; just like electricity.

> Similar to the days when electricity was first being adopted, some now argue that broadband is so necessary to the economic welfare of contemporary society it should at least be regulated—if not operated as a utility; just like electricity.

Telecommunications and Broadband

Telecommunications is the term used when describing a communication system, whether it is an analog or digital system, which transmits some form of information through a signal or frequency—and can travel great distances. It combines what was once limited to voice communications as found in the telephone, and suggests a broader array of applications which includes voice, data, and video as found in today's TV. Connections can be made through a set of wires, cable, fiber, microwave, satellite, as well as over-the-air radio signals that can both transmit and receive.

Broadband, whether it is designed to be wired (fixed) or wireless signals (mobile), is a collection of electromagnetic or simply radio frequencies that carry a signal or group of signals from one point to another or to a multitude of points to one another. The electromagnetic frequencies in which voice, data, or video signals are carried through a wire or through the air is simply referred to as spectrum.

Why is Broadband Important?

Telecommunications is of course critical to contemporary life, as we know it. Governments in particular have a need to communicate vast amounts of information as well as provide for data collection, commerce across all boundaries, critical mapping intelligence, financial transactions, policy formulation and collaboration, scheduling of transportation, tracking of government vehicles and shipments, research, critical infrastructure, facility monitoring security systems, staff assignments and alerts, and national security interests. Federal, state, and local governments depend on broadband for critical communications, which include, police, fire, and rescue, as well as utility and transportation systems. In 2009, recognizing the growing importance of broadband, Congress, through its American Recovery and Reinvestment Act of 2009, directed the Federal Communications Commission (FCC) to develop a National Broadband Plan. The FCC went to great lengths to solicit and incorporate public participation. It did so by conducting thirty-six public workshops held at the FCC, which involved over 10,000 in-person or online attendees. Based on this initial input, the FCC issued 31 public notices, which generated some 23,000 comments totaling about 74,000 pages from more than 700 parties. Also, nine public hearings were held throughout the country to further clarify the issues addressed in the plan. For more information see the National Broadband Plan website.

The National Broadband Plan was released in March 2010 and contained seven major areas that it deemed "national purpose," which included Health Care, Education, Energy and the Environment, Economic Opportunity, Government Performance, Civic Engagement, and Public Safety. The National Broadband Plan website listed over ninety action steps and provides for a quarterly broadband report along with benchmarks (Broadband.gov).

The plan's executive summary states "Like electricity a century ago, broadband is a foundation for economic growth, job creation, global competitiveness and a better way of life. It is enabling entire new industries and unlocking vast new possibilities for existing ones. It is changing how we educate children, deliver health care, manage energy, ensure public safety, engage government, and access, organize and disseminate knowledge" (ibid.).

Figure 6.5 National Broadband Progress Report

Source: The National Broadband Plan website

Like electricity a century ago, broadband is a foundation for economic growth, job creation, global competitiveness and a better way of life. It is enabling entire new industries and unlocking vast new possibilities for existing ones. It is changing how we educate children, deliver health care, manage energy, ensure public safety, engage government, and access, organize, and disseminate knowledge.

The plan took a wide and comprehensive view of broadband today and where the nation needs to be in the next decade and beyond. It also endorsed the following six long-term goals, which are:

1. At least 100 million US homes should have affordable access to actual download speeds of at least 100 megabits per second and actual upload speeds of at least 50 megabits per second.
2. The United States should lead the world in mobile innovation, with the fastest and most extensive wireless networks of any nation.
3. Every American should have affordable access to robust broadband service, and the means and skills to subscribe if they so choose.
4. Every American community should have affordable access to at least 1 gigabit per second broadband service to anchor institutions such as schools, hospitals, and government buildings.
5. To ensure the safety of the American people, every first responder should have access to a nationwide, wireless, interoperable broadband public safety network.
6. To ensure that America leads in the clean energy economy, every American should be able to use broadband to track and manage their real-time energy consumption.

While many of the plan's recommendations involve new or modified regulations, laws, or guidelines, Congress did not appropriate any funds for any of the plans recommendations. The plan nevertheless serves as a blueprint for further thought as well as action by all government entities. The plan strikes a balance between two related but different sides of broadband. One is the issue of *demand*, which refers to citizen acceptance and actual usage of broadband. It addresses such factors as to whether broadband is available, accessible, and affordable. According to the Pew Internet Family Life Foundation, approximately 20 percent of Americans do not have access to or use broadband. For more information see Pew Research Internet Project (2013). The other of the two factors is *supply* and here the plan addresses the need for more abundant and faster broadband as well as the reasons why. Supply also involves investment in better technologies, infrastructure, and capacity.

According to the Pew Internet Family Life Foundation, approximately 20 percent of Americans do not have access to or use broadband.

Broadband has become a critical ingredient for economic development generally, and in particular it enables innovation to occur in education, commerce, medial care, public safety, and civic improvement in government at all levels. The Broadband.gov website offers citizens a tremendous amount of information. For example, its broadband map provides citizens the opportunity to enter their address and see which companies serve that address, both wired and wireless (or both) and their advertised speeds. The National Broadband Map can display eight different maps:

1. Maximum advertised speed test available
2. Type of technology available
3. Numbers of providers
4. Broadband provider service areas
5. Broadband availability across demographic characteristics
6. Consumer broadband test verses actual or typical speeds
7. Community Anchor Installations (twenty-five closest)
8. National Broadband Map (NBM) users feedback map and data (crowd-sourced).

The US is not alone in its quest to promote better broadband as even the poorest nations recognize the importance of broadband, and especially when one looks at its usage and comparisons when compared with other countries, the US lags in just about every category.

Among several indicators of how well the US is doing with broadband adoption, the US standing has been well behind that of many countries. In one report the ITIF found that the US ranks fifteenth in households subscribing to wired broadband, and number eleven in households with access to a computer that subscribes to wired broadband (Bennett, Stuart, Atkinson 2013).

In Ookla's *Global Download Index* (2014), the US ranked number thirty.

When it comes to upload speeds, the US ranks forty-first in the world. In Ookla's *Quality Index*, the US is ranked second, and the US is ranked in twenty-first place in the *Broadband Cost Index*. The US ranks twenty-first in Ookla's *Promise Index*, which is the actual broadband speed calculated between promised or advertised speeds verses actual experience. For more information see Ookla (2014).

With broadband, there is most always a bi-directional pathway; simply referred to as download and upload speeds. A download speed was at one point in time more important than upload speeds. Americans download music, documents, games, articles, pictures, videos, and movies. On most Sunday evenings, the online movie provider, Netflix, often consumes over thirty percent of all Internet traffic in the US due to heavy demand for

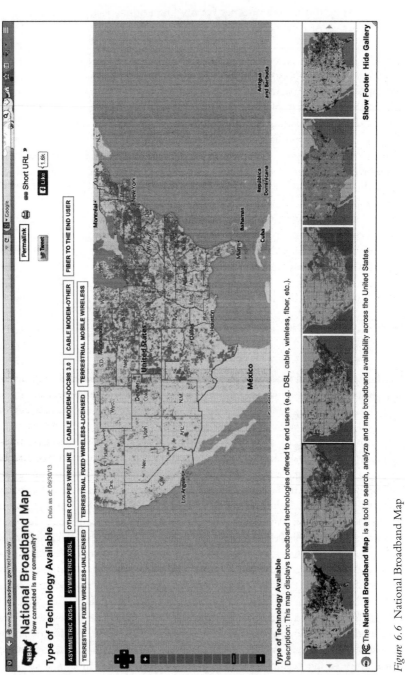

Figure 6.6 National Broadband Map

Source: Broadband.gov

Global Download Speed Rankings	
Hong Kong	81.80 Mbps
Singapore	66.85 Mbps
Romania	57.46 Mbps
South Korea	54.01 Mbps
Lithuania	49.80 Mbps
Sweden	49.59 Mbps
Switzerland	48.53 Mbps
Netherlands	46.22 Mbps
Andorra	41.69 Mbps
Taiwan	41.13 Mbps

Figure 6.7 Ookla global download speed rankings

Source: Ookla 2014

online movie streaming. By comparison, broadband upload speeds used to be viewed as that of a "special request line." When someone requests an online video, document, music, or movie, the request requires far less bandwidth than the actual downloaded content. Today upload speeds are quickly playing a more important role as citizens and government alike are collaborating and sharing greater amounts of content through text and video which requires a tremendous amount of bandwidth. Ookla is but one organization that measures broadband metrics in a real-time environment based on actual minute-by-minute usage. Other studies and indexes, while deriving data from other means, have the US lagging when compared to other countries across the globe. Why is this important one may ask? The answer lies with the quickly evolving nature of the information-age economy. Broadband competition is focused on speed, customer growth, content development, and acquisition, as well as service delivery. High-speed broadband provides much needed instant communications and information, all this in an ever competitive environment. Broadband speeds matter, for example, in the world of publicly traded stock transactions. Today, the overwhelming amount of stock transactions in any given day are automated by computers or "machines" that are programmed to buy and sell under specific circumstances. With high-stakes investments made every second, every millisecond counts. No wonder a few super computer stock service companies have physically located within close proximity to the major stock exchanges' central systems as they boast that they can shave fractions of a second off stock trades. This translates into a company saving millions of dollars (or more) as a result of a slight fractional time advantage over those who rely on basic broadband connectivity.

> Today upload speeds are quickly playing a more important role as
> citizens and government alike are collaborating and sharing greater
> amounts of content through text and video which requires a tremendous
> amount of bandwidth.

The need and advantage of greater speeds goes far beyond the previous
example of stock trading companies as new applications such as remote medical training and operations, distance learning, public safety, transportation
systems, and even flying remote unmanned vehicles all require dependable
and fast broadband connectivity.

The US Government through its policies and regulatory structure has
largely taken a hands-off approach, believing instead that market forces as
opposed to regulatory intervention remain the best policy for sustainable
longer-term growth and overall improvement.

What is the Government's Interest in Broadband?
Getting into the Act

Early regulations focused on rules, regulations, and pricing of telegraph services, telephone service, and television. They also established the practice of
requiring a person or entity to apply for a license in order to operate a radio,
and later, TV service. Because most telecommunications services operate across state borders, it made sense for the federal government to oversee
and enforce the regulatory environment. The Federal Radio Act of 1912
had regulatory power over mostly what we call today AM Radio. The Federal Radio Act of 1912 was later replaced by the Federal Radio Act of 1927
that had the authority to grant and deny licensing, assign frequencies, and
power levels for each license holder. The Act divided the country into five
regions, each represented by a commissioner. The Act included not only
broadcast radio it also had authority over maritime radio and amateur radio
rules, regulations, and licensing. Initially telecommunications was regulated
through the Interstate Commerce Commission (ICC). Since the ICC (which
was disbanded in 1995) was mostly focused on the growth of the railroad
industry, Congress saw the need to separate out telecommunications and
created the Telecommunications Act of 1934, which called for the creation
of the independent Federal Communications Commission (FCC). Rules also
focused on the qualifications of ownership and, in the case of radio and television, rules to make sure there was no central concentration of ownership
by just a few, and there were rules to prevent frequency interference between
broadcast stations. In the early days of what we now call telecommunications, regulations aimed at creating a competitive environment, laid out how
systems operated, promoting a productive use of spectrum, and monitoring

the cost and pricing of services to the public, and the quality and type of services offered.

Cable TV, once regarded as a medium that could deliver basic TV programming through cable, filled a need to provide basic TV service to areas where over-the-air broadcast signals could not reach. Initially cable TV was regulated through local authorities because cable was considered "local." Given the expense of stringing cables to homes and businesses, it made no economic sense to have more than one cable operator in any given community. Cable companies operated as regulated monopolies and had to apply for a cable franchise, typically through a local city or county. The cable industry had to have the local authorities review and approve any rate increases. As part of most cable franchise agreements, cable operators either offered or were required to provide local governments with channels of their own called public, educational, and government access channels, or simply PEG channels. Of course cable today has grown to include far more than re-broadcasting basic network television. Contemporary cable provides telephone service, movies, entertainment, broadband, music, sporting events, premium movie channels as well as on-demand movies and entertainment for an extra price. While cable companies continue to provide local news programming, there has been much consolidation within the seven largest companies with the most number of subscribers—Comcast, Time Warner, Verizon FIOS, Cox Communications, AT&T Universe, Charter Communications, and Cablevision.

While cable got its initial start serving markets just outside the range of a typical TV station, there were many areas in the country that had neither cable or wireless services—that is until advances in satellite technology came about. Today satellite companies include Dish, Direct TV, HughesNet. There are also satellite companies that primarily offer broadband services such as Dish, Exede, HughesNet, and WildBlue. As market forces and technologies in the cable environment began to heat up, Congress passed the Cable Communications Act of 1984 which was designed to promote competition and deregulation of the cable industry. Like its telecommunication cousins, the federal government entered the field because of the volume of commerce crossing state and local boundaries. Local governments lost their near complete control of cable TV regulation and had little choice but to accept what Congress termed a delicate balance between who should exercise the most power over local cable operations. The Act provided municipalities and other local governing bodies principal authority to grant and renew cable franchise licenses. The regulations were also designed to protect cable operators from unfair denials of license renewals while at the same time the regulations stipulated federal standards for renewals. The rationale of the Act was to remove excessive burdens and regulations as well as local politics to better ensure a greater competitive marketplace. As with most forms of deregulation, the opportunities for growth mostly benefited the larger media companies who now had a consistent regulatory structure that paved the way for dramatic growth and consolidation.

Twelve years later, Congress passed the Telecommunications Act of 1996, which was the first major overhaul of the original Communications Act of 1934. The 1996 Act represented a major shift in the way telecommunications was governed from a regulatory perspective and included for the very first time the Internet when it came to broadcast and spectrum allocations. It also addressed the issue as to how the federal government was going to regulate "telecommunications" with that of "data communications." Traditional telephone communications was once heavily regulated while the emerging data communications (the Internet) was not. The plan addressed the issues of what government can do in order to influence the broadband ecosystem. Chief among them was to design policies that ensure robust competition and, as a result, maximize consumer welfare, innovation, and investment. Outside of the purview of the regulatory body, the plan promotes the reform of laws, policies, standards, and incentives in order to maximize the benefits of broadband in sectors government influences significantly, such as public education, health care, and government operations.

The 1996 Act represented a major shift in the way telecommunications was governed from a regulatory perspective and included for the very first time the Internet when it came to broadcast and spectrum allocations.

Telework

A good example of the federal government's interest in broadband is the issue of telework, the ability to work at home either on a limited basis or full-time. The Telework Enhancement Act of 2010 specifies roles and responsibilities for the Office of Personnel Management, General Services Administration, Office of Management and Budget, Department of Homeland Security, National Archives and Records Administration, and others to provide overall guidance to Federal Executive agencies, creating baseline expectations for agency programs and helping agencies implement those programs as effectively as possible. The Act also aims to improve Continuity of Operations and ensure essential federal functions are maintained during emergency situations as well as promote management effectiveness through telework. It also aims to reduce transit costs and environmental impacts and to enhance the work-life balance of federal workers (see the Linkedin.com website). For more information see the Telework Research Network website.

The Global Workplace Analytics and the Telework Research Network issued an update to its annual forecast for government-wide telework savings, and based on the Office of Management and Budget data, federal telework could save fourteen billion annually.

Telework for all its aim and goals could not exist without broadband to the home or to a remote business location.

Towards Deregulation, No Longer Saved by the Bell

Before broadband and telecommunications became somewhat synonymous, the connecting or switching of actual telephone calls from one point to another was quite labor intensive where operators were required to make the connection. This was especially true when making what was once called long-distance; calls that were relatively expensive when compared to local calls.

As telephone systems were being built out, most of what connected people to each other was copper wires strung over great distances on telephone polls. The regulatory landscape evolved into seven regional companies referred to as "baby bells" and all connected to one company called AT&T. AT&T was formed in 1885 to connect the local bells and in 1913 AT&T agreed to become a regulated monopoly, where prices and policies were wholesale rates by the Federal Communications Commission. Consumers could not purchase a phone from the phone company, it was considered a "rental." All the research, development, and innovation involving the growth of the nation's telephone infrastructure was the responsibility of Bell Laboratories, simply called Bell Labs. The regulatory structure of its day insured reliable service that came with quality assurance guaranties (quality of service or QoS) and a set of standards that provided for one of the most powerful and reliable systems in the world.

However, advances in technology began to overwhelm and threaten the once superior monopoly. Entrepreneurs became frustrated at being left

Figure 6.8 An early 1930s rotary dial tethered phone

out of the telecommunications business and the once superior telephone monopoly was being threatened from all sides. Competition began to develop in 1956 when the courts overruled an FCC ban on an add-on phone device called the Hush-a-Phone. Tom Carter, an entrepreneur and inventor, challenged the FCC with his device that snapped onto a telephone and made it possible for the user to speak in a whisper. It was called the "Telephone Silencer." The Hush-a-Phone court decision paved the way for acoustically coupled terminals where one could take a standard telephone handset and place it into a cradle thus providing computer connectivity (albeit primitive by today's standards) over a telephone line. Soon after, Carter had another invention that was called the "Carterphone." The Carterphone was a device that allowed for patching radio signals into the AT&T network. In 1968, the Federal Communications Commission allowed the Carterphone and other devices to be connected directly to the AT&T network, as long as they did not cause harm to the system. As a result companies began developing and selling telephones, fax machines, and answering machines—which until then were only sold by one company. The decision also allowed a small startup company called MCI to build microwave towers that could carry telephone signals between Chicago and Saint Louis.

On January 1, 1984, a Federal Court ordered AT&T to give up its twenty-two local Bell companies and established seven regional Bell Operating Companies. Since that time, the seven regional companies have been dramatically reduced to mergers and acquisitions that came along with the new competitive regulatory structure. AT&T spun off its research and equipment manufacturing operations and became a long-distance carrier, but now AT&T would face fierce competition from the likes of what were then emerging new companies such as MCI and Sprint. Initially, the Regional Bell Operating Companies, simply called RBOCS, were limited to local service only.

Prior to 1996, the US telecommunications regulatory structure was anchored in the Communications Act of 1934. The Telecommunications Act of 1996 required RBOCS to provide competitors with access to their local lines at regulated wholesale rates. In return, RBOCS could offer long-distance service if they were able to demonstrate there was local competition in their market. The march towards a greater telecommunications marketplace would continue with a 2004 FCC ruling in which electric power companies could use their wiring for Internet service, including voice over Internet Protocol (IP) or simply VoIP. The FCC also ruled that other companies providing computer-to-computer VoIP services should not be subject to the same regulations as phone companies. The highly competitive and confusing marketplace has taken many interesting twists and turns and in January 2005, AT&T agreed to be sold to an RBOC, Southwestern Bell, that had earlier purchased another RBOC, Pacific Bell. This new entity changed its name to AT&T. Within a relatively short period of time, Verizon purchased MCI and Sprint purchased Nextel. In turn the new ATT purchased

BellSouth making ATT one of the largest telecom providers in the US. The telephone industry has undergone massive changes in both technology and its regulatory environment. The evolution in the telephone set the stage for providing the initial infrastructure that would soon make way for the World Wide Web or what we commonly refer to as the Internet.

Local Governments' Role in Broadband

Much of this chapter has centered on, one way or another, the role of the federal government. Nevertheless, local governments play an important role too. They are closest to their citizens and often hear complaints about poor or no broadband coverage in certain areas, or hear about issues having to do with accessibility or affordability. Many communities have tried very hard to provide broadband or Wi-Fi to entire communities or simply designated hotspots. They have blanketed public buildings such as libraries, schools, senior homes, and other public institutions with Wi-Fi. Many efforts have been met with stiff opposition from cable and commercial wireless providers who have gone as far as to try to ban such systems in the state legislature. It has even been reported that the Internet Service Providers lobby has won limits on public broadband in twenty states (ARS Technica 2014a).

Google, better known for its search engine as well as Gmail, is very involved in providing broadband to targeted cities. In some cases Google is looking to partner with local governments in providing super-fast connectivity referred to as gigabyte speeds. One city went so far as renaming itself in hopes of attracting Google's attention. Despite all the legislative actions against having municipalities owning and or operating their own broadband systems, local governments continue to experiment in a landscape filled with defunct muni projects that failed due to a number of economic factors. In some cases their attempts caused incumbent providers with a strong incentive to aggressively build out systems just to stay ahead of the municipality and ultimately drive them out of business.

Some ten years ago, the State of Utah created the Utah Telecommunication Open Infrastructure Agency (UTOPIA) (Utah Telecommunication Open Infrastructure Agency website). UTOPIA was designed to be a state-of-the-art fiber-optic network supported by its member communities and built to benefit residents and business. This network allows subscribers to connect to the world in ways they have never experienced before, where broadband choices are quite limited, providing blazing fast Internet speeds, phone, and television services. UTOPIA's eleven service areas represent nearly 28 percent of all communities in the US that can enjoy 1 gigabit service on a publicly-owned network—100 times faster than the national average of 8Mbps (ARS Technica 2014b). Thus far Utah has not found any willing partnerships with existing ISPs as had been hoped and UTOPIA has faced ten years of financial challenges.

Figure 6.9 Optical fiber can carry as much as 1.05 petabytes per second

On the other hand, the City of Chattanooga has been referred to as "Gig City" and claims to have one of the least expensive high-speed Internet services in the United States. The speed that citizens enjoy is about fifty times faster than the national average. The system is taxpayer owned and has become a very powerful economic engine for both the city and the region (Wyatt 2014b).

Despite the legal haggling and downright defeats, local governments enjoy a number of important roles that include:

- **Zoning requirements**—Local governments can insist that any new construction of dwellings or roads, or digging up or repairing existing structures, should include a requirement to install fiber cable or conduits for immediate or later use.
- **Anchor tenant**—Local governments can and are serving as "anchor tenants" thus becoming a large consumer of telecommunications services. This provides the local government with added leverage for concessions for not only themselves, but for their citizens. This might translate into better service or improved pricing or coverage.
- **Public-private partnerships**—Local governments are in a unique position to form public-private partnerships that can lead to better coverage and improved services.
- **Economic incentives and development**—Local governments are in a unique position to view a city differently than a private company might.

Making sure there is abundant and reliable broadband is critical towards economic development. Having this known asset is very important in not only attracting new businesses to the area, but to retain the businesses they already have.

- **Consumer information and education**—Local governments can and should provide consumer information and education services. Each broadband provider is quite good about stating their coverage areas and pricing, but there is often no one place to go to see how prices and coverage areas stack up against the competition.

- **Consumer protection**—Like consumer information, consumer protection can be provided to citizens who have complaints with their broadband providers.

- **Provider of last resort**—Realizing the significance of broadband, local governments can provide broadband through their own system, or throughout their public institutions, or provide subsidized broadband to special needs citizens.

- **Protect and plan for energy emergencies**—Local governments can leverage their broadband systems in order to best respond to pending emergencies. This can be accomplished with internal priority access in time of emergencies—usually an option offered by commercial providers. They can develop and deploy comprehensive plans that might utilize all broadband companies to broadcast critical information in times of emergencies.

Coming to Terms

There are a number of terms that require some definitions to assist those who are not familiar with the telecommunications, broadband, and the Internet evolution.

Broadband: Broadband or high-speed Internet access allows users to access the Internet and Internet-related services at significantly higher speeds than those available through "dial-up" Internet access services. Broadband speeds vary significantly depending on the particular type and level of service ordered and may range from as low as 200 kilobits per second (Kbps), or 200,000 bits per second, to 30 megabits per second (Mbps), or 30,000,000 bits per second. Some recent offerings even include 50 to 100 Mbps. Broadband services for residential consumers typically provide faster downstream speeds (from the Internet to computer) than upstream speeds (from computer to the Internet). For more information see the Federal Communications Commission website.

Coaxial Cable: A type of wire that consists of a center wire surrounded by insulation and then a grounded shield of braided wire. The shield minimizes electrical and radio frequency interference. Coaxial cabling is the primary type of cabling used by the cable television industry and is also widely used for computer networks, such as Ethernet. Although more expensive than standard telephone wire, it is much less susceptible to interference and can carry much more data. For more information see the Webopedia website.

Dial-Up: Dial-up refers to an Internet connection that is established using a modem. The modem connects the computer to standard phone lines, which serve as the data transfer medium. When a user initiates a dial-up connection, the modem dials a phone number of an Internet Service Provider (ISP) that is designated to receive dial-up calls. The ISP then establishes the connection, which usually takes about ten seconds and is accompanied by several beeping and buzzing sounds. After the dial-up connection has been established, it is active until the user disconnects from the ISP. Typically, this is done by selecting the "Disconnect" option using the ISP's software or a modem utility program. However, if a dial-up connection is interrupted by an incoming phone call or someone picking up a phone in the house, the service may also be disconnected. For more information see the TechTerms website.

DSL: Digital Subscriber Line: a technology that allows high-speed transmission of data, audio, and video, over standard telephone lines; a form of broadband transmission.

For more information see the Free Dictionary website.

Fiber Cable: This is a cable made up of super-thin filaments of glass or other transparent materials that can carry beams of light. Because a fiber-optic cable is light-based, data can be sent through it at the speed of light. Using a laser transmitter that encodes frequency signals into pulses of light, ones and zeros are sent through the cable. The receiving end of the transmission translates the light signals back into data that can be read by a computer.

Because fiber optics are based entirely on beams of light, they are less susceptible to noise and interference than other data transfer mediums such as copper wires or telephone lines. However, the cables are fragile and are usually placed underground, which makes them difficult and expensive to install. Some fiber-optic cables are installed above ground, but if they break, they often need to be completely replaced, which is very costly. Copper wires can be spliced and mended as many times as needed and are much easier to fix or repair than glass fiber-optic cables. For more information see the TechTerms website.

FIOS: This is Verizon's proprietary fiber to the home or business product offering.

Gigabyte Connectivity: Describes the relative connection speed measured as gigabytes per second.

GSM: This is now considered third generation 3G or Global System for Communications.

The Internet: An electronic communications network that connects computer networks and organizational computer facilities around the world. For more information see the Merriam-Webster website.

Internet Protocol (IP): The primary network protocol used on the Internet, developed in the 1970s. On the Internet and many other networks, IP is often used together with the Transport Control Protocol (TCP) and referred to interchangeably as TCP/IP.

LTE: LTE stands for the fourth generation global standard or 4G LTE, Long-Term Evolution. LTE was designed to increase the capacity of high-speed data through digital signal processing.

RBOC: As a result of the break-up of the AT&T regulated monopoly, seven regional operating Bell companies were created from AT&T's original twenty-two, which were simply referred to as RBOCs.

Telecommunications: The electronic systems used in transmitting messages, as by telegraph, cable, telephone, and television. For more information see the Free Dictionary website.

Comparative Speeds & Storage—Understanding Bit and Bytes

Electromagnetic frequencies are carried over wires and cables, as well as in the air via radio signals. Data is measured by speed and how much it takes to move data from one point to another. Data can also be measured by how many bytes can be stored on a particular medium, such as a DVD disk, a portable or network drive, etc. Everything we send and store, unless erased, is stored somewhere. Data storage can take many forms such as a page, document, book, picture, song, or video. These distinctions are expressed in terms that are measured as kilobytes all the way up to yottabytes. By themselves these terms have little relative meaning unless you compare them with objects we are familiar with.

Data can be measured by how many bytes of data can travel from point "A" to a point "B" in seconds or even milliseconds. Data is also measured by the amount of space that is required to store data. So for example, a signal rated as traveling at 56 Kbs, would be 56 kilobytes of data per second. By comparison, 40 Mbs would be 40 megabytes of data per second.

Kilobyte (KB): A kilobyte is 1,024 bytes
Megabyte (MB): 873 pages of plaintext, or four books
Gigabyte (GB): 894,784 pages of plaintext, 4473 books, 640 webpages, 341 digital pictures
Terabyte (TB): 916,209,689 pages of plaintext, 4,581,298 books, 655,360 webpages, 349,525 digital pictures
Petabyte (PB): 938,249,922,368 pages of plaintext, 4,691,249,611 books, 671,088,640 webpages, 357,913,941 digital pictures
Exabyte (EB) 960,767,920,505,705 pages of plaintext, 4,803,839,602,528 books, 687,194,767,360 webpages, 366,503,875,925 digital pictures
Zettabyte: (ZB) 983,826,350,597,842,752 pages of plaintext, 4,919,131,752,989,213 books, 703,687,443,750,000 webpages, 375,299,970,000,000 digital pictures
Yottabyte: 1,007,438,183,012,190,978,921 pages of plaintext, 5,037,190,915,060,954,894 books, 720,575,937,500,000,000 webpages, 384,307,166,666,666,666, digital pictures
For more information see Computer Hope.

To try and put things in perspective, to store a yottabyte on terabyte-sized hard drives would require ten billion city block-sized data centers, as big as the states of Delaware and Rhode Island.

The US is currently building a facility in a remote part of the State of Utah that will house the nation's largest database for national security information and will be the very first facility to store a yottabyte or more of data.

Figure 6.10 Understanding bits and bytes

VoIP: This is a technology that allows telephone calls to be made over computer networks like the Internet. VoIP converts analog voice signals into digital data packets and supports real-time, two-way transmission of conversations using IP. VoIP calls can be made on the Internet using a VoIP service provider and standard computer audio systems. Alternatively, some service providers support VoIP through ordinary telephones that use special adapters to connect to a home computer network.

Rules of the Road or Digital Highway: Understanding the Regulatory Environment (FCC, Commerce Dept., RUS, ITU)

Telecommunication systems depend on spectrum that has become both scarce and finite. There are three major federal bodies and one international body that play a key role in regulating and promoting telecommunications.

The Federal Communications Commission was created in 1934 as a result of the Telecommunications Act of 1934 and is an independent Federal Commission that is overseen by Congress. Today the FCC is responsible for regulating the nation's public airways, which include all radio, TV, cable, public safety, utilities, aviation, maritime, data-only services, telemetry, monitoring, and amateur radio. The FCC also has a consumer protection interest, and takes action against improper use of telephony such as robot and telemarketing calls and spam, and promotes affordable telecommunications services.

Figure 6.11 Federal Communications Commission website

Source: www.fcc.gov

One of the most notable consumer protection actions the FCC took was to require number portability between carriers. Prior to FCC action cell phone carriers would make it more difficult to switch to another carrier because the consumer would lose the number that they had. The FCC believed that consumers should not be held "captive" to a carrier they did not want to stay with and believed that carriers should focus instead on better customer services so that people would be more inclined to stay. Today, when consumers change carriers they can take their number with them thanks to the FCC.

Our nations' airwaves are limited and are considered a natural resource and as such require that we utilize the airwaves wisely, safely, and in the best interest of the public—not hoard them for speculation purposes. Hoarding refers to the potential for someone or some company to lease or purchase spectrum in the hope of using or selling it at some point in the future—as one might do with real estate. If hoarding was allowed to occur, the public would not be served by having valuable spectrum sitting idle and such a practice might also have the tendency to artificially raise its value by creating artificial demand. Since radio frequencies are finite, once they are allocated, they are mostly gone. The FCC allocates spectrum by type of service and telecommunications carriers are required to obtain a license for each of the pieces of spectrum they operate in.

> Our nations' airwaves are limited and are considered a natural resource and as such require that we utilize the airwaves wisely, safely, and in the best interest of the public—not hoard them for speculation purposes.

The FCC also administers the Universal Service Fund. Universal service is the principle that all Americans should have access to communications services. Universal service is also the name of a fund and the category of FCC programs and policies to implement this principle. Universal service is a cornerstone of the law that established the FCC, the Communications Act of 1934. Since that time, universal service policies have helped make telephone service ubiquitous, even in remote rural areas. The Telecommunications Act of 1996 expanded the traditional goal of universal service to include increased access to both telecommunications and advanced services—such as high-speed Internet—for all consumers at just, reasonable, and affordable rates. The Act established principles for universal service that specifically focused on increasing access to evolving services for consumers living in rural and insular areas, and for consumers with low incomes (Federal Communications Commission website). The FCC also administers the e-rate program, a multi-billion dollar program that is the common name for the Universal Service Fund. The e-rate is funded through the Universal Service Fund that supports eligible schools and libraries to fund broadband projects and connectivity (ibid.). The goal of the program is to bring every school and library in America into the information age (see the Universal Service Administrative Company website). Additional principles called for increased access to high-speed Internet in the nation's schools, libraries, and rural health care facilities. The FCC established four programs within the Universal Service Fund to implement the statute. The four programs are:

1. Connect America Fund (formally known as High-Cost Support) for rural areas.
2. Lifeline (for low-income consumers), including initiatives to expand phone service for Native Americans.
3. Schools and Libraries (E-rate).
4. Rural Health Care.

For a comprehensive look at frequency assignments in the US see the Federal Communications Commission website.

The National Telecommunications & Information Administration is part of the US Department of Commerce. The stated principle mission of the NTIA is to be responsible for advising the President on telecommunications and information policy issues. NTIA's programs and policy-making

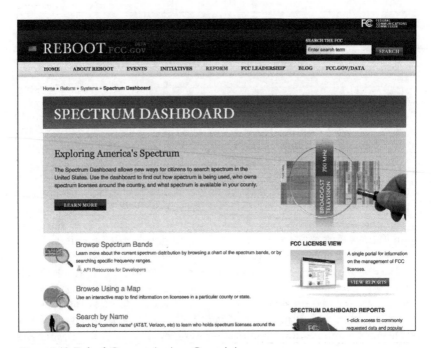

Figure 6.12 Federal Communications Commission

Source: www.reboot.fcc.gov

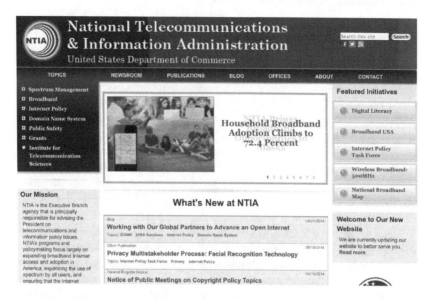

Figure 6.13 National Telecommunications & Information Administration

Source: www.ntia.doc.gov

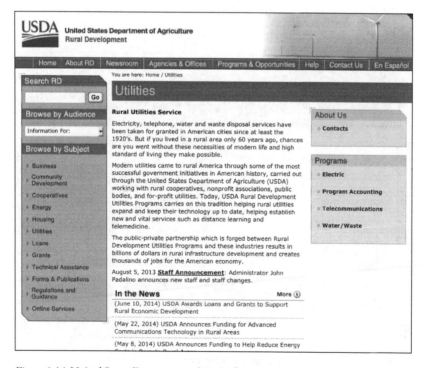

Figure 6.14 United States Department of Agriculture

Source: www.usda.gov

focus is largely on expanding broadband Internet access and adoption in America, expanding the use of spectrum by all users, and ensuring that the Internet remains an engine for continued innovation and economic growth. NTIA and the FCC share in the National Broadband Map, as well as digital literacy initiatives, broadband promotion, and broadband adoption research.

Housed within the US Department of Agriculture, the Rural Utility Service (RUS) has been instrumental in expanding the reach of broadband throughout rural America. This is the same department that played a leadership role in bringing electricity, telephone, water, and waste disposal services to rural America since the early 1900s. Most recently RUS has provided grants and contracts regarding rural broadband as well as serving as the principal federal advocate.

The International Telecommunication Union (ITU) is the United Nations specialized agency for information and communication technologies—ICTs. The ITU is the international organization that allocates global radio spectrum and satellite orbits, and develops the technical standards that ensure networks and technologies are allowed to seamlessly interconnect. Through its mission and policies, the ITU also strives to improve access to ICTs to underserved communities worldwide. (Globally, the term ICT is still used whereas in the US it is simply referred to as IT.)

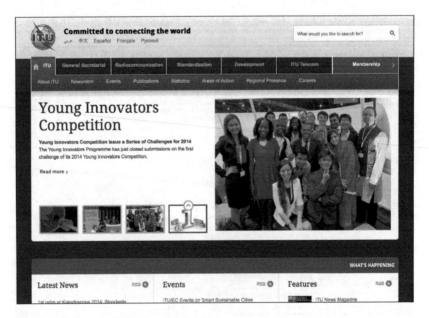

Figure 6.15 International Telecommunication Union

Source: www.itu/int

Mobile Evolution

Most people prefer to use cordless phones, bluetooth headsets or hands-free communications whether in the office, the car, or at home—society is moving away from being tethered by cords. In April 1972, a Motorola engineer produced the first handheld cell phone. The prototype's capacity was thirty minutes of what we now refer to as "talk time" and it took ten hours to recharge the device. The first generation using cellular technology (1G) began in the US in 1983. Early consumer phones were clunky "bag phones" which literally attached to a canvas bag, came equipped with a portable roof-mounted antenna, and a charger cord that plugged into what used to be referred to as a car's "cigarette lighter" power socket. Bag phones never contained a battery, because they were heavy enough without a battery and, if purchased, the battery would cost at least as much as the phone itself.

The growth of cell phones was dramatic and cell phone service was no longer just for the wealthy. The FCC stepped in to ensure a competitive environment and realized that the analog systems that had become so popular were not very spectrum-efficient. The first generation used up a lot of spectrum—leaving little room for longer-term growth. Moving to a digital environment the FCC developed a migration path for carriers to move to a new spectrum that allowed for much greater spectrum efficiency and growth. Digital cellular service began in the 1990s and has grown in subscriber numbers as well as usage. In 2014, smartphones now outsell traditional cell phones. The public enjoys not only making phone calls, but also sending text messages, pictures, videos, and watching movies and sporting events all on their phone. To maintain a robust wireless environment, the

Figure 6.16 The ITU plays a critical role in the global community

federal government had to be creative in granting mobile licenses that were so highly valued. With scarcity of spectrum approaching, the FCC was given a new mandate—offer new mobile licenses through an auction process.

HDTV

Somewhat similar to the growth of analog cell phone use, television also used large amounts of analog spectrum for broadcast TV. Not only was this becoming quite inefficient, newer technologies offered dramatically improved services with less spectrum.

As compression technologies improved, the ITU formed a group to look at how HDTV might replace analog TV. An international group was formed consisting of equipment manufactures, broadcasters, and regulatory organizations to further explore ways to bring HDTV to market. The first HDTV broadcast took place in July 1996. Given the dramatically superior video and audio quality of HDTV, Congress mandated a switch from analog broadcasts in the US to become effective February 17, 2009. This change created quite a concern among consumer groups who were troubled by the number of homes without HDTVs, cable, or satellite service. Congress approved a provision requiring the distribution of digital-to-analog converter boxes within a specified time frame. Despite the many provisions offered to protect consumers, the transition did not go as smoothly as some had hoped or promised. Today, most citizens enjoy their relatively new larger screen devices and many can't image what it was like before HDTV.

This is an excellent example of how equipment manufacturers, broadcasters, legislators, and regulators, with many different interests, were able to work together which ultimately led to success for all. Aside from issues of changing deadlines, on-air antenna issues, shortage of converter boxes, overall cost to convert, etc., there was the issue of what to do with the millions of TVs and computer monitors that were about to be replaced.

Disposing of the "Old"

With the unprecedented growth of the lightweight flat screen for both TVs and computers, millions of "old" heavy TV screens and monitors had to be disposed of. Most of this discarded equipment contained dangerous chemicals used in the wiring that, if left exposed, could cause harm to humans. At first most of the discarded equipment found its way to third world countries where the very poor were often employed to dismantle the equipment for usable parts and scrap. Suffice to say millions of tons of used electronics have been discarded, and given the changeover in technologies many of the parts that could be modified or re-used are no longer viable. The nation's landfills are filled with vast amounts of used electronics and at one time overwhelmed local governments who felt the brunt of the digital revolution. The problem continues today with leaders like Apple who argue that there is a demand for sleekly designed computers, phones, and tablets. In order to meet the demand

Figure 6.17 Disposing of old technologies remains a real challenge to the environment

for lighter and smaller equipment, batteries will no longer be user replaceable. This will most likely result in having more equipment meet a premature death rather than going through the process of trying to have new batteries installed. Many experts argue that the real solution is for manufacturers to be more responsible in designing devices with earth-friendly components and making them last longer too. This has become a worldwide dilemma.

On the Horizon

Public Safety and FirstNet

Ever since 9/11 when it came to light that public safety radios did not work very well inside the World Trade Center along with problems of interoperability among the various agencies, there have been numerous studies and commissions to rectify the issues. This was not the first time shortcomings in public safety radio communications were made public, however, 9/11 provided the public safety community and the general public with new energy and a sense of urgency for changes to be made. The 9/11 Commission had made as one of its recommendations the creation of a separate public safety communications network. With strong public support, the public safety community called for not only better radio equipment but also to develop for the very first time a national public safety network that would operate on common frequencies, and be located on a common block of radio spectrum. In 2012, after several false starts, Congress allocated 20 megahertz to public safety once called the "D" block. FirstNet is an independent authority housed with the NTIA that is governed by a fifteen member board whose mission is to build out the first national responder network that will incorporate voice, data, and video into one cohesive network using the LTE (long-term evolution) technology. Under the plan, each state has its own staff assigned to FirstNet responsibilities. Local governments also have a large role to play too. For more information see the FirstNet website.

Alerting the Public

Given the penetration of broadband devices, reaching out to the public via smart devices has become a reality if not a necessity. With each new idea, there needs to be an accompanying policy such as what will be the nature of alerts, frequency, specified locations, reaching physically challenged individuals, as well as the costs for monitoring and administering. Most broadband carriers have agreed to the National Emergency Alert System whereby they can pass along emergency notifications about imminent life-threatening emergencies. In 2014, the US Weather Service experienced system failures leading to geographic areas that were never alerted to an impending weather emergency. Because technology scales so well to massively large groups, any failure can impact hundreds of thousands of people if not millions.

Since 2003, many local governments have begun to use social media as a way to reach and communicate with citizens. Early attempts at using social media, such as Facebook, Twitter, and even YouTube were centered around "broadcasting" information they felt was important. It didn't take long for government to realize the fact that citizens wanted to communicate back too.

In 2014, US telecom providers began to deploy Text to 911 emergency systems. This is but another example of how government is utilizing technology in ways never contemplated just a few years ago.

Net Neutrality

Over the years a battle has been growing between Internet service providers ISPs. ISPs such as Verizon, Comcast, ATT, Cox, and Time Warner believe that since they have invested billions of dollars in infrastructure they should be free to enter into special agreements with those willing and able to pay more for improved services. If allowed, companies like Netflix or Amazon might have to pay extra to stream their content on what some have referred to as an express line on the web. Neutrality embraces the principle that all traffic on the Internet should be treated equally, without discriminating in quality of service or pricing. A number of leading consumer groups have expressed their fear that Internet providers will devote more bandwidth to the highest bidder, leaving the rest of the Internet to possibly slower or inferior services. Consumer advocates worry that as content providers pay more—the higher costs will be passed on to the consumer. The ISPs claim that they are committed to an open Internet and the issue appeared to have been somewhat resolved until January of 2014, when a Federal Court of Appeals in the District of Columbia struck down a ban on ISPs' ability to negotiate deals for premium or specialized services. This is a complicated proceeding that goes back to 1996. While deciding the current ban was invalid, the Federal Court ruling stated that the FCC still has some basic authority "to promulgate rules governing broadband providers' treatment of Internet traffic." The Court also upheld existing FCC rules that require broadband companies to disclose how they manage their networks (Porter 2012). For more information see *The New York Times* website articles on net-neutrality.

The bottom line is that implications of the ruling will not be felt right away and the FCC has already issued a proposed rulemaking process aimed at clarifying net-neutrality. The Communications Act of 1996 made assumptions as to what constituted telecommunications and what constituted an information provider—both are regulated quite differently.

> The Communications Act of 1996 made assumptions as to what constituted telecommunications and what constituted an information provider—both are regulated quite differently.

Towards a New Telecommunications Regulatory Structure?

Much of the regulatory structure governing both telecommunications as well as the Internet tend to be playing catch-up to the rapid change of events. Even with the reforms in the Telecom Act of 1996, telecommunication is still heavily regulated with the goal of ensuring reliability, promoting competition, and expanding access. The FCC has said it will consider new rules that take into account that we are in a transition period where every type of communication is moving towards Internet Protocol. Many broadband networks like Skype and Vonage have proven that broadband companies can provide very good Internet calling services as well as more traditional services. Expect a new regulatory structure to emerge in the 2015–16 time frame.

The Internet of Things or Everything

The Internet of things is a relatively new term used to describe the connection of multiple devices to the Internet, thus moving from the Internet of peer to peer to include such devices as sensors, monitors, RFID tags, thermostats, meters, medical devices, home appliances, transportation systems, and more. It is still too early to see how the Internet of things actually will play out, but there appears to be more and more devices that are being connected every day with entirely new functionality. Add to this the new

Internet addressing protocol, IPv6, Internet addresses even for the tiniest of devices, will have plenty room to be mapped and grow (Digital Communities 2014).

Discussion Questions

1. Describe what your personal and or professional life would look like if you were totally without broadband and the Internet for over a day, a week, a year?
2. How has the Internet changed the way governments operate? Name at least five positives and five negatives.
3. Describe the role of government in deciding broadband and Internet policy, what seem to be the leading guiding principles?
4. Should the federal government seek greater control of the Internet in terms of online commerce and taxes?
5. Can you name one or more public-private partnerships that can serve as positive examples for future partnerships?
6. What steps can state and local governments take to ensure better broadband deployment and coverage?
7. Where do you see the "Internet of Things" going? How might this impact your office or home?
8. Where do you stand on the issue of net-neutrality? Can you list at least five pros and cons?
9. What do you see as the limits of broadband communications? Can you elaborate?
10. What might the Internet look like in five to ten years?

References

ARS Technica. 2014a. "ISP Lobby Has Already Won Limits on Public Broadband in 20 States." Accessed October 17, 2014. http://arstechnica.com/tech-policy/2014/02/isp-lobby-has-already-won-limits-on-public-broadband-in-20-states/.

ARS Technica. 2014b. "Utah bill Would Stop Regional Fiber Networks from Expanding." Accessed October 17, 2014. http://arstechnica.com/tech-policy/2014/02/utah-bill-would-stop-regional-fiber-networks-from-expanding/.

CNET. 2014. "US Official: The Internet Can Stand on its Own Now." Accessed October 17, 2014. http://www.cnet.com/news/commerce-department-official-the-net-can-stand-on-its-own-now-q-a/.

Digital Communities. 2014. "Cisco Live: The Internet of Everything." Accessed October 17, 2014. http://www.digitalcommunities.com/articles/Cisco-Live-Internet-of-Things-vs-Internet-of-Everything.html.

Internet Society. 2013. "Brief History of the Internet." Accessed October 17, 2014. http://www.internetsociety.org/internet/what-internet/history-internet/brief-history-internet.

Ookla. 2014. *Global Download Index*. Accessed October 17, 2014. http://www.netindex.com/value/allcountries/.

Pew Research Internet Project. 2013. "Broadband and Smartphone Adoption Demographics." Accessed October 17, 2014. http://www.pewinternet.org/Infographics/2013/Broadband-and-smartphone-adoption.aspx.

Porter, Eduardo. 2012. "Keeping the Internet Neutral." *The New York Times.* Accessed October 17, 2014.http://www.nytimes.com/2012/05/09/business/economy/net-neutrality-and-economic-equality-are-intertwined.html?pagewanted=all.

Wyatt, Edward. 2014a. "US to Cede Its Oversight of Addresses on Internet." *The New York Times.* Accessed October 17, 2014. http://nyti.ms/1ks1gpe.

———. 2014b. "Fast Internet Is Chattanooga's New Locomotive." *The New York Times.* Accessed October 17, 2014. http://nyti.ms/1inJjqU.

Digital Destinations

Amaze. http://www.amaze.com/Images/The%20Mobile%20Imperative%20-%20White Paper_tcm22-4921.pdf

Broadband.gov. http://www.broadband.gov

Cisco New Mobile World Order. http://www.cisco.com/web/about/ac79/docs/sp/New-Mobile-World-Order.pdf

Computer Hope. http://www.computerhope.com/issues/chspace.htm

Definition of Broadband. http://en.wikipedia.org/wiki/Broadband

E-Rate. Universal Service Fund. http://www.USac.org/sl/

Federal Communications Commission. http://www.fcc.gov/encyclopedia/universal-service

———. http://www.fcc.gov/guides/getting-broadband

———.http://transition.fcc.gov/learnnet/

FirstNet. http://www.ntia.doc.gov/page/about-firstnet

Free Dictionary. http://www.thefreedictionary.com/telecommunication

ICANN. http://www.icann.org/en/about/welcome

Internet 2. http://www.internet2.edu/

IPv4 verse IPv6. http://mashable.com/2011/02/03/ipv4-ipv6-guide/

Linkedin.com. http://www.linkedin.com/company/telework-research-network

Merriam-Webster. http://www.merriam-webster.com/dictionary/internet

National Broadband Plan. http://www.broadband.gov/plan/

National Telecommunications & Information Administration. http://www.ntia.doc.gov/category/firstnet

———. http://www.ntia.doc.gov/files/ntia/publications/fact_sheet_promise-9-27-13.pdf

The New York Times. Net Neutrality. http://www.nytimes.com/2014/01/15/technology/appeals-court-rejects-fcc-rules-on-internet-service-providers.html

———. http://bits.blogs.nytimes.com/2014/01/14/the-nuts-and-bolts-of-network-neutrality/?emc=eta1

———. http://www.nytimes.com/2014/02/02/US/fcc-says-it-will-double-spending-on-high-speed-internet-in-schools-and-libraries.html?hpw&rref=education

———. http://www.nytimes.com/2014/04/24/technology/fcc-new-net-neutrality-rules.html?emc=edit_th_20140424&nl=todaysheadlines&nlid=57856652

———. http://www.nytimes.com/2012/05/09/bUSiness/economy/net-neutrality-and-economic-equality-are-intertwined.html?pagewanted=all

———. http://www.nytimes.com/2014/05/16/technology/fcc-road-map-to-net-neutrality.html

Pew Research Center. http://www.pewinternet.org/

Senator Stevens (R–Alaska) Broadband Remarks. http://en.wikipedia.org/wiki/Series_
of_tubes

TechTerms. http://www.techterms.com/definition/fiberopticcable

Telecommunications Act of 1996. http://en.wikipedia.org/wiki/Telecommunications_
Act_of_1996

Telework Research Network. http://www.telework.gov/Index.aspx

————. http://www.telework.gov/guidance_and_legislation/telework_guide/telework_
guide.pdf

————. http://www.telework.gov/Reports_and_Studies/Annual_Reports/2013telework
report.pdf

Universal Service Administrative Company. http://www.USac.org/default.aspx

Universal Service & E-Rate. http://www.fcc.gov/encyclopedia/universal-service

Utah Telecommunication Open Infrastructure Agency. http://www.utopianet.org/
about-utopia/

Webopedia. http://www.webopedia.com/TERM/C/coaxial_cable.html

Who Owns the Internet? http://computer.howstuffworks.com/internet/basics/who-
owns-internet3.htm

The Whole Picture: Where America's Broadband Networks Really Stand. http://www2.
itif.org/2013-whole-picture-america-broadband-networks.pdf

Further Reading

Diaz, Jesus. 2010. "The One Hundred Trillion Dollars Hard Drive." *Gizmodo*. 7 June.

Press, Larry. 2009. "Broadband Policy: Beyond Privatization, Competition, and Independent Regulation." *First Monday*. Vol. 14. No. 4.

Santorelli, Michael J. 2010. "Regulatory Federalism in the Age of Broadband: A US
Perspective." *Policy and Internet*. Issue 3.

Strickland, Jonathan. 2008. "Who owns the Internet?" HowStuffWorks.com. Accessed
October 17, 2014. http://computer.howstuffworks.com/internet/basics/who-owns-
internet.htm.

Tapia, Andrea Hoplight and Alison Powel. 2009. "Reforming Policy to Promote Broadband Networks." *Journal of Communication Inquiry*. Vol. 33.

Titch, Steven and Leonard Gilroy. 2011. "The Year 2010 in IT Outsourcing, Network
Neutrality, and Federal Broadband." *Reason Foundation*. February.

7 Managed Software and Hardware Services

Once Upon a Cloud

Back in 2004 when someone referred to a cloud they were probably referring to the weather. Today, cloud and cloud-based solutions are the talk of anyone connected with the information technology field. This chapter will review what the cloud really is, how it is changing the way IT is managed, the significance of cloud computing, as well as the implications for the future. Cloud-based services are not an all or nothing proposition as there are many options from which to choose.

Many Clouds: Many Definitions

Students in a graduate class in 2012 were asked how many of them used cloud-based services. Out of 28 students, only three stated that they had any personal experience with the cloud. However, when popular "online" services were explained as being cloud-based services, the class was surprised by the amount of cloud services they were actually using. The entire class had in one way or another experienced a cloud type service—that in its simplest definition is like using someone else's computer hard drive located somewhere else. Overall, many citizens do not realize how many cloud-based services are already in use and commonly accepted, albeit through different names and descriptors. Take, for example, that just about anyone with a mobile device and or a social media presence is actually using a cloud service. Such services were simply not promoted based on the term *cloud*. Google Play, iTunes, Picassa, Flickr, Skype, Dropbox, YouTube, Gmail, Face-Book, and Linkedin are all examples of consumer-oriented cloud services. These services can be accessed almost anywhere and from multiple types of devices just as long as there is good broadband connectivity. Today we store, retrieve, and share photos, videos, and documents. We access emails, music, movies, reports, and operate software from remote locations. This is all happening by typing in an IP address or clicking on a dynamic link, or pressing a mobile app button. For the most part we have no idea where our "stuff" is located—and perhaps which state, or nation, but rest assured they are in a cloud someplace.

Software providers like Microsoft and Adobe, and Symantec's Norton AntiVirus, mostly sold their software products via disks found in boxes purchased in a store or perhaps, online. Today, most software companies are quickly moving away from physical copies (disks) and instead offering downloads directly to the intended device or devices. For example, Microsoft's Office 365 can be purchased for an annual fee that can include up to five devices for the same price. Of the many advantages to the user, Microsoft promises to update its features on a continuous basis. One key advantage is that consumers no longer have to be as concerned about having the latest and greatest—just as long as you continue to pay your annual fee. Google on the other hand with all of its 23-plus service offerings, including Google Docs, has always been cloud-based. YouTube (owned by Google) has billions of videos stored in the cloud, but once again, does anybody know where and does anyone really care? (Shark 2012)

Cloud computing, or cloud-based solutions, is much more a concept than an actual product or service. There are perhaps as many definitions of the cloud as there are clouds in the sky. Similarly, as with what we find in the heavens, cloud computing can be grouped into types and variations. The cloud in the IT setting has the potential to significantly alter the government technology enterprise as well as just about every government program, service, and office operation. The selling of cloud-based services to the public was rather easy and aside from actual cloud storage services like iCloud, or OneDrive, the services were promoted on the basis of what they do and what the benefits are to the consumer, and the term cloud was almost never mentioned. However, for federal, state, and local governments,

Figure 7.1 Many clouds–many definitions

it was, and is, a much more complicated environment. Furthermore, unlike most consumer cloud offerings that are generally free, there is a real cost to businesses and government.

The Government Case

We know from the previous chapters that government collects, analyzes, stores, and publishes data. Much of the data is considered personal–birth certificates, drivers' licenses and related information, federal, state, and local tax payment records, and medical records. When a consumer signs up for a service that is online (cloud-based) one is often asked to check off a box that specifies that you have read the statements and or agree to the terms and limitations. Essentially consumers are signing a "terms of service" (TOS) policy that mostly protects the provider against any liabilities and far less so the consumer. Government agencies' handling of sensitive data assumes an enormous burden in having to protect all types of confidential and important data. As you will see in Chapter 10, even the best government security systems—despite all of their internal safeguards—can still become vulnerable.

Cloud-based services have become increasingly popular for a number of reasons. Factors include saving money and using only the computing power that is required at any given time and the ability to scale data operations thus provisioned only when needed. The cost of cloud services can be spread over a larger user base. Finally, data centers are expensive to maintain, and governments at all levels have been under great pressure to do more with less. Cloud services are very dependent upon having superior broadband capabilities along with competitive cost of data storage.

The Center of Data and the Cloud

All data centers are built with excess capacity in mind; they must plan for growth. This is due to the fact that computer centers have to plan for increased data needs over the lifespan of the equipment. A new data center may open today operating at 60 percent capacity with the understanding that each year the requirements to store and use more data will only increase. There has been a growing trend to consolidate data centers within governments as well as to "virtualize" the number of servers in order to be more efficient and cost-effective. Simply put, a "virtual" server is a software solution that operates within a physical server (a computer box) as if it was a stand-alone box. A physical server (a box), comes equipped with a motherboard, internal wiring, connectivity, storage drives, cooling fans, much like any desktop computer. A virtual server is loaded as software on the physical server and since it lacks any physical properties of its own, it is designed to utilize the physical space of its host as if it had its own physical structure and can do so in harmony with other virtual servers. So instead of buying a new server (computer box) every time a new application requires one, the first question to be asked is, can it be "virtualized?" However, a server containing many virtualized servers will certainly reach its capacity at some point in time, thus there are physical limits to virtualization.

One might conclude that with data center consolidation and virtualization, the problem of growth and capacity can be solved. The answer is less than clear, as regardless of server consolidation and server virtualization, data centers are still expensive to maintain. They require special security, both physical and virtual, they require round-the-clock monitoring, and they require great amounts of energy to operate the equipment as well as maintain a strict temperature and humidity controlled environment. So, the pressure for governments to operate more efficiently and effectively continues to grow and in some cases, the cloud is becoming an attractive opportunity for which to explore new options. Technology applications and requirements never stand still. For consumers, cloud-based services are commonplace, often free or low cost and optional however, at the federal government level they're now required.

There has been a growing trend to consolidate data centers within governments as well as to "virtualize" the number of servers in order to be more efficient and cost-effective.

Defining a Phenomenon

Cloud computing, or cloud-based services, has been around for many years, under different names. Names of earlier "pre-cloud" offerings included managed online services, software as a service, contracted data and or data processing services, outsourced data services, and excess IT capacity for lease. Aside from the many cloud-based services and applications, the cloud is most often used to describe a data center that is located at a distance and usually connected through the Internet that delivers services for a fee. Services might include a specific type of application that requires computing power, authentication of user, data storage, transactional services, online form submissions between entities or on behalf of a customer, payment collection, and communication between various authorized users at multiple locations. Cloud computing is really about using someone else's computing and network infrastructure, whether it is a consumer, business, or government agency, each might utilize multiple services from the same provider.

The management analysis and consulting firm Gartner defines public cloud computing as a style of computing where scalable and elastic IT-enabled capabilities are provided as a service to external customers using Internet technologies—i.e., public cloud computing uses cloud computing technologies to support customers that are external to the provider's organization. Using public cloud services generates the types of economies of scale and sharing of resources that can reduce costs and increase choices of technologies. From a government organization's perspective, using public cloud services implies that any organization (in any industry sector and jurisdiction) can use the same services (e.g., infrastructure, platform, or software), without guarantees about where data would be located and stored.

Source: Gartner Definition of Public Cloud Computing

The National Institute of Standards and Technology (NIST) refers to cloud computing as evolving paradigm (NIST 2011). In defining cloud computing, NIST is quick to point out that it is not intended to be either prescriptive or restrictive regarding any type of cloud deployment.

NIST's definition (2011) states:

Cloud computing is a model for enabling ubiquitous, convenient, on-demand network access to a shared pool of configurable resources (e.g., networks, servers, storage, applications, and services) that can be rapidly provisioned and released with minimal management effort or service provider interaction. This cloud model is composed of five essential characteristics, three service models, and four deployment models.

NIST's five essential cloud model characteristics:

1. *On-demand self-service:* A consumer can unilaterally provision computing capabilities, such as server time and network storage, as needed automatically without requiring human interaction with each service provider.
2. *Broad network access*: Capabilities are available over the network and accessed through standard mechanisms that promote use by heterogeneous thin or thick client platforms (e.g., cell phones, tablets, laptops, and workstations).
3. *Resource pooling*: The provider's computing resources are pooled to serve multiple consumers using a multi-tenant model, with different physical and virtual resources dynamically assigned and reassigned according to consumer demand. There is a sense of location independence in that the customer generally has no control or knowledge over the exact location of the provided resources but may be able to specify location at a higher level of abstraction (e.g., country, state, or data center). Examples of resources include storage, processing, memory, and network bandwidth.
4. *Rapid elasticity*: Capabilities can be elastically provisioned and released, in some cases automatically, to scale rapidly outward and inward

commensurate with demand. To the consumer, the capabilities available for provisioning often appear to be unlimited and can be appropriated in any quantity at any time.

5. *Measured service*: Cloud systems automatically control and optimize resource use by leveraging a metering capability at some level of abstraction appropriate to the type of service (e.g., storage, processing, bandwidth, and active user accounts). Resource usage can be monitored, controlled, and reported, providing transparency for both the provider and consumer of the utilized service. (Typically this is done on a pay-per-use or charge-per-use basis). (Ibid.)

The NIST definition of cloud computing includes three service areas:

1. *Software as a Service (SaaS)*. The capability provided to the consumer is to use the provider's applications running on a cloud infrastructure. The applications are accessible from various client devices through either a thin client interface, such as a web browser (e.g., web-based email), or a program interface. The consumer does not manage or control the underlying cloud infrastructure including network, servers, operating systems, storage, or even individual application capabilities, with the possible exception of limited user-specific application configuration settings.

2. *Platform as a Service (PaaS)*. The capability provided to the consumer is to deploy onto the cloud infrastructure consumer-created or acquired applications created using programming languages, libraries, services, and tools supported by the provider. The consumer does not manage or control the underlying cloud infrastructure including network, servers, operating systems, or storage, but has control over the deployed applications and possibly configuration settings for the application-hosting environment.

3. *Infrastructure as a Service (IaaS)*: The capability provided to the consumer is to provision processing, storage, networks, and other fundamental computing resources where the consumer is able to deploy and run arbitrary software, which can include operating systems and applications. The consumer does not manage or control the underlying cloud infrastructure but has control over operating systems, storage, and deployed applications; and possibly limited control of select networking components (e.g., host firewalls) (NIST 2011).

Finally, the NIST definition of cloud computing includes four deployment models:

Private cloud. The cloud infrastructure is provisioned for exclusive use by a single organization comprising multiple consumers (e.g., business units). It may be owned, managed, and operated by the organization, a third party, or some combination of them, and it may exist on or off premises.

Community cloud. The cloud infrastructure is provisioned for exclusive use by a specific community of consumers from organizations that have shared concerns (e.g., mission, security requirements, policy, and compliance considerations). It may be owned, managed, and operated by one or more of the organizations in the community, a third party, or some combination of them, and it may exist on or off premises.

Public cloud. The cloud infrastructure is provisioned for open use by the general public. It may be owned, managed, and operated by a business, academic, or government organization, or some combination of them. It exists on the premises of the cloud provider.

Hybrid cloud. The cloud infrastructure is a composition of two or more distinct cloud infrastructures (private, community, or public) that remain unique entities, but are bound together by standardized or proprietary technology that enables data and application portability (e.g., cloud bursting for load balancing between clouds). (Ibid.)

The NIST definition provides a rather comprehensive lens from which to describe and better understand cloud-based solutions. There are many variations to a cloud. The novelty, or special considerations, for cloud computing is starting to dissipate as it evolves into standard operating procedures for consumers, businesses, and government.

Federal Government Cloud Forecast

In 2009, Vivek Kundra was appointed by President Obama to become the nation's first Chief Information Officer, serving from 2009 through August 2011. Having advocated cloud computing initiatives at the District of Columbia as its Chief Technology Officer, he brought his vision for cloud computing to the federal government. President Obama was sworn in as President for his first term in January 2009. Not wasting any time, in April 2009 the first Cloud Computing Program Management Office (PMO) was established at the General Services Administration (GSA). The Cloud Computing PMO was responsible for coordinating the federal government's cloud computing efforts in key areas, such as security, standards and acquisition, and is developing the governance approaches necessary to effectively engage with federal agencies for the safe and secure adoption of cloud technology.

On July 1, 2010, Mr. Kundra testified before the House Committee on Oversight and the Government Reform Subcommittee on Government Management, Organization, and Procurement, regarding "Cloud Computing: Benefits and Risks of Moving Federal IT into the Cloud" (CIO.gov. 2010). In his prepared remarks he said,

As the world's largest consumer of information technology, the federal government spends approximately $80 billion annually on more than 12,000 systems at major agencies. Fragmentation of systems, poor project execution, and the drag of legacy technologies in the federal government have presented barriers to achieving the productivity and performance gains that can be found in the private sector's more effective use of technology. For example, over the past decade, while the private sector was consolidating data centers, the federal government increased its data centers from 432 to over 1,100, leading to redundant investment, reduced energy efficiency, and poor service delivery.

Cloud computing has the potential to greatly reduce inefficiencies, increase data center efficiency and utilization rates, and lower operating costs. It is a model for delivering computing resources—such as networks, servers, storage, or software applications.

There was a time when every household, town, farm, or village had its own water well. Today, shared public utilities give us access to clean water by simply turning on the tap; cloud computing works in a similar fashion. Just like water from the tap in your kitchen, cloud computing services can be turned on or off quickly as needed. Like at the water company, there is a team of dedicated professionals making sure the service provided is safe, secure, and available on a 24/7 basis. When the tap isn't on, not only are you saving water, you aren't paying for resources you don't currently need.

Given the backdrop of record deficits in the federal government budget as well as improvements in technology in the private sector, this was an opportune time to address government technology reform. In February 2010, the Department of Homeland Security launched the Federal Data Center Consolidation Initiative (FDCCI) aimed at consolidating the federal government's fragmented data center environment. Through the FDCCI, agencies were required to formulate detailed consolidation plans and technical roadmaps to eliminate a minimum of 800 data centers by 2015.

In February 2011 Kundra issued the *Federal Cloud Computing Strategy* which contained a "*Cloud First*" strategy for all federal government agencies to follow. The report stated this "*Cloud First* policy is intended to accelerate the pace at which the government will realize the value of cloud computing by requiring agencies to evaluate safe, secure cloud computing options before making any new investments" (Kundra 2011). The *Federal Cloud Computing Strategy* further articulated the need for federal agencies to think and act differently when it comes to using and procuring technology. The initiative provided a decision framework for agencies to consider and follow regarding migration from current systems to the cloud. It also provided case examples that helped illustrate the migration framework The initiative also laid out a governance model to follow while addressing the need for a trustworthy environment as well as streamlining the IT procurement process.

Finally the initiative recognized the need for standards and called upon NIST to develop over time a set of uniform standards for all federal agencies to follow.

The data consolidation effort was designed to reverse what had been an ongoing trend to simply build more data centers with almost no planning or coordinating with any other agency. The *Cloud First* initiative was to serve as a practical framework for future planning and action. The plan also served to promote a relatively new concept for government agencies to follow. For many government IT professionals and the network they maintain and work so hard to secure, the cloud concept was initially met with great skepticism, doubt, and to some, as a threat to their career.

EFFICIENCY	
Cloud Benefits	**Current Environment**
• Improved asset utilization (server utilization > 60-70%) • Aggregated demand and accelerated system consolidation (e.g. Federal Data Center Consolidation Initiative) • Improved productivity in application development, application management, network, and end-user	• Low asset utilization (server utilization < 30% typical) • Fragmented demand and duplicative systems • Difficult-to-manage systems
AGILITY	
Cloud Benefits	**Current Environment**
• Purchase "as-a-service" from trusted cloud providers • Near-instantaneous increases and reductions in capacity • More responsive to urgent agency needs	• Years required to build data centers for new services • Months required to increase capacity of existing services
INNOVATION	
Cloud Benefits	**Current Environment**
• Shift focus from asset ownership to service management • Tap into private sector innovation • Encourages entrepreneurial culture • Better linked to emerging technologies (e.g. devices)	• Burdened by asset management • De-coupled from private sector innovation engines • Risk-adverse culture

Figure 7.2 Cloud benefits: efficiency, agility, innovation

Source: *Federal Cloud Computing Strategy* (Kundra 2011)

In Figure 7.2, a benefit-driven framework is provided that explains the "current" environment against the benefits of cloud computing. The chart also shows three key information technology drivers, efficiency, agility, and innovation.

Figure 7.3 lays out a framework for migrating to the cloud designed for departments and agencies to follow. It is important to point out that the initiative does acknowledge and provide for flexibility and allows room for adjustments. Each federal government agency finds itself in a unique position with special needs and requirements. If an agency recently built a brand new data center, it would make little sense to simply abandon it and migrate to the cloud.

In August 2013, the federal government's top technology managers were called to Capitol Hill to explain some disappointing results regarding the FDCCI. While 500 federal data centers did indeed close, the actual new number of data centers rose by 3,700 (Forbes 2013). Essentially it was discovered that for every data center that was closed, seven new ones had been discovered. The answer to this revelation had more to do with the definition of what constitutes a "data center." It was discovered that federal agencies were counting everything from large standard data centers to individual servers that were housed in a room or closet. As a result of the miscounting of data centers, the Office of Management and Budget had to officially clarify how a data center should be classified and what constitutes a core data center—which was the goal of the consolidation initiative in the first place.

Select	Provision	Manage

• Identify which IT services to move and when
 	
  – Identify sources of value for cloud migrations: efficiency, agility, innovation
 	
  – Determine cloud readiness: security, market availability, government readiness, and technology lifecycle
	• Aggregate demand at department level where possible
	
	• Ensure interoperability and integration with IT portfolio
	
	• Contract effectively to ensure agency needs are met
	
	• Realize value by repurposing or decommissioning legacy assets and redeploying freed resources
		• Shift IT mindset from assets to services
		
		• Build new skill sets as required
		
		• Actively monitor SLAs to ensure compliance and continuous improvement
		
		• Re-evaluate vendor and service models periodically to maximize benefits and minimize risks

Framework is flexible and can be adjusted to meet individual agency needs		

Figure 7.3 Decision framework for cloud migration

Source: *Federal Cloud Computing Strategy* (Kundra 2011)

Figure 7.4 Cloud solutions have unlimited applications and connections

Source: Federal Data Center Consolidation Initiative 2011

The Cloud Commissions

In 2010 the TechAmerica Foundation created a "Cloud Commission" that was comprised of seventy-one companies and organizations that included cloud users and cloud businesses and with the encouragement of the Federal CIO. Their report entitled *Cloud First, Cloud Fast: Recommendations for Innovation, Leadership, and Job Creation* was published in 2011 (TechAmerica Foundation 2011). The report was important because it identified the needs and obstacles that had to be addressed by both business and government for realizing greater efficiencies as well as remaining competitive globally. In its rather optimistic foreword, the report stated, "Cloud technologies are transforming the way computing power is bought, sold and delivered. Rather than purchasing licenses or hardware, users may now obtain computing power as a service, buying only as much as they need, and only when they need it."

The group's report filled in many gaps found in the initial federal government's cloud strategy by identifying a number of key issues that had to be addressed in order to achieve greater (and faster) adoption. These key issues include the need to update US laws (e.g., the 1986 Electronic Communications Privacy Act) to reflect changing technology and legal needs. Second was the need to establish clearer rules and processes on data breach disclosures to maximize transparency. Third, there was the need for an identity management ecosystem as envisioned by the National Strategy for Trusted Identities in Cyberspace (NSTIC) which is well underway. Fourth they identified the need for reliable and sufficient broadband bandwidth. They also identified the need for clarity around the rising issues regarding transnational data flows. And finally, the report discussed the need for ongoing industry and academic research to advance cloud computing technologies and the cultural issues that often limit the deployment of new technologies.

Without trust, cloud adoption will not occur smoothly or effectively. Further, one must create an environment where there is a greater appreciation and understanding of transactional data flows, transparency, and applying transformational policies, practices, and finally, people skills, for successful cloud adoption. Because the federal government has such an impressive investment in information technology systems, it stands to reason that changing the dynamics of security, access, procurement, and business processes, requires a new paradigm in federal IT management.

While the federal government has its own unique challenges regarding cloud adoption, state and local governments are often less encumbered by one-size-fits-all policies yet have their own issues. To help address these differences, the TechAmerica Foundation created the State and Local Government Cloud Commission in 2011, and released its report in early 2012. TechAmerica Foundation's *The Cloud Imperative: Better Collaboration, Better Service, Better Cost* (for state and local government) (2012) examined five key aspects of cloud computing:

1. Issues for State and Local Government—Key concerns and benefits of cloud computing for governments.
2. Technology for Cloud Computing—Key technical issues to consider when moving to cloud computing.
3. Implementing the Cloud—A four-stage management structure for transition to cloud.
4. Acquiring the Cloud—Procurement vehicles, business models, funding streams, and contractual terms for cloud.
5. Case Studies and Success Stories—Examples of how state and local governments are acquiring and using cloud.

Cloud computing, or cloud-based services, represents a significant shift in how government IT is managed. By 2020, the term "cloud" most likely will not be an issue unto itself. Nevertheless, there are legitimate concerns regarding the shift from owning data and infrastructure to managing data and infrastructure in the cloud.

Many state and local governments have ventured into the cloud by first identifying applications that are the most cloud-appropriate or adoptable. This would include having emails hosted and managed by an outside company instead of hosting and maintain email services themselves. Companies such as Microsoft, Google, and Rackspace are examples of a few companies

Figure 7.5 Consumer cloud storage companies

Figure 7.6 Local governments, by necessity, are turning to cloud-based solutions to help save money

Source: Siobhan Duncan

that offer email hosted solutions. State and local governments are also turning to cloud-based companies that provide data warehousing, data storage and retrieval services, and contract for services like application and, perhaps, license processing and call-center augmentation. Election and voting authorities,

---

Managed Services Case-in-Point

Many local governments struggled with localized crime reporting to their citizens. They often lacked the staff expertise, and often found that it took more time and resources with little to show for their efforts. Sensing a need to leverage local police crime data and place on localized interactive maps, both online and via mobile apps, a company called Crime Reports was created. Today it is the largest company of its kind and is funded by local police entities that recognize the benefit for utilizing their cloud-based infrastructure. Instead of each local police agency developing their own mapping and cataloging system and supporting it 24/7, one company can do it better and more affordably since the actual costs are spread amongst thousands of localities. For more information see CrimeReports.com

---

Figure 7.7 Managed cloud solutions case-in-point

who only require peak data processing power during certain times of the year (or once every four years), can now purchase the extra processing power as needed and thus reduce the need to maintain equipment that is designed for peak periods when peak period capacity is rarely needed.

Cloud computing is also about managed services. Many parks and recreation departments use cloud-based companies to process their activities. Citizens are not aware that when they click on certain links such as applying for a fishing or hunting license, or to reserve basketball or tennis courts they might actually be processed by an outside company. Managed services are designed to be seamless and follow the necessary legal and administrative policies and procedures as if the application was processed at a government's facility. Using someone else's expertise and staff can save money or provide better services than a government entity could ever hope to make available.

Cloud computing will continue to be an invaluable resource for state and local governments in their efforts to rationalize and optimize computing resources. Cloud computing should be seen as an IT innovation that can support rationalization and optimization of business services as well as IT services. Due diligence prescribes the necessity of exploring and evaluating jurisdictional issues in order to ensure long-term sustainability and growing adoption of collaborative government operations in state and local government.

One might be tempted to downplay the significance of cloud computing. After all, data is data, with the only difference being that the data is being operated and located on someone else's infrastructure. The National Association of State Chief Information Officers (NASCIO 2011) in the third in its series *Capitals in the Cloud*, points out some of the risk factors when it comes to cloud computing scenarios which can trigger disputes and litigation that include, but are not limited to, the following:

- data protection and privacy
- sharing data residence with other service provider customers
- outright theft of data
- hackers
- unintentional release of data
- sending, storing, processing of data in multiple jurisdictions
- censorship
- computer crime
- contracts
- copyright
- defamation and libel
- discrimination
- fraud
- harassment
- intellectual property
- taxation
- trade secrets
- trademark
- inter-tenant data penetration, corruption, modification.

State and local governments have always had to deal with these issues, but because cloud computing emphasizes and encourages multi-user environments, each of these issues requires very careful thought, strategies, and policies to prevent unauthorized access from government employees as well as to those on the outside that are constantly probing for ways to access

Figure 7.8 Cloud-based solutions have unlimited possibilities

government data. When it comes to cloud computing the devil is truly in the details. Government mangers must be absolutely certain that they understand the cloud provider contracts and their provisions, as well as their performance and legal obligations.

Cloud Matters and Factors

Cloud computing represents a completely new way of thinking and managing information technology. Chief Information Officers initially were hesitant to embrace cloud computing for several reasons, however, they are generally more and more confident and hopeful. Despite growing optimism for cloud computing, a number of issues still must be addressed such as:

1. Can a government entity legally move government-protected data that generally contains personally identifiable information (PII)?
2. If there is a data loss or breach in the cloud, who is legally responsible?
3. What types of protection are provided to ensure data protection and integrity?
4. What types of data back-ups are provided, what is the frequency?
5. Can data encryption be provided, and how and where?
6. Can a cloud server be based in a "foreign" country?
7. What types of disaster recovery techniques are employed?
8. What happens if a cloud company goes out of business or merges with another?
9. How difficult would it be if a government entity wanted to move its cloud services to another vendor? What is involved?
10. What penalties can be imposed if a cloud vendor fails to live up to their contractual obligations?
11. Who actually owns the data that is in the cloud?
12. How will access user authentication and control be established, checked, and enforced?
13. What type of quality of service (QoS) is guaranteed?
14. What kind of power back-up system is used and how quickly can service be restored, and under what conditions?
15. When it comes to on-demand provisioning for peak usage, how quickly can this be initiated, by whom and under what conditions?
16. What is the availability of the cloud service provider for help?

As noted throughout the chapter, cloud computing is a new and different way to think and operate. It involves data centers, stand-alone applications, and third party service providers. It is now being utilized to connect various platforms from legacy mainframe computers to laptops and mobile devices. If a new city or business were to be created from scratch, would they even bother to purchase and maintain their own data centers and associated infrastructure? After all, computer systems are nothing but tools that enable governments to be more productive and to be able to process data and information in ways that no human could possibly perform. In the end it's all about results, such as did I receive my payment on time or was my application processed in a timely manner?

The City of San Diego which was followed by the County of San Diego has outsourced most of their information technology services in order to reduce overheads and costs. They claim that they benefit from gaining greater flexibility by paying for services they actually need and leave it to the outside service providers to find and maintain the necessary human technology talent. Both the City and County of San Diego each maintain their CIOs, but their job responsibilities are vastly different from that of their more traditional counterparts. Their job is to manage contracts and work with chosen vendor staff. Clearly, there are both advantages and disadvantages to hiring out IT services.

Many state and local governments complain about the lack of flexibility they have in dealing with their technology staff given the current state of civil service laws. Public managers have voiced concern about having to keep protected IT staff whose skills were once very much valued but, however, may no longer be needed due to changing technologies. It can be a daunting task to try to get workers to be re-trained and to embrace new skill sets. The other issue regarding staffing is finding the right skill sets among new applicants and then being able to pay them a competitive wage. The human resource is very much in play when it comes to moving operations in the cloud or contracting for cloud-based services.

Most state and local government agencies still operate as they have for the past twenty-five years. Not only do they have to contend with human resource issues, many continue to operate under outdated procurement polices and procedures making it even more difficult to migrate operations and applications to the cloud. It is incumbent upon the cloud companies to provide strong assurances that privacy, access, and security are at least as good, if not better, than that of any government entity. More importantly they have to prove it through demonstrated experience and best practices.

The Federal Government Cloud Blueprint

In 2014, Fedramp.gov was launched as a separate website. Previously it had been part of the CIO Council website.

From 2011 on, the Office of Management and Budget (OM), along with the General Services Administration (GSA) and Department of Homeland Security (DHS) sought to better promote cloud computing and, in particular, wrestled with the paramount issue of security. Thus cloud computing offers a unique opportunity for the federal government to take advantage of cutting edge information technologies to dramatically reduce procurement and operating costs and greatly increase the efficiency and effectiveness of

Figure 7.9 Cloud.cio.gov homepage

services provided to its citizens. Consistent with the President's International Strategy for Cyberspace and Cloud First policy, the adoption and use of information systems operated by cloud service providers (cloud services) by the federal government depends on security, interoperability, portability, reliability, and resiliency.

In a memo to all federal agencies (OMB 2011), OMB provided a comprehensive set of instructions with a rationale for cloud adoption and security. The coordination and adoption was also a main focus of the Federal CIO as well as the Federal CIO Council.

FedRAMP's mission and purpose can be summed up as:

1. Establishes federal policy for the protection of federal information in cloud services;
2. Describes the key components of FedRAMP and its operational capabilities;
3. Defines executive department and agency responsibilities in developing, implementing, operating, and maintaining FedRAMP; and
4. Defines the requirements for executive departments and agencies using FedRAMP in the acquisition of cloud services.

Today it is common to see major cloud providers seeking acceptance into the FedRAMP system and the list of companies is growing quickly.

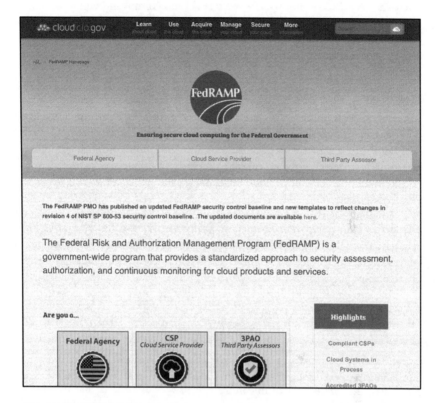

Figure 7.10 FedRAMP homepage

Storm Clouds Ahead

The private sector has always promoted a very sunny and bright future for cloud computing and cloud-based services. There have been a number of cloud outages and a few isolated cases of hacking. When it comes to government data processing, cloud computing becomes far more complicated than one might expect. Every government data application is usually as massive as it is unique. They are dependent on numerous subsystems that query and check against information in other databases. Suffice it to say that government requirements for cloud computing—especially found in legacy systems—are far more complex than would be found in the comparatively simple consumer-based versions. FedRAMP is a major initiative aimed at securing the cloud in the federal domains. However, in the end, government agencies are still responsible for protecting data and information regardless of where it is housed. This places a great deal of responsibility on public administrators who have the ultimate burden of assessing risk in moving to the cloud.

By the year 2020, if not sooner, the term cloud computing will most likely evaporate into thin air, as it will evolve into normal business practices. On the other hand, the need to manage data and information systems will remain, it simply will matter far less where the true IT infrastructure lies.

Discussion Questions

1. Name the number and types of cloud-based services you use either for personal use or for professional use at the office or in the field.
2. Look up at least five different definitions of cloud computing applications and describe the common elements and differences.
3. Explain or discuss how cloud computing can help governments improve their operations.
4. What are the dangers and or limitations of cloud computing?
5. What laws need to reviewed or modified to allow for greater cloud usage?
6. How secure is cloud computing? What do we know about its safety record?
7. How can change management techniques be used to address staff that are fearful of cloud computing?
8. What types of government services might lend themselves to a managed service provided by a company or even another government entity?
9. Can you identify any weakness in the FedRAMP initiative?
10. Can you identify at least three major security breaches that involved government and the cloud? If yes, what was the cause and where there any similarities?

References

CIO.gov. 2010. "Vivek Kundra Testimony on Cloud Computing." Accessed October 17, 2014. https://cio.gov/vivek-kundra-testimony-on-cloud-computing/.

Federal Data Center Consolidation Initiative. 2011. *Data Center Consolidation Plan & Progress Report*. October. Accessed October 17, 2014. https://www.dhs.gov/sites/default/files/publications/DHS_FDCCI_Report_Oct_2011_Final508.pdf.

Forbes. 2013. "The Surprising Truth about Federal Data Center Consolidation." Accessed October 17, 2014. http://www.forbes.com/sites/oracle/2013/08/13/the-surprising-truth-about-federal-data-center-consolidation/.

Kundra, Vivek. 2011. *Federal Cloud Computing Strategy*. February 8. Accessed October 17, 2014. https://www.dhs.gov/sites/default/files/publications/digital-strategy/federal-cloud-computing-strategy.pdf, pages 29, 30.

NASCIO. 2011. *Capitals in the Clouds Part III—Recommendations for Mitigating Risks: Jurisdictional, Contracting and Service Levels*. Lexington, KY. Accessed October 17, 2014. http://www.nascio.org/publications/documents/NASCIO_CloudComputing_PartIII.pdf.

NIST. 2011. "Definition of Cloud Computing." Special Publication 800-145. September, 2011. Washington, DC.

OMB. 2011. *Memorandum for Chief Information Officers.* December 8. Accessed October 17, 2014. http://www.whithouse.gov/sites/default/files/omb/assests/egov_docs/fedreampmemo.pdf.

Shark, Alan. 2012. *Cloud-Based Solutions. The Seven Trends that will Transform Local Government Through Technology.* Public Technology Institute, Alexandria, VA.

TechAmerica Foundation 2011. Cloud Commission Report. *Cloud First, Cloud Fast: Recommendations for Innovation, Leadership, and Job Creation.* Accessed October 17, 2014. https://www.techamerica.org/techamerica-foundation-cloud-commission-report/.

TechAmerica Foundation. 2012. *The Cloud Imperative: Better Collaboration, Better Service, Better Cost.* Accessed October 17, 2014. http://www.techamericafoundation.org/slg-cc-download.

Digital Destinations

Crime Reports. https://www.crimereports.com/

Federal CIO Council Cloud Information. http://cloud.cio.gov/

Federal Cloud Computing Front & Center. https://cio.gov/cloud-computing-front-and-center/

Federal Cloud Computing Strategy. https://cio.gov/wp-content/uploads/downloads/2012/09/Federal-Cloud-Computing-Strategy.pdf

Federal Cloud Computing Update: Best Practices for Acquiring IT as a Service. https://cio.gov/cloud-computing-update-best-practices-for-acquiring-it-as-a-service/

The Federcal CIO Council's website for cloud computing information. http://www.cloud.cio.gov

The Federal Government's cloud initiative. http://www.fedramp.gov

Gartner Definition of Public Cloud Computing. http://www.gartner.com/it-glossary/public-cloud-computing

NASCIO. http://www.nascio.org/committees/EA/download.cfm?id=145

TechAmerica Foundation. http://www.techamerica.org/Docs/fileManager.cfm?f=taf_slg_cc_summary.pdf

———http://www.techamerica.org/Docs/fileManager.cfm?f=taf_slg_cc.pdf

Further Reading

NASCIO. 2011. *Capitals in the Clouds—The Case for Cloud Computing in State Government Part I: Definitions and Principles.* Lexington, KY. Accessed October 17, 2014. http://www.nascio.org/publications/documents/NASCIO-Capitals_in_the_Clouds-June2011.pdf.

———. 2011. *Capitals in the Clouds—The Case for Cloud Computing in State Government Part II: Challenges and Opportunities to Get Your Data Right.* Lexington, KY. Accessed October 17, 2014. http://www.nascio.org/publications/documents/NASCIO_Cloud Computing_PartII.pdf.

———. 2011. *Capitals in the Clouds Part III—Recommendations for Mitigating Risks: Jurisdictional, Contracting and Service Levels.* Lexington, KY. Accessed October 17, 2014. http://www.nascio.org/publications/documents/NASCIO_CloudComputing_PartIII.pdf.

————. 2012. *Capitals in the Clouds Part IV—Cloud Security: On Mission and Means.* Lexington, KY. Accessed October 17, 2014. http://www.nascio.org/publications/documents/NASCIO_CloudComputing_PartIV.pdf.

————. 2013. *Capitals in the Clouds Part V: Advice from the Trenches on Managing the Risk of Free File Sharing Cloud Services.* Lexington, KY. Accessed October 17, 2014. http://www.nascio.org/publications/documents/NASCIO_CloudComputing_PartV.pdf.

TechAmerica Foundation. (n.d.) *Commission on the Leadership Opportunity in US Deployment of the Cloud (CLOUD²).* Accessed October 17, 2014. http://www.techamerica-foundation.org/cloud-commission.

8 Geospatial Systems and Planning

Mapping and Visualizing the Future

If you've ever been lost in a foreign land, you know that finding your way to your destination isn't nearly as scary as it might seem—provided there are people around to show you the way. It takes gumption to stop someone on the street and ask for directions, but once you've mustered the courage to disrupt someone you don't know, the answer is usually quickly had. One surprise for those who've never been lost abroad in a land where a foreign language is spoken is that communicating directions is quite possible despite language barriers.

This is because, once the desired destination has been adequately conveyed, directions can be given using gestures and descriptions that do not require common language, only a common sense of spatial relations. It's easy to point someone in the right direction, and nowadays, even easier to pull out your smartphone, pull up a digital map, and show someone the way, regardless of linguistics.

Historians like J.B. Harley and David Woodward point out that mapping occurred before written languages and numeric systems (Harley and Woodward 1987). More importantly, they explain that "there have been relatively few mapless societies in the world at large" (ibid.). It follows that mapping has played a role in the governance of societies of all sizes, structures, and distinctions throughout time. Maps are something humans have an innate understanding about, and governments, inherently tied to geography, have long had a special interest in maps.

It should come as no surprise that some of the most dramatic strides in the public sector's pursuit of technology-based tools made in the last few decades have involved the digitization and manipulation of mapped information. Maps transcend the barriers of knowledge, experience, and even language. They offer instantly comprehensible insights about relationships in an objective way. They leave only the interpretation of the facts up to the viewer; everything else is plain to see. For this reason, they offer an opportunity to bring government departments, whole governments, and citizens together to solve problems—literally putting every stakeholder on common ground.

Geospatial Data-Powered Decision Making

In contemporary government, as in the private sector, there is a clear and undeniable demand for better decision-making. It's easy to recognize that better understanding the dynamics of current situations is a critical factor in the pursuit of that goal. A clear picture of the current state of systems lends itself to a more accurate imagining of future states at various intervals, and helps convey the extent to which a change in the system recasts projected future states. But the relative clarity of that current state view can quickly be obscured by a number of confounding factors. How hard is it to gather the right information about the current state? How easy is it to interpret the information? Which people, each with different biases, can be exposed to that information to make an individual judgment about the right next steps? The wrong answers to questions like these can render all the data in the world inert, and leave humans to make decisions that are as poorly informed as they might have been decades or even centuries ago. Modern mapping technologies seek to cure all of these insufferable blinders and decision-making snares. While they may look interesting or pretty, or simply be exciting to create, the maps discussed in the following sections of this chapter all serve a very specific purpose: to bolster decision making by increasing understanding and interpretation of geographically organized information. Modern digital mapping is interesting enough to captivate on its own, but the information and knowledge it can relay make it a hundred times more powerful than it is good-looking. As William Huxhold wrote in 1991 when describing the value of GIS, "good decisions require good information" (Huxhold 1991). Government systems for mapping information provided that then, and although the technology behind them has advanced dramatically since that writing, they still provide good information. That they are enabling the business of government to be done with greater intelligence and insight is the core value of geospatial systems.

What is GIS?

Geographic Information System (GIS) is a term used to describe any location-based visualization technology tool designed to demonstrate correlations between virtually any information that can be mapped. "In the strictest sense, a GIS is a computer system capable of assembling, storing, manipulating, and displaying geographically referenced information (that is data identified according to their locations)," according to The United States Geological Survey (USGS), a federal agency (USGS 2007). GIS, as a term, can also be used to describe a diverse set of systems, geospatial data, or even a team of people. The USGS, which by virtue of its focus on the geography of the United States uses GIS as part of its core business, has the following mission: "The USGS serves the nation by providing reliable scientific information to describe and understand the Earth; minimize the loss of life and property from natural disasters; manage water, biological, energy and mineral resources; and enhance and protect our quality of life" (ibid.).

Meet the Deep Data Map

If the USGS has such a weighty role to play in the lives of American citizens, and it uses GIS as a base tool to do so, it is easy to get a sense of how powerful GIS can be. But the practical applications of GIS extend far beyond federal agencies with a focus on geography and the mapping of resources. Today, virtually every public sector entity in the country can gain valuable insights by deploying a GIS.

Spatial Data and Attribute Data

Throughout history, maps have been useful for their ability to relay *spatial data*—information correlating to a point or points in space. Thanks to a basic map's ability to convey spatial information, we can see that driving from Washington, DC, to Arlington, Texas, covers only about half the distance to San Diego, California. And, if we calculate the distances using powerful spatial data sets within geospatial systems that also include major roadways in this country—such as those made widely available through Google Maps or in-car global positioning systems (GPS)—we can see that the distance between San Diego and Arlington, and between Arlington and Washington, DC, are equal within a few miles of each other. The large data sets that can be processed in a GIS make spatial calculations fast and easy to perform.

Spatial data can be very precise and can include both discrete objects, such as the X on a pirate map or a river, as well as continuous fields indicating homogenous information about a whole region, like elevation or temperature. These different types of spatial data can be combined to generate very accurate maps locating everything from potholes to natural landmarks to viewing health statistics in any given area. Figure 8.1 (Centers for Disease Control and Prevention) is a GIS map used by the Centers for Disease Control and Prevention.

GIS can offer powerful visualization of spatial data sets, and allow sets to be displayed or hidden from view with the click of a button, making it easy to see only the information required by the user. These spatial data can be viewed over time in animations or even fed into a GIS in real-time when tracking moving objects such as livestock on a farm or range. But the addition of *attribute data* to GIS brings a never-before-seen depth of field to mapping that is only possible through digitization. Attribute data is metadata associated with instances of spatial data in a GIS. For example, imagine a GIS that includes the spatial data needed to indicate the location of every oil derrick in Texas. The addition of attribute data to that GIS

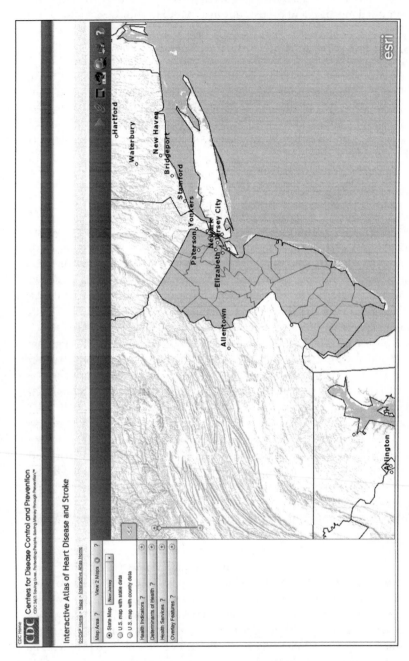

Figure 8.1 Centers for Disease Control and Prevention website

Source: www.nccd.cdc.gov

would give users the ability to click each derrick (or interact with it in some other way) so as to reveal additional information about it, such as the year the well was drilled, the owner, or the number of months remaining before it should be inspected again. The depths of this attribute data are only limited by the amount of information available for inclusion in the GIS. Figure 8.2 shows how attribute data can even be photographic, in this case helping the public works and law enforcement teams in Riverside, California, identify multiple occurrences of graffiti created by the same criminal. Where paper maps could once only relay spatial data, requiring an additional resource—perhaps a listing of further information—correlated to points on the map for additional information, GIS constitutes a quantum leap forward if only for its ability to provide attribute data (see the American City and County website).

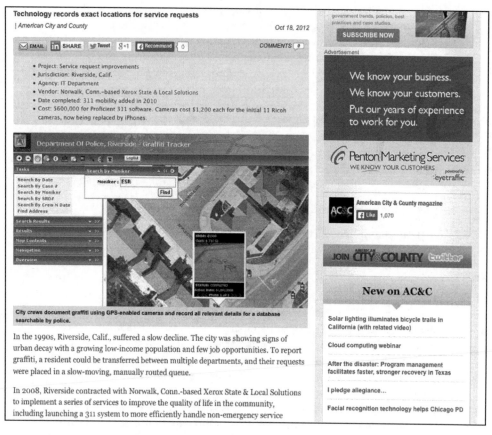

Figure 8.2 American City and County website

Source: www.americancityandcounty.com

Raster and Vector Graphics

While the ability to incorporate attribute data into a GIS marks a sea change in the amount of information maps can hold, the digitization of traditional map elements and widespread availability of bird's eye view photography have also enabled more information to be relayed through GIS. Where maps for specific uses could once only be created as illustrations meant to represent actual land-masses and regions, satellite and aerial imaging now make bird's eye photography widely available and easy to incorporate into a GIS. *Raster*, or pixel-based, images can be included in GIS today with a few clicks. By virtue of the fact that these images include subtle details only photography can capture, they can make it simple for users to orient themselves on the map. For example, if a certain bend in a river always features whitewater rapids, that bend can be quickly located on an aerial photo of the region. In contrast, *vector*, or shape-based, illustrations can make up the entirety of a GIS map, as shown in Figure 8.3 or only the spatial elements overlaid on top of a raster base map as shown in Figure 8.4. This flexibility makes it easy to view the information displayed alone and free from clutter or in the context of a bird's eye photo.

Both of these images were generated by Google Maps, an openly available GIS designed for consumer use, which can be accessed from most Internet browsers at maps.google.com. This technology made a huge splash when Google announced the inclusion of "Street View," on May 25, 2007 (Class Action Complaint 2010). Beginning as a small set of spatial data points in Google Maps that could be clicked to view a full 360-degree panorama of raster photography taken from that location, Street View has since expanded to include panoramic images as attribute data for points along roads and paths all over the globe. To learn more about Street View, see Google (2014).

The Value of Layered Data

With all the different ways to display information in a GIS, it follows that virtually any data set with geographic markers can be visualized in a GIS. This fact makes a GIS an incredibly useful tool for public managers and governments, which by virtue of the work they do, have a tendency to generate the kinds of data sets and stores of information that are usefully displayed in a GIS. However, these data sets, when viewed independently, often still require much interpretation. This is why modern governmental GIS enables users to view multiple data sets, structured as "layers" of data, in the same visualization. While it might prove useful to view a map of all the potholes in a city, prioritizing the order in which they are repaired would be much easier if a color-coded map of the most-traveled roads in the city was layered on top of it. It's exactly this kind of logic that has resulted in the layering of data sets in GIS systems, and, of course, having the power to see a multiplicity of factors at once makes for much more robust decision making. One data set can provide context for other sets, revealing correlations and even causation. Figure 8.5

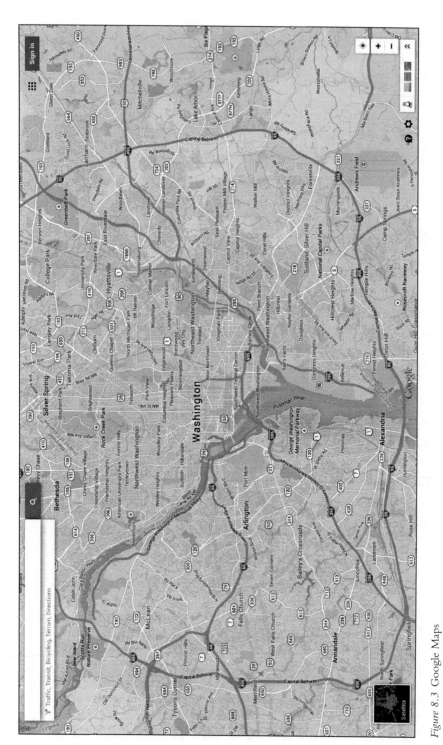

Figure 8.3 Google Maps

Source: Google Maps 2013

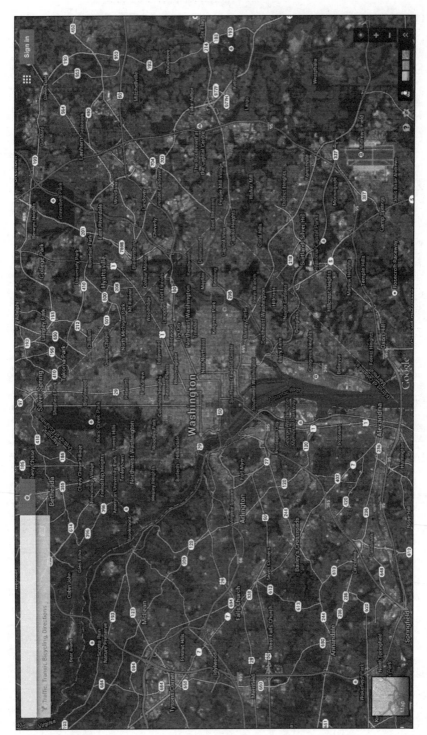

Figure 8.4 Google Maps

Source: Google Maps 2013

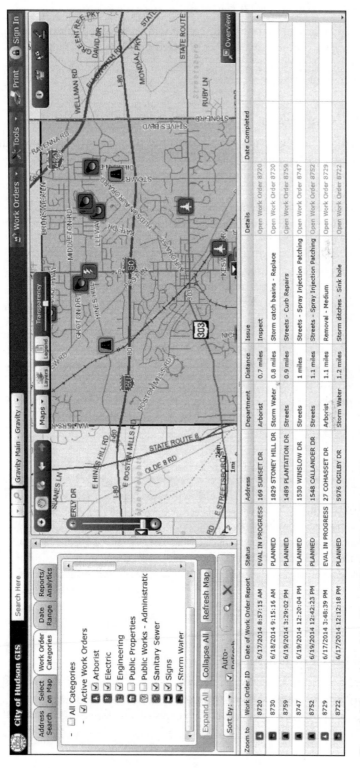

Figure 8.5 Screenshot of the City of Hudson Work Orders GIS

Source: http://gis.hudson.oh.us/workorders/

is an image generated by the public facing GIS created by City of Hudson, Ohio, to display different work orders created by its citizens. The left-hand side allows citizens to display or hide many layers of data, each associated with a different type of work order.

The Impact of GIS on Government

While Google and many others in the private sector have made powerful use of geospatial systems and GIS technology, there is an argument to be made for the idea that no industry has been revolutionized by their power more than government. Governments big and small have implemented GIS across the United States, and are using this technology to make a wide variety of decisions. As of 2003, GISs had reached near ubiquity among large local governments. Some 97 percent of local governments serving over 100,000 people had incorporated GIS. Perhaps more surprising is the fact that 88 percent of governments serving between 50,000 and 100,000 citizens were using GIS at that point, and over half of all the small local governments (56 percent) with fewer than 50,000 citizens were using GIS (Sarkar 2003). Short of the Internet or the telephone, it's hard to think of any high technology tool that has experienced such rapid widespread adoption in the public sector—modern computer systems enabling GIS didn't emerge until the 1960s. Of course, GIS is widely used at state and federal levels today, just as it is in large cities. The universal adoption of GIS technology for decision-making has many causes, not the least of which being that it is so elegant and unbiased as to support the most basic purposes of government.

As of 2003, GISs had reached near ubiquity among large local governments. Some 97 percent of local governments serving over 100,000 people had incorporated GIS. Perhaps more surprising is the fact that 88 percent of governments serving between 50,000 and 100,000 citizens were using GISs at that point, and over half of all the small local governments (56 percent) with fewer than 50,000 citizens were using GIS.

Source: Dibya Sarkar 2003

GIS and the Purpose of Government

In his 2003 book *America's Founding Fathers: Their Uncommon Wisdom and Wit*, author Bill Adler explains that "[Thomas] Jefferson believed that the entire purpose of government is to enable the people of a nation to live together in safety, security and happiness, and that the government exists for the interests of the governed, not for the governors" (Adler 2003). To many in the public sector, these Jeffersonian ideals and other basic principles about the goals and purposes of government no doubt serve as inspiration. It's no secret that many government workers are motivated by the service they provide to citizens. Governments and government workers have long strived to improve that service, and to *advance*, not just uphold, the values of government service. Whether those values have shifted or not, modern parlance describes a few of them using the following new (or at least newly applied) terms that serve to indicate the shifting relationships between governments and citizens in the pursuit of improved government services: transparency, accountability, and citizen engagement.

How GIS Supports Transparency, Accountability, and Citizen Engagement

As the way government work gets done advances and new technologies enable different forms of communication and interaction between citizens and their governments, the lexicon used to describe these shifting relationships also changes. What follows is a quick look at three new terms used to describe the purpose of government, along with explanations and examples describing how GIS is supporting each of them.

Transparency

In contemporary American government, greater dissemination of information enabled by the Internet and other powerful tools of mass communication has led, in turn, to greater demand for clarity about how governments serve their citizens, extending to the point of full disclosure. It has become common to describe this clarity and the demand for disclosure as *transparency*. Today, GISs are supporting transparency by giving citizens more access to information about the business of government. This information certainly serves to build trust between citizens and their governments, and it can lead to improved safety and security, which Adler posits was paramount to Jefferson's ideas about the purpose of government. For example, demands for transparency might posit that, if governments have record of the whereabouts of known criminals and crimes, then they should share those with the people. The website CrimeReports.com, created by a private-sector company called PublicEngines, does just that, aggregating recent reports of criminal activity from municipalities across the country, and displays them all in different layers (associated with different types of crimes) in a publically accessible GIS map. For more information see CrimeReports (2013). Figure 8.6 shows an image of this web-based GIS depicting crimes in Lower Manhattan and Brooklyn.

Figure 8.6 CrimeReports website

Source: CrimeReports 2013

Accountability

If the role of government is to protect the interests of the "governed, not the governors," as Jefferson appears to have believed, then contemporary governments have a duty to demonstrate how citizen tax dollars are being spent—and to enable citizens to hold them accountable for the effectiveness of government work. *Accountability* is a word used to describe this duty. A GIS can support accountability by clearly and quickly conveying the areas and points of interest where tax dollars are being spent. This fact is well demonstrated by the website Recovery.gov, created by the Recovery Accountability and Transparency Board established as part of the American Recovery and Reinvestment Act of 2009. This comprehensive site gives the American people a clear view into how and where funds associated with the Act are being spent. Figure 8.7 shows a handful of the many map-based information displays hosted on Recovery.gov.

Citizen Engagement

Thanks, in part, to the rise of mass communication technologies like social media, and to the proliferation of citizen-owned devices that make communicating en masse easier than ever, there has also been a rise in demand for *citizen engagement* meant to shorten the feedback loop between the governments that serve citizens and the people being served. An example of GIS enabling the proliferation of citizen-generated information and feedback about service quality is the private sector created SeeClickFix mobile application, which allows citizens to send photo images of non-emergency issues within their communities to local governments that adopt the technology. This so-called E 311 program and others like it are making it easier than ever for citizens to communicate service needs to their governments. Figure 8.8 shows an image from SeeClickFix.com demonstrating how SeeClickFix enables governments to monitor real-time citizen-generated data in GIS.

An example of GIS enabling the proliferation of citizen-generated information and feedback about service quality is the private sector created SeeClickFix mobile application, which allows citizens to send photo images of non-emergency issues within their communities to local governments that adopt the technology. This so-called E 311 program and others like it are making it easier than ever for citizens to communicate service needs to their governments.

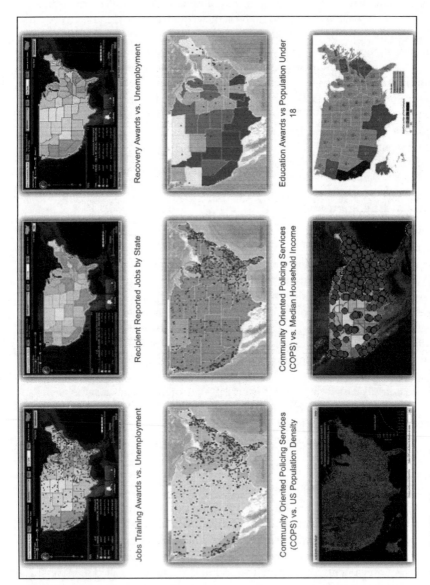

Figure 8.7 The American Recovery and Reinvestment Act website

Source: Recovery.gov

Figure 8.8 SeeClickFix website

Source: SeeClickFix 2014

GIS and the Business of Government

While it's important to consider how new technology tools like GIS can enable governments to improve their ability to uphold the core values and ideals of public service, it is equally important to consider their ability to support government's ability to do its work more efficiently and effectively—to improve the business of government. As Eric Anderson, City Manger of Tacoma, Washington, points out in the first chapter of *The GIS Guide for Local Government Officials* (2005), "Public policy is about values, but it's also about knowing what's going on and how people are affected by policies. This requires powerful information, delivered to decision makers in a transparent, understandable form that results in the best policy possible." Anderson goes on to argue that GIS can provide exactly that kind of information, transparency, and understandability. Armed with this powerful knowledge, public administrators on all levels can glean incredible insight into the business of government and, therefore, improve it. What follows are just a few examples of how this is possible.

Saving Time and Money

By painting a clear picture of current situations and conveying system dynamics thanks to its ability to display multiple, interrelated data sets at once, GIS can enable savings of all kinds at all levels of government. Take for example Alameda County, California, which had the goal of streamlining its election workflows to save time and money. Building on the San Francisco Bay's GIS, special tools were created for election staff that enabled them to select optimal polling locations and consolidate precincts. According to Tim Dupuis, the Chief Technology Officer of Alameda County, "making the switch to GIS means precinct consolidation that traditionally took six election technicians up to three weeks to complete now takes three technicians one to three days to complete" (Thomas, Parr, Hinthorne 2012).

Increasing Productivity and Efficiency

Technologies like email have saved public and private sector organizations countless dollars by enabling faster written communication. By the same token, GIS technology has been shown to improve government operations by making implementations simpler to monitor and plain old paperwork less cumbersome. In short, GIS can enable more modern communication, productivity, and efficiency. As an example, the City of Colorado Springs, Colorado, installed a GIS to improve public works efforts to repair road signs that ultimately improved productivity and efficiency. Historically, the asset management process in Colorado Springs involved multiple documents flowing through many siloed departments in a number of different buildings. "A typical work order for a sign repair was taking nearly fifty hours from start to finish, costing the city approximately 30,000 hours of staff time annually" (Thomas, Parr, Hinthorne 2012). Switching to a GIS-based system for asset management reduced that time to complete a work order to about 18 minutes (Ibid.).

At first glance, GIS can appear to be a costly and time-consuming way to make "pretty pictures," but the data-driven decision making enabled by GIS has demonstrated value in many settings and in the context of a wide range of strategic operational imperatives—those listed are just two examples. Many more can be found in the book titled, *Measuring Up: The Business Case for GIS* (Thomas, Parr, Hinthorne 2012). Whatever a government organization is trying to do as a business, better information and better understanding of the information available can absolutely lead to improvements. A GIS can enable the discovery and dissemination of information critical to decision-making across a wide range of business goals.

Making the Case for GIS

GIS is more useful and usable today than ever before. The emergence of open source GIS systems, which are freely available to the public, and massive advances in vendor capabilities, are enough to demonstrate as much.

Where once installing a GIS involved investment in massive, dedicated hardware in the form of workstations, today, many GIS systems can run on typical computers and even mobile devices with the data they display accessed through the cloud. Data scientists and engineers manipulating large data sets may always use dedicated, high-power workstations, but for many applications, using GIS is as simple as opening a browser window. What's more, GIS systems are cheaper than ever to deploy and more flexible and powerful thanks to the widespread proliferation of geo-tagged data. With regular training and upkeep, they can be incredibly useful and easy to use.

Where once installing a GIS involved investment in massive, dedicated hardware in the form of workstations, today, many GISs can run on typical computers and even mobile devices with the data they display accessed through the cloud.

GIS in Emergency Situations

Some of the most eye-opening use cases for GIS occur when they are used in emergency situations; these are scenarios that convey the value of GIS immediately and undeniably. As you'll read in the case study at the end of this chapter, the benefits witnessed by New York City (and seen by the world) during the rescue efforts that took place in the wake of September 11 raised nationwide awareness about the value of GIS almost overnight. Of course, GIS doesn't just help communities recover from disasters, natural or manmade. GIS can also be a powerful tool in predicting natural disasters by enabling the analysis of location-based data ahead of time. This is something the National Oceanic and Atmospheric Association (NOAA), a scientific organization within the United States Department of Commerce, does regularly, analyzing weather data constantly, and making much of it available in GIS form online (NOAA.gov 2014). An example of a weather map image that displays information designed to convey safety concerns can be seen in Figure 8.9 which illustrates the type of data that is available to the public 24/7.

Believe it or not, the use of GIS for predicting weather disasters and phenomena is not limited to the federal government. For example, the State of Alabama Department of Homeland Security, Google Maps, and a number of Alabama's counties teamed up in 2006 to create Virtual Alabama, a unified, state-wide GIS designed to better enable tornado preparedness and recovery. By 2010, all 67 counties in Alabama were supplying data and imagery to the program. Virtual Alabama has won numerous awards for its civil service (Shark 2012). Examples of GISs serving people in emergency situations have

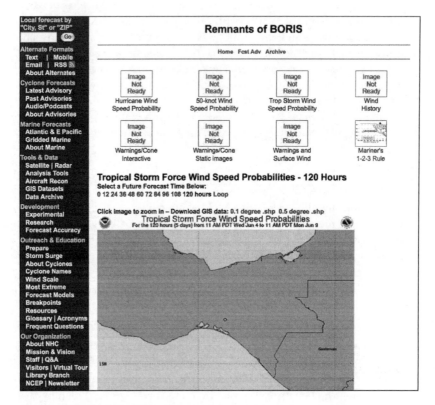

Figure 8.9 National Hurricane Center website

Source: National Hurricane Center 2013

become numerous, and have certainly enabled public administrators to witness and convey their value as sources of information and insight. However, the way to extract optimal value from a GIS is to deploy it across silos so it can support decision making across the entire enterprise.

Enterprise GIS and Beyond: Sharing Knowledge, Decision Making, and Funds

Governments are not independent and autonomous; they should not act as though they are, and GIS supports the kind of collaboration that revolutionizes the way interdepartmental work gets done in government. In contemporary terms, GIS is about data gathering and sharing. Governments are often better at gathering data than using data. Today, practical GIS deployment is as much about finding valuable data and information already owned by the organization as it is about generating new data, and putting it to work for public administrators and citizens. If the base technology required to deploy a GIS is enough to get one department started, that same technology is typically designed to be scalable so other departments and systems may benefit. Small, incremental investments are often all it takes to add new layers to a GIS or even new functionality. Delivering a GIS that can support the entire government enterprise does not have to mean making a massive financial investment. More importantly, deploying GIS across the enterprise often means adding layers of data comprised of sets that are already available within the organization, and that may be going unutilized. Put simply, if GIS can help a single department work smarter, it can certainly help whole organizations collaborate more effectively.

By combining internal resources, GIS can support the full range of departments in a government while also supporting their collective efforts. However, taking an additional step back, GIS can also support the collaboration and shared efforts that must occur between local governments, among clusters of state governments, or even across a group of state, local, and federal organizations. In many cases, state and federal mandates require that local government IT systems support decision-making and GIS can fill those needs, and foster greater federal and state government collaboration, with the goal of delivering better government services. (Anderson 2005).

Like many technologies, GIS is not a solution but a tool to enable better solutions. Effective use of GIS involves regular sharing of data, frequent training, and opportunities to collaborate. It is not a one-and-done investment, but a new way of enhanced government operations that requires ongoing efforts to support it and derive new value from it. Full-scale GIS adoption takes continued dialogues about how it's being utilized and how it might be deployed to solve other problems. It requires true organizational buy-in and support, as well as executive-level sponsorship. With those commitments, it can be an incredibly powerful tool for the delivery of better services and improved quality of life for citizens—not to mention work that's less tedious and more rewarding for public sector employees.

The Future of GIS

Thanks to widespread adoption, the future of GIS has, in many ways, already arrived. GIS data are his only getting richer and more useful as time passes, while GIS developments for visualizing and plotting data also become easier and easier to operate. One example of the new heights data richness is reaching can be found in the realm of LiDAR, a set of laser systems used to generate three-dimensional renderings that can be used in GISs. Specialists are deploying three-dimensional GIS integrations thanks to data gathered by LiDAR systems for all kinds of applications, bringing a new wave of accuracy and imaging thoroughness to GIS. 3D systems like LiDAR are also bringing virtual reality into the GIS conversation, enabling a wider range of decisions to be influenced by visual information that can be viewed from any side and every vantage point. (To learn more about LiDAR, be sure to check out the USGS website dedicated to it.)

In addition to the data richness created by technologies like LiDAR, opportunities for *mashups*—systems that incorporate data from disparate sources across the private and public sectors—are also emerging, creating new information systems and visualizations to support decision making. Examples of this can already be seen in cities like Boston, Massachusetts, where efforts have been made to combine private sector-owned bicycle-sharing data with public sector-owned transit department data (Psaty 2012).

> In addition to the data richness created by technologies like LiDAR, opportunities for *mashups*—systems that incorporate data from disparate sources across the private and public sectors—are also emerging, creating new information systems and visualizations to support decision making.

Perhaps even more revolutionary are trends that involve rich data sets being generated not by private companies or public sector initiatives but by citizens themselves. The smartphones many Americans carry in their pockets are able to gather incredibly rich, location-specific data that can reveal things about what citizens need from their governments. With more and more sensors being included in smartphones, from GPS technology, to digital compasses, to cameras, the opportunities for citizens to act as sensors, gathering real-time data and sharing it, are seemingly endless. What if smartphones could measure air pollution levels? What if the headphones that came with these smartphones could sense a user's pulse or body temperature? The public health implications would be incredible. Of course, as the opportunities for government to use citizens as sensors emerge, greater dialogues about privacy will necessarily be escalated, but the opportunities are easy to imagine and get excited about—on both sides.

Although there will always be those in government who adore spreadsheets and find them easy to interpret, the power of data visualization will not be ignored. The proliferation of rich data will likely bring easier-to-use GISs. Recent innovations have already put GIS into the cloud and onto standard computers where it once required dedicated hardware and workstations. Further advances will surely make data sets easier to add and access, maps faster to generate and share, and information critical for decision making more readily available. Intelligent pattern recognition systems will likely get smarter and easier to deploy, making valuable insights and causation more readily apparent, and data errors and flaws more obvious. New and unique ways of visualizing data making it more easily shared or interpreted will also come into use. For the public administrators of today and tomorrow, the power of GIS lies in the fact that maps are a universal language. GIS and other visualizations are powerful not just for what they can tell us, but for their ability to tell everyone the same things—to provide starting points for discussion and debate that involve more shared insight and base knowledge. This fact positions GIS as a continued demonstration of what government can be and has already become—better, faster, more efficient, and hopefully, more well informed.

Case Study: GIS—A Hero On September 11

As smoke poured out from a towering heap of twisted metal in Lower Manhattan, emergency responders worked to put out a fire that had been burning for days. But unlike the first few days following the September 11 attacks, the firemen were now looking to do more than extinguish fires and make rescues—they were hoping to avoid a second devastating explosion.

Moments earlier, a relatively unheard-of system known as GIS helped find fuel repositories located directly beneath the rubble. The maps generated by the system helped the firemen prevent the gas tanks from overheating, just in time (Francica 2011).

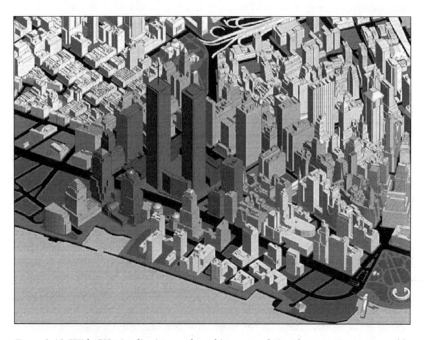

Figure 8.10 With GIS visualizations such as this one on their side, rescue teams were able to quickly understand the level of devastation at Ground Zero, and to make better decisions about how to move forward with rescues and recovery efforts

Source: http://seeclickfix.com

This is simply one of many lifesaving roles GIS played in the wake of September 11. Massive amounts of critical data were mapped and used to coordinate many of the response initiatives, making GIS an invaluable resource to numerous teams and departments throughout the recovery efforts.

While the use of GIS in a crisis of this capacity was novel at the time with many of the processes and tools being developed on the fly, the true value of GIS was brought to the attention of the world and the use and function of geospatial sciences in government were forever altered (Kevany 2011).

Responding to a Crisis with GIS

Before the attacks on September 11, New York City was no stranger to GIS. Having started GIS development during the 1980s through the department of city planning, the system had snowballed into many other departments. In fact, in the early 1990s NYC initiated the construction of a base map by combining all of the maps built by individual departments (Francica 2011). This single, comprehensive map could be used by any department across the city to access a broad spectrum of data to use for various applications.

Fast-forward to September 11, 2001, and in the chaotic moments following the attacks, these same departments were unexpectedly thrust into a frenzied state of disarray. Data was dispersed, departments were fragmented, and the GIS offices were inaccessible due to infrastructure breakdowns and evacuations. Nonetheless, key decisions needed to be made—and they needed to be made quickly.

Because of its familiarity and comfort with GIS, when the first tower came crashing to the ground on that horrific morning, the city didn't hesitate to involve GIS in the response efforts (Francica 2011). GIS was instantly called upon to organize the manifold of information spread throughout the city and present the data in a visual, quick-to-understand way, enabling informed decision-making amid chaos.

With the help of the Office of Emergency Management (OEM) and under the leadership of Al Leidner, the Director of the Department of Information Technology and Telecommunications (DoITT), the entire GIS community of NYC came together to help coordinate the efforts of emergency response teams rushing to the scene and others who needed to make large-scale decisions (Kevany 2011).

As shown in Figure 8.11, debris and rubble covered the streets near Ground Zero. Evacuation routes had eliminated access to both of the two GIS offices and all of the data inside, so the first couple days were spent organizing teams and bringing the necessary individuals together, while simultaneously meeting the initial demands for maps. On the first day, this meant teaming up with Hunter College—a hub of GIS activity in NYC—and delivering building blueprints to response teams. On the second day, the teams generated maps of every utility failure throughout the city, mapping electricity, water, telephone, and gas outages (Francica 2011).

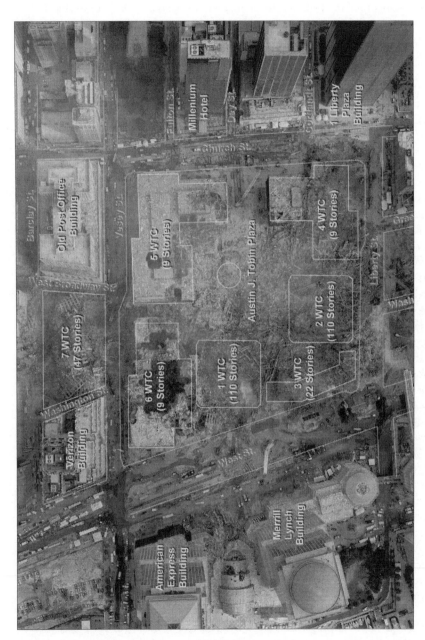

Figure 8.11 GIS planning map of the former World Trade Center's footprint

Source: NOAA September 2011

Come the third day, OEM had erected a makeshift headquarters at Pier 92, five miles from Ground Zero. Software and hardware were borrowed from across the city and data from an array of sources was accumulated to develop complex mapping with added layers, helping to meet specific needs. Equipped with multiple workstations and staffed by a range of GIS professionals working day and night, this center was responsible for generating maps vital to response (Kevany 2011).

From the police department to the fire department to FEMA and the American Red Cross, agencies from all over the city and state relied on these location-based data compilations to make pivotal decisions (GIS Monitor 2001). In the end, nearly 3,000 people tragically lost their lives during and after the attacks, but the capabilities enabled by GIS saved countless more and helped avert multiple compounding catastrophes.

Many of the processes for collaborating between departments and individuals, compiling the data, generating the maps, and delivering them to emergency responders were developed organically during the first few weeks, as none of the GIS workers were trained in crisis response. These off-the-cuff workflows and improv tools used to direct the city's disaster response efforts are the primary building blocks for GIS in crisis management today. And the pitfalls of GIS at the time, such as the lack of field-to-office communications, were recognized and have been erased by modern techniques and technologies over the past twelve years (Kevany 2011).

But the most important contribution made by the GIS workers in NYC after the attacks goes beyond evolving processes—as significant as they may be. The greatest outcome of those early efforts was that GIS was forced into the spotlight, receiving attention on a global scale. Its merit was well chronicled and governments that witnessed its ability to guide decision-making couldn't ignore its worth.

Today, GIS is considered a critical component of almost every government agency and viewed as an enterprise-wide function—due in large part to the events succeeding that fateful day in history (Robinson 2002).

Discussion Questions

1. What is a GIS and what is the core value of any GIS for public administrators?
2. Why is the ability of GISs to display multiple layers of data incredibly valuable?
3. What are the three newly applied terms discussed in this chapter that are used to describe the purpose of government?
4. How do GISs support those governmental goals, in brief?
5. How can GISs support the business objective of governments?
6. Why do emergency situations make the value of GISs readily apparent?
7. Why can an enterprise GIS be more powerful than a number of disparate GISs operating independently within an organization?

8. What new potential value are citizen smartphones and tablets bringing to GISs and other government decision-making tools?
9. What examples can you describe where a state or local government is utilizing GIS for greater productivity or citizen engagement?
10. Where is further research and experimentation still needed?
11. Can you describe a GIS application that falls short of your expectations? Why?
12. Can you describe and explain how GIS can greatly assist in public management in any one of the following areas: health, transportation, public safety, parks and recreation, other?

References

Adler, Bill. 2003. *America's Founding Fathers: Their Uncommon Wisdom and Wit.* Taylor Trade Publishing, Lanham, MD. Page 92.

Anderson, Eric. 2005. *The GIS Guide for Local Government Officials,* ed. Cory Fleming. ESRI Press, Redlands, CA.

Class Action Complaint. 2010. Electronic Privacy Information Center. Accessed October 17, 2014. https://epic.org/privacy/googlespyfi/Keyes.pdf.

CrimeReports. 2013. "Screenshot of the View of Lower Manhattan." Accessed September 25, 2013. https://www.crimereports.com/.

Francica, Joe. 2011. "A Look Back at 9/11 and GIS in NYC–An Interview with Al Leidner, New York City's GIS Director in 2001." *Directions Magazine,* September. Accessed October 17, 2014. http://www.directionsmag.com/podcasts/podcast-gis-and-9-11-an-interview-with-al-leidner-new-york-citys-gis-d/198245.

GIS Monitor. 2001. "GIS in the Trenches." *Professional Surveyor Magazine,* September 27. Accessed October 17, 2014. http://www.profsurv.com/magazine/article.aspx?i=70632.

Google. 2014. "Behind the Scenes – Street View." Accessed October 17, 2014. http://www.google.com/maps/about/behind-the-scenes/streetview.

Google Maps. 2013. "A Map of Washington D.C. from Google Maps." Accessed October 23, 2013. https://maps.google.com/maps?q=Washington,+DC&hl=en&sll=38.833289,-76.934509&sspn=1.362839,2.779541&oq=washing&hnear=Washington,+District+of+Columbia&t=m&z=11.

Harley, J.B. and David Woodward. 1987. *The History of Cartography, Volume 1.* (First paragraph of Chapter 1.) Accessed October 17, 2014. http://www.press.uchicago.edu/books/HOC/HOC_V1/HOC_VOLUME1_chapter1.pdf.

Huxhold, William. 1991. *An Introduction to Urban Geographic Information Systems.* Oxford University Press, New York.

Kevany, Michael. 2011. "GIS in the World Trade Center Response: 10 Years After." *International Archives of the Photogrammetry, Remote Sensing and Spatial Information Sciences.* Vol. 38, No. 21. Pages 137–42. Accessed October 17, 2014. http://www.int-arch-photogramm-remote-sens-spatial-inf-sci.net/XXXVIII-4-C21/137/2011/isprsarchives-XXXVIII-4-C21-137-2011.pdf.

National Hurricane Center. 2013. "Screen Shot of a Map Hosted on the National Hurricane Center on 10/25/2013." Accessed October 25, 2013. http://www.nhc.noaa.gov/refresh/graphics_ep2+shtml/145641.shtml?tswind120#contents.

Psaty, Kyle. 2012. "Mayor's Office and MBTA 'Challenge' Local Developers; will they Heed the Call?" *Boston.com*, January 23.

National Oceanic and Atmospheric Administration (NOAA). 2014. "NOAA's Mission: Science, Service, and Stewardship." Accessed October 17, 2014. http://www.ppi.noaa.gov/mission/.

Robinson, Brian. 2002. "GIS Vision Fades at Local Level." *FCW*, May 16. Accessed October 17, 2014. http://fcw.com/Articles/2002/05/16/GIS-vision-fades-at-local-level.aspx?Page=2.

Sarkar, Dibya. 2003. "Local Governments Use GIS." *FCW*, December 11. Accessed October 17, 2014. http://fcw.com/articles/2003/12/10/local-governments-use-gis.aspx.

SeeClickFix.com. 2014. "A Screen Shot of the Government Management." Accessed October 17, 2014. http://gov.seeclickfix.com/.

Shark, Alan. 2012. *Seven Trends That Will Transform Local Government Through Technology.* Public Technology Institute, Alexandria, VA. Page 112.

Thomas, Christopher, Brian Parr, and Britney Hinthorne. 2012. "Saving Livestock Saves Millions." *Measuring Up: The Business Case for GIS.* Esri Press, Redlands, CA. Page 8.

United States Geological Survey. 2007. "What is a GIS?" Accessed October 17, 2014. http://webgis.wr.usgs.gov/globalgis/tutorials/what_is_gis.htm.

Digital Destinations

American City and County website. http://www.americancityandcounty.com

Centers for Disease Control and Prevention. http://nccd.cdc.gov/dhdspatlas/viewer.aspx?state=NJ

ESRI. http://www.esri.com/industries/government/federal

———. http://www.esri.com/industries/localgov

———. http://www.esri.com/industries/stategov

LiDAR. http://lidar.cr.usgs.gov/

National Oceanic and Atmospheric Administration (NOAA). http://www.noaa.gov/index.htmlNational

Recovery.gov. http://www.recovery.gov/arra/Transparency/Pages/Maps.aspx

US Geological Survey. http://www.usgs.gov/

9 Assessing and Measuring IT Performance

The printing press was arguably the beginning of the information revolution, so it's possible to argue Johannes Gutenberg was the grandfather of modern IT. When Gutenberg invented the moveable type printing press, his first project, in 1454, was a reproduction of the Bible (Kovarik 2011). Gutenberg invented the press to serve a specific purpose: more widely distributing something that already existed—books. Gutenberg was enabling the world's people to share volumes of information with one another for a far lower cost than had been possible previously. So, from the beginning, information technology was an enabler, catering to and supporting larger priorities.

Of course, electricity and, later, computing took information to new heights. The electric calculator enabled more reliable, more accurate calculations, but it did not make new calculations possible. The fundamentals of mathematics remained unchanged. The idea that the primary role of IT was, for centuries, focused on enabling improvements in communications came to a head in the late 1980s and early 1990s. In the decades leading up to that time, IT professionals were viewed as support players (Groysberg, Kelly, McDonald 2011). In the minds of many people who dealt with IT professionals, IT was about supporting pre-existing initiatives and enabling new efficiencies. The IT team was a silo, bolted onto its organization and treated like an afterthought by decision-makers in both the public and private sectors. Often, IT departments were kept out of sight, and only called upon to solve problems. In the decades leading up to the mid 1990s, IT was synonymous with the notion of the "help desk." It supported the business, like the cleaning staff that appeared after hours, but did not drive it.

However, in the late 1990s and early 2000s, the role of IT in the private sector began to shift. As the demand for computer-based efficiency emerged in the 1980s for-profit organizations began to bring IT into more conversations seeking greater solutions. It became critical for research and development, marketing, sales, product development, and other core functions of private sector businesses. Soon, IT leaders began to take positions in the executive suite. Chief Technical Officers (CTOs) and Chief Information Officers (CIOs) became commonplace. Meanwhile, the public sector, through a combination of inertia and uninitiated leadership, stayed the course, maintaining the status quo. An IT gap between the private and public sectors began to widen.

"Our IT people take their jobs very seriously."

Figure 9.1 IT is no longer a back-room operation

During the Obama Administration, the Performance.gov website, which was created to promote greater transparency among the federal government's branches and agencies, as well as the American people, states the following:

> The Federal government spends nearly eighty billion annually on information technology. This technology supports every mission our government performs—from defending our borders to protecting the environment. IT is essential for the government to do its work, and it is essential that we have access to the latest and most innovative technologies. However, compared to the technology-driven productivity gains seen in the private sector, the Federal government has not received commensurate return from its over $500 billion in IT investments over the past ten years. Under the leadership of the Federal Chief Information Officer (CIO), the Administration has led the effort to close the gap in effective technology use between the private and public sectors, create a more efficient Federal IT footprint, and more effectively secure our Federal assets.

When viewed as a whole, this excerpt demonstrates two things. First, that many in the public sector still see IT as a supporting player—not a star athlete in the game of advancement. Second, the excerpt acknowledges that in no uncertain terms the public sector is far behind the private with regard to performance and effectiveness. Many believe that the distance between public and private sector IT is continuing to widen. The problem is getting worse, not better. Plainly stated, this is a fact that nearly every public administrator will likely have to face in the coming decades.

Many believe that the distance between public and private sector IT is continuing to widen. The problem is getting worse, not better. Plainly stated, this is a fact that nearly every public administrator will likely have to face in the coming decades.

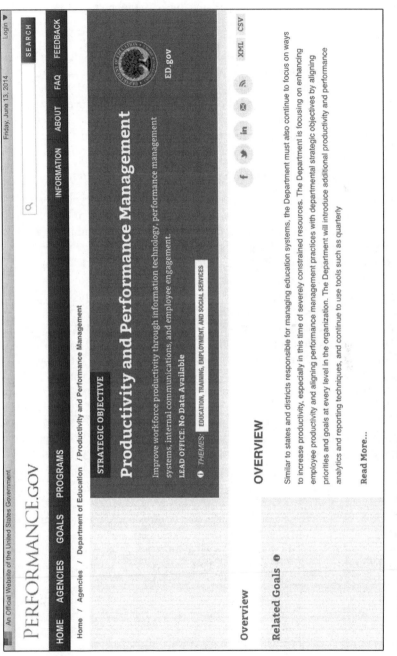

Figure 9.2 Performance.gov tracks federal IT productivity and performance

Source: Performance.gov website

However it is possible for public sector entities to stem the rising tide of comparative inefficiency. Although there are many steps government IT leaders can take to close the gap, perhaps the single biggest question these leaders are facing is how, exactly, to tell when government IT investments are successful, and more importantly, how to tell when they are beginning to go awry. As the private sector has learned, and many business leaders have espoused in one simple maxim, measurement is the key to management. In other words, if the public administrators of the future are interested in actively closing the public-private IT gap, or at least slowing the divergence, they'll need to first be able to successfully measure the productivity, performance, and efficiency of public sector IT. This, it turns out, is no easy task.

Exploration in Public Sector Performance Management

In order to candidly and directly discuss the concept of IT performance measurement, it helps to clearly define it. *Performance measurement* can be defined as, "measurement on a regular basis of the results (outcomes) and efficiency of services or programs" (Hatry 1999). To draw a simple analogy, the graded report cards children have long brought home with them from school at regular intervals is a great example of classic performance measurement. This is but one of three standard ways performance is measured in the private sector. Measurement can be performed against a standard such as an average, as is often the case with student report cards. It can be evaluated in the context of the competition in much the same way the rankings in a multi-day cycling race can be evaluated at any given moment during the race. Or, it can be performed against pre-defined goals, which might involve varying levels of collaboration between the evaluators and those being evaluated.

Performance measurement can be defined as "measurement on a regular basis of the results (outcomes) and efficiency of services or programs."
Source: Hatry 1999

The trouble with these forms of performance measurement in government is that every government, local, state, or federal, is unique in comparison to others. Measuring against a standard such as an average can introduce insurmountable flaws in the analysis. Similarly, without the ability to compare apples to apples, measurement against the so-called "competition" can also be quite troublesome. This leaves, as the sole option, measurement against stated goals. Unfortunately, in government, this can be as fluid a measuring stick as any that has ever been created. This is because setting pre-defined goals about what an IT team should be able to accomplish in a given time or with a given budget requires input from every stakeholder. Those being held accountable for the performance will almost invariably try to lower expectations during those discussions, while those charged with holding IT accountable on the other side of the table will be inclined to set the bar high to make the relative success of the project all the more convincing to elected officials and the public.

Standing in stark contrast to the fuzzy methods for measuring public sector performance are those used to gauge performance in the private sector. Although performance and productivity are not synonymous—*productivity* can be defined as the rate at which goods or services are delivered by a given organization—as long as free trade has existed, productivity measurement has been a great measure of effectiveness in the private sector. Even before the assembly line and other innovations drove productivity way up for many businesses, it was easy for a trader to look at how many outputs were produced, what the cost of producing those goods was, and how much revenue resulted from their sale in an effort to gauge effectiveness. Productivity is easy to measure in the private sector, because all businesses, in all markets, serving all manner of customers and clients, regardless of distinction between providing goods or services have had the ability to measure their productivity universally by calculating profits. This is not the case in the public sector, and that fact has resulted in both difficulty measuring public sector performance across entire governments and the deficit in governmental IT performance, as well. Simply put, "Private companies are driven by competition, and, regardless of the average productivity rate, high-achieving companies should out-compete lower-achieving ones. Such a performance lever is largely missing from government, which could have dramatic long-term consequences" (Wirtz 2001).

> "Private companies are driven by competition, and, regardless of the average productivity rate, high-achieving companies should out-compete lower-achieving ones. Such a performance lever is largely missing from government, which could have dramatic long-term consequences."
>
> Source: Wirtz 2001

Of course, these difficulties measuring the performance of government, and in turn, government IT, have not prevented those in the United States federal government from trying to measure performance.

The Federal Productivity Measurement Program (FPMP)

The Federal Productivity Measurement Program operated from 1967 to 1994, and gathered productivity metrics for a wide range of federal offices and agencies over that twenty-seven year period (Fisk and Forte 1997). Launching at a time when private sector productivity and performance were under close scrutiny by business leaders hoping to compete with a more global economy, the FPMP marked the first large-scale effort to measure productivity across the federal government. For the sake of consistency, productivity was measured in terms of outputs. "The procedure was to apply fixed, base-year labor weights—specifically, unit labor requirements—to each output activity and sum the results" (Fisk and Forte 1997).

As part of the FPMP, each federal agency with 200 employees or more was asked to provide data annually on its outputs, as well as the labor used to produce those outputs and the compensation paid to the employees producing those outputs (Fisk and Forte 1997). In theory, this extension of the way many private businesses measure productivity—through return-on-investment (ROI) analysis—was meant to help evaluators and federal agency leaders compare like measures across organizations, or at least within the same organization, as time passed.

Although oversight of the project was managed by a number of different federal organizations over the years, including the Office of Management and Budget (OMB), which was the original agency tasked with coordinating the effort, the analysis remained fairly consistent for two decades. Over the course of the project, about 69 percent of executive branch civilian employees were represented in the research (Fisk and Forte 1997). Five indexes were measured as part of this exploratory effort in hopes of painting a picture of the federal government's overall productivity (Fisk and Forte 1997):

1. Output
2. Labor input
3. Compensation per employee year
4. Output per employee year
5. Unit labor cost.

These measures strived to quantify the value the federal government provides to the American people in a clear, relatable way. How much work did a specific service require? How expensive was it to pay those workers? What were they producing, as individuals and whole organizations? These were the questions the FPMP sought to answer. Unfortunately, the difficulty in measuring productivity and performance by simple ROI calculations such as these can be felt in these realms, as well.

A World Apart: Comparing Public and Private Productivity

The FPMP taught federal leaders a great deal about where specific difficulties arise in public sector performance management. First, the simple fact that much government business is not delivered in exchange for revenue (nor does it have a clear cut total cost) causes fundamental problems in attempts to measure productivity. What is the value of the services each branch of the United States military delivers? What is the cash value of what a city mayor accomplishes in a given year?

Donald Fisk and Darlene Forte, two former directors of the FPMP put a fine point on this challenge in an article they authored for the May, 1997 issue of *Monthly Labor Review*, a publication aimed at documenting key labor-related learning that has been circulated by the Bureau of Labor Statistics (BLS) since 1915. The article was titled, "The Federal Productivity Measurement Program: Final Results." Wrote the authors,

> Unlike the situation in the private sector, where there are streams of prices and revenues, it is not possible to measure government output (with the possible exception of enterprise services) using a deflated-value technique (in which revenue is divided by price to yield a quantity measure).

Another critical point of differentiation noted by the authors relates to the fact that businesses can typically calculate output succinctly where public sector organizations cannot. Output, or the total goods and services produced by a specific organization, can be very difficult or even impossible to measure in the public sector, because so much of what government provides are services. For example, how does one measure the output of a state police force, where fewer arrests are certainly a goal, but fewer arrests might actually make that police force look less productive?

---

[b]usinesses can typically calculate output succinctly where public sector organizations cannot. Output, or the total goods and services produced by a specific organization, can be very difficult or even impossible to measure in the public sector, because so much of what government provides are services.

Source: Fisk and Forte 1997

The FPMP stuck to its original output-based plan for nearly three decades despite obvious indicators that its strict definition of productivity was limiting the view of the project's analysts. Fisk and Forte (1997) go on to explain that a lack of output clarity was just one of the factors that prohibited federal agencies from participating in the FPMP: "The decision whether to include an agency in the data base reflected the availability of organizational data, how well the conceptual questions concerning the measurement of the agency's output could be resolved, and the organization's willingness to participate."

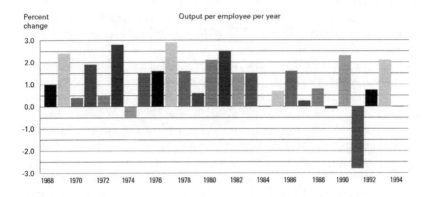

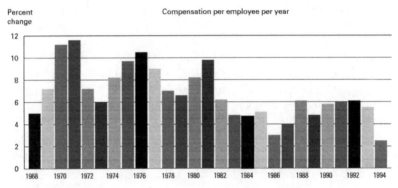

Figure 9.3 Performance.gov example of productivity per employee

Source: Performance.gov website

It's clear that any efforts to measure the productivity of government should be more holistic, and that the concept of clear cut outputs may well be an example of something that works well for the private sector, which the public sector cannot learn from. In some ways, productivity is now viewed as only a small piece of the puzzle in the private sector as well. Performance measurement is, by most definitions, meant to provide more clarity about what is provided, not what is produced, and so performance measurement involves the more complex task of addressing more than just outputs. It must also attempt to understand outcomes. This is a subtle distinction, but an important one. In fact, some economists view productivity measurement as but one piece of the greater puzzle of performance measurement.

> Performance measurement is, by most definitions, meant to provide more clarity about what is provided, not what is produced, and so performance measurement involves the more complex task of addressing more than just outputs. It must also attempt to understand outcomes.

"[Productivity] is, in some ways, subsumed by a broader current effort called performance measurement, which is intended to gauge social and other benefits brought about by government programs and spending," says Ronald Wirtz (2001).

The FPMP served leaders by teaching them about measuring productivity (and the larger measures associated with overall performance), but unfortunately, the data collected didn't result in many changes to the operations of the participating organizations. It was a fact-finding mission. Even with all the learning the FPMP uncovered with regard to public sector productivity measurement, it did little to illuminate how the public sector might think about productivity measurement in IT. However, there was one insightful revelation about IT's relationship to productivity in the *Monthly Labor Review* article referenced earlier, which again was published in 1997. Fisk and Forte write, "The computer was often cited as the driving force behind the increasing output per employee year." (Fisk and Forte 1997). By the time the FPMP project lost funding, it had become clear that IT advancement tends to improve productivity across the enterprise as it does in finance and accounting (Fisk and Forte 1997).

IT Performance in Focus: Regulations for the Computer Age

The productivity and performance measurement revelations the FPMP supplied to government leaders across the public sector as a whole certainly applied and still apply to government IT. But beyond those general lessons, another exploratory initiative running concurrently for almost as long put a specific emphasis on IT. The Office of Technology Assessment (OTA) sought to uncover the potential value IT could bring to the federal government, and in turn, state and local governments too.

The Office of Technology Assessment

The OTA was a Congressional office that operated from 1972 to 1995, which existed to help Congressional members and committees understand complex technologies. It served as an internal consulting group of sorts, providing thought leadership about how to leverage technology and innovation to improve public services and increase efficiency (Daly 2013).

A group of six Senate members and six House members, each consisting of three republicans and three democrats, presided over the OTA during its twenty-three years as an agency. This so-called Technology Assessment Board also included a nonvoting director (Daly 2013). Together, this group and the rest of the agency produced over 750 reports on a wide range of issues facing science and technology during the OTA's existence (Daly 2013).

Although these reports added a great deal of insight to federal decision making, the OTA's funding was not renewed and the office was shut down on September 29, 1995. Critics of the OTA argued it was a duplication of efforts being undertaken by other agencies in an era where everyone had a responsibility to understand how technology might impact decisions. Proponents argued the OTA was positioned to help the public sector adapt to the advancing Internet Age. Although the OTA was dissolved, its end raised public discourse about the federal government's responsibility to keep up with technology. That same discourse helped the federal government move forward in the next decade-and-a-half.

> Although the OTA was dissolved, its end raised public discourse about the federal government's responsibility to keep up with technology. That same discourse helped the federal government move forward in the next decade-and-a-half.

In the years leading up to and immediately following the retirement of the FPMP and the OTA, a veritable tsunami of new legislation set new rules and expectations about federal productivity and performance management. All of this reform was aimed at improving management, efficiency, and accountability. New best practices also emerged, as well as initiatives designed to help save money across the federal government through the adoption of standards and universal approaches to technology.

Moving Forward in Pursuit of Performance Management and Technology

Much of the federal legislation that passed in the last decade of the 20th century applied to the way IT investments were made and maintained, and additional thinking has yielded improved results in the realm of IT performance measurement that has already echoed through the state and local levels of government. As the conversation about how IT can be most effective in government has unfolded, both inside chamber walls and outside of them, the added value IT can offer as a core department in an organization has gained popular awareness. IT managers have moved into the C-Suite as CIOs and CTOs, and IT is being integrated more wholly across organizations at every level.

Of primary importance is contemporary thinking around the simple fact that IT projects applied to increase efficiency and performance across an entire government or agency are much more effective in moving the needle than single projects aimed at treating the problems of individual departments. This aligns with the takeaways from the FPMP that implied more comprehensive metrics—metrics related to outcomes more than outputs—should be adopted. While it's true that innovation often happens in small steps, patchwork solutions don't work to move an organization forward as a whole. Investments that act as temporary Band-Aids to spot treat problems, ignoring larger organizational impairments, have been widely vilified at all levels of government—and for good reason.

IT Investments for the Whole Enterprise

The concept of enterprise-wide IT is no longer novel. For example, Shannon Tufts writes, "State governments throughout the United States are using enterprise approaches to achieve high levels of return on investments, greater customer satisfaction, and increased cost-savings" (Tufts 2011). Much of the work IT departments do still enables greater efficiencies for processes that were established long before the Internet Age took hold. But many organizations no longer view IT solely as an enabler of efficiency. Enterprise IT leaders can make a big impact when strategy leverages economies of scale by delivering comprehensive technology solutions across an organization. Today, IT leaders can jump in the driver's seat, creating or influencing the purchase of technology designed to revolutionize an organization, to drive it forward. This new attitude towards IT and the new position it's taken in the enterprise is due to a number of compounding factors, including legislation, the development of strong IT leadership in government, and influence and learning from the private sector.

Let's explore some of the new points of focus that organizations in both sectors have targeted in an effort to continue the development of standard methods for achieving efficiency in IT.

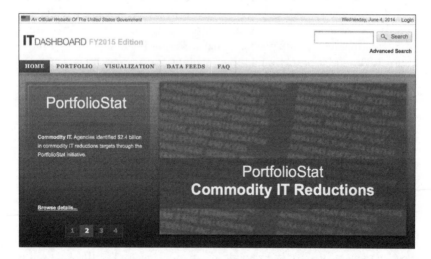

Figure 9.4 IT Dashboard.gov; good source to view IT performance statistics

Source: IT Dashboard website

Governance

In order to ensure alignment, public sector organizations at all levels have developed scorecards to guide decision-making. Sound governance ensures that the right people are incorporated into the decision-making process. It promotes clear identification of decision-making rights for IT investments, as well as outlining clear processes under which IT decisions can be made (NASCIO 2008). Key areas of focus on the topic of governance include but are not limited to the following (Office of the State Auditor of Colorado 2012):

1. Strategic Alignment
2. Value Delivery
3. Resource Management
4. Risk Management
5. Performance Measurement.

Accountability

As higher-level IT leaders have emerged in government, accountability has become a bigger priority for IT than it ever was before. In order for IT to play a critical role in the business of government, IT leaders and their managers must be willing to assume responsibility in the same way leaders in more traditional roles do. A handful of pieces of legislation that were passed in the 1990s were designed to improve performance accountability across the board, impacting IT performance and accountability. First, the Chief Financial Officers Act (1990) established CFOs in federal agencies and created greater accountability for the finances of each federal agency. Also, the Government Performance and Results Act (1993) required agencies to think more strategically and to take steps to better measure performance. Finally, the Government Management Reform Act (1994) was established, calling for agency financial statements and a government-wide financial statement that reflect results. The Government Performance and Results Act broke new ground by requesting that federal agencies:

1. Develop five-year strategic plans with mission statement and long-term goals.
2. Document yearly performance goals.
3. Prepare annual performance reports.

Investing Wisely

Procurement reform has been a hot topic in public sector IT offices, as well as the offices of private vendors with the capabilities to serve the federal state and local governments. The federal government has suffered the most. As a result, legislators have enacted a great deal of procurement reforms in recent decades.

The Federal Acquisition Streamlining Act (1994) shifted procurement strategy from lowest bid to best value, which helped to ensure that more of the technology the government invests in is cutting edge and will not be obsolete the moment it's delivered. The Act clearly articulated a mandate for continued value-based performance evaluation during the design and build phases, as well as in later support stages of a given contract. The Act states that, "the head of each executive agency should achieve, on average, ninety percent of the cost and schedule goals for major and non-major acquisition programs of the agency without reducing the performance or capabilities of the items being acquired." In other words, even if federal agencies cannot gauge the relative success or failure of their vendors by clear competitive measures, these agencies should at the very least hold vendors accountable for delivering what was promised.

Later, the Clinger-Cohen Act (1996) introduced federal IT reforms for acquiring, using, and eliminating technologies, paving the way for the Federal Enterprise Architecture—a universal, federal-wide plan for closing the private-public IT gap—in 1999. The Clinger-Cohen Act made enterprise-wide performance and strategic alliance a priority for federal IT. The Act also mandated that all agencies appoint a CIO to be the central person accountable for IT efforts, and established a series of responsibilities designed to promote governance, accountability, and architecture within the organization (NASA Audit Report 2000).

Enabling Success

Another major priority for many public and private sector IT leaders has been to pass legislation that creates new freedoms for them to make the right decisions. Additionally, both sectors have witnessed the establishment of organizations designed to share best practices in an effort to share knowledge and learning about IT management. The National Association of State CIOs (NASCIO) and other governmental organizations are playing a key role in supporting successful performance management at various levels. Additionally, the Federal Financial Management Improvement Act (1996) helps agencies monitor their own budgets, and thus their performance, by providing better support to help them compare spending to results.

Avoiding Unintended Consequences

Finally, individuals inside and outside of government organizations have promoted ongoing discussions focusing on the ethical obligation of policy makers to take steps to ensure ostensibly beneficial technologies aren't also going to result in pollution, public health risks, or social degradation (Malloy 2013). Of course unintended consequences cannot always be foreseen, but this does not mean IT leaders shouldn't turn over every stone as a project ramps up in an effort to prevent them.

Classic Business Metrics and the Big Picture

Given these new points of focus, all of which are areas government IT leaders are targeting for measurement and improvement, it's clear that enterprise-wide IT has come a long way since the FPMP kicked off in 1967. These are more sweeping and strategic targets, and each of them poses its own confounding factors for a given organization. As a result, leaders may find them too nebulous to grasp and too daunting to attempt to measure and optimize. However, they evolved from the need for a more outcome-based approach to management, and there are less complex ways of approaching IT performance measurement and management, which extend classic performance measurement approaches.

Writes Tufts (2011),

> As technology investments become more mission-critical and given budgetary pressures to reduce government expenditures, CIOs must embrace other aspects of performance measurement, such as service quality, outcomes and financial impact (cost-benefit). These metrics will provide accurate and reliable information about the true value and return on investments associate with IT investments to senior elected and appointed officials.

As technology investments become more mission-critical and given budgetary pressures to reduce government expenditures, CIOs must embrace other aspects of performance measurement, such as service quality, outcomes and financial impact (cost-benefit). These metrics will provide accurate and reliable information about the true value and return on investments associate with IT investments to senior elected and appointed officials.

Source: Tufts 2011

It is possible to extend classic concepts like *costs*, defined as initial investments plus ongoing expenses over the life of a project, and *benefits*, defined in financial terms as a representation of all monetary and non-monetary achievements, into more progressive targets of measurement (Tufts 2011). Classic business case metrics like these can be dangerous when deployed as the sole performance indicator, because managers will inevitably make decisions intended to satisfy those performance metrics; it's easy to lose

Figure 9.5 Performance metrics are required to better assess IT project accountability

focus on the bigger picture of government services when the only metric being evaluated does not promote the improvement of every aspect of those services.

In an attempt to dissuade staff from becoming fixated on simple, classic business case metrics, refined classic examples of business measures can be used, like *total cost of ownership* (TCO), which the research firm Gartner defines as, "a comprehensive assessment of information technology or other costs across enterprise boundaries over time" (Gartner 2014). In many cases, attempts to quantify and sum costs across the full lifetime of an investment are made in an effort to ensure a TCO metric is comprehensive. Return on investment (ROI) is another comprehensive, classic example of business metrics that attempt to measure effectiveness and efficiency across a whole enterprise. Gartner defines ROI as, "financial gain expressed as a percentage of funds invested to generate that gain." Metrics like these can help align the efforts of a staff with the holistic goals of the organization—curbing the tendency of individuals to lose sight of the organization's strategic mission and big picture goals.

Value–Based Performance Metrics for the Public Sector

While the private sector can provide valuable insight into the development of more successful IT projects and initiatives, the public sector faces unique challenges when it comes to performance measurement (as was discussed earlier in this chapter). As a result, tomorrow's public administrators may need to find metrics that are better suited as public sector indicators of success or failure. In government, where success must be measured by outcomes and not just outputs, value-based metrics like internal effectiveness, internal efficiency, customer satisfaction, and learning and innovation have been promoted by thinkers like Tufts (2011).

Whether tomorrow's public administrators attempt to measure IT performance by simple, classic methods, by their extensions, by value-based metrics, by more nebulous metrics, or by any combination of these, enterprise analysis of IT performance certainly requires a dedication to rigor, full buy-in on the idea that enterprise architecture is a superior approach, and a willingness by all stakeholders to set reasonable, rational goals for IT. This will ensure that the goals put forth at the outset of a project are attainable in the eyes of all stakeholders, and also enable the measurement of success against those pre-idefined goals.

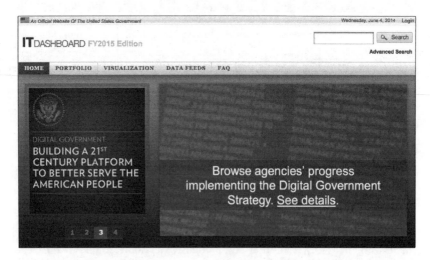

Figure 9.6 IT Dashboard.gov

Source: IT Dashboard website

The Process of IT Management

Given the many attempts to control IT performance in terms of costs and effectiveness there appears to be a greater emphasis on a holistic approach that, when combined as a whole, provides future public managers with a new framework for action. There are perhaps five areas that are all inherently related which are:

1. **Better upfront IT planning.**
   Many programs experience failures due to poor planning either from unrealistic Congressional or administrative mandates, lack of time to adequately plan, and/or poorly trained staff.
2. **More intelligent IT purchasing decisions.**
   The procurement of IT services (hardware and software) is often burdened with overly complicated purchasing requirements that tend to favor larger tech companies at the expense of smaller ones with perhaps a greater potential for success. Recent e-procurement polices have improved the process and provide for greater flexibility.
3. **Greater IT program and project transparency.**
   Opening up the process to the public is certainly a growing trend in the federal government as well as state and local governments too. Many states and localities provide open data portals that provide the public with information on how well projects are doing, budget projections, and sometimes flag problems. Nonprofit organizations such as the Center for Effective Government and Citizens Against Government Waste serve as a watchdog for the general public. On the federal front, with the initiation of IT Dashboard, Data.gov and Performance.gov the public now has a better idea as to how well their government is doing than ever before. There is certainly room for improvement in terms of timeliness and accuracy of information, but these initiatives are a great start.
4. **Better project and program management.**
   There is a growing recognition for more government employees to be better trained as well as certified in program and project management in order to assist them in carrying out their staff responsibilities.
5. **Built-in continuous monitoring and evaluation.**
   Performance measurement generally, and more particularly in IT management, is gaining in attention as new metrics and key performance indicators are increasingly becoming more common than not. Most Congressional initiatives require that agencies report how well their projects are doing on a routine basis.

Finally, the General Accountability Office (GAO) has issued numerous reports that evaluate various aspects of program and project effectiveness. GAO reports and studies are generally regarded as both excellent and comprehensive. The

Figure 9.7 Performance.gov

Source: IT Dashboard website

Office of Management and Budget (OMB) is also involved in improving IT management, as is the Federal CIO Council.

The Future Of IT Performance Management

In the beginning, IT was an enabler. This will still be true in the future, as new efficiencies are made possible through technology. But in the future, IT will also play a much bigger strategic role in guiding the activities and efforts of governments at all levels. Thanks to state and federal governments creating many best practices in IT performance management, local governments will be able to deploy IT in smarter, more comprehensive ways, measuring its effectiveness and the efficiency it creates through a tailored dashboard of metrics. Classic business case metrics will be taken into account, but more holistic measures will deliver quality services by aligning with the true goals of government. The idea that there is one simple way to measure IT performance will have been abandoned, and a greater number of public administrators will be knowledgeable about the range of metrics at their disposal. In performance management, goals will be set, metrics will be tracked, and perhaps even a new central agency like the OTA will be tasked with ensuring accountability and advising the public sector on technology investments. Procurement rules will allow room for smaller players to win contracts, while also doing a better job of holding vendors of all sizes accountable for their performance. The performance of vendors will certainly still roll up into the performance of the IT department responsible for managing those vendors. Procurement and decisions to sustain technologies or sunset them will be

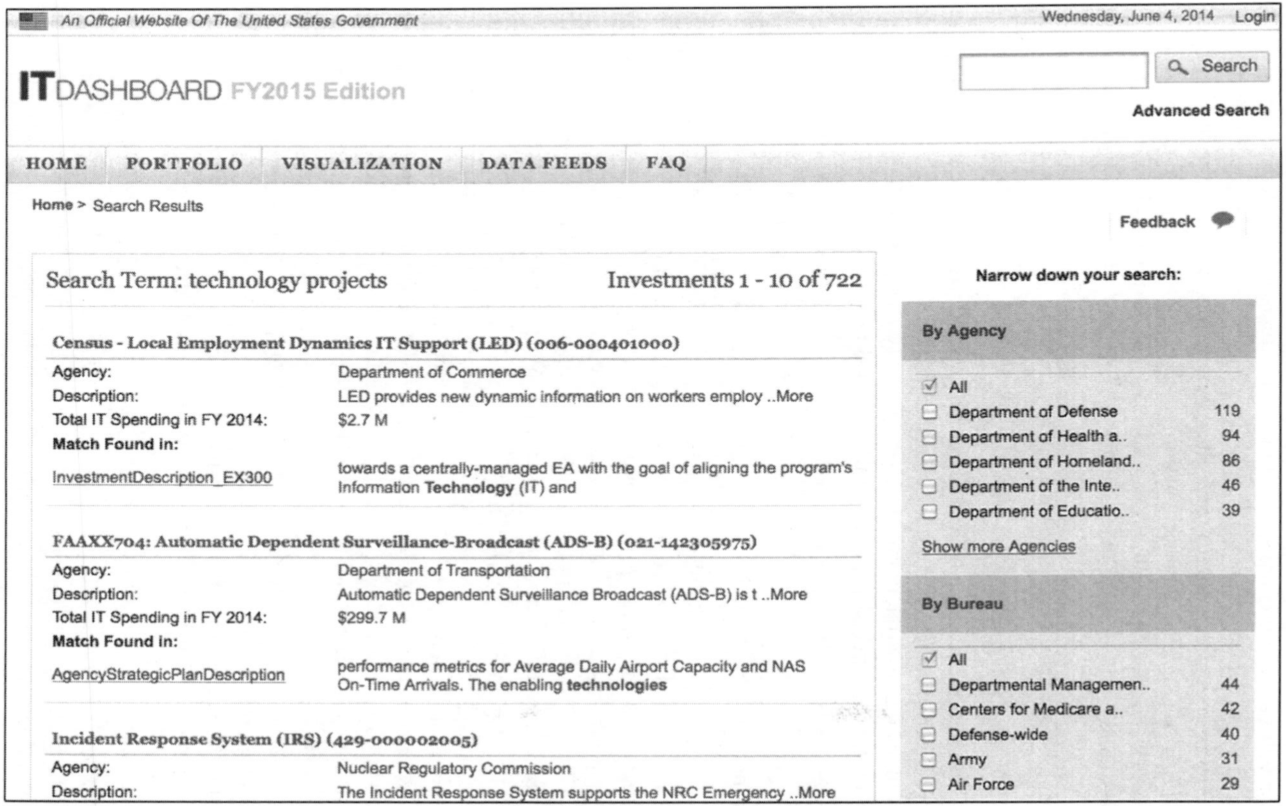

Figure 9.8 IT Dashboard.gov, example of IT investments

Source: IT Dashboard website

based more on metrics and performance than political agendas. The private sector will take a more active role in enabling increased efficiency through technology at all governmental levels. The gap between public and private sector efficiency will begin to close after decades of gaping ever wider. With continued dialogues, relentless pursuit of better performance metrics, and more private sector insights on the horizon, the future of IT performance measurement, and in turn, management, will be much brighter.

Thanks to state and federal governments creating many best practices in IT performance management, local governments will too be able to deploy IT in smarter, more comprehensive ways, measuring its effectiveness and the efficiency it creates through a tailored dashboard of metrics.

Discussion Questions

1. Describe the role IT played in the early stages of its evolution as a department in both private and public sector organizations.
2. What are the three general approaches to performance measurement that can be applied to a wide range of scenarios and evaluations?
3. What is the name of the productivity management project that measured executive branch outputs from 1967 to 1994?
4. Fill in the blanks: Outputs are typically evaluated as part of _____ measurement while the more holistic measure of outcomes is associated with _____ measurement.
5. What are three points of focus that have resulted from a more universal adoption of enterprise-wide IT in government?
6. Define costs and benefits, and describe the relationship they share to one another.
7. What is the risk of relying solely on simplistic, classic business case metrics?
8. Describe the benefits of value-based performance metrics, and explain what sets them apart from classic business case metrics.

References

Daly, Jimmy. 2013. "The Forgotten Office of Technology Assessment." *FedTech*, December 2. Accessed October 17, 2014. http://www.fedtechmagazine.com/article/2013/12/forgotten-office-technology-assessment.

Federal Acquisition Streamlining Act. 1994. Bill. Subtitle B, Part A. Accessed October 17, 2014. http://www.gpo.gov/fdsys/pkg/BILLS-103s1587enr/pdf/BILLS-103s1587enr.pdf.

Fisk, Donald and Darlene Forte. 1997. "The Federal Productivity Measurement Program: Final Results" *Monthly Labor Review*, May. Page 19. Accessed October 17, 2014. http://www.bls.gov/mfp/mprff97.pdf.

Groysberg, Boris, Kevin L. Kelly, and Bryan McDonald. 2011. "The New Path to the C-Suite." *Harvard Business Review*, March. Accessed October 17, 2014. http://hbr.org/2011/03/the-new-path-to-the-c-suite/ar/1.

Hatry, Harry. 1999. *Performance Measurement: Getting Results.* Urban Institute Press, Washington, DC. Page 3.

Kovarik, Bill. 2011. *Revolutions in Communication: Media History from Gutenberg to the Digital Age.* The Continuum International Publishing Group, New York. Page 18.

Malloy, Timothy. 2013. "Integrating Technology Assessment into Government Technology Policy." UCLA School of Law Research Papers Nos. 13–18. Accessed October 17, 2014. http://papers.ssrn.com/sol3/papers.cfm?abstract_id=2288158.

NASA Audit Report. 2000. "Audit Report: NASA's Organizational Structure for Implementing the Clinger-Cohen Act." July 17. Page 2. Accessed October 17, 2014. http://oig.nasa.gov/audits/reports/FY00/pdfs/ig-00-038.pdf.

NASCIO. 2008. "IT Governance and Business Outcomes—A Shared Responsibility between IT and Business Leadership." National Association of State CIOs. Page 2. Accessed October 17, 2014. http://www.nascio.org/publications/documents/NASCIO-ITGovernanceBusinessOutcomes.pdf.

Office of the State Auditor of Colorado. 2012. "Information Technology in Colorado State Government." August. Page 4. Accessed October 17, 2014. http://www.leg.state.co.us/OSA/coauditor1.nsf/All/9B472AB97A36350C87257A5C007AE62C/$FILE/2185%20IT%20in%20State%20Final%20Aug%2016%20KM.pdf.

Tufts, Shannon. 2011. "Measuring Technology Investment Success and Impact" ed. Alan Shark in *CIO Leadership for State Governments—Emerging Trends and Practices.* PTI, Alexandria, VA. Page 220.

Wirtz, Ronald. 2001. "Icebergs and Government Productivity." *Fedgazette*, June 1. Accessed October 17, 2014. http://www.minneapolisfed.org/publications_papers/pub_display.cfm?id=3446.

Digital Destinations

CAGW. http://www.marketwatch.com/story/cagw-releases-statement-on-2014-gao-report-on-federal-software-licenses-2014-05-23

CBO. http://www.cbo.gov/topics/results?topic=178&field_display_pubtype_value_many_to_one=All&congressional_session=All&budget_function=All

CIO Council. https://cio.gov/deliver/techstat/https://cio.gov/performance-metrics-and-measures/

Energy. http://energy.gov/cio/downloads/basic-performance-measures-technology-projects

GAO. http://gao.gov/products/GAO-04-49

———. http://gao.gov/modules/ereport/handler.php?m=1&p=1&path=/ereport/GAO-14-343SP/data_center_savings/Information_technology/24._Information_Technology_Investment_Portfolio_Management

Gartner IT Glossary. http://www.gartner.com/it-glossary/total-cost-of-ownership-tco

IT Dashboard. https://www.itdashboard.gov/

OMB. http://www.whitehouse.gov/sites/default/files/omb/assets/memoranda_2010/m10-27.pdf

OMB Watch/Center for Effective Government. http://www.foreffectivegov.org/search?keys=IT+Performance

Performance.gov. http://technology.performance.gov/

10 Network and Cybersecurity

Every day modern society as we know it becomes increasingly dependent on being connected to the Internet through a vast array of networks. It follows then—the more we become dependent—the more we have to lose if something were to go wrong due to a deliberate act of sabotage, someone's ignorance, criminal activity, or perhaps an act of God, or even an act of war. This chapter will examine the critical importance regarding what public managers must do to better protect our nation's digital infrastructure. The days of simply relying on a data processing manager to ensure security on a local network have long since gone. Today's environment requires a new form of governance; one that relies on shared responsibility. In 2009,

Figure 10.1 Cybersecurity awareness is everyone's responsibility

President Obama declared the cyber threat to be "one of the most serious economic and national security challenges we face as a nation" and also stated "America's economic prosperity in the 21st century will depend on cybersecurity" (White House 2009).

In 2009, President Obama declared the cyber threat to be "one of the most serious economic and national security challenges we face as a nation" and also stated "America's economic prosperity in the 21st century will depend on cyber security" (White House 2009).

Network and Cybersecurity

Network and cybersecurity are often used interchangeably and are certainly related but also quite different. Let's begin with the term "network." In simpler times a network might have described a computer system mostly isolated from the outside environment. It would have been nearly and entirely self-contained—except perhaps for a central connection to another source via a cable or high-speed telephone line. Today, computer networks are comprised of numerous interconnected systems with most connecting to and through the Internet. Access to the Internet can be made from almost any workstation and from every smart mobile device, be it a phone, laptop, or tablet. All Internet traffic is carried over many networks spanning the globe; often with a trip or two via a satellite connection, along fiber pathways, underground and above ground, to and from one destination to another within milliseconds. With the growth of connection points comes added risk.

Every network, regardless of type, has some form of security built into it, whether it is hardware or software or both. There is also the need for human intervention and constant monitoring and evaluation. Cybersecurity has become the term of choice to describe the overarching focus on securing all aspects of the digital infrastructure, more or less the sum of its parts. Certainly one of the key elements of cybersecurity is the computer or communications network, or a combination of interconnected networks. According to the Merriam-Webster dictionary, cybersecurity is defined as *measures taken to protect a computer or computer system (as on the Internet) against unauthorized access or attack* (see Merriam-Webster website). Mr. Leon Panetta, former head of the CIA and Defense Department, warned in 2012 about the real potential for a Pearl Harbor type surprise cyber attack that could threaten our very existence without firing a conventional or nuclear weapon (Bumiller and Shanker 2012). Indeed, a number of leading politicians and military officials believe the next battle or war may be fought over a cyber attack. Moreover, the weapons that will be used will involve cyber warfare as opposed to the use of conventional weapons.

In its Internet Security Report, Internet security company Symantec reported a 42 percent increase in targeted attacks in 2012. It also reported that

32 percent of all mobile device hacking resulted in the loss of information (see Symantic website). Panda Security reported that there were no less than 82,000 malware threats every day in 2003 (Bradley 2014). According to the *Cisco 2014 Security Report*, attacks are not only on the rise, but they are also becoming increasingly more sophisticated. The Cisco report states:

- Attacks against infrastructure are targeting significant resources across the Internet.
- Malicious actors are using trusted applications to exploit gaps in perimeter security.
- Investigations of multinational companies show evidence of internal compromise. Suspicious traffic is emanating from their networks and attempting to connect to questionable sites (100 percent of companies are calling malicious malware hosts) (Cisco 2014).

Between 2011 and 2013, every major newspaper in the US had been hacked—*The Wall Street Journal, The New York Times*, and *The Washington Post*. During this period Wells Fargo Bank, Bank of America, and Capital One Bank were also hacked. At the close of 2013, Target reported over Seventy million credit card records were hacked which eclipsed a large number of relatively smaller store hackings. Perhaps most disturbing is the fact that the CIA, the Pentagon, the State Department, and NASA have all been hacked in some form or fashion too. In some cases the attacks amounted to what is called a denial of service (DOS) attack where remote computers have been compromised and thus overwhelm websites rendering them useless. Other attacks have taken the form of what could be called *digital graffiti*. Some attacks that have been reported further highlight the potential for identity theft or the outright theft of funds. Not long ago, most cyber attacks went unreported. The reporting of security breaches was something to be avoided because there was a perceived stigma that revealing them was a sign of internal weakness and could lead to mistrust from citizens and or customers alike. Today, one finds a new culture where quite the opposite is true as most significant hacking does get reported which is highly encouraged by all authorities. The thinking here is that the more that gets reported, the more one can learn from each incident and where this information can be used and shared to help prevent similar attacks elsewhere.

Every moment of every day, all kinds of computer and mobile devices belonging to businesses, governments, and citizens are being probed for vulnerabilities, deficiencies, and weaknesses. People generally have a difficult time imaging how this can happen, mainly because they think as humans with all their limitations. However most attacks, while initially designed by humans, are actually carried out by software programs and botnets that automatically troll the Internet looking for opportunities or areas from which to exploit. This explains how such probing can occur with unmanageable frequency and speed. These types of malicious activities and programs never stop to eat or sleep.

Most attacks, while initially designed by humans, are actually carried out by software programs and botnets that automatically troll the Internet looking for opportunities or areas from which to exploit. This explains how such probing can occur with unmanageable frequency and speed.

In 2013 a security expert developed an experiment where they designed what looked like two very real water utilities that appeared in every fashion, as any water utility would appear on the Internet—with the exception that they were actually decoys. In a matter of hours they were discovered and probed. Over the experiment's 28-day appearance, researchers were able to document 39 attacks from among 14 nations, with some being quite serious. Had these water utilities been real, the attackers might have been able to compromise the systems which could have lead to stopping the pumps altogether, or modifying the pressure—each resulting in catastrophic system failure (Higgins 2013). Imagine the nation's electric generation stations, power grids, plus oil and gas utilities, and how such cyber tinkering could disrupt or destroy our way of life.

One of the strangest and disturbing hacker attacks occurred in February 2013 when the US Emergency Alert System (EAS), which serves as a secure national public warning system, was hacked into. In two separate but related attacks that occurred in Michigan and Montana, hackers were able to get into the EAS system and interrupt regular TV programming and began broadcasting an audio message alerting viewers, "bodies of the dead are rising from their graves and are attacking the living." Preceding the ominous message one could hear the unmistakable emergency alert tones. While somewhat amusing to some, what would have happened if the hackers had chosen something more believable which could have lead to local or national panic (Constantin 2013)? If this type of hack were to happen more frequently, perhaps with different false messages, the public would have no way of distinguishing the real from the unreal and render the EAS system practically useless. Just as disturbing, how could a secure federal emergency warning system be hacked into in the first place?

Most intrusions can be grouped into six areas; (1) people playing pranks on others or organizations, (2) defacing websites with digital graffiti or political propaganda, (3) malicious intent with the goal of harming others or corporate and or government interests, (4) criminal activity in order to steal trade secrets or extract money—credit card theft, embezzlement, and identity theft, (5) political intent to slander, embarrass, or disgrace a person or organization, perhaps with misinformation, (6) an enemy intent on sabotaging the critical infrastructure of a city, country, or nation.

What makes some of the attacks so frustrating is the ability for those with hostile intentions to be able to perform their actions under the cloak of anonymity while remaining largely hidden. Current laws that govern cyber intrusions have yet to keep up with the quickly changing landscape. Some attacks are known to have originated in nation-states where laws are lax or non-existent, and where governments are often reluctant or incapable of combating cyber crime.

What makes some of the attacks so frustrating is the ability for those with hostile intentions to be able to perform their actions under the cloak of anonymity while remaining largely hidden. Current laws that govern cyber intrusions have yet to keep up with the quickly changing landscape.

Many successful attacks have been made possible by flaws in systems that were once considered impenetrable, as well as human ignorance and carelessness, or people were simply unable to keep up with the latest protection systems and procedures. Recognizing the growth of cyber attacks against federal agencies and critical infrastructure, the GAO issued a report *Cyber Security—National Strategy, Roles, and Responsibilities Need to Be Better Defined and More Effectively Implemented* which included a set of recommendations for protecting federal infrastructure and agencies (GAO 2013).

As shown in Figure 10.2, the number of incidents reported by federal agencies to the US Computer Emergency Readiness Team had increased 782 percent from 2006 to 2012.

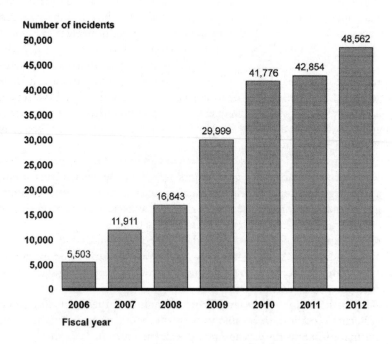

Figure 10.2 Incidents reported by federal agencies in fiscal years 2006–12

Source: GAO 2013

The GAO report examined federal government actions' pertaining to cybersecurity policies and directives from 2000 to 2012 and notes while much progress had been made over the years, there remain a number of troubling deficiencies.

The report summarizes the types of threats in three basic areas, which are:

- Threats to national security include those aimed against the systems and networks of the US government, including the US military, as well as private companies that support government activities or control critical infrastructure. These threats may be intended to cause harm for monetary gain or political or military advantage and can result, among other things, in the disclosure of classified information or the disruption of operations supporting critical infrastructure, national defense, or emergency services.
- Threats to commerce and intellectual property include those aimed at obtaining the confidential intellectual property of private companies, the US government, or individuals with the aim of using that intellectual property for economic gain. For example, product specifications may be stolen to facilitate counterfeiting and piracy or to gain a competitive edge over a commercial rival. In some cases, theft of intellectual property may also have national security repercussions, as when designs for weapon systems are compromised.
- Threats to individuals include those that lead to the unauthorized disclosure of personally identifiable information, such as taxpayer data, Social Security numbers, credit and debit card information, or medical records. The disclosure of such information could cause harm to individuals, such as identity theft, financial loss, and embarrassment (ibid.).

The GAO report points out that as of 2013 there is still no single document that comprehensively defines the nation's cybersecurity strategy. In its absence a number of key documents have been adopted that have served as a national strategy over the past decade. While the federal government's response to cybersecurity strategy has evolved over time, it is still not fully defined or implemented.

Federal agencies face many challenges from both internal as well as external sources. Most experts agree that implementing and maintaining sound security controls is of paramount importance in ensuring government agency systems are not compromised. Conversely, ineffective security controls and systems could lead to:

- loss of theft or resources, including money and intellectual property;
- inappropriate access to and disclosure, modification, or destruction of sensitive information;
- use of computer resources for unauthorized purposes or to launch attacks on other computer systems;
- damage to networks and computer equipment;
- loss of business due to lack of customer confidence;
- increased costs from remediation (GAO 2013).

The GAO identified and classified nine sources of cyber threats to Federal agencies and critical infrastructure. (GAO.gov).

Table 1: Sources of Adversarial Threats to Cybersecurity

Threat source	Description
Bot-network operators	Bot-network operators use a network, or bot-net, of compromised, remotely controlled systems to coordinate attacks and to distribute phishing schemes, spam, and malware attacks. The services of these networks are sometimes made available on underground markets (e.g., purchasing a denial-of-service attack or services to relay spam or phishing attacks).
Criminal groups	Criminal groups seek to attack systems for monetary gain. Specifically, organized criminal groups use spam, phishing, and spyware/malware to commit identity theft, online fraud, and computer extortion. International corporate spies and criminal organizations also pose a threat to the United States through their ability to conduct industrial espionage and large-scale monetary theft and to hire or develop hacker talent.
Hackers	Hackers break into networks for the thrill of the challenge, bragging rights in the hacker community, revenge, stalking, monetary gain, and political activism, among other reasons. While gaining unauthorized access once required a fair amount of skill or computer knowledge, hackers can now download attack scripts and protocols from the Internet and launch them against victim sites. Thus, while attack tools have become more sophisticated, they have also become easier to use. According to the Central Intelligence Agency, the large majority of hackers do not have the requisite expertise to threaten difficult targets such as critical U.S. networks. Nevertheless, the worldwide population of hackers poses a relatively high threat of an isolated or brief disruption causing serious damage.
Insiders	The disgruntled organization insider is a principal source of computer crime. Insiders may not need a great deal of knowledge about computer intrusions because their knowledge of a target system often allows them to gain unrestricted access to cause damage to the system or to steal system data. The insider threat includes contractors hired by the organization, as well as careless or poorly trained employees who may inadvertently introduce malware into systems.
Nations	Nations use cyber tools as part of their information-gathering and espionage activities. In addition, several nations are aggressively working to develop information warfare doctrine, programs, and capabilities. Such capabilities enable a single entity to have a significant and serious impact by disrupting the supply, communications, and economic infrastructures that support military power—impacts that could affect the daily lives of citizens across the country. In his January 2012 testimony, the Director of National Intelligence stated that, among state actors, China and Russia are of particular concern.
Phishers	Individuals or small groups execute phishing schemes in an attempt to steal identities or information for monetary gain. Phishers may also use spam and spyware or malware to accomplish their objectives.
Spammers	Individuals or organizations distribute unsolicited e-mail with hidden or false information in order to sell products, conduct phishing schemes, distribute spyware or malware, or attack organizations (e.g., a denial of service).
Spyware or malware authors	Individuals or organizations with malicious intent carry out attacks against users by producing and distributing spyware and malware. Several destructive viruses and worms have harmed files and hard drives, and reportedly have even caused physical damage to critical infrastructure, including the Melissa Macro Virus, the Explore.Zip worm, the CIH (Chernobyl) Virus, Nimda, and Code Red.
Terrorists	Terrorists seek to destroy, incapacitate, or exploit critical infrastructures in order to threaten national security, cause mass casualties, weaken the economy, and damage public morale and confidence. Terrorists may use phishing schemes or spyware/malware in order to generate funds or gather sensitive information.

Figure 10.3 Nine sources of cyber threats

Source: GAO analysis of data from the National Institute of Standards and Technology, United States Computer Emergency Readiness Team, and industry reports

At the end of December 2013, the third largest retailer in the US, Target, experienced a major security breach. Over forty million consumers' credit information was stolen and a total of seventy million customer records including addresses, telephone numbers, and other pieces of personal information were essentially stolen. According to published reports, Target's management was alerted days earlier to malware embedded in Target's payment systems. A year earlier, a high-tech security company was hired to monitor Target's network and detected the presence of malware. It was later discovered this breach occurred through a heating contractor's system working for Target. The security firm indeed detected something very sinister and sounded a series of alerts to Target's headquarters. As unexplainable as it sounds, Target's internal security executives failed to act, and it wasn't until the US Department of Justice notified the retailer about the breach that they began to react and

Table 2: Types of Cyber Attacks

Types of attack	Description
Cross-site scripting	An attack that uses third-party web resources to run a script within the victim's web browser or scriptable application. This occurs when a browser visits a malicious website or clicks a malicious link. The most dangerous consequences occur when this method is used to exploit additional vulnerabilities that may permit an attacker to steal cookies (data exchanged between a web server and a browser), log key strokes, capture screen shots, discover and collect network information, and remotely access and control the victim's machine.
Denial-of-service	An attack that prevents or impairs the authorized use of networks, systems, or applications by exhausting resources.
Distributed denial-of-service	A variant of the denial-of-service attack that uses numerous hosts to perform the attack.
Logic bombs	A piece of programming code intentionally inserted into a software system that will cause a malicious function to occur when one or more specified conditions are met.
Phishing	A digital form of social engineering that uses authentic-looking, but fake, e-mails to request information from users or direct them to a fake website that requests information.
Passive wiretapping	The monitoring or recording of data, such as passwords transmitted in clear text, while they are being transmitted over a communications link. This is done without altering or affecting the data.
Structured Query Language injection	An attack that involves the alteration of a database search in a web-based application, which can be used to obtain unauthorized access to sensitive information in a database.
Trojan horse	A computer program that appears to have a useful function, but also has a hidden and potentially malicious function that evades security mechanisms by, for example, masquerading as a useful program that a user would likely execute.
Virus	A computer program that can copy itself and infect a computer without the permission or knowledge of the user. A virus might corrupt or delete data on a computer, use e-mail programs to spread itself to other computers, or even erase everything on a hard disk. Unlike a worm, a virus requires human involvement (usually unwitting) to propagate.
War driving	The method of driving through cities and neighborhoods with a wireless-equipped computer—sometimes with a powerful antenna—searching for unsecured wireless networks.
Worm	A self-replicating, self-propagating, self-contained program that uses network mechanisms to spread itself. Unlike viruses, worms do not require human involvement to propagate.

Figure 10.4 GAO report of sources of adversarial threats to cybersecurity

Source: GAO analysis of data from the National Institute of Standards and Technology, United States Computer Emergency Readiness Team, and industry reports

reach out to their customers. The high-tech company Target had hired uses, among many things, a highly sophisticated system that operates a sandbox system that mimics Target's system and is therefore able to use sophisticated intrusion monitoring systems that can spot and isolate a problem before it enters the real system. As bad as the breach was, in the end, consumers still had the choice as to whether or not they wanted to continue shopping at Target. Early indications revealed that shoppers were angry and sales were significantly down.

In February 2014, 145 million eBay customers were placed at risk as hackers were able to get into the system thus causing eBay to issue a plea for each customer to change their password. It was later found that hackers were able to penetrate the eBay systems by exploiting weaknesses with passwords found in a few corporate employees' accounts. Unfortunately, the trend for hackers gaining access to systems is growing—and with each exposure seeming to dwarf the last.

Had these malware attacks affected a government agency, citizens might be angry, but unlike a retail store or online service provider experience, they lack the option to shop around for another government agency. In other words the consequences are far worse for government agencies. After all, democratic societies rely on trust.

The Target and eBay breaches will provide many lessons in the years to come, but it must not be overlooked that both companies utilized highly sophisticated monitoring systems, and in the case of Target, it appears a group of employees within its information technology department knew something was up—but failed to recognize the severity. Perhaps one lesson is that while it is important to have the best monitoring systems in place, one can never rely entirely upon other individuals or automated systems. The human element simply can't be overlooked and employees at all levels must be prepared to act swiftly and at all times. Cyber crime does not take breaks of any kind. For an excellent review of what happened at Target see Riley, Lawrence, and Matlack (2014).

> While it is important to have the best monitoring systems in place, one can never rely entirely upon other individuals or automated systems. The human element simply can't be overlooked and employees at all levels must be prepared to act swiftly and at all times.

Presidential and Congressional Initiatives (2000–14)

Since 2000, there are have been a number of key cybersecurity initiatives that have been promulgated by the President and Congress. In 2000, President Clinton issued the *National Plan for Information Systems Protection*. This plan served as an important first step in recognizing key threats against the nation's

Figure 10.5 Preventing cyber attacks has become a top priority for the federal government as well as the US Military

information systems as well as critical assets from future cyber attacks. The plan identified risks that were generally associated with the nation's growing dependence on computers and networks directly tied to critical services. This initiative recognized for the first time the need for the federal government to take a leadership role. The plan identified specific actions and milestones to help the federal government both prepare for and prevent cyber attacks.

The Federal Information Security Management Act of 2002 (FISMA), which was part of the E-Government Act of 2002, created a framework for ensuring the effectiveness of information security controls that support federal government operations. This Act assigned specific responsibilities to federal agencies, including the OMB and NIST. According to FISMA, the term information security means protecting information and information systems from unauthorized access, use, disclosure, disruption, modification, or destruction in order to provide integrity, confidentiality, and availability. FISMA required agency officials to conduct annual reviews of each agency's information security programs and report the results to the OMB. Other specific goals included:

- periodic assessments of the risk and magnitude of harm that could result from the unauthorized access, use, disclosure, disruption, modification, or destruction of information systems;

- policies and procedures that (1) are based on risk assessments, (2) cost-effectively reduce information security risks to an acceptable level; (3) ensure that information security is addressed throughout the lifecycle of each system; and (4) ensure compliance with applicable requirements;
- security awareness training to inform personnel of information security risks and their responsibilities in complying with agency policies and procedures, as well as training personnel with significant security responsibilities for information security;
- periodic testing and evaluation of the effectiveness of information security policies, procedures, and practices, to be performed with a frequency depending on risk, but no less than annually, and that includes testing of management, operational, and technical controls for every system identified in the agency's required inventory of major information systems;
- procedures for detecting, reporting, and responding to security incidents (GAO 2013).

Critics of FISMA have argued that the Act, with all its good intentions, was fundamentally flawed in that FISMA focused too much on measures for security planning as opposed to measuring information security. There is common agreement however, that despite its flaws, FISMA serves as a solid framework and foundation for further action.

In 2003, under President Bush, the *National Strategy to Secure Cyberspace* was released. This plan, while similar to its predecessor, provided a framework for organizing and prioritizing efforts to protect the nation from cyber attacks and outlined five national priorities, which are

1. Develop and maintain a National Cyberspace Security Response system.
2. Develop and maintain a National Cyberspace Threat and Vulnerability Reduction Program.
3. Develop and maintain a National Cybersecurity Awareness and Training program.
4. Secure Governments' Cyberspace.
5. Develop and maintain a National Security and International Cyberspace Security Cooperation.

Both the 2000 plan and the 2003 plan had much in common that demonstrated a rather consistent ongoing commitment towards cybersecurity planning.

During his second term in 2008, President Bush issued the *National Security Presidential Directive 54/Homeland Security Presidential Directive 23* that established what is now referred to as the Comprehensive National Cybersecurity Initiative (CNCI). The CNCI created a set of 12 projects all aimed at safeguarding the executive branch's information systems with the goal of reducing potential vulnerabilities, as well as protecting and anticipating future threats. The CNCI's 12 projects were:

1. **Trusted Internet Connections**: Reduce and consolidate external access points with the goal of limiting points of access to the Internet for executive branch civilian agencies.
2. **Einstein Two**: Deploy passive sensors across executive branch civilian systems that have the ability to scan the content of Internet packets to determine whether they contain malicious code.
3. **Einstein Three**: Pursue employment of an intrusion prevention system that will allow for real-time prevention capabilities that will assess and block harmful code.
4. **Research and Development Efforts**: Coordinate redirect research and development (R&D) efforts with a focus on coordinating both classified and unclassified R&D for cybersecurity.
5. **Connecting the Centers**: Connect current cyber centers to enhance cyber situational awareness and lead to greater integration and understanding of the cyber threat.
6. **Cyber Counterintelligence Plan**: Develop a government-wide cyber counterintelligence plan by improving the security of the physical and the electromagnetic integrity of US networks.
7. **Security of Classified Networks**: Increase in security of classified networks to reduce the risk of information they contain being disclosed.
8. **Expand Education**: Expand education efforts by constructing a comprehensive federal cyber education and training program, with attention to offensive and defensive skills and capabilities.
9. **Leap-Ahead Technology**: Define and develop enduring leap-ahead technology, strategies, and programs by investing in high risk, high reward research and development and by working with both private sector and international partners.
10. **Deterrence Strategies and Programs**: Define and develop enduring deterrence strategies and programs that focus on reducing vulnerabilities and deter interference and attacks in cyberspace.
11. **Global Supply Chain Risk Management**: Develop a multi-pronged approach for global supply chain risk management while seeking to better manage the federal government's global supply chain.
12. **Public and Private Partnerships "Project 12"**: Define the federal role for extending cybersecurity into critical infrastructure domains and seek to define new mechanisms for the federal government and industry to work together to protect the nation's critical infrastructure.

In 2009, President Obama ordered a thorough review of the federal government's capabilities in regard to defending the nation's information and communications infrastructure. This review also included a comprehensive approach to cybersecurity. Thus, the White House cyberspace policy review was released in May 2009 where it recommended the President create a national cybersecurity coordinator. As a result of the policy review, President Obama determined that the CNCI and its associated activities should evolve towards developing key elements of a broader, updated national strategy (GAO 2013). In 2012, the White House Security Coordinator, with cooperation from the DHS, DOD, NIST, and OMB had identified three priority areas for improved federal cybersecurity (ibid.), which were:

1. **Trusted Internet connections:** Consolidate external telecommunications connections and ensure a set of baseline security capabilities for situational awareness and enhanced monitoring.
2. **Continuous monitoring of federal information systems:** Transform the otherwise static security control assessment and authorization process into a dynamic risk mitigation program that provides essential, near real-time security status and remediation, increasing visibility into system operations and helping security personnel make risk management decisions based on increased situational awareness.
3. **Strong authentication:** Increase the issue of federal smartcard credentials such as Personal Identity Verification and Common Access Cards that provide multifactor authentication and digital signature and encryption capabilities, authorizing users to access federal information systems with a higher level of assurance.

While the GAO report provided an excellent review of federal directives, its bottom line warned that the federal government in 2013 still lacks a comprehensive cybersecurity strategy and clear lines of authority and accountability.

In 2012, President Obama championed the Cybersecurity Act of 2012. One of the main thrusts of the proposed law was to help and require private businesses to better protect the nations' business and infrastructure from cyber attacks. Many do not realize that 99 percent of the electricity used by the military comes from civilian sources. And 90 percent of military voice and Internet communications travel over commercial networks (Carter and Holl Lute 2012). The dependence on commercial Internet and telecommunications providers is more like 100 percent for federal, state, and local governments. While the Bill was bipartisan and watered down numerous times by the administration in order to gain greater support, it failed to get the necessary votes. The Republican Senate, who sided with the private sector, argued strenuously that the Act's requirements would be too burdensome. The original version of the Bill had called for mandatory standards but in an attempt to gain more votes, the Bill's language was changed to optional standards for the computer systems that oversee the nation's critical infrastructure—such as power grids, dams, and transportation systems. In the same year, the US House of Representatives passed a Cybersecurity Bill of its own, despite the fact the

President had said he would veto it. The administration opposed the legislation because they felt it called for too much sharing of information between government and business (Schmidt 2012). After a lot of recriminations from all sides, 2012 ended without any legislative action on cybersecurity.

Many do not realize that 99 percent of the electricity used by the military comes from civilian sources. And 90 percent of military voice and Internet communications travel over commercial networks (Carter and Holl Lute 2012). The dependence on commercial Internet and telecommunications providers is more like 100 percent for federal, state, and local governments.

In February 2013, taking a different approach, the President issued Executive Order 13636, "Improving Critical Infrastructure Cybersecurity." The order called for the development of a voluntary, risk-based Cybersecurity Framework aimed at helping organizations manage cyber risk. In the spirit of cooperation, over 3,000 individuals and companies were invited and participated thus contributing to the Framework. The Cybersecurity Framework, officially titled, "Framework for Improving Critical Infrastructure Cybersecurity" was issued through NIST and was passed in February, 2014. All parties acknowledge that this is simply a first but important step in better protecting the nation's 16 critical infrastructure sectors, which include financial services, communications, utilities, transportation, and energy.

When it comes to cybersecurity, government policies need to balance the need for security with civil liberties. The Framework recognizes the role that the protection of privacy and civil liberties plays in creating greater public trust, and includes a methodology to protect individual privacy and civil liberties when critical infrastructure organizations conduct cybersecurity activities.

The Framework's core consists of five concurrent and continuous functions, which are, Identify, Protect, Detect, Respond, and Recover. When considered as a whole, these five functions are designed to provide a high-level, strategic view of the lifecycle of an organization's management of cybersecurity risk.

The *Framework Core* provides a set of activities to achieve specific cybersecurity outcomes, and references examples of guidance to achieve those outcomes. The Core is not designed simply to be a checklist of actions to perform. Instead, it presents key cybersecurity outcomes identified by industry as helpful in managing cybersecurity risk. The Core comprises four elements: Functions, Categories, Subcategories, and Informative References, depicted in Figure 10.6.

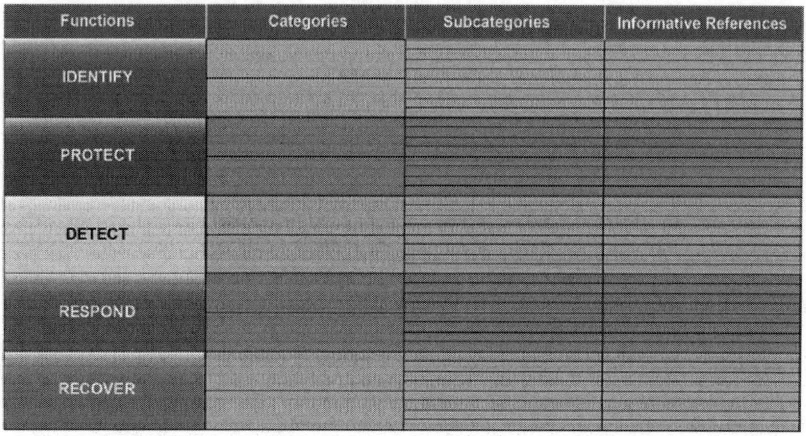

Functions	Categories	Subcategories	Informative References
IDENTIFY			
PROTECT			
DETECT			
RESPOND			
RECOVER			

Figure 10.6 Framework Core structure

Source: National Institute of Standards and Technology 2014

The Framework is essentially a way of thinking, planning, and acting. Some may find it lacking in detail, but the approach was intentional in that it makes it easier for companies to better understand their processes and risk assessment. The NIST Framework defines each of the elements of the Core, which are:

- **Identify**—Develop the organizational understanding to manage cyber-security risk to systems, assets, data, and capabilities. The activities in the Identify Function are fundamental for effective use of the Framework. Understanding the business context, the resources that support critical functions, and the related cybersecurity risks enables an organization to focus and prioritize its efforts, consistent with its risk management strategy and business needs. Examples of outcome Categories within this Function include: Asset Management; Business Environment; Governance; Risk Assessment; and Risk Management.
- **Protect**—Develop and implement the appropriate safeguards to ensure delivery of critical infrastructure services. The Protect Function supports the ability to limit or contain the impact of a potential cybersecurity event. Examples of outcome Categories within this Function include: Access Control; Awareness and Training; Data Security; Information Protection Processes and Procedures; Maintenance; and Protective Technology.
- **Detect**—Develop and implement the appropriate activities to identify the occurrence of a cybersecurity event. The Detect Function enables timely discovery of cybersecurity events. Examples of outcome Categories within this Function include: Anomalies and Events; Security Continuous Monitoring; and Detection Processes.

- **Respond**—Develop and implement the appropriate activities to take action regarding a detected cybersecurity event.
- **Recover**—Develop and implement the appropriate activities to maintain plans for resilience and to restore any capabilities or services that were impaired due to a cyber security event.

Learning from the legislative battles that preceded it, the Framework avoids recommending any regulations or approving any incentives. Instead, the Framework appeals to the best interests of companies in the private sector. It is designed to be high level so that CEOs should be better prepared to ask about their companies' security practices as well as those of their suppliers, partners, and customers. Cybersecurity needs to have both knowledge and support from the top from public as well as private organizations. Figure 10.7 describes a common flow of information and decisions at the following levels within an organization:

- Executive
- Business/Process
- Implementation/Operations.

The executive level communicates the mission priorities, available resources, and overall risk tolerance to the business/process level. The business/process level uses the information as inputs into the risk management process, and then collaborates with the implementation/operations level to communicate business needs and create a Profile. The implementation/operations level communicates the Profile implementation progress to the business/process level. The business/process level uses this information to perform an impact assessment. Business/process level management reports the outcomes of that impact assessment to the executive level to inform the organization's overall risk management process and to the implementation/operations level for awareness of business impact.

The Roles of Federal Agencies Regarding Cybersecurity

While every federal agency operates under various acts, frameworks, guidelines, and regulations, there are a few key agencies that have the responsibility to monitor, coordinate, inform, and develop responses to cyber threats and crimes in addition to protecting the nation's critical infrastructure. There are over a hundred federal offices that have a cybersecurity focus of some sort. The following is simply a sampling of some of the key agencies and their offices that play a key role in cybersecurity.

Office of Management and Budget (OMB)

The OMB is the administration's key agency, which among its many responsibilities, issues operational guidance on cybersecurity initiatives regarding implementation, monitoring, sharing, reporting, and evaluation. OMB works with most federal agencies.

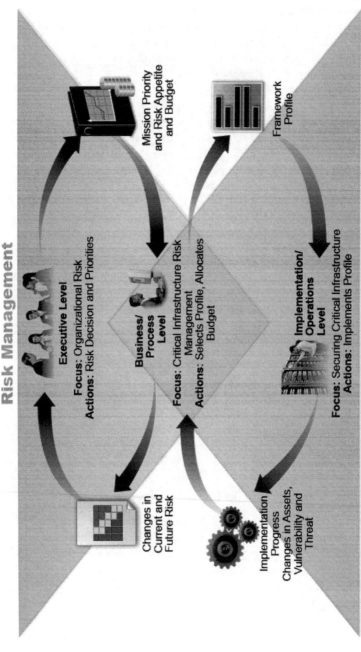

Figure 10.7 NIST risk assessment model

Source: National Institute of Standards and Technology 2014

National Institute of Standards & Technology (NIST)

- The Computer Security Division (CSD), a component of NIST's Information Technology Laboratory (ITL), provides standards and technology to protect information systems against threats to the confidentiality, integrity, and availability of information and services. For more information see the CSD website.
- National Strategy for Trusted Identities in Cyberspace (NSTIC). The NSTIC mission is to help individuals and organizations utilize secure, efficient, easy-to-use, and interoperable identity credentials to access online services in a manner that promotes confidence, privacy, choice, and innovation. For more information see the NSTIC website.

Department of Homeland Security

- United States Computer Emergency Readiness Team (US-CERT). US-CERT is part of DHS' National Cybersecurity and Communications Integration Center (NCCIC). The Department of Homeland Security's United States Computer Emergency Readiness Team (US-CERT) leads efforts to improve the nation's cybersecurity posture, coordinate cyber information sharing, and proactively manage cyber risks to the nation while protecting the constitutional rights of Americans. US-CERT strives to be a trusted global leader in cybersecurity—collaborative, agile, and responsive in a dynamic and complex environment. For more information see the US-CERT website.
- National Cybersecurity and Communications Integration Center (NCCIC). The Department of Homeland Security is responsible for protecting our nation's critical infrastructure from physical and cyber threats. Cyberspace has united once distinct information structures, including our business and government operations, our emergency preparedness communications, and our critical digital and process control systems and infrastructures. Protection of these systems is essential to the resilience and reliability of the nation's critical infrastructure and key resources; therefore, to our economic and national security.

The National Cybersecurity & Communications Integration Center (NCCIC), within the Office of Cybersecurity and Communications, serves as a centralized location where operational elements involved in cybersecurity and communications reliance are coordinated and integrated. NCCIC partners include all federal departments and agencies; state, local, tribal, and territorial governments; the private sector; and international entities. The center's activities include providing greater understanding of cybersecurity and communications situation awareness vulnerabilities, intrusions, incidents, mitigation, and recovery actions.

Secret Service—National Threat Assessment Center

As part of its protective responsibilities, the United States Secret Service has long held the view that the best protective strategy is prevention. The goal of the Secret Service's threat assessment efforts is to identify, assess, and manage persons who have the interest and ability to mount attacks against Secret Service protectees. After the completion of the Secret Service's first operationally relevant study on assassins and near assassins (i.e., the Exceptional Case Study Project) in 1998, the agency created the National Threat Assessment Center (NTAC).

The mission of NTAC is to provide guidance on threat assessment, both within the Secret Service and to its law enforcement and public safety partners. Through the Presidential Threat Protection Act of 2000, Congress formally authorized NTAC to provide assistance.

NTAC also provides research on threat assessment and various types of targeted violence as well as training on threat assessment and targeted violence to law enforcement officials. For more information see the Secret Service website.

Department of the Treasury

The overall mission of cybersecurity at the Department is to assure the appropriate protection of cyber information, services, and assets. Security is critical to Treasury's daily operations and fulfillment of its mission, which relies on protection of both sensitive unclassified and national security systems throughout the Department. The Federal Information Security Management Act of 2002 (FISMA) provides the overall information security policy framework and sets cybersecurity requirements for systems throughout the federal government. Treasury often partners with and implements requirements from other national authorities, such as the Office of Management and Budget, the National Institute of Standards and Technology, the Committee on National Security Systems, and the Office of the Director of National Intelligence. Each Bureau operates and maintains an information security program consistent with federal and departmental requirements.

Department of Justice

Domestically, the Department of Justice works on numerous cases and with other federal agencies in both preventing cyber crime as well as punishing cyber criminals to the full extent of the law. The Department of Justice, through the International Criminal Investigative Training Assistance Program (ICITAP), is working diligently with foreign nations all over the world to develop professional and transparent law enforcement institutions that protect human rights, combat terrorism and corruption, and reduce the threat of transnational crime, including cyber crimes.

One of the areas that ICITAP is focused on improving is cybersecurity. In Eastern Europe, for example, Department of Justice officials are working with law enforcement agencies in nations that make up the US–GUAM (Georgia, Ukraine, Azerbaijan, and Moldova) Framework Program. ICITAP helped develop a Virtual Law Enforcement Center, which links the four member countries through a secure video and criminal information network.

The Federal Bureau of Investigation (FBI) leads the national effort to investigate high-tech crimes, including cyber-based terrorism, espionage, computer intrusions, and major cyber fraud. To stay in front of current and emerging trends, the FBI gathers and shares information and intelligence with public and private sector partners worldwide. For more information see the FBI website.

Department of Defense

US Cyber Command is an armed forces command subordinate to United States Strategic Command The Command is charged with pulling together existing cyberspace resources, creating synergy, and synchronizing warfighting effects to defend the information security environment. The Cyber Command centralizes command of cyberspace operations, organizes existing cyber resources, and synchronizes defense of US military networks. Each of the armed forces maintains its own cyber warfare office and command. For more information see the Army Cyber website.

It is important to note that there are a number of nonprofit institutions and organizations that focus on cybersecurity as well. Chief among them is Carnegie Mellon's CyLab that has become a world leader in both technological research and the education of professionals in information assurance, security technology, business, and policy, as well as security awareness among cyber-citizens of all ages. For more information see the CyLab website. The Center for Internet Security and its MS-ISAC (Multi-State Information Sharing & Analysis Center) is another example. For more information see the MS-ISAC (website). The MS-ISAC is a focal point for cyber threat prevention, protection, response, and recovery for the nation's state, local, tribal, and territorial governments. The MS-ISAC, 24x7 cybersecurity operations center provides real-time network monitoring, early cyber threat warnings and advisories, vulnerability identification and mitigation, and incident response. The Identity Theft Resource Center is another nonprofit organization that among the many roles it plays in this area also publishes useful breach data information. For more information see the Identity Theft Resource Center website.

The Nationwide Cyber Security Review is a voluntary self-assessment survey designed to evaluate cybersecurity management within state, local tribal, and territorial governments. For more information see the NSR website.

There are of course many more organizations that would fall within this important mission-driven area where nonprofits help fill specific voids between the public, government, and private enterprise.

Data Compliance Regulations

As mentioned in chapter four, the federal government has numerous requirements that aim at protecting data such as the Privacy Act of 1974. Before electronic records, protecting and discarding paper files—especially classified and top-secret information—was rather straightforward. Federal law sets forth a set of standards for securing paper files as well as shredding or destroying records, files, and equipment that hold critical information. Electronic files pose a more complicated set of procedures. The Department of Defense has standards of its own and on the civilian side there is NIST and the National Archives and Records Administration. There are even standards and requirements for deleting records referred to simply as "digitally shredding" documents. When it comes to computer systems, many people fail to realize that when data is deleted in a conventional manner, the information is not completely erased and may still be recoverable with special software. The delete function in most operating systems merely removes the traditional access to the file, but does not immediately remove the content data itself.

> When it comes to computer systems, many people fail to realize that when data is deleted in a conventional manner, the information is not completely erased and may still be recoverable with special software. The delete function in most operating systems merely removes the traditional access to the file, but does not immediately remove the content data itself.

Another issue regarding electronic records is the ability to tell if a file or record has been copied, and if so by whom, and where? There are rules that address records management as it pertains to making copies, but it is less than clear as to how the rules are actually carried out.

> Electronic Data Shredding or "e-shredding" is a phrase used to describe the process of permanently removing electronic data from digital devices. This technology is often compared to paper document shredding, but on a digital level.

When it comes to security, there are two major initiatives that stand out above the rest; the Health Insurance Portability and Accountability Act (HIPAA) of 1996, and the other involves protecting credit card transactions better known as PCI Compliance.

HIPAA

One of the primary goals of HIPAA is to protect the confidentiality and security of health care information. It also provides for the protection of individually identifiable health information that is transmitted or maintained in any form or medium. The privacy rules affect the day-to-day business operations of all organizations that provide medical care and maintain personal health information (see the HHS.gov website).

PCI

The *Payment Card Industry Data Security Standard* (PCI DSS) is a set of requirements designed to ensure that all companies that process, store, or transmit credit card information maintain a secure environment. The Payment Card Industry Security Standards Council (PCI SSC) was launched on September 7, 2006 to manage the ongoing evolution of the Payment Card Industry (PCI) security standards with focus on improving payment account security throughout the transaction process. The PCI DSS is administered and managed by the PCI SSC, an independent body that was created by the major payment card brands (Visa, MasterCard, American Express, Discover, and JCB). Government agencies either accepting direct credit card payments or utilizing third party vendors to collect payment on behalf of a government agency must comply with PCI standards and requirements (see the PCI Security Standards Council website).

CJIS Compliance

The Criminal Justice Information System (CJIS) provides state, local, and federal law enforcement and criminal justice agencies with access to critical, personal information such as fingerprint records, criminal histories, and sex offender registrations. In order to prevent unauthorized access to this extremely sensitive information, a security policy governing the access to the CJIS database was enacted on January 1, 2011. CJIS compliance information was set in a mandate released by the FBI. The mandate sets forth the minimum requirements for securing access to the data included within CJIS (FBI 2014). The policy requires "Advanced Authentication," or multi-factor authentication, to be implemented across all those agencies that access the information contained in the CJIS database. CJIS compliance will affect many organizations and many departments. Public safety, judicial, and correctional institutions must comply or face administrative sanctions and/or criminal penalties (FBI website).

State and Local Government

In 2013–14, two surveys found that the top concern for Chief Information Officers at the state level as well as cities and counties was cybersecurity CIO top10, NASCIO 2013a). State and local governments are not immune to cyber attacks, in fact in a number of ways they might be considered more vulnerable. Unlike the federal government that receives guidance from the White House, OMB, NIST, and the Department of Homeland Security, state and local governments are left to their own policies and resources. In 2011 it was revealed that the State of Texas Comptroller's office discovered that 1.3 million records were left on the state website unprotected for over a year (Shannon 2011). What happened in Texas was not an outside the perimeter security breach—rather it was simply employee carelessness. This does not mean, however, that states are not active when it comes to cybersecurity awareness and policies. In 2003, California became the first state in the country to require data breach notifications (OAG.ca.gov 2014). As with the federal government, state government cyber governance is quite fragmented, with each independent agency pursuing security somewhat differently and with little to no coordination. The Golden State, despite all of its cybersecurity focus, *may have* experienced a large data breach regarding credit card transactions involving its state motor vehicle department. In March 2014, despite the continued denial from the department, major credit card companies such as MasterCard issued a breach alert and asked citizens to scrutinize their credit card statements. This serves as a good example of the difficulty in identifying and assigning blame and responsibility. When a security breach occurs, who is to blame? Can a public manager rightly blame a contractor? The answer might be yes but the overall responsibility always lies with the government.

In 2011 it was revealed that the State of Texas Comptroller's office discovered that 1.3 million records were left on the state website unprotected for over a year (Shannon 2011). What happened in Texas was not an outside the perimeter security breach—rather it was simply employee carelessness.

In 2012, South Carolina suffered a massive breach by a foreign national involving 3.6 million records of citizens who had filed tax returns since1998. Initially the Governor had stated publically that this incident was "regrettable, bizarre, and unavoidable." With outrage mounting, the Governor had to push back and began engaging in a more informed damage control strategy. It's hard to imagine a high-ranking public official telling its citizen's that the breach was "unavoidable" (Carolinalive.com 2012). If the public is expected to place their trust in government online services, they have a right to expect that their information is protected to the highest standards. In the case of South Carolina, key data was not encrypted and access to the data was comparatively weak. The state government also blamed the Federal IRS for not requiring social security number encryption (which at the time it had not). Beyond the state blaming the IRS, they did not have any encryption requirements of their own and they lacked strong user controls, plus they maintained outdated equipment going back to the 1970s.

Security Breach Notification Policies

A data breach can be defined as an event in which an individual name plus Social Security Number (SSN), driver's license number, medical record, or a financial record/credit/debit card is potentially put at risk—either in electronic or paper format (Identify Theft Resource Center 2014).

In 2014, the National Conference of State Legislators (NCSL) reported that forty-seven states have enacted legislation requiring private or government entities to notify individuals of security breaches of information involving personally identifiable information (PII). (Only Alabama, New Mexico, and South Dakota do not have a law to date.) States such as New York provide definitions of security breaches as well as penalties for non-compliance. It also requires that when the public is notified of a security breach, the state attorney general, the department of state, and the state office of information technology services must also be notified. A security breach affecting private information of 500 or more persons requires the entity to report to the media. It is less clear when a state or local government should notify the proper federal agencies such as the FBI or Department of Homeland Security, or the Treasury Department.

What happened in California, Texas, South Carolina, and elsewhere, provides for a serious wake-up call that requires government agencies at all levels to review their equipment, security practices, policies, and work with one another to share in best practices. Along with each breach comes a painful lesson.

In the first 4.5 months of 2014 there were 233 data breaches affecting 5,171,507 records. This represents a 17.7 percent increase over the same period a year ago. (Identity Theft Resource Center 2014).

No business or government official wants to succumb to the thought that breaches are "unavoidable," however, despite best efforts they do occur. Every federal, state, and local government agency has a tacit, if not legal, responsibility to inform other agencies and ultimately the public in the event of

Category	Percent of Total Breaches 2013
Insider Theft	11.7%
Hacking	26.1%
Data on the Move	13%
Accidental Exposure	7.5%
Subcontractor	14.3%
Employee Negligence	9.3%

Figure 10.8 Data breaches in 2013

Source: Identity Theft Resource Center 2014

a breach—and the quicker the better. Even if not presently required, every agency should develop a Breach Response Policy. The policy would contain internal requirement for understanding and mitigating any breach, as well as a compliance component that usually requires notifying federal and state officials in a timely manner. Last, breach response policies assign specific tasks and responsibilities to certain officials, which include notifying other government officials and agencies, the public, and possibly the media. Most responsible businesses and governments who have experienced a breach have gone so far as to offer the compromised public free credit monitoring for at least a year or more by a recognized credit monitoring company. Such services are helpful in monitoring and identifying attempts at unauthorized use of credit cards, credit information, and/or identity theft. These remedies come with a heavy cost, often in the millions of dollars. However, the cost of failing to act is far worse and can contribute to the erosion of public trust and participation.

Providing quick and concise notifications helps in numerous ways:

- It may cut off further breached damage
- It may greatly assist law enforcement agencies in catching or, at least, identifying the perpetrators
- Early alerts empower citizens to carefully manage their online accounts and records and may compel them to change their passwords or obtain new credit card account numbers
- It may help in alerting others to the nature and type of breach that could help prevent similar breaches elsewhere.

The bottom line is that security breaches are not "unavoidable" but accidents do occur, and every government has to be prepared for the worst-case scenario.

Many states, aside from protecting their digital infrastructure from cyber threats have created cybersecurity awareness websites aimed at alerting and educating the public.

Many states, aside from protecting their digital infrastructure from cyber threats, have created cybersecurity awareness websites aimed at alerting and educating the public. The National Association of State Chief Information Officers (NASCIO) published the *NASCIO Cybersecurity Awareness Resource Guide* in 2013 (NASCIO 2013b). In 2012, NASCIO published the *2012 Deloitte-NASCIO Cybersecurity Study—State Governments at Risk: A Call for Collaboration and Compliance* (NASCIO 2012). The study focused on four key areas, which are:

1. **The Cybersecurity budget-strategy connection:** Insufficient funding remains a huge challenge.
2. **Cybersecurity authority and governance:** States operate in a highly distributive model having little direct authority over agency security strategies, activities, and resources.
3. **Preparedness for emerging threats:** The wealth of personally identifiable information (PII) as well as sensitive business data makes states attractive targets for cyber criminals and hackers.
4. **Compliance—a lever for CISO Leadership:** There continues to be a ever-growing stream of new cybersecurity regulatory requirements and follow-up audits. There is a growing need for better coordination and leadership.

Local governments have their share of cybersecurity issues too, though they have not received as much national attention. Most of what has been reported through 2014 has been lapses in security systems as well as cyber

	Percent
Adopted a cybersecurity framework based on national standards and guidelines	78%
Acquired and implemented continuous vulnerability monitoring capabilities	78%
Developed security awareness training for workers and contractors	78%
Established trusted partnerships for information sharing and response	75%
Created a culture of information security in your state government	73%
Adopted a cybersecurity strategic plan	61%
Documented the effectiveness of your cybersecurity program with metrics and testing	47%
Developed a cybersecurity disruption response plan	45%
Other	6%

Figure 10.9 Characterizations of the current status of the cybersecurity program and environment in state government

Source: NASCIO 2013c

	Percent
Increasing sophistication of threats	83%
Lack of adequate funding	77%
Inadequate availability of security professionals	55%
Emerging technologies	42%
Lack of visibility and influence within the enterprise	25%
Lack of support from business stakeholders	21%
Inadequate competence of security professionals	19%
Lack of clarity on mandate, roles and responsibilities	13%
Lack of legislative support	12%
Other	10%
Lack of executive support	6%

Figure 10.10 What major barriers does your state face in addressing cybersecurity?

Source: NASCIO 2013c

crime where cyber gangs have stolen millions of dollars from unsuspecting and unprepared local government employees. There have been a number of state initiatives that involve local governments to help protect and better coordinate cyber prevention reporting and strategies.

While much has been done, and CIOs at the state level are painfully aware of the challenges that lie ahead, Figure 10.10 shows just how much and what areas require further attention and resources.

Threats From Within

While so much focus has been directed to cyber threats from outside the perimeter, there is growing concern about what happens inside the perimeter. Many public employees are left to think someone else is protecting their data and systems without realizing the vigilant role they must play too. Network security experts worry that the weakest link in a system may be an unsuspecting employee. When one looks at the types of internal threats they can be grouped in the following four categories:

> Many public employees are left to think someone else is protecting their data and systems without realizing the vigilant role they must play too. Network security experts worry that the weakest link in a system may be an unsuspecting employee.

1. **Lax environment, carelessness, rules are often ignored**. Assuming management is aware of the required cybersecurity procedures and safeguards, without their constant oversight and review, employees may be

prone to non-compliance. It is imperative that managers at all levels create a culture that demonstrates management commitment to following through on ensuring cybersecurity rules are adhered to and not ignored. For example, management efforts to require stronger passwords or scheduled password changes has often been met with passive resistance. Employees have been known to leave their passwords on sticky notes pasted to a monitor or kept underneath a keyboard. Computers have been left on throughout the day, unattended, where someone could easily obtain unauthorized access. People take home digital files that are against policies and procedures in laptops, thumb drives, and tablets. Aside from violating policies, confidential records are at risk when taken out of a secure environment, or at risk if a device containing government data is lost or stolen. Employees, who willingly violate cybersecurity safeguards, usually are so focused on completing their work and assignments they become increasingly oblivious to anything that they perceive as taking away from their prime mission. Most employees know better, they simply don't believe anything bad is going to happen to them if they ignore some of the safeguards imposed on them.

2. **Ignorance**. Unlike carelessness and working in a lax environment, an alarming number of public employees are unaware of the procedures that they are expected to follow, or how every worker places others at risk when they don't follow at least the most basic cyber precautions.

When it comes to employees, ignorance or lack of awareness, abounds. There are plenty of common security myths and misconceptions, such as:

- **"I don't have anything anyone would ever want."** This is a serious breach in understanding. It may be true the employee has nothing of value, but bad guys and botnets alike are constantly searching for points of entry into the main system. Once they find a weakness, like a password or code, they can use your system like someone would use a back door.
- **"I have the best antivirus software installed."** Once upon a time, this might have been true; however, there are thousands of new threats launched every day. Experts warn that virus protection is but one element in a secure network, and it requires constant updating with the latest defensive definitions. Most experts advise using more than one virus and malware protection program. There are many security suites available that are designed to guard against phishing, worms, malware, and trojan horses, to name a few. It is up to the systems administrator to decide and enforce across the enterprise.
- **"I don't use Windows, so I'm safe."** There is growing evidence that no system is safe from harmful malware. Often, simply going to a website can infect a device, and we are seeing some malicious software being imbedded in pictures that are being shared from device to device. Even if a system does not appear to be infected,

it may still be a carrier of malware to other systems workers may be communicating with.

- **"My network has a great firewall, so I am safe."** This would be like saying the Titanic was unsinkable during its maiden voyage. Firewalls are important, but in today's environment where there are multiple points of entry, firewalls are just one line of defense.

- **"I only visit safe sites, so I'm okay."** Visiting certified safe sites is a good practice, but even "safe sites" have been known to pass along malware at times. Keeping up-to-date protection programs with multiple layers is the best defense.

- **"My network administrator is the one in charge of my data."** Best practices prescribe that each individual should be responsible for his or her data. Many still have important files stored on local drives where network administrators have no access. Some employees continue to store data on unencrypted USB drives, and added to the advent of smartphones and smart tablets, there is no way a centralized system can be responsible for all data and files.

- **"I have had my password for years, and nothing has ever happened."** Password protection is like the master key to your front door. With so much at risk, one cannot be too careful with passwords. The days when a four-digit combination would suffice are gone; today, the minimum password should be at least eight characters with a capital letter or two, and at least one number. It can take a couple of hours to find a password with just four digits compared to a few days for an eight-character password. Most systems now require two-factor authentication and password attempt timeouts that after repeated tries locks the account.

- **"No one cares about our information."** As mentioned earlier, there are literally millions of automated botnets that scour the Internet seeking weak or soft spots from which to capture information, passwords, codes, secret documents, or worse. The interest in a user's computing device may very well be to use it as a gateway into a system where a hacker could plant malicious code or steal valuable passwords and other critical information found elsewhere.

- **"Data security is an IT function."** One cannot overstate the need to ensure that everyone is made aware that data and system integrity is everyone's responsibility.

3. **Disgruntled employee(s).** Before advanced computer systems were commonplace, a disgruntled employee posed little security risk to the organization. Given today's highly sophisticated systems, a disgruntled employee could inflict great harm to an agency. Many business and public organizations now require managers to be ever-vigilant for unusual

employee behavior. There have been numerous cases where a disgruntled employee has attempted to sabotage a project or program, or bring down an entire organization. Managers must also be on the lookout for suspicious behavior where an employee may profess, directly or indirectly, varying forms of disagreement with an organization's mission. The same is true for an employee showing signs of unusual behavior.

4. **Internal espionage/criminal activity**. Threats to our nation's critical infrastructure are continuous—with outside forces constantly probing for weakness in various systems. Until recently, internal threats to security were not well understood. Two highly visible and damaging examples illustrate this point. First of all, more attention is now being directed towards internal threats. In 2013, Pfc. Bradley Manning—who leaked one of the largest cache of classified documents in US history—was sentenced to thirty-five years in prison. Manning served as a US Army intelligence analyst and turned over thousands of classified documents to WikiLeaks, an organization that believes that governments have few rights in withholding information from the public. The second example is Edward Snowden, an American computer specialist who was a former employee of the CIA and a former contractor for the National Security Agency (NSA) who disclosed thousands of classified documents to several media outlets. At the time of the data theft, he served as a civilian analyst attached to the CIA, and was able to steal thousands of classified documents. Believing he was doing the right thing, he exposed, as well as uncovered, the existence of numerous global surveillance programs that the general public was not aware of causing incalculable and lasting damage to the nation's cybersecurity agencies.

Both Manning and Snowden serve as painful reminders that despite all of the automated protection systems that are supposedly in place, there always remains a high risk that an employee may decide to take matters into their own hands. Regardless of one intentions or motives, this can cause great harm to the nation's security and its ability to maintain confidential records, critical information, as well as communications among diplomats across the globe. While citing the high visibility using the Manning and Snowden examples, there have been many other individuals who have been caught stealing trade, military, as well as top-secret government documents.

Identity Management

Identity management is another area that is gaining attention throughout all sectors of business and government. In an ever-interdependent digital world, possessing trusted identities has become an enormous challenge to the future of what has been called e-democracy. How can we be sure that when you receive an email or an official looking document it is indeed from the person or organization they say they are? When someone sends in an application, payment, affidavit, or even a vote, it is of paramount importance that there is a standard method for verification. Trusted identities initiatives also include the need to ensure privacy as a central ingredient in establishing trust. In 2011, President Obama signed the National Strategy for Trusted Identities in Cyberspace (NSTIC) to address two challenges that can affect economic growth online: (1) the insecurity and inconvenience of static passwords and (2) the cost of transactional risks that arise from the inability of individuals to prove their true identity online. The strategy was to be carried out by the NIST's National Strategy for Trusted Identities in Cyberspace (see the NSTIC website).

> In an ever-interdependent digital world, possessing trusted identities has become an enormous challenge to the future of what has been called e-democracy.

NSTIC is charged with developing a user-centric "Identity Ecosystem" built on the foundation of private sector identity providers. In 2011, the administration took another key step towards realizing the vision of NSTIC. The Federal CIO issued a Memorandum for Chief Information Officers of Executive Departments and Agencies detailing requirements for accepting externally-issued digital credentials This means that solutions from firms like Equifax, Google, PayPal, Symantec, and others—all of whom have had their credentialing solutions certified to meet federal security and privacy requirements—can be trusted identity providers for certain types of federal applications. This policy advances federal efficiency. For example, a citizen who is a veteran, a college student, and a taxpayer would no longer have to obtain separate digital credentials at each agency website, but instead should be able to use the ones he or she already has. For example, a university-issued

Figure 10.11 Digital logons will rely more and more on biometrics

credential could be used across sites hosted by the Departments of Veterans Affairs, Education, and the Treasury thus allowing the federal government to streamline the customer experience and recognize real cost savings. Moreover, by using accredited identity providers, federal agencies will be able to ensure that citizen information is treated with privacy and security online (White House 2011). This policy when fully implemented envisions an Internet ID that could eventually make passwords for online accounts obsolete.

In an information technology environment, identity management is about access and controls as it pertains to information usually found on a network. For example, only those with a top security clearance would have access to certain files, while those with higher clearances might have access to even more. Conversely, those without the required clearances or authorizations would have more limited access to information. Since governments have a principal responsibility for protecting information and privacy, safeguards regarding access to information are critical.

In 2008, the Identity, Credential, and Access Management (ICAM) program was created whose mission focused on addressing challenges, pressing issues, and design requirements for digital identity, credential, and access management, and defining and promoting consistency across approaches for implementing ICAM programs as reflected in the FICAM Roadmap and Implementation Guidance (FICAM Roadmap website). The FICAM Roadmap was developed

Figure 10.12 ID Management.gov website

Source: https://www.idmanagement.gov

as an outline for a common framework for ICAM within the federal government and to provide supporting implementation guidance for federal agencies as they plan and execute a segment architecture for ICAM management programs. For more information see the ID Management website.

Among the key federal ID initiatives are:

- **Federal Public Key Infrastructure**
  Federal Public Key Infrastructure (FPKI) provides the government with a common infrastructure to administer digital certificates and public-private key pairs, including the ability to issue, maintain, and revoke public key certificates. FPKI leverages a security technique called Public Key Cryptography to authenticate users and data, protect the integrity of transmitted data, and ensure non-repudiation and confidentiality.
- **Homeland Security Presidential Directive 12**
  Driven by the creation and signing of Homeland Security Presidential Directive 12 (HSPD-12), the Personal Identity Verification (PIV) card was adopted as the standard credential for federal employees and contractors for access to federal information systems and federally controlled facilities. The PIV card is a key element in implementing ICAM by assisting the federal government in moving towards strong authentication. This page provides federal agencies with information regarding policies, procedures, requirements, and purchasing HSPD-12 products. Specific PIV card requirements are introduced in FIPS 201, a standard developed by the National Institute of Standards and Technologies (NIST) in response to HSPD-12.
- **Identity, Credential, and Access Management**
  Since its creation in fall 2008, the Identity, Credential, and Access Management (ICAM) program has focused on addressing challenges, pressing issues, and design requirements for digital identity, credential, and access management, and defining and promoting consistency across approaches for implementing ICAM programs as reflected in the FICAM Roadmap and Implementation Guidance (FICAM Roadmap website). The FICAM Roadmap was developed to outline a common framework for ICAM within the federal government and to provide supporting implementation guidance for federal agencies as they plan and execute towards developing a system architecture for ICAM management programs.

Cybersecurity Governance, the Sum of the Parts

The battle for cybersecurity rages on and continues to challenge the very best of networked systems. The "bad guys" are forever seeking even the tiniest of weaknesses overlooked by those who should know better. Sound strategies require a holistic approach to protecting business and government systems, often referred to as cybersecurity governance. Cybersecurity governance requires everyone to play a defined role in protecting our nations' various systems, sort of like a "digital neighbor watch." The Chief Information Security Officers and other cybersecurity officials have their work cut out for them, but they need to be supported by updated equipment, polices and procedures, and continuous employee awareness programs. The elements of cybersecurity governance therefore include (1) External threat strategy and assessment, (2) Data integrity and security, (3) Internal threat awareness polices and programs, as well as (4) Privacy, (5) Governance, and (6) Ethics.

Employee Awareness

Most government employees are unaware of the risks they pose without even knowing. One informal survey noted that in some offices, 35 percent of employees keep their passwords written down on sticky notes that are stuck to their monitors or underneath their keyboards. When one looks at the 2013 listing of the "worst passwords" it is no wonder network security officers are appalled.

25 Worst Passwords of 2013		
1. 123456	14. letmein	The length and composition of a good password referred to as strong usually consists of no less than eight characters with a combination of upper and lower case letters, symbols and numbers. The length and type definitely can make a huge difference, for example: A six character, single case password has 308 million possible combinations which can be cracked in just minutes. Combining upper and lower case and using 8 characters instead of 6 = 53 trillion possible combinations. Substituting a number for one of the letters yields 218 trillion possibilities. Substituting a special character one gets 6,095 trillion possibilities. Finally, using a special high-speed computer that is GPU-based, it can scan billions of passwords per second.
2. password	15. photoshop	
3. 12345678	16. 1234	
4. qwerty	17. monkey	
5. abc123	18. shadow	
6. 123456789	19. sunshine	
7. 111111	20. 12345	
8. 1234567	21. password1	
9. iloveyou	22. princess	
10. adobe123	23. azerty	
11. 123123	24. trustno1	
12. admin	25. 000000	
13. 1234567890		

Figure 10.13 Worst passwords of 2013

Source: Mashable.com 2014

With such incomprehensible speed, one can't but wonder if passwords are still relevant, regardless of complexity? The answer is that most systems only allow for a limited amount of password attempts before locking out the user. Second, intrusion prevention systems can detect unusual patterns that will automatically shut off access too. Finally, new forms of system access are being tried such as special government-issued swipe cards, fingerprint readers, iris scans, and two-factor authentication. With two-factor authentication, employees, in order to gain access to systems and files, are required to have, as the name implies, two forms of verifiable credentials. This could take the form of a password in combination with a fingerprint reader, or a call back with a special number that is sent to one's mobile device.

With the growth of the mobile workforce, more employees are carrying information with them in the form of laptops, smartphones, tablets, and portable storage devices such as USB drives. Each device poses a different type of potential threat and each requires a strict policy that must be followed by all. Equipment can be stolen, copied, or simply used to gain access to sensitive information stored elsewhere. Mobile devices, to be reasonably secure, require encryption and other forms of protection.

Sample of Basic Mobile Device Policy categories
- Type of secure passwords?
- Encryption of files and records?
- Access to files and records? (in-office & remote)
- Restrictions on types of information that can be placed on portable devices?
- Citizen privacy protection?
- When workers leave?
- Laptop and portable storage policies?
- Portable device policies?
- Back-up policies?
- Portable device cut-off & destroy systems?
- Cyber and network security safeguards on every device
- Secure wireless communication protocols
- Portable device cut-off & destroy systems?
- Blocked Internet Sites?
- Policy on social network sites?
- Rules for laptop data protection and encryption
- Security training policies?
- Security clearances? (Who should have and what criteria?)
- Network security audits? (By whom and frequency?)
- How are files shared among staff and other agencies? What security precautions are in place?

Figure 10.14 Sample of mobile device policy categories

Phishing and Other Tactics

There have been numerous documented instances where a public official has been tricked into believing an email message is real when in fact it is a ruse to help extract critical information such as passwords and other sensitive information. Phishing schemes have extracted millions of dollars from unwitting public managers and citizens alike. Phishing schemes are effective because they appear to be authentic emails from trusted sources. The trend towards tricking individuals will not go away and will in fact get worse. There are a number of good online and in-person programs designed to educate workers about the perils of phishing and what to look for and how to avoid being scammed. The bottom line here is that we can no longer simply rely on a central IT staff to protect employees with the latest antivirus or malware software. Employees must be trained on a periodic basis and be encouraged to take greater responsibility for their actions.

Cybersecurity and network operations must also take into consideration procedures for keeping systems operational during storms, power outages, and other physical threats to their critical operations. It used to be completely adequate to have back-up electrical support for up to seventy-two hours. Nowadays experts are recommending back-up systems that can operate for much longer periods of time. Individual employee and agency files and data require not only routine back-ups but also redundant systems in case one system is down. Many local governments utilize remote storage systems, and in some cases have relationships with other jurisdictions to store and retrieve critical data in case of emergencies. Simple questions remain however, such as how are fuel tanks serviced in times of emergency and how is fuel kept fresh when it is well. And even with additives, fuel has a limited shelf life. More information can be found under topics such as energy assurance and energy resiliency. For more information see the Energy.gov website.

Keeping employees up to date with the latest information is also tantamount to the success of any written policy. The need for ongoing training and education needs to be a continuous process of written guidelines, updates, and hands-on demonstrations. Some will argue there is simply no time—experts will argue that it is necessary and time well spent.

> Keeping employees up to date with the latest information is also tantamount to the success of any written policy. The need for ongoing training and education needs to be a continuous process of written guidelines, updates, and hands-on demonstrations.

Experts agree that we can never let our guard down. Every system and network must have a strategy for prevention, intervention, and restoration. Every government agency needs to continuously review its equipment, software, programs and policies, and requires ongoing employee cybersecurity awareness training.

Discussion Questions

1. How have cyber and or network security policies and procedures changed over the last five years?
2. How would you apply the Framework for Cybersecurity work in your organization or one that you may be familiar with?
3. How often do you change your passwords? Are they generally considered "strong"? What other safety measures are used?
4. Does your organization have polices and procedures for working with mobile devices? What are your policies regarding downloads and adding software applications?
5. When were your organization's security policies last reviewed?
6. Have you participated in a Cybersecurity Awareness Program? What if anything did you learn?
7. Can you identify any security weaknesses that still exist in your organization, or one that you are familiar with? If yes, why do they still exist, and what would it take to remedy them?
8. What types of energy resilience programs exist in your government agency or jurisdiction if the power goes out? If you are familiar with them, are they adequate? Why or why not?
9. Can you identify and explain the nine sources of cyber threats to federal agencies and critical infrastructure?
10. What more can the federal government do to better protect the nation's critical infrastructure?
11. What can state governments do to better protect citizens in regard to cyber crime and cybersecurity?
12. What role can and should local governments play in protecting their records and infrastructure?

References

24-7pressrelease.com. 2014. "Security Is Top Priority for Local Government IT Executives in 2014." Accessed October 17, 2014. http://www.24-7pressrelease.com/press-release/security-is-top-priority-for-local-government-it-executives-in-2014-375584.php.

Bradley, Tony. 2014. "Report: Average of 82,000 New Malware Threats per Day in 2013." *PCWorld.* Accessed October 17, 2014. http://www.pcworld.com/article/2109210/report-average-of-82-000-new-malware-threats-per-day-in-2013.html.

Bumiller, Elisabeth and Thom Shanker. 2012. "Panetta Warns of Dire Threat of Cyberattack on US." *The New York Times.* Accessed October 17, 2014. http://www.nytimes.com/2012/10/12/world/panetta-warns-of-dire-threat-of-cyberattack.html?pagewanted=all&_r=0.

Carolinalive.com. 2012. "SC Gov Haley to Give Update on Hacked Tax Returns." Accessed October 17, 2014. http://www.carolinalive.com/news/story.aspx?id=827638#.U625rKijThg.

Carter, Ashton B. and Jane Holl Lute. 2012. "A Law to Strengthen Our Cyberdefense.," *The New York Times.* August 1.

Cisco. 2014. *Cisco 2014 Security Report.* Accessed October 17, 2014. http://www.cisco.com/web/offers/lp/2014-annual-security-report/index.html?.keycode=000350063.

Constantin, Lucian. 2013. "Emergency Alert System Devices Vulnerable to Hacker Attacks, Researchers Say." *Computerworld.* Accessed October 17, 2014. http://www.computerworld.com/s/article/print/9236758/emergency_alert.

FBI. 2014. *CJIS Security Policy.* Accessed October 17, 2014. http://www.fbi.gov/about-us/cjis/cjis-security-policy-resource-center/view.

GAO. 2013. "Cyber Security—National Strategy, Roles, and Responsibilities Need to Be Better Defined and More Effectively Implemented." Accessed October 17, 2014. http://www.gao.gov/assets/660/652170.pdf.

Higgins, Kelly Jackson. 2013. "Decoy ICS/SCADA Water Utility Networks Hit By Attacks." *InformationWeek.* Accessed October 17, 2014. http://www.darkreading.com/attacks-breaches/decoy-icsscada-water-utility-networks-hi/240151010.

Identity Theft Resource Center. 2014. "Data Breaches." Accessed October 17, 2014. http://www.idtheftcenter.org/id-theft/data-breaches.html.

Mashable.com. 2014. "The 25 Worst Passwords of 2013." Accessed October 17, 2014. http://mashable.com/2014/01/22/worst-passwords-2013/.

NASCIO. 2012. *2012 Deloitte-NASCIO Cybersecurity Study—State Governments at Risk: A Call for Collaboration and Compliance.* Accessed October 17, 2014. http://www.nascio.org/publications/documents/Deloitte-NASCIOCybersecurityStudy2012.pdf.

NASCIO. 2013a. *2014 State CIO Top 10.* Accessed October 17, 2014. http://www.nascio.org/publications/documents/NASCIO_StateCIOTop10For2014.pdf.

NASCIO. 2013b. *Nascio Cybersecurity Awareness Resource Guide.* Accessed October 17, 2014. http://www.nascio.org/publications/documents/NASCIO_CyberSecurityResourceGuide2013.pdf.

NASCIO. 2013c. *The 2013 State CIO Survey.* Accessed October 17, 2014. http://www.nascio.org/publications/documents/2013_State_CIO_Survey_FINAL.pdf. Pages 10-11.

National Institute of Standards and Technology. 2014. "Framework for Improving Critical Infrastructure Cybersecurity." Accessed October 17, 2014. http://www.nist.gov/nstic/.

OAG.ca.gov. 2014. "Cybersecurity in the Golden State." Accessed October 17, 2014. https://oag.ca.gov/cybersecurity.

Riley, Elgin, Dune Lawrence, and Carol Matlack. 2014. "Missed Alarms and 40 Million Stolen Credit Card Numbers: How Target Blew It." *Bloomberg Businessweek.* Accessed October 17, 2014. http://www.businessweek.com/articles/2014-03-13/target-missed-alarms-in-epic-hack-of-credit-card-data.

Schmidt, Michael S. 2012. "Cybersecurity Bill Is Blocked in Senate By G.O.P Filibuster." *The New York Times.* August 3.

Shannon, Kelley. 2011. "Breach in Texas Comptroller's Office Exposes 3.5 Million Social Security Numbers, Birth Dates." *DallasNews.* Accessed October 17, 2014. http://www.dallasnews.com/news/state/headlines/20110411-breach-in-texas-comptrollers-office-exposes-3.5-million-social-security-numbers-birth-dates.ece.

White House. 2009. "Remarks by the President on Securing Our Nation's Cyber Infrastucture." Accessed October 17, 2014. http://www.whitehouse.gov/the-press-office/remarks-president-securing-our-nations-cyber-infrastructure.

White House. 2011. "Administration Releases Strategy to Protect Online Consumers." Accessed October 17, 2014. http://www.whitehouse.gov/the-press-office/2011/04/15/administration-releases-strategy-protect-online-consumers-and-support-in.

Digital Destinations

Army Cyber. http://www.arcyber.army.mil/org-uscc.html

CSD. http://nist.gov/itl/csd/index.cfm

CyLab. https://www.cylab.cmu.edu

Energy.gov. http://energy.gov/oe/services/energy-assurance

FBI. http://www.fbi.gov/about-us/investigate/cyber

FICAM Roadmap. www.idmanagement.gov/ficam-roadmap-update

HHS.gov. http://www.hhs.gov/ocr/privacy/hipaa/understanding/summary/

Identity Theft Resource Center. http://www.idtheftcenter.org

IDManagement.gov. https://www.idmanagement.gov

Merriam-Webster. http://www.merriam-webster.com/dictionary/cybersecurity

MS-ISAC. http://msisac.cisecurity.org

Nationwide Cyber Security Review. https://msisac.cisecurity.org/resources/ncsr/

National Strategy for Trusted Identities in Cyberspace (NSTIC). http://www.nist.gov/nstic/

NCCIC. https://www.dhs.gov/about-national-cybersecurity-communications-integration-center

PCI Security Standards Council. https://www.pcisecuritystandards.org/security_standards/

Secret Service. http://www.secretservice.gov/ntac.shtml

Symantic.com. http://www.symantec.com/security_response/publications/threatreport.jsp

US-CERT. http://www.us-cert.gov/

Further Reading

Schmidt, Howard A. 2011. "Advancing the National Strategy for Trusted Identities in Cyberspace: Government as Early Adopter." *The White House Blog.* October 14. Accessed October 17, 2014. http://www.whitehouse.gov/blog/2011/10/14/advancing-national-strategy-trusted-identities-cyberspace-government-early-adopter.

11 Managing Knowledge and Data Management

Knowledge is, in many ways, an abstract concept. Public administrators first considering the role knowledge plays in a public manager's duties are apt to write it off as less concrete and therefore less important. But knowledge management (KM) may very well constitute the single biggest opportunity tomorrow's public managers have to create a lasting impact on the communities and individuals whom they serve. Applying what we know about KM becomes more critical for two central reasons: the baby boomer retirement mass exodus, and the influx of "millennials" who tend to change jobs far more often than any group before them. In both examples, people along with their knowledge are walking out the door.

The dotcom bubble of the late 1990s and the sudden proliferation of digital data widely characterized as "big data" in the late 2000s vaulted both the problem of knowledge management and its study into the spotlight. Between 1986 and 2007, the world's technological capacity to store information multiplied by a factor of more than 100, leaping from about 2.6 exabites of storage capacity to about 295 exabites (Hilbert and Lopez 2011). IBM and Cisco have both arrived at the conclusion that 90 percent of the world's data has been generated in the last two years (IBM 2014). Senior executives, public and private, are facing the growing problem of data proliferation on a global scale.

> IBM and Cisco have both arrived at the conclusion that 90 percent of the world's data has been generated in the last two years. Senior executives, public and private, are facing the growing problem of data proliferation on a global scale (IBM 2014).

KM is more than an abstract idea about ideas. It is a well-established field of management science. Stated plainly, KM is a method for working smarter—a goal managers everywhere are fond of espousing to subordinates. KM enables teams and individuals to learn from everyone who has done the job before them. With help from leading thinkers like Michael Stankosky, the co-founder and co-director of The Institute for Knowledge

Figure 11.1 People create 2.5 quintillion bytes of data every day

and Innovation at the George Washington University, much work has been done to demonstrate the role KM is playing and can play in both public and private institutions, driving innovation forward and preventing the loss of mission-critical information and systems.

To be sure, knowledge loss is something that's affecting federal, state, and local governments, as well as federal agencies, nonprofits, and for-profit businesses in the private sector, too. Take, for example, the fact that much of the knowledge required to repeat NASA's 1969 moon landing and the historic first steps on the moon has been lost or rendered indecipherable without the contextual and personal knowledge of the 400,000 engineers who worked on it (Kim 2005). The scenario is almost tragic. Think of all the money spent. History was made, but without the proper documentation structure in place, it was also lost. The loss of knowledge can lead to efforts to reinvent solutions that have already been discovered, answering queries and solving problems that have already been addressed. Reinventing the wheel is both expensive and, by definition, inefficient. KM, as a management science, is designed to limit this kind of institutional loss.

There are many current social factors impacting, and in some cases, propelling the loss of knowledge in today's American public and private institutions. Perhaps the largest is the aging and retirement of the baby boomer generation—those "born from mid-1946 to 1964." (US Census Bureau 2011). The baby boomer generation has "79 million people" in it, and represents roughly "26 percent" of the US population (Barry 2010). This means that "[b]y 2030, when all the Baby Boomers will have turned 65, fully 18 percent of the nation's population will be at least that age" (Cohn and Taylor 2010). Baby Boomers constitute a large portion of the senior leadership in today's organizations, simply by virtue of their age and experience. As this group reaches retirement age and leaves the workforce, boomers will potentially take with them many valuable insights and large portions of the wisdom associated with their roles.

Another workforce factor posing a serious risk of knowledge loss is the fact that many young people are spending less time working for the same employer than young people of past generations. The median number of years America's youngest workforce generation, the Millennial Generation, spends employed by a given institution is just two years (Frank 2012). There are many factors driving the decrease in a typical young person's tenure with each employer, but the net effect is a combination of knowledge loss and fragmentation. In short, knowledge is leaking out of institutions at an alarming rate, walking out the door in the form of employees young and old, departing for reasons endemic to modern American society.

> Knowledge is leaking out of institutions at an alarming rate, walking out the door in the form of employees young and old, departing for reasons endemic to modern American society.

The Problem of Knowledge Management

KM has been studied formally for decades, as organizations sought to preserve critical efficiencies and intellectual property, and informally for thousands of years, as entrepreneurs sought to pass business contacts and trade techniques on from one employee to another. To be sure, the idea that preserving ideas is important is not novel.

Common concerns on the minds of public management executives might include:

- Managing and storing data efficiently.
- Protecting data and preventing it from falling into the wrong hands.
- Making useful, open data more accessible to the public.
- Improving the work done daily, monthly, and annually with data.
- Using data to inform decision-making and efforts to innovate.
- Analyzing data to provide better services to the public.
- Predicting and solving problems before they even arise.

These questions and many more like them are driving dialogues and new thinking about data and knowledge management at all levels of government. When one considers the size of the criminal database managed by the Federal Bureau of Investigation (FBI), or the citizen statistics database managed by the United States Census Bureau (USCB), or the scientific research database managed by the National Science Foundation (NSF), it becomes easy to see how, today, the role of government is inextricably linked to data. Even in the smallest towns and municipalities, moral and legal responsibilities to accumulate, secure, and share data exist. Government data must be protected, verified, and put to use for the good of the people being served.

Modernity means tackling new responsibilities for data management in the public sector, and it also means new complexities. As shared services and government outsourcing become more popular solutions to the problems the public sector is facing, the potential for knowledge loss associated with data also grows, in some ways compounding the challenges the modern public sector is facing. Luckily, humans have gotten much better at managing data and information during the era of "big data," and more importantly, we've gotten better at *synthesizing* it.

Defining Knowledge Management

The American Productivity & Quality Center (APQC) has developed a widely-referenced definition for KM. According to the APQC, KM can be defined as, "a systematic effort to enable information and knowledge to grow, flow and create value" (O'Dell and Hubert 2011). It helps to conceptualize knowledge in the context of data, where knowledge is the synthesis or interpretation of data.

As illustrated in Figure 11.2, when analyzed, data becomes information. Moving up the pyramid, applied information becomes knowledge, and when knowledge is combined with experience, wisdom is generated. With all the data on Earth, there is certainly more knowledge today than there's ever been, but it's growing at a slower rate, by the relational definition implied in the knowledge pyramid. Knowledge is also relatively more valuable to organizations because of the processes that must be undertaken to create it—hence the need to capture knowledge, store it, and put it to work for the organization.

Figure 11.2 Knowledge management pyramid

Source: Blankenship 2011

Why Knowledge Management Matters

For busy managers, holistic KM initiatives can often seem like idealistic pursuits, tangential to critical goals. But being attentive and thoughtful about an organization's knowledge can serve to solve a multiplicity of problems. Beyond its being interesting and available to managers in both public and private sectors, a clear line can be drawn between KM and the business goals critical to various organizational components of both private enterprises and public administration. As a point of entry, KM efforts can provide solutions to business initiatives being created completely independent from formal KM strategies and structures.

Typical administrative goals that KM efforts can solve or help solve for independent departments and teams in an organization:

- Training new hires faster (Human Resources).
- Recording project lessons learned to inform future projects (Operations).
- Forming technical and process efficiencies (Information Technology).
- Reducing waste generated by staffs (Sustainability).
- Predicting cost-structure changes (Finance).
- Fostering mentorship between experienced and inexperienced staffs (Management).

When senior managers step back from their tactical objectives and examine overarching strategies that might solve multiple issues and process dysfunctions across departments, it's easy to see that KM strategies and structures can provide sound, sweeping solutions, as well.

Common organizational strategic goals that KM addresses:

- Minimizing knowledge gaps.
- Reducing training times for new hires.
- Developing new organization-wide competencies.
- Preventing repeated errors across interdepartmental processes.
- Unifying processes across independent teams.
- Retaining knowledge after employee departures.

With all the problems and inefficiencies knowledge management can solve, it can certainly still involve wasted efforts. Capturing, cataloging, and storing knowledge takes both time and money. Like any investment, KM efforts can go sideways or prove fruitless. If not carefully planned out and managed, these efforts can distract from the critical business of the day. And prioritizing them undoubtedly means de-prioritizing other initiatives. So how can public administrators ensure their KM efforts start off on the right foot and stay relevant? By remaining continuously and rigorously focused on *critical* knowledge.

Uncovering Valuable Knowledge

Perhaps the biggest key to success in KM is recognizing that it is not a panacea for all organizational ills. Like many major organizational initiatives a public manager might undertake, KM is meant to serve the greater strategic imperatives in the organization. It's good for addressing specific issues or goals, not for tackling all of them at once. By the same token, KM efforts are not meant to record the totality of wisdom, knowledge, information, and data in an organization. For example, tasking every employee with labeling and saving to a publicly accessible server every email they send and receive—in case someone else in the organization might find some gem therein useful—would be obviously impractical and might even undermine the privacy the team has become accustomed to, and in turn, its sense of teamwork. In contrast, deploying a KM directive requesting that any emails in which processes are explained to new hires be documented and saved to a common location might prove very fruitful. In short, KM is best deployed with specific strategic intent.

> Perhaps the biggest key to success in KM is recognizing that it is not a panacea for all organizational ills.

Another common misconception about KM is that it should be designed to mirror the structure of the organization it's serving. After all, there's surely knowledge behind every door in every great organization, right? Of course, the short answer is yes. There's knowledge inside every department and under every hat. But trying to record all of it would quickly become cripplingly cumbersome. Beginning by recording random bits of knowledge from every department would result in little forward momentum. And much of the knowledge captured would likely never be referenced. Just because knowledge exists, does not make it valuable to an organization.

The simple, universal truth is this. It is impossible to capture all knowledge, so it is critical to capture important knowledge first. How an organization prioritizes its KM efforts should be heavily influenced by the priorities driving the organization as a whole. This means an early-stage KM prototype or initiative will be well served by finding the intersections where critical knowledge is required or shared, and beginning there. Beyond that, anyone participating in a KM process should view it as an attempt at innovation and therefore an initiative worth testing, learning from, re-prioritizing, and re-applying. Minor failures are simply part of the process of creating. Many notably successful KM efforts were developed over time using iterative approaches, including NASA's, which is discussed in depth at the end of this chapter. The trick, it seems, is growing your KM initiative in a way that makes sense for your organization—one that makes doing business more efficient and effective in the long term, not less. Given that adopting even a pilot KM

Figure 11.3 It's critical to focus only on what knowledge is most important

program requires new effort and diverted attention in the short term makes that task much harder than it might sound.

> It is impossible to capture all knowledge, so it is critical to capture important knowledge first. How an organization prioritizes its KM efforts should be heavily influenced by the priorities driving the organization as a whole.

Typifying Knowledge: Tacit vs. Explicit

When it comes to discovering the most valuable knowledge and therefore the most critical knowledge to the organization, it helps to understand the different types of knowledge that exist in modern institutions, private and public. When asked to think about where to find valuable knowledge in a business context, many new to KM immediately go to processes, procedures, and facts about the business—the details of its operational underpinnings. This type of knowledge

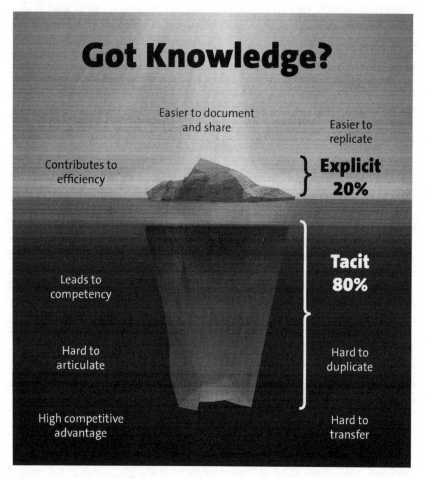

Figure 11.4 Explicit and tacit knowledge

Source: Blankenship 2011

is certainly important to an organization. It's called *explicit knowledge*, which is "also known as *formal* or *codified* knowledge" (O'Dell and Hubert 2011).

Every organization also relies heavily on one other type of knowledge that is as important if not more, and much harder to find and capture. This other type of knowledge is made up of all the experience and wisdom obtained by employees based on their past exposures to people and processes. This deeper type of knowledge, which is represented in Figure 11.4 by the portion of the iceberg found beneath the surface, is known as *tacit knowledge*, often thought of as, "*informal* or *uncodified* knowledge" (ibid.).

Tacit knowledge can be critically important to an organization's operation. Consider a past job you've had. When you think about all the components of that job you learned in passing, or from informal conversations with co-workers, it's easy to see how much genuine knowledge might not have been encapsulated in the company handbook. Tacit knowledge may be siloed in the mind of the only engineer in the local water department who knows where the key shut offs are buried, or the retiring nuclear weapons expert scheduled to leave just before a project is completed.

Critical knowledge can come in the form of both explicit knowledge and tacit knowledge, so the ability to recognize both types and to identify opportunities to capture both forms is of key importance to KM strategists. Other key imperatives for these strategists include the ability to scope the amount of valuable knowledge in an organization and to locate it in the minds and processes most critical to an organization's continued functioning and growth. To deal with these challenges, the practice of knowledge mapping has emerged as a standard exercise undertaken by knowledge managers planning KM strategies and evaluating the performance of KM efforts.

Critical knowledge can come in the form of both explicit knowledge and tacit knowledge, so the ability to recognize both types and to identify opportunities to capture both forms is of key importance to KM strategists.

Knowledge Mapping

When strategizing around any multi-layered or otherwise complex system, it often helps to create a visual. As grade school students, we are taught that there are many different ways to visually plan a piece of expository writing. Some people prefer outlines, while others prefer spider diagrams or flow charts. Knowledge maps are equally subject to personal preference. The valuable tacit and explicit knowledge in an organization can be mapped visually using any one of a number of structures. With that in mind, the American Productivity & Quality Center has developed a generalized set of steps for mapping knowledge (O'Dell and Hubert 2011).

The APQC's steps to mapping knowledge, taken directly from the book *The New Edge in Knowledge* (O'Dell and Hubert 2011) are:

1. Specify the process or focus area through which the critical knowledge flows. This is the scope of the map.
2. Specify the reason (i.e., the call to action) for mapping the knowledge.
3. Map the process or focus area.
4. Identify key decision points and cross-functional hand-offs.
5. Locate owners and stakeholders of highly valued activities.
6. Identify sources and recipients of critical knowledge.
7. Identify important knowledge assets needed for each step of the process.

8. Create an inventory of types of knowledge (explicit and tacit) used and needed.
9. Identify gaps, lack of connectivity, and information overload.
10. Develop a plan for reviewing, validating, and sharing the findings from your map.

Of course, many KM projects and initiatives require multiple knowledge maps dedicated to different strategic goals or disparate operational systems. The scope of all of these maps combined is the scope of the KM system as a whole, and the target areas pinpointed in each map are the critical points of knowledge flow in the project or initiative. Following the flow of knowledge can also be particularly useful in isolating areas where further investigation is required. These areas are often called *knowledge gaps*. These are the areas where KM process improvements are waiting to be found.

Strategies for Knowledge Management

In truth, no KM system is complete or perfect, so the process improvements revealed by sound gap analyses will always be present, even in mature KM systems. This is because KM systems and their strategies are architected on the shifting bedrock of the organizations that they serve. Priorities are constantly changing in the public sector as administrations rise and fall, and as time passes and goals are either reached or abandoned in favor of more pressing ones. If great KM strategies are designed to serve the key strategic imperatives of their organizations, it follows that the leaders of KM initiatives should expect their strategies to experience forced adaptation at least as often as the organization as a whole changes. This means that the flow of knowledge through an organization will likely never be perfect, though it can operate at peak performance under its given constraints. It can be useful to envision the type of knowledge flow that the most efficient and complete KM systems might create, if only to inspire the pursuit of excellence in practice.

With the best KM system in place, knowledge flow might be represented by the diagram in Figure 11.5.

Here, knowledge in a hypothetical organization flows constantly in a clockwise direction. First, knowledge is created through natural business processes and moments of accomplishment. Next, it's identified as something with a high likelihood of being re-used and becoming valuable knowledge in the identification phase. The knowledge is validated as current, accurate, and useful in the next phase. It's documented in a way that's concise and labeled using a practical, logical taxonomy. It's published in a location where those who might need it might easily retrieve it. Then, in the retrieval phase, it's found by someone else in the organization to whom it has a use. That person puts it to work, applying the knowledge, either with the help of the individual or team that originally created the knowledge, or without them—it was vetted and well documented in earlier phases. Finally, the re-use of knowledge allows the organization to focus on newer, more pressing problems, where creation may begin anew.

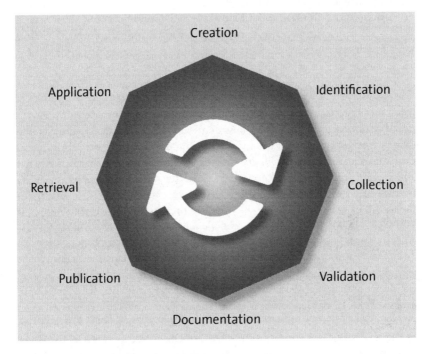

Figure 11.5 Knowledge flow chart

To handle the practical task of enabling this type of knowledge flow in the long term, a comprehensive KM strategy is often deployed. These strategies are made up of interrelated but individually defined processes and structures that support one or many stages of knowledge flow.

Here follows a hypothetical example of a comprehensive KM strategy at the federal level as explained by Linda Blankenship on March 5, 2013 in a class video presentation to Rutgers students:

- **Codification**—Includes a standard system of naming and labeling units of knowledge, as well as procedures, checklists, and inventories of knowledge, all of which serve to support documentation and retrieval.
- **Collaboration**—Encourages the sharing of knowledge across individual teams performing the same functions, as well as across departments and roles, supporting knowledge identification, collection, and validation efforts.
- **Alternative Resources**—Include agencies, rotational staffs, cross-training, and even retirees returning to the workforce part-time or on a project basis, all of which serve to impart and seed new knowledge.
- **Process Improvements**—Include operational improvements that are sources of new, valuable knowledge, as well as capital investments in automation and smarter systems, which can result in KM system growth and adaptation.

- **Education and Training**—Includes classroom and simulation formats, on-the-job training, mentoring, and apprenticeships, all of which create opportunities for knowledge creation, and disseminate critical knowledge quickly.

Systems of Knowledge Retention

If it's simple to envision the ideal flow of knowledge through an organization, beginning to understand the systems and strategies deployed to enable that flow means making a mental step in the direction of practical application, and that, in turn, entails increased complexity. Returning to what has already been presented, we know that knowledge creation happens as a natural part of an organization's growth and development, and that it occurs in the minds of workers (tacit knowledge) and processes of doing work (explicit knowledge). We also know that knowledge mapping provides a customizable, dynamic, and repeatable exercise for finding critical knowledge within an organization. Next in the ideal flow of knowledge comes collection.

Collection often requires a system of communication that makes it easy for those with valuable knowledge to be able to store and share it, to raise awareness of it, or that enables those tasked with collecting knowledge to engage those creating knowledge. The collection of knowledge can be done in practice using everything from video cameras to record work being done, to simple logs where new practices and solutions can be detailed. Of course, the individuals participating in the documented collection of knowledge can certainly be the same people engaged in knowledge creation.

> Collection often requires a system of communication that makes it easy for those with valuable knowledge to store and share it, or that enables those tasked with collecting knowledge to engage those creating knowledge.

Validation is often done collaboratively, and marks a good phase in the flow of knowledge to address the importance of teamwork and collaboration in knowledge management. If only subject matter experts close to the knowledge in question are granted the ability to validate knowledge, then the set of knowledge viewed as valuable in the KM system would certainly look different from the set selected by third-party knowledge managers tasked with the oversight of KM systems. That set of valuable knowledge, of course, might look much different from one deemed valuable by a group of senior executives, focused on strategic objectives. Validation, along with many other phases of a KM system—not to mention the operation and installation of a KM system in the first place—is best done by an interdepartmental team that brings a diverse set of priorities and experience to the table while still being able to share the same vision for successful KM. This team often includes an executive-level sponsor, something that will be covered in-depth later in the chapter.

> Validation is often done collaboratively, and marks a good phase in the flow of knowledge to address the importance of teamwork and collaboration in knowledge management.

Knowledge as Content

Humans are unbelievably good at saving things. Where we tend to fall short is in the retrieval of them after they've been saved. Consider the way you organize files saved in your computer or in the cloud. Do you have a system for labeling your files and for organizing them in folders? Could you find everything you've ever saved in a moment's notice? Most importantly, could you teach a friend how to find anything on your computer using only one example to educate them?

In generations past, children were all taught the Dewey Decimal System, which Melvil Dewey introduced in 1876; it was designed from inception to create a universal way for libraries to organize their volumes (Dewey 1876). The system has been widely used since the late 1800s to organize books kept in libraries, based on their relation to other books in a given section.

Of chief importance to the documentation, publication, retrieval, and application phases of the idealized knowledge flow introduced in the last section is the way that an organization's knowledge is documented and stored. Think of a KM system as needing its own library, of sorts. *Codification*, or a system of rules used to keep a set of knowledge organized, is central to the structure required to document, publish, retrieve, and ultimately, to apply knowledge. Sound codification often includes *taxonomy*, a system of categories used to make knowledge more easily locatable, and may include any number of directories to help users find the knowledge they're seeking in a given knowledge repository. In libraries of printed books, the Dewey Decimal System is the codification; the sections into which books are grouped constitute the library's taxonomical structure.

> *Codification*, or a system of rules used to keep a set of knowledge organized, is central to the structure required to document, publish, retrieve, and ultimately to apply knowledge. Sound codification often includes *taxonomy*, a system of categories used to make knowledge more easily locatable, and may include any number of directories to help users find the knowledge they're seeking in a given knowledge repository.

Taxonomies must make sense for the types of knowledge being gathered by an organization. And the greater systems of codification must be determined not just by the logic that makes sense to KM system organizers, but by the logic that those seeking knowledge in the KM system will apply. Knowledge repositories are only as valuable as the knowledge in them is findable. For this reason, KM strategists are well advised to put careful thought into the usability of their repositories.

Knowledge kept in repositories is often formatted as digital content. Given the nuance, context, and specific application implicit in the makeup of knowledge, often more complex than a single data point, which can be kept logically in a the single cell of a spreadsheet, this digital content can appear in many forms.

Examples of the many digital content formats knowledge can be encapsulated in:

- **Video Files:** Good for providing context, relaying critical distinctions, and being quick to consume; but file sizes tend to be large, so repositories need to include large storage capacities.
- **Text Documents:** Good for providing detail, being easy to update and requiring little storage space; but the value of the knowledge encapsulated can be limited by the quality of the writing.
- **Wikis:** Good for fostering collaborative knowledge sharing, being easy to update, and encouraging critical discussion of knowledge; but the format can be daunting for the uninitiated.
- **Bulletin Boards:** Good for fostering critical discussion of knowledge, being easy to update, and helping users and the organization pinpoint key knowledge creators and enablers; but the format requires moderation since its conversational nature can lead to meandering debate, undermining taxonomy.

These are just a few of the various shapes digital content can take within KM systems. Every content format has strengths and weaknesses, and for this reason, many mature KM systems capture and codify knowledge in a variety of formats, deploying multiple content management systems to support them. Additionally, many enterprise-level software solutions for KM exist, some of which are specifically designed for public sector organizations. Of course, different organizations have different strategic goals necessitating a wide range of KM systems to support them. Some KM systems are very complex, and some are simple. More powerful software solutions don't necessarily create more powerful KM systems, and no IT solution should constitute the totality of a KM system. Unfortunately, many KM efforts fail when stakeholders conclude that what they need is simply a technology investment and nothing more. KM software and IT systems are not a viable replacement for well-considered, strategic, human-led efforts to

Figure 11.6 Technology alone can't replace human-led efforts to manage systems

capture knowledge and enable knowledge flow. They only serve to support these efforts.

Of course IT solutions and software created either in-house or by enterprise providers can provide incredible support if properly selected and deployed. A good technology investment can deliver powerful functionality for the documentation, storage, and retrieval of knowledge content within a greater KM system. Perhaps the most powerful factor to consider is the semantic search functionality included in such technology. Going back to the analogy proposed earlier in the chapter, where a simple personal computer is presented as a repository, and all the files within it as knowledge content, it's easy to see why all modern computer operating systems include quick access to search fields powering systems that can scan a computer's entire hard drive or connected cloud storage system quickly based on a word or phrase. Semantic search has become the retrieval method of choice for digital users in applications ranging from locating emails in an archive to discovering specific information on the vast World Wide Web. Enabling these search functionalities are systems of keywords known as *metadata,* which provide taxonomical or categorical data about the information they're attached to. Tagging content with metadata or meta-tags is a great way to help computer systems decipher what the content is about—and people find what they're searching for.

Semantic search has become the retrieval method of choice for digital users in applications ranging from locating emails in an archive to discovering specific information on the vast World Wide Web. Enabling these search functionalities are systems of keywords known as *metadata,* which provide taxonomical or categorical data about the information they're attached to.

Not all KM systems require complex, software-based content repositories, but they can be a powerful addition. High-tech content management systems can offer a true resource to turn to, available to everyone in an organization at any time of the day or night. When paired with good KM communication strategies, they can foster a sharing culture and break down silos. These technologies provide repositories where knowledge is easily found and a variety of content types can be stored. The systems themselves can be custom-structured in ways that make sense for an organization, and that can often serve the dual role of supporting important legal requirements regarding record retention. On the downside, technology solutions like these often require substantial financial investments, which only pay themselves back when paired with equally substantial cultural investments. KM content management systems often require regular attention from at least one manager, sometimes many, to usher the programs into further levels of maturity. More importantly, KM success almost always requires buy-in from many stakeholders, and without it, powerful technologies can quickly be rendered inert. Not every organization is ready to adopt KM; those that shun standard operating procedures, business processes, and policies are not great candidates, culturally. KM requires a concerted effort and real support, not just lip service. So how can public managers who recognize the value of KM solicit the kind of support they need to create successful KM systems? The answer is often found by focusing on the value that a KM system can deliver to the organization.

Making the Case for Knowledge Management

Experts have pinpointed a handful of key points where KM initiatives can either advance to greater levels of adoption by their institutions, or burn out. To be sure, ushering a KM initiative from the germ of an idea to a fully formed and institutionalized KM system takes work. Figure 11.7 shows the critical points at which KM efforts are often either adopted or abandoned. It's easy to see how big a role internal selling can play in KM adoption.

Executive-level buy-in is of critical importance every time an initiative designed to support the highest strategic priorities of an organization is put in place. This is because executives often shoulder the responsibility of driving major strategic initiatives. Since KM efforts are tasked with supporting these kinds of strategic initiatives, having executive-level buy-in is almost always key to the success of KM efforts. The good news is that, in many cases, KM efforts

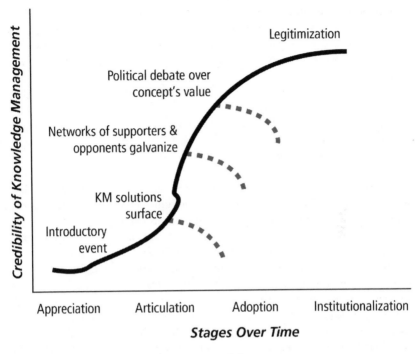

Figure 11.7 Lifecycle of institutionalizing knowledge management concept

Source: DeLong 2004

are first promoted by lower tier employees, not Chief Information Officers (CIOs), or other members of the executive suite. In these scenarios, executives aren't required to lead KM initiatives, but simply to sponsor them and to help maintain their prioritization among others on the senior leadership team.

The best way to solicit executive sponsorship for a KM program is to form a value proposition—designed to highlight the purpose and value of KM in the context of the organization and its strategic initiatives—that can drum up support for KM throughout the organization, especially at the highest levels. One method for uncovering a sound KM value proposition is by focusing on the following questions from the APQC.

> The best way to solicit executive sponsorship for a KM program is to form a value proposition—designed to highlight the purpose and value of KM in the context of the organization and its strategic initiatives—that can drum up support for KM throughout the organization, especially at the highest levels.

Questions for developing a KM value proposition modified from private sector questions found in *The New Edge in Knowledge* (O'Dell and Hubert 2011):

1. Does your current knowledge allow you to serve citizens well now?
2. What knowledge will you need to help you innovate and meet long-term goals?
3. What public services can be improved if knowledge and expertise is better shared and transferred?
4. Are there current and pending challenges or issues that are knowledge-related?
5. What will success look like?

These questions and others like them can help public managers understand the roles KM could play in supporting high-level strategies, and therefore, better align them with the key strategic goals being promoted by senior leaders. Ultimately, the goal is to be able to explain how each functional group within the organization will benefit from a KM initiative.

There are as many KM value propositions as there are organizations. A well-designed and viable KM initiative is well suited for the goals it is meant to serve. Extraneous KM efforts are the fastest route to obsolescence in KM and quickly lead to KM system failure. As has been previously discussed in this chapter, KM systems are only as effective as they are useful. Moreover, the greater the number of stakeholders in an organization supporting a KM initiative's success, the higher its chances are of succeeding. In short, KM is a team sport and should be played like one.

Non-Technical and Cultural Systems for Knowledge Retention

A lack of organization-wide buy-in can be a sign of a lack of understanding about the value of KM in general, or it can be the result of the fact that the organization truly does not require a KM system. An honest evaluation of the organization is required to determine the value that might be delivered using knowledge maps and other methods of evaluating knowledge creation and loss within the organization. Luckily, there are plenty of less formal (or less technical) knowledge-sharing practices that can be deployed individually if knowledge loss is only a small issue. Of course, these kinds of systems can also play roles as components of full-scale KM systems.

Part-time or Temporary Retiree Involvement

Many public institutions are finding that bringing long-time employees back in for temporary or part-time roles can mean recovering valuable lost knowledge.

Organizational Learning and Training Programs

Systems designed to educate employees, whether classroom-based or online, have a long precedence in bringing employees up to speed on explicit knowledge, and are often met with less skepticism. They are great for developing a base level of shared knowledge across an organization, as well as building specialized knowledge among individuals or teams.

One-on-One Mentoring

Advisor and mentor programs take advantage of the natural interest many people have in helping someone along in their career—and in learning from those more experienced in a field. When true mentor relationships are fostered, tacit knowledge can be transferred very effectively.

One-to-Many Mentoring

Group settings can also provide great opportunities for learning. Internal classroom sessions and storytelling initiatives are popular forms of one-to-many knowledge exchange. Believe it or not, basic storytelling can be a great way to transform tacit knowledge into explicit knowledge. This practice has been adopted by NASA, the World Bank, and IBM, among others (DeLong 2004).

Communities of Practice

A great many organizations have developed informal communities—both real and virtual—of employees working on similar problems and sharing interests. These are widely referred to as *communities of practice*, and they can be a great way of transferring both explicit and tacit knowledge and developing databases of specific questions and answers.

Getting Started with Knowledge Management

While executive-level sponsorship and cultural initiatives are important to the successful adoption of a KM initiative, the process of institutionalizing a full KM system must ultimately begin with efforts to isolate the most valuable knowledge and record it. From the outset, most KM strategists find themselves working to build structures for organizations that are by no means permanent in their structures, needs, and strategic imperatives. Simply put, organizations change, and so do KM systems. For this reason, KM initiatives often involve a test-and-learn approach from the outset. Iteration is a key ingredient in building a successful, long-lasting KM system, so the first steps should be viewed simply as first efforts. When trying to establish startup systems for KM and knowledge retention, many practitioners explore gaps revealed during knowledge mapping exercises, comparing them to ideal states of knowledge flow. How does knowledge flow in the organization now? What would improved knowledge flow look like? How can we reach this ideal state? What systems might support that transition? These are all questions that can be useful to those analyzing gaps against desired states of knowledge flow.

After such exercises have been undertaken, the next steps often involve developing a pilot knowledge retention system where team members can record their knowledge as content and host it in a digital repository using a system of codification. There are two common exercises that constitute good starting places for any KM strategist trying to get the ball rolling with the actual recording of knowledge in a repository, both of which are recommended by the Kirkpatrick Model of training developed by Donald Kirkpatrick in the 1950s (Blankenship 2011).

The Wiki Approach

Many find content that can be augmented or updated by many authors useful. This is often done using wikis, where articles can be edited by anyone else with access. Those contributing don't always need expertise, since others in the system are free to make corrections—a detail that can help foster a sense of collaboration among contributors. These kinds of repositories can be grown quickly, but the content's organization and quality can suffer since there isn't a single editor charged with approving all the content and labeling it properly using a pre-defined taxonomy (ibid.).

The Review Process Approach

In this system, knowledge content is created and sent to a single editor or a group of editors charged with validating it, tagging it properly, and posting it to the repository. In this system, the content is often more consistent, as is its organization. However, the review process approach can result in a bottle-necking effect where content is waiting to be approved for too long. Those contributing and using knowledge from the repository can grow impatient and become discouraged by the lack of efficiency.

Knowledge Management and the Future

Advanced KM strategists can go way beyond gap analyses and knowledge mapping as methods of pinpointing intersections of knowledge loss. Administrators of mature KM systems can even build systems that predict points of knowledge loss based on retirement schedules, skills inventories, and estimations of future needs for essential roles (DeLong 2004). At this level of maturity, KM can do much more for a public sector organization than stem the loss of critical knowledge. Mature KM systems can enable the flow of knowledge so well that they actually drive government innovation and enable new creativity. Breakthroughs, well documented, communicated consistently, and utilized by team members, lead to more breakthroughs. In these systems, continuous improvement can be supported by the KM system. Figure 11.8, developed by the APQC, shows levels of maturity commonly witnessed in KM systems.

In their most advanced forms, KM systems support dynamic knowledge, where even wisdom flows from one team member to others at regular

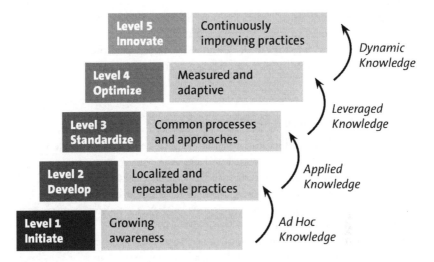

Figure 11.8 Levels of knowledge management maturity

Source: O'Dell and Hubert 2011

intervals. In the future, this could serve to create a sort of collective intelligence within organizations, where knowledge workers gain valuable knowledge from their work, at ever-increasing rates. In tomorrow's knowledge economy, this kind of work will surely prove the most fulfilling for knowledge workers. More importantly, this kind of system will enable rapid innovation and knowledge flow, limited only by the advances in IT that are arriving ever more rapidly as societies are vaulted into the future. It seems very likely that optimal knowledge sharing will play a critical role in the arrival of optimal government systems and services.

Case Study: NASA's Process Based Mission Assurance Knowledge Management System (PBMA-KMS)

Explorations into the depths of space, images of the universe's most mysterious phenomena, spacecraft touching down on distant planets—NASA has the power to stretch the human imagination and feed mankind's innate curiosity. But behind every one of NASA's 100-plus missions per year is an enormous network of nearly 80,000 civil service and contract workers following complex work processes across multiple departments (NASA Missions 2014, NASA Employee Orientation 2014).

During the late 1990s, NASA initiated its first KM system, Process Based Mission Assurance, to aid in the formation of a universal approach to mission safety and assurance that could be used by every employee in NASA's wide-ranging workforce, on every mission.

Today, this system is still growing, and is recognized as a model of KM for organizations in all fields—especially government. The following case study provides an overview of the system's creation and evolution based primarily on the research and writings of J. Steven Newman and Stephen M. Wander in "NASA's Pioneering PBMA Knowledge Management System" (Newman et al. 2002).

Leveraging Knowledge for Mission Success

NASA has eighteen centers and research facilities throughout the country (Wilson 2013). It is across this scattered network, where more than 17,000 NASA employees and countless more government contractors work to answer basic questions about aerospace exploration and how to improve the quality of life on Earth (NASA AES Report 2012). This research often calls for highly involved missions—the complexity of which is compounded by the fact that each program involves the disparate work of numerous departments. And if that isn't enough, while passing through the hands of hundreds of workers from aeronautical engineers to computer scientists, every step requires near flawless or flawless execution.

NASA's Office of Safety and Mission Assurance (OSMA) is the department responsible for ensuring each phase of the mission lifecycle—starting with concept development and ending with deployment. OSMA adheres to rigorous safety, quality, and compliance standards that aim to guarantee success (Office of Safety and Mission Assurance 2013).

During the late 1990s, after a series of mission failures, NASA recognized the need to shore up its Mission Assurance program (Newman et al. 2002). The gaps between separate departments needed to be bridged and a universal, unfailing process for applying safety and mission assurance at every stage of each mission needed to be developed.

In 1999, OSMA initiated the development of a KM system, known as PBMA-KMS (Newman et al. 2002). The original goal of this system was to provide workers at every stage in the mission lifecycle access to proven best practices and case studies containing useful safety and mission assurance information. In other words, knowledge needed to be captured, shared, accessed, and used to guarantee a unified mission assurance process across all departments and hand-offs.

With an overarching KM goal defined, the content that would translate this vision into a reality was decided on and gathered. While the PBMA-KMS team initially focused on best practices and case studies, the collection effort soon grew well beyond these original goals. Throughout the development of the system, the team collected countless artifacts—in the form of explicit and tacit knowledge—related to mission assurance such as policies, standards, test requirements, and verification processes. This collection of knowledge constituted nearly everything any NASA team member would need to execute effective mission assurance practices, regardless of department or lifecycle phase.

The functionality required to deliver this knowledge to the NASA community was also carefully considered. PBMA-KMS coordinators made certain the content and users guided the decision about which technology and delivery methods would work best, leading to the PBMA-KMS being built entirely in a web portal accessible by all NASA employees. Within this portal, content delivery methods included libraries, repositories, and collaboration environments, to name a few.

In 2001, PBMA-KMS was officially introduced, becoming the first NASA KM system deployed across all departments. Since its inception, the NASA community has enjoyed limitless access to knowledge aiding in the implementation of safety and mission assurance practices throughout a mission's lifecycle.

Presently, the PBMA web portal consists of many KM tools including:

- **Best Practice Library**
  Hundreds of best practice resources such as handbooks, procedure documents, and techniques that provide mission assurance guidance.
- **Video Nugget Library**
  Videos of experts designed to add a personal perspective to various topics and surround them with context.
- **Program Profiles**
  Information and details about past safety and mission assurance processes to give program and project managers examples of previous practices.
- **System Failure Case Studies**
  Collection of case studies used to demonstrate where things can go wrong and what to avoid.
- **Communities of Practice**
  Over 700 discussion groups comprised of individuals from multiple departments built to share insights, offer advice, and resolve problems.

These tools, and many others, have helped bring every department under one unified system of processes and provided easy access to invaluable mission assurance insight, discussion, and best practices.

Over the years, needs continue to change and, as such, so too does the system's content and functionality. NASA continually grows and adapts PBMA-KMS, looking for better ways to capture and share critical mission assurance knowledge. This constant evolution is perhaps the biggest reason the system continues to be an enduring resource essential to the success of every awe-inspiring NASA mission to this day.

Discussion Questions

1. Why is knowledge retention important to organizations today?
2. What are the two types of knowledge?
3. Why is the flow of knowledge critical to organizational growth and adaptation?

4. Why is a KM system's codification critical to its success?
5. What are some types of knowledge repositories and what kinds of knowledge content do they store?
6. Name some non-technical or cultural knowledge management systems.
7. What are the two common approaches to getting started with knowledge management?
8. Describe the value a mature knowledge management system can create for an organization.

References

Barry, Dan. 2010. "Boomers Hit New Self-Absorption Milestone: Age 65." *The New York Times*. December 31. Accessed October 17, 2014. http://www.nytimes.com/2011/01/01/us/01boomers.html?pagewanted=all&_r=0.

Blankenship, Linda. 2011. "Knowledge Management and Retention," in *CIO Leadership for State Governments—Emerging Trends and Practices*. PTI, Alexandria, VA.

Cohn, D'Vera and Paul Taylor. 2010. "Baby Boomers Approaching 65—Glumly." *Pew Research & Social Demographic Trends*, December 20. Accessed October 17, 2014. http://www.pewsocialtrends.org/2010/12/20/baby-boomers-approach-65-glumly/.

DeLong, David. 2004. *Lost Knowledge: Confronting the Threat of an Aging Workforce*. Oxford University Press, New York.

Dewey, Melvil. 1876. *Dewey Decimal Classification*. Kingsport Press, Kingsport, TN. Accessed via Project Gutenberg Ebook, September 27, 2013. http://www.gutenberg.org/files/12513/12513-h/12513-h.htm.

Frank, Lydia. 2012. "Gen Y on the Job. Research Compiled from a Survey Given to 500,000 Millennial Workers between July 2011 and July 2012." August 21. Accessed October 17, 2014. http://www.payscale.com/gen-y-at-work.

Hilbert, Martin and Priscila Lopez. 2011. "The World's Technological Capacity to Store, Communicate and Compute Information." *Science Magazine*, April 1. Accessed October 17, 2014. http://www.sciencemag.org/content/332/6025/60.

IBM. 2014. "What Is Analytics?" Accessed October 17, 2014. http://www.ibm.com/smarterplanet/us/en/business_analytics/article/it_business_intelligence.html.

Kim, Moonja P. 2005. "Knowledge Retention Enhances Performance-Based Management." Accessed October 17, 2014. http://www.dcma.mil/communicator/fall05/4_business_processes/DCMA_Comm_v05n03_pp49-51.pdf.

O'Dell, Carla and Cindy Hubert. 2011. *The New Edge in Knowledge*. John Wiley & Sons, Inc., Hoboken, NJ.

US Census Bureau. 2011. "The Older Population: 2010." Accessed October 17, 2014. http://www.census.gov/prod/cen2010/briefs/c2010br-09.pdf.

Case Study Sources

NASA AES Report. 2012. "National Aeronautics and Space Administration: 2012 Annual Employee Survey Results." Accessed October 17, 2014. https://searchpub.nssc.nasa.gov/servlet/sm.web.Fetch/NASA_2010_AES_Report.pdf?rhid=1000&did=739126&type=released.

NASA Employee Orientation. 2014. "Contractor Employees." NASA. Accessed October 17, 2014. http://employeeorientation.nasa.gov/contractors/default.htm.

NASA Missions. 2014. "NASA's Alphabetical List of Missions." NASA. Accessed October 17, 2014. http://www.nasa.gov/missions/index.html#.UkQy5tKsiSo.

Newman, J. Steven, Stephen M. Wander, William Vantine, and Paul Benfield. 2002. "Introducing the NASA Process Based Mission Assurance Knowledge Management System." Joint ESA-NASA SPace-Flight Safety Conference. Accessed October 17, 2014. http://articles.adsabs.harvard.edu/full/2002ESASP.486. . .39N.

Office of Safety and Mission Assurance. 2013. "Office of Safety and Mission Assurance." NASA, June 3. Accessed October 17, 2014. http://www.hq.nasa.gov/office/codeq/.

Wilson, Jim. 2013. "NASA Centers and Facilities." NASA, July 28. Accessed October 17, 2014. http://www.nasa.gov/about/sites/index.html#.UkOppNKeqSo.

Additional Resources

Basiulis, Karen E. 2009. "The New Reality of the American Workforce: Knowledge Management as a Retention Tool." *Contract Management* 49, 11: 76–85.

Dalkir, Kimiz. 2011. *Knowledge Management in Theory and Practice*. MIT Press, Cambridge, MA.

Green, Annie, Michael Stankosky, and Linda Vandergriff. 2010. *In Search of Knowledge Management: Pursuing Primary Principals*. Emerald, Bingley, UK.

Hislop, Donalk. 2013. *Knowledge Management in Organizations: A Critical Introduction*. Oxford University Press, USA.

Jennex, Murray E. 2007. *Knowledge Management in Modern Organizations*. IGI Global, Hershey, PA.

Lytras, Miltiadis D., Meir Russ, Ronald Maier, and Ambjörn Naeve, eds. 2008. *Knowledge Management Strategies: A Handbook of Applied Technologies*. Information Science Reference, Hershey, PA.

McInerney, Claire R. and Michael E.D. Koenig. 2011. *Knowledge Management (KM) Processes in Organizations: Theoretical Foundations and Practice*. Morgan & Claypool Publishers, San Rafael, CA.

Rahman, Hakikur ed. 2009. *Social and Political Implications of Data Mining: Knowledge Management in E-Government*. Information Science Reference, Hershey, PA.

Stankosky, Michael. 2011. *Creating the Discipline of Knowledge Management*. Taylor & Francis, New York.

Wallace, Danny P. 2007. *Knowledge Management: Historical and Cross-Disciplinary Themes*. Libraries Unlimited, Westport, CT.

Yen-Ku Kuo and Kung-Don Ye. 2010. "How Employees' Perception of Information Technology Application and Their Knowledge Management Capacity Influence Organizational Performance." *Behaviour & Information Technology* 29, 3: 287–303.

Digital Destinations

Department of the Navy Knowledge Management Policy and Initiative. http://www.doncio.navy.mil/TagResults.aspx?ID=33

Federal Knowledge Management Initiative Mission. https://sites.google.com/site/fmwgroupnasa/vision

Institute for Knowledge and Innovation. http://www.linkedin.com/groups/Institute-Knowledge-Innovation-GWU-1097047/about

Institute for the Study of Knowledge Management in Education. http://www.iskme.org/

Service Component Reference Model (SRM): Digital Asset Services: Knowledge Management. http://www.whitehouse.gov/sites/default/files/omb/assets/omb/egov/a-4-4-digit-knowledge.html

12 The People Factor—Managing the Human Resource Function in a Technology Environment

When the US Constitution went into effect on March 4, 1787, many things about the world—and the nascent US government—were very different (Rogers 2011). Relaying a message from Philadelphia to New York required a three-day ride by horseback. The country was without the Internet, telephones, electricity, or even a capital city.

Over the last 200-plus years, government has adapted to technological ubiquity, transforming alongside innovations from the private sector. Today, the ways government workers do work and the types of work they do—the "human factors" related to the intersection of government and technology—are shifting faster than ever. Never-before-seen job titles are part of this shift. Even the ways people communicate inside government are changing. This shift is occurring most visibly at the federal and state levels, where the largest workforces exist and the biggest technological investments are made. Of course, local governments are adapting, as well.

> Today, the ways government workers do work and the types of work they do—the "human factors" related to the intersection of government and technology—are shifting faster than ever. Never-before-seen job titles are part of this shift.

A core driver of this shift in the way the business of government gets done is technology. Specifically, the rapid transformation of IT is altering the landscape of communication upon which much of the government's work is built. Closely connected to the evolution of IT is the ability of individuals and groups to adopt that technology innately, which precipitates greater cultural and societal advances that, in turn, propel innovation in both the systems governments use to get work done and the technologies used to do it. Compounding the complexity of this governmental adaptation are ever-decreasing budgets and rapidly shifting worker demographics. This complexity all boils down to a cycle that involves forces from government workers, government organizations, and technologies—all pushing in the direction of efficiency, and more importantly, improved services.

Figure 12.1 The human element in IT cannot be overlooked, people still matter

Technology's human factor is causing dramatic and sweeping changes inside government organizations big and small. These changes can be an intimidating departure from the status quo, but they also create new opportunities for tomorrow's public managers to harness the power of this change to create more effective teams, systems, and government organizations. Tackling the future of collaboration and work by understanding and embracing the social and technological shifts that are happening can mean the difference between success and failure.

Incorporating the Technology Professional into Government

Among the most tangible technology-driven shifts happening inside government organizations across the country is the arrival of a wide range of new technology professionals, with various titles and backgrounds, into organizations of all sizes and responsibilities. The incorporation of IT professionals has been wholesale, and is reflected in some form or another in every government organization in the country. According to the Bureau of Labor Statistics (BLS), "IT management positions" were the number three occupational series in the federal government in 2004, with 64,209 jobs, making them one of the largest and most universal job function clusters in the United States government today (Crosby 2004). It's not often that universal new positions are created in government, let alone whole departments—as have been witnessed by organizations incorporating robust IT teams into their operations. These IT teams are far different from their help desk predecessors of the late 1980s and early 1990s. IT professionals inside government organizations are no longer limited to simply resetting computer passwords and wiring the building with CAT5 network cables. Today, technology professionals falling into the IT chain of command are building mobile applications designed to help workers be more efficient on the go and constructing complex technology resources with varying levels of security access and encryption— not to mention the technologies they're building and maintaining to enable e-government and m-government, as detailed in Chapter 3. Of course, these same teams are still responsible for making hardware updates and helping their colleagues reset passwords and recover lost documents, but thinking of IT's function as simple, rudimentary, or detached from the core business of operating and advancing the organization is a crude misstep in today's technology-enabled public sector. Exploring some of the most rapidly arriving and evolving types of IT roles emerging in the public sector should illustrate this fact.

According to the Bureau of Labor Statistics (BLS), "IT management positions" were the number three occupational series in the federal government in 2004, with 64,209 jobs, making them one of the largest and most universal job function clusters in the United States government today.

Source: Crosby 2004

The Chief Information Officer

Although the role of the Chief Information Officer (CIO) in government, including the role of the Federal CIO position was discussed in depth in Chapter 2, the CIO has become the most visible and prominent technologist in government today, so it seems prudent to mention that today's public sector CIO holds a very important and often misunderstood station in the organization. While it might seem readily obvious that the job of a federal agency's Chief Financial Officer (CFO) is to manage funds and understand the financial underpinning's of the agency in question, the function of the CIO is often more difficult to understand. This seems largely due to the fact that information is a more abstract component of an organization's operation and advancement. Everyone understands what it means to manage money and budget, because they are part of our everyday lives. Relatively few people understand what it means to build and maintain computer and information technology.

Today's public sector CIO is often tasked with prioritizing and overseeing the full array of technologies used by the organization, both for internal

Figure 12.2 The IT team operates much as a musical symphony

use (as is the focus of this chapter) and external, organization-to-constituent, use. This means keeping tabs on everything from the security and usability of the computers sitting on every public servant's desk to decision-making about how best to update legacy technologies or integrate new technologies and information systems into the organization. The CIO's job also involves ensuring that the technology being used by the organization is useful and is being used by employees whose work might be expedited or enabled by it. CIOs can even be responsible for overseeing security, a job that occasionally has its own private sector equivalent in the Chief Security Officer (CSO), or for overseeing the development of new technology, which is often the responsibility of the Chief Technology Officer (CTO) in the private sector. Suffice it to say that the job of the government CIO is only getting bigger and more complex, and that one of the most critical components of the role is to play the part of the conductor in the technological symphony that the modern public sector IT department represents.

A newer position is emerging with addition of the Chief Innovation Officer. The focus on innovation is an attempt to have someone chiefly in charge of looking at current government business processes and seeking ways to innovate by measureable improvements. As the saying goes there is only so much one can do in repaving the "cow paths" of the past as opposed to seeking new pathways that are relatively free from "this is the way we have always done it."

The Software Specialists

If the IT team in a public organization can be represented by a symphony, with the CIO holding the conductor's wand, the software specialists on the team might play any number of roles from percussionist to violin or trumpet soloist. This is because software engineers and software architects often build and maintain the foundation of the technology in an organization—known as the *information architecture*—and software developers create single- or multi-purpose applications for use by citizens or team members. The software specialists keep the beat upon which the whole technology stack is constructed, as well as creating the tools that make working easier and more efficient. They are also often heavily involved in policy and planning roles at the higher levels, devoting their know-how to capital planning and information security management. Down the chain of command, they can be responsible for building websites and Internet resources, and even providing support as it relates to technology. The BLS predicts that nationwide software developer jobs will grow by 30 percent between 2010 and 2020, a much faster rate than the average for all occupations, which is just 14 percent (BLS website).

The Data Specialists

The newest breed of technologists appearing universally in both public and private sector organizations are the data specialists. Their roles are still shaking out in many ways, as governments and private businesses find new and unique ways to extract insights and knowledge from data sets during the proliferation of digital data known as "big data," discussed at length in Chapter 11. Of course, to many data professionals, the word "big" in the phrase big data is a red herring, because many federal agencies and government organizations have dealt with large data sets for a long time. But the term big data also implies that the size of the data sets is becoming so big that it's contributing to the problem data specialists have to deal with, which necessitates new specializations to manage data and databases. These new role players possess unique skills ranging from the visualization of data to the science of it, which incorporates many fields including mathematics, pattern recognition, and advanced machine learning. Database managers are the most traditional data-related role players in the symphony, ensuring that every piece of music's various parts and individual sheets are accurate and that they come together to create a complete song. Without them, the organization's databases would quickly fall into chaos, and all of the valuable information and knowledge buried in public sector data sets could never be extracted. They validate, structure, and cull data to put it to work, and they also guard it. The BLS predicts nationwide database administrator jobs will grow by 31 percent between 2010 and 2020, a much faster rate than the average for all occupations (BLS website).

> The newest breed of technologists appearing universally in both public and private sector organizations are the data specialists. Their roles are still shaking out in many ways, as governments and private businesses find new and unique ways to extract insights and knowledge from data sets during the proliferation of digital data known as "big data."

Special Consideration for Technologists

Technologists in government organizations often shoulder a multiplicity of responsibilities, with much overlap. The software specialists described in the previous section often develop applications that make use of data, and the data specialists often build software applications that process data. For example, in the private sector, roles are often defined more by an individual's skill set and primary function as part of a team than anything else, so it follows that the same sort of flexibility is needed at the government level if organizations are to make the most of their internal technologists. This constitutes a departure from many other departments in government organizations, where the roles have been traditionally well defined by comparison. Tomorrow's public managers need to recognize that, due to the nature of the work they do and the unique new roles they play, technologists require special consideration in their roles, classifications, and the ways they work. There's already precedence for this at the federal level; "the US Office of Personnel Management (OPM) relaxed some regulations to allow federal agencies to meet their staffing needs . . . during the late 1990s, when federal agencies sought to hire and keep IT professionals to do Year 2000 conversions" (Mastracci 2009).

> Technologists are far from a commodity in today's economy. In fact, these new specialists are in such demand that it's become common in the private sector to hire them based solely on their demonstrable skills in working with technology; innovative technology companies like Facebook and Google fully reject traditional measures of merit like experience and formal education as part of their hiring practices regarding software and data specialists.

Technologists are far from a commodity in today's economy. In fact, these new specialists are in such demand that it's become common in the private sector to hire them based solely on their demonstrable skills in working with technology; innovative technology companies like Facebook and Google fully reject traditional measures of merit like experience and formal education as part of their hiring practices regarding software and data specialists. Local governments are already finding it increasingly difficult to retain and hire information technology staff because of the competitive nature of the positions. It seems likely that many public sector organizations will also need to adopt the same new measures of qualification, assuming they have not already, if they intend to recruit and retain skilled technologists.

Additionally, competitive pay is a critical determining factor for any organization vying for these sought-after specialists. As was observed by Ingraham, Moynihan and Selden, "The reality of the marketplace is that there is a strong competition for talent, and the public sector must compete with the private sector for human resources with increasingly complex skills" (Ingraham, Selden, Moynihan 2000). Given that both the public and private sectors are competing in the same market for technologists, those individuals will no doubt expect equal or near equal salaries to perform the same functions in government that they are well compensated to perform in the free market.

Some government organizations have already had to alter their pay scales in order to attract them; the OPM enabled this when it released updated policies regarding attracting and retaining IT specialists in 1998, which included the payout of bonuses and increased salaries. "The new interim regulations will give agencies the authority to pay up to 10 percent of an employee's rate of basic pay (up to 25 percent with OPM approval) to a group or category of employees, like computer programmers and system engineers, with specialized skills," wrote the OPM in a press release about the change (Mastracci 2009).

Additionally, research has indicated that prospects for job security and advancement are also critically important to these workers (Mastracci 2009). Flexible work schedules and improved work-life balance are important to many workers in contemporary government, but technologists appear less concerned about these topics, based on Mastracci's research.

Additionally, research has indicated that prospects for job security and advancement are also critically important to these workers (Mastracci 2009). Flexible work schedules and improved work-life balance are important to many workers in contemporary government, but technologists appear less concerned about these topics, based on Mastracci's research. Ultimately,

Figure 12.3 IT is always a 24/7 operation

technology is a 24/7 component of government, unlike many of the governmental components that predate the rise of digital information and modern IT structures and systems. Technology workers and the ways they work seem to reflect this shift to a government that is "always on." Nonetheless, tomorrow's public managers will need to continue to work to meet the needs of technologists working in government, and to understand the things that motivate them to select government jobs over those in the private sector. A sense of civic obligation and the fulfillment it offers is certainly present in many government sector technologists, but new types of workers and work necessitate fresh ways of thinking about managing these workers. This will be true even after current efforts to boost internal technologists are long past, and human capital markets shift dramatically in new and unpredictable directions.

Weighing Technology Contracting Against In-House Development

Many of the software systems created for governments and government agencies in past decades have been developed, delivered, and maintained by contractors. While this practice is sure to continue into the future, there are many circumstances in which it will prove preferable to create, update, and work with technology as part of the internal function of the organization. This is already the case in organizations where developing new technology has become part of the organizational DNA. For example, the National Security Agency (NSA), the Central Intelligence Agency (CIA), and the Federal Bureau of Investigation (FBI) are all known to work with both contractors and in-house technologists to perform cyber surveillance and to counteract cyber crime and cyber terrorism. The US Bureau of Labor Statistics (BLS) and the US Bureau of the Census are both deeply rooted in statistical data analysis and maintain data specialists on both contract and internal bases.

Contracting can be a very efficient and effective way of delivering new technology; it offers private sector agility and standards for quality. Additionally, outsourced IT work can mean improved services, because contractors can be quickly and easily dismissed for failing to deliver on stated goals or agreed-upon levels of service quality—something that's not necessarily true inside government organizations with antiquated policies on hiring and firing.

Technology contracting, specifically in the software space, has been criticized as an inefficient and outdated way of solving problems and delivering improved services in government organizations. This is because modern software development often involves *rapid iteration*—a process by which new versions of the same software are released in short intervals, with each new version attempting to better solve the needs of the software user.

Source: Lathrop and Ruma 2010

However, technology contracting, specifically in the software space, has been criticized as an inefficient and outdated way of solving problems and delivering improved services in government organizations (Lathrop and Ruma 2010). This is because modern software development often involves *rapid iteration*—a process by which new versions of the same software are released in short intervals, with each new version attempting to better solve the needs of the software user. As the needs and application of the software shift, so does the software solution. Building a complete piece of software based on a written Request for Proposals (RFP) ignores this methodology, and more importantly, amplifies misalignments between the stated requirements of that software and the actual needs of the users, in this case, government employees. This is to say that technology, especially software, built in-house can often be maintained more efficiently and can certainly be updated faster than software built by contractors. There are also further problems in the realm of technology contracting related to the fact that highly complex technical systems built by one contractor can be difficult for other contractors or internal teams to update over time. This results in complications at the procurement level.

Despite the various supporting and critical arguments about technology contracting, it seems unlikely to disappear entirely from the public sector any time soon. Tomorrow's public administrators need to recognize, however, that both outsourced and internally developed technology solutions come with their respective difficulties and benefits. Thoughtful consideration about which route to go will be warranted more and more as procurement rules shift and new opportunities to build technology in-house are created. Simply outsourcing technology without consideration will no longer be an option. More importantly, efforts to better understand the need, and to articulate it carefully to whichever technologist or team of technologists are tasked with solving for that need is, and will be, critically important. Breaking down barriers between users and the technologists developing the tools they need is, and will be, critical to creating technologies that are useful and used. When there is a question of how and where to build new technology for internal use in government, the answer and a great many others can often be found by enabling better communication between the user and the technology developer.

The Technology-Enabled Worker

Technology professionals aren't the only ones affecting the way governments innovate and incorporate technology into daily work.

Figure 12.4 The changing of the guard-the next generation of leadership is coming

A Changing of the Guard

The next generation of workers now entering the workforce, known as the Millennial Generation, is also bringing in entirely new skills, values, and attitudes regarding technology and its role in the workplace. In the public sector, children of the baby boomer generation are filling many of the roles left behind by members of that retiring generation, and they're looking to do the work of their parents much differently.

> Millenniums are different than those before them, having grown up with the latest technologies and devices. They are more restless than their predecessors and are often look at jobs differently with the idea of changing jobs far more often than before.

With these Millenniums providing an insatiable appetite for new technology inside the workforce, organizations both public and private are finding new ways to enable individuals to work more efficiently and more autonomously through technology. When something needs to be understood, it is quickly Googled. When an internal question related to HR or a worker's role presents itself, that worker, more and more, simply turns to the organization's Intranet for an answer. Contemporary workers are enabled by their own skills to work better and learn faster on their own, and that's changing the way work gets done inside government organizations in widespread and far-reaching ways. Millenniums are different than those before them, having grown up with the latest technologies and devices. They are more restless than their predecessors and are often look at jobs differently with the idea of changing jobs far more often than before. This will place new pressures on government to develop innovative ways to retain valued workers or at least develop provisions that when they leave, much of their knowledge stays with the organization. Millenniums view technology quite differently, and are much more prone towards working in a collaborative and self-empowering environment.

The Digital Native at Work in Government

Many in the Millennial Generation have been called *Digital Natives* because they grew up in a world where technology was constantly in their hands—and if not, at least within arm's reach. They were educated on computers and gained access to the Internet in their formative years, facts that seem to make them more innately capable of adopting new technologies and integrating them into their daily lives. While the idea of the Digital Native does not apply to every member of the Millennial generation, individuals in this cohort grouping have been characterized as "native speakers of the digital language" (Prensky 2001). Brought about by being born into a life of complete technological immersion, every aspect of this generation's lifestyle—behaviors, values, and norms—was and is shaped by technology, and this is carrying over into the workplace (Tapscott 1999).

This influx of technologically savvy workers is changing the work-technology relationship in a multitude of ways—many of which are leading to faster, smarter, more efficient ways of working. With around one out of every four workers in America currently belonging to the Millennial Generation, public and private organizations have already felt the impact (Toossi 2012). By 2020, that number will swell to more than 40 percent, meaning the influence of these employees on the workplace will continue to manifest itself in nearly every aspect of every job (ibid.).

> With around one out of every four workers in America currently belonging to the Millennial Generation, public and private organizations have already felt the impact (Toossi 2012). By 2020, that number will swell to more than 40 percent, meaning the influence of these employees on the workplace will continue to manifest itself in nearly every aspect of every job (ibid.).

Digital Natives possess many tendencies and behaviors that result from living a life intertwined with technology. For instance, these workers expect answers to be instant and knowledge to be quickly obtained. They also expect to have access to the tools necessary to do their jobs. This has helped usher in a new expectation as to how and where employees can access information and set a higher standard for efficiency and convenience.

Figure 12.5 Google and other search engines have helped drive expectations about information accessibility and the instant availability of answers among Digital Natives

Source: Google.com

Additionally, extensive experience in social networking platforms allowing for two-way communication and constant connectivity to others through various communication technologies has bestowed this generation with a unique desire for collaboration. While many baby boomers prefer to work independently, Digital Natives thrive when working with others and are most productive as part of a network (Mason, Barzilai-Nahon, Lou 2008). This presents a clashing of work styles, but also introduces the possibility of a more productive work environment where the potential for collective knowledge and teamwork are fully realized and leveraged.

> While many baby boomers prefer to work independently, Digital Natives thrive when working with others and are most productive as part of a network (Mason, Barzilai-Nahon, Lou 2008). This presents a clashing of work styles, but also introduces the possibility of a more productive work environment where the potential for collective knowledge and teamwork are fully realized and leveraged.

Perhaps the most significant impact Digital Natives have on today's workplace is an expectation and yearning for new technology, as well as a capacity to learn and adapt to it. In organizational settings Digital Natives have the power to both initiate the procurement of innovative technologies, and the ability to aid in the diffusion of them amongst all workers, as older employees commonly turn to these individuals to make sense of foreign or relatively novel technologies (Myers and Sadaghiani 2010). This is evidenced in the rising acceptance of the bring-your-own-device movement and the ways in which these mobile technologies have been integrated into the work environment.

This transformation of technology's role in the workplace won't end with the hiring of the last Digital Native. As technology continues to evolve at an exponentially quicker pace, the differences between generations will also quicken. Lee Rainie, director of the Pew Research Center's Internet and American Life Project, explains it best saying, "College students scratch their heads at what their high school siblings are doing (Stone 2010)." Each year, waves of more and more technologically-versed workers will enter the public and private workforce, carrying with them new ways of approaching technology and forcing organizations to find new ways to accommodate and leverage this added knowledge.

> Each year, waves of more and more technologically-versed workers will enter the public and private workforce, carrying with them new ways of approaching technology and forcing organizations to find new ways to accommodate and leverage this added knowledge.

Figure 12.6 Bring Your Own Device (BYOD) is a great employee incentive if properly
managed

The Self-Service Intranet

As Digital Natives and other tech-savvy employees have entered the workforce, a greater demand for the ability to solve problems and answer questions
independently has emerged. On the other side of this demand, HR professionals and managers eager to streamline workflow and enable new standards
for productivity have worked to deliver more information meant to answer
these questions via secure internal networks known as *Intranets*. The most
popular enterprise Intranet solution among international businesses at the
time of this publication was Microsoft's SharePoint, with one survey showing
that 39 percent of respondent organizations were using the software (Apprio
2013). SharePoint has also been widely adopted among governments and
government organizations as the preferred Intranet provider. Other options
including building a custom Intranet, and adopting other enterprise solutions
meant to enable employees to answer their own questions about the organization and the way things are meant to operate.

Common organizational uses of Intranets include:

- providing document management services
- managing business records

- powering enterprise search
- publishing Intranet content
- publishing Internet websites
- delivering business intelligence and insights
- creating business applications
- enabling workflow processes
- supporting team collaboration.

Another popular organizational resource arriving on the scene in recent years is the *shared drive*, a form of cloud storage that allows internal team members to access shared files from within an organization's private network. Enterprise content management systems described in Chapter 11 are also enabling individual workers to acquire key knowledge and insights about their work without much help from team members. Shared drives, content management systems, and Intranets, which are frequently used together or even integrated, can be deployed by IT teams in ways that make them accessible via the Internet or mobile applications so work can be performed remotely. This makes these resources accessible the moment they're needed.

With all this information at the fingertips of employees, added layers of security are often required to protect confidential data and information from falling into the wrong hands. However, as described in Chapter 10, this fact does not pose such interminable threats as to render self-service technologies too risky. Careful consideration about security has simply become part of the job description for IT professionals installing self-service technologies and executives leading the charge to adopt them.

As time passes and systems mature, these technologies and portals seem to be becoming more social and more usable. Intuitive interfaces are becoming increasingly common as these self-service technologies become more popular, encouraging adoption from among the ranks and creating movement in the direction of internal ubiquity. To be sure, self-service technologies have proven themselves useful, and as a result, they have become popular in both public and private sectors. However, the power of self-service technology has been eclipsed, in many ways, by the power of collaborative technology in the workplace. The same Intranets used to make it easier for individuals to do their work alone have been vaulted into the world of the modern social web, also known as *Web 2.0*, since the rise to prominence of social media platforms like Facebook, Twitter, and others, beginning in the early 2000s and continuing through present day.

The power of self-service technology has been eclipsed, in many ways, by the power of collaborative technology in the workplace. The same Intranets used to make it easier for individuals to do their work alone have been vaulted into the world of the modern social web, also known as *Web 2.0*, since the rise to prominence of social media platforms like Facebook, Twitter and others, beginning in the early 2000s and continuing through present day.

The Technology-Enabled Team

Without a doubt, a common goal among public managers driving the adoption of Intranets today is the support of team collaboration. The same Digital Natives driving demand for self-service are also driving demand for collaborative technologies meant to enable virtual teams to work together in better unison. After all, three out of four people in the Millennial Generation are connected to social networks, so it follows that they'd want to use technology to engage others at work (Lenhart et al. 2010). Unfortunately, this poses unique problems for governments and government agencies that have traditional, hierarchical structures and siloed departments.

Breaking Down Barriers to Collaboration

Departmental and organizational silos can be very palpable in governments of all sizes, and they can drive costs and inefficiencies. Take, for example, a hypothetical local government in the process of purchasing a new fleet of maintenance trucks from a local car dealer that has not yet purchased its annual business license from the city. Perhaps the siloed business-licensing department knows that the payment is outstanding, but the city councilor driving the purchase, or worse, the silo in charge of purchasing, does not. If everyone had access to the same knowledge about the car dealer, the city's business could all be dealt with in the same meeting. But since it does not, the city spends money on the vehicles without collecting the licensing fee, and money that could be on the city's books is not present, resulting in lost revenues. Months later, when the business-licensing department or tax department catches up to the dealer, following numerous calls and communications, an additional meeting is set up to finalize the licensing transaction. This kind of story plays out all the time in modern government.

Now consider an alternative situation in which everyone in the local government uses the same software to track all touch points with the car dealership and every other small business in town. This type of collaborative technology might even reveal that the tax silo has been attempting to collect licensing fees from the dealership for the last two years to no avail. Of course, the dealership wants to sell the maintenance trucks to the city, so a single meeting clears up all the pending transactions.

These types of software have come into wide use in the private sector, where businesses have been able to remove the silos from their daily operations. So-called Customer Relationship Management software provided by companies like Salesforce help businesses ensure they are making all the right contacts with their sales prospects without overwhelming them or sending them materials that prospects are not interested in. This is the type of thinking that the public sector should be learning from to streamline efficiency and cut costs.

Telecommuting to Improve Government Collaboration

One realm of technology-enabled collaboration where the federal government has kept up with the pace of change is in enabling *telework* among workers. The Telework Enhancement Act of 2010 established new flexibilities and guidelines for federal agency employees working remotely from home or while traveling. The Act's stated purpose was to, "require the head of each executive agency to establish and implement a policy under which employees shall be authorized to telework" (Public Law 111-292 2010). The Act defines telework as, "a work flexibility arrangement under which an employee performs the duties and responsibilities of such employee's position, and other authorized activities, from an approved worksite other than the location from which the employee would otherwise work" (ibid.).

This relatively new law is important because it represents the federal government's recognition that telework can be as efficient or even more efficient than working together inside an office. It also signifies recognition that the federal government can save money typically dedicated to real estate, energy, and other infrastructure by enabling virtual collaboration. Moreover, the federal government can also insulate itself from the impacts of terrorism and natural disasters by making telework a common practice; employees of the federal government can work from anywhere, thanks to the Act, no matter what the circumstances. Enabled by new technologies and supported by the rules the Act puts forth to help managers and their team members develop a

Figure 12.7 Thanks to the Telework Enhancement Act of 2010, many federal employees now enjoy improved work-life balance. Working from home enables them to spend more time with family, and improves the functioning of the government during crises

mutual understanding about expectations for teleworking employees, virtual collaboration is a more powerful force in government today than ever before. (To learn more about telework in the federal government, visit www. Telework.gov, a website created by the OPM and the US General Services Administration.)

Virtual collaboration, at its core, is a great way to pursue the better, faster, smarter work the private sector has simultaneously enabled through innovation and adopted. Collaboration enables organizations to pursue improved efficiency, productivity, and innovation—to bring new ideas to bear by bringing people together. But if technology is enabling collaboration, how do tomorrow's public administrators decide which collaborative technologies to adopt and which to ignore? This question has a perplexing and complex answer.

> Collaboration enables organizations to pursue improved efficiency, productivity, and innovation—to bring new ideas to bear by bringing people together. But if technology is enabling collaboration, how do tomorrow's public administrators decide which collaborative technologies to adopt and which to ignore?

The Additive Nature of Collaboration Technologies

In the early 1980s, the telephone was the preferred communication technology of nearly all organizations, private and public. Fax machines, which allowed individuals to scan and send documents to one another remotely, were also popular. These technologies enabled instant communication, though mail-based communications were still popular for many reasons. Today, numerous additive technologies have been adopted by organizations to better enable collaboration and communication. Email has taken over the lion's share of internal and external communication for many organizations, while some still promote phone-based conversations. Many organizations still send and receive faxes, despite the relative ubiquity of technology that enables the delivery of documents via email. And, of course, the oldest mode of communication and collaboration in business and government, face-to-face conversation, has maintained a critical role in the way business of all types gets done. More modern collaboration technologies seem to arrive every day. For example, there's Microsoft's Yammer, which enables teams to post short messages and share links in real-time feeds, and Google Docs, a set of cloud-based, real-time collaboration file types that can be simultaneously edited by remote individuals over the Internet. Looking ahead, new collaboration technologies will continue to emerge, adding even greater nuance to the collaborative technologies organizational leaders have to choose from.

Tomorrow's public administrators will be faced with an ever-widening array of options to enable their teams to communicate internally among the local team and with other teams in the organization, as well as externally with other organizations and citizens. The best leaders among them will understand the features and best use cases of each technology when setting expectations, and be thoughtful about the ones they select—perhaps even soliciting collaborative feedback from their team members as part of the process of selection.

Questions worth asking to select the right collaboration technology:

1. How often and in what circumstances will we need to use this technology?
2. Can we use a technology we have already adopted to enable this collaboration?
3. Will this collaboration be synchronous or asynchronous?
4. Will the collaboration need to happen in front of everyone on the team, or just a select subset of team members? Will the subsets shift over time?
5. Will this collaboration tool enable us to automatically document information we need to record for legal or knowledge management purposes?

These questions and their answers cannot be taken lightly. Negative impacts can be felt when the wrong collaboration technologies are adopted, or when outdated collaboration technologies are retained for too long. Efficiency, job satisfaction, and a team's sense of connectedness can be hampered. Even when perfectly viable technologies are selected, there are negatives to technology-enabled telework, in addition to positives. Tomorrow's public administrators will be well served to keep these pluses and minuses in mind as they think about when and how to enable telework and virtual collaboration among team members.

Common detractors to the perceived value of telework:

*   A team's sense of organizational commitment may be lower.
*   Encourages too much professional autonomy, the exact opposite of collaboration.
*   Can create a perceived lack of visibility between workers and managers.

Common benefits perceived by those engaging in telework:

*   Improved work-life balance.
*   Connects disparate workers in a personal way.
*   Enables fresh voices to join in the collaboration.

> Negative impacts can be felt when the wrong collaboration technologies are adopted, or when outdated collaboration technologies are retained for too long.

The Future of Technology-Enabled Collaboration

Ultimately, virtual collaboration enabled by telecommuting can serve to bring thinkers and problem-solvers to the virtual table together to consider issues and find resolutions. Reductions in isolating factors beyond the silos that exist within government organizations, along with increased government transparency, can allow other governments and organizations into the conversation as shared services are enabled. Technologists and creative problem-solvers from the private sector can be invited onto virtual teams to help tackle issues and deliver services as public-private partnerships are enabled. This collaboration can even extend to create connections between governments and citizens, bringing the individuals being served into the collaboration. The nation's first Federal CIO, Vivek Kundra, summed it up when he said, "We've got to recognize that we can't treat the American people as subjects but as a co-creator of ideas" (Kash 2009).

Managing the Introduction of New Technologies and Systems

Humans are well known for being resistant to change. Even the Digital Natives among us can find new technologies hard to accept or adopt when we don't see the purpose or feel it solves a problem. Change for the sake of change is perceived simply as more work to do or red tape. More and more, the introduction of new technologies in the form of enterprise solutions, contracted solutions, and custom-builds is becoming part of the government process. Due to the rapid acceleration of technology adoption, public administrators can benefit from understanding the principles and best practices of change management as they apply to the integration of new technology in the private sector.

First and foremost, public managers must get better at selecting and strategizing the creation of technologies to ensure that they truly meet the needs of internal users. Thoughtful deliberation about whether technology adoption is truly needed is paramount. New technologies are too often viewed as solutions in and of themselves, both in the private and public sectors. This practice is akin to buying a helicopter to solve a painfully long commute. If you don't know how to fly a helicopter, and have nowhere to land it, you've invested in a solution that doesn't solve your problem, wasting money without making any headway. The fact that technology can only be as useful as it is good at solving an organization's problem or problems cannot be overemphasized. This means carefully understanding those problems first.

The fact that technology can only be as useful as it is good at solving an organization's problem or problems cannot be overemphasized. This means carefully understanding those problems first.

Evaluating Current States and Envisioning Future States

One common practice among change managers in the private sector involves carefully analyzing the current state of the business—understanding where it's failing and where it's succeeding. When that process has been undertaken thoroughly, problems become glaringly obvious. Developing desired future states with the help of the executive leadership constitutes the second half of this two-step process. It often involves factoring in strategic goals for innovation, customer service, product or services quality, and other factors that help businesses differentiate themselves in marketplaces. Public managers can learn from these processes, and draw similar conclusions about what getting from the current state to the desired future state means.

Fostering Cultures of Adaptation

It's been widely posited that the most adaptable private sector organizations are those that build adaptation into their DNA by enabling employees of all ranks to introduce changes and by making it clear always that change is simply part of the business. Venture-backed technology startups—many of the same companies building contracted technology for governments—are famous for their adaptability. Many of them, as well as larger private organizations known for handling change well, do so by creating a shared vision for what the company is out to accomplish. Public managers can apply this thinking to government organizations by upholding the sense of public duty and any other values considered endemic to the organization as things that will never change. When the technologies or systems they use to accomplish those goals—the same goals as always—change, the idea is that change is less disruptive for the team. In other words, the organization is still trying to get to the cheese at the end of the maze; only the route to that cheese has changed.

Practicing Company-Wide Transparency

Another trait many companies in the private sector that are good at managing change posses the ability to keep all members of the organization abreast of changes. Combined with a dedication to setting honest expectations among all team members about how changes are going to be undertaken, how the process of change will being measured, and later, how well the organization is making the shift, this dedication to transparent communication can help organizations return from the brink of extinction or worse. Public sector organizations rarely maintain that internal transparency is a core tenet, and in many cases true transparency is impossible at these organizations. The necessity of security clearances and varying degrees of secrecy in government organizations precludes transparency. However, removing silos and making efforts to be more transparent can make adapting to change easier as everyone feels a sense that they have an important role to play in that adaptation. Adopting internal technologies is no exception.

One factor the public sector has an advantage in when it comes to adopting new technologies is the fact that it's good at interpreting and understanding new rules and regulations. Governments are seasoned veterans of change. Moving forward, it will be important to channel that skill to support the learning of new technologies and systems. The more public sector organizations can develop standard processes for learning about new technologies and how to use them, as they have with new rules and regulations, the better those institutions will be at making critical leaps with regard to new technology and systems.

> One factor the public sector has an advantage in when it comes to adopting new technologies is the fact that it's good at interpreting and understanding new rules and regulations. Governments are seasoned veterans of change in this regard. Moving forward, it will be important to channel that skill to support the learning of new technologies and systems.

The Human Element of Technology and the Future

Simply re-organizing the same old roles or attaching flashy new names to the same old responsibilities is not enough to effect internal governmental adaptation. For government to innovate, the way it works internally must innovate. In the next fifty years, as the pace of change quickens, it will not be enough for governments and government agencies to undertake innovative initiatives. A fundamental change will have to take place in the DNA of these organizations—in the people they hire, the job functions those people perform, and the technologies they use to do their work better, smarter, and faster.

Tomorrow's public managers will have to help remove silos within their organizations, and manage telecommuting teams undertaking real-time collaboration. Sometimes those teams will be comprised of contractors and private sector advisors, as well as government employees. New ways of working, new access for team members, and better collaboration through technology will be required. If government efficiency is to grow on pace with the demand for it, then new technologies and additional modes of communication will have to be adopted that allow each team member to do more to drive the organization forward as an individual and in collaboration with others. This does not have to mean putting to a vote the decisions traditionally made by the leaders of the organization, nor should it require a wholesale re-creation of the fundamentals upon which America's governmental system is founded. But it will undoubtedly mean finding new ways to get government work done.

More than just the DNA of organizations will have to change, too. Many of the factors that define how these organizations are allowed to work must grow to meet new needs. The rules and regulations limiting adaptation will require reform. In many federal- and state-level organizations, unions and antiquated work rules are the biggest limiting factors hampering internal innovation. Unlike many private enterprises, governments and government agencies still have last-in first-out rules, and other systems that can no longer be supported in the new age of information. Merit systems are outdated, as are many of the methods used to measure the qualifications and effectiveness of government workers.

Without reform, there is a very real risk that government will erode as outsourcing becomes a more and more viable passageway around antiquated rules. This will shrink government and put more government work in the hands of private enterprise. Organizations that are not allowed to adapt are at risk of disappearing, and tomorrow's public managers must prioritize adaptation with an urgency that reflects this fact. Even in government, the choice will be to evolve or go extinct.

Case Study: The City of Riverside, California—A City of Innovation

If you were to take a stroll through downtown Riverside, California, you'd bear witness to one of the most technologically advanced cities in the world. From a Wi-Fi network covering nearly every corner of the city, to a Traffic Management Center capable of correcting real-time traffic hang-ups, to a highly developed, multi-layered GIS system, Riverside is nothing short of cutting edge (Innovation and Technology 2012).

But a decade ago, the city was far from the inventive marvel it is today. Low-tech industries made up the majority of its economy and low-wage workers constituted the majority of its workforce (Tillquist 2004). While the city was home to a number of colleges and universities, upon graduation these highly educated residents were packing up and heading for greener, more modern pastures (Awards 2012).

In dire need of a change, Riverside's government officials set out to reinvent the very identity of the city by striving to become a center of innovation and high technology. By consulting with private sector partners, bringing in a complete staff of IT professionals, and maintaining a steadfast commitment to continued innovation, Riverside met and surpassed expectations.

The Road to Innovation

Rooted alongside the Santa Ana River in Southern California, this once thriving city was trudging into the 21st century. If the city were to regain its competitive standing among great American cities, Riverside officials knew a change towards a more technologically-driven city was necessary. To truly change the core of Riverside's character, technology and innovation needed to permeate every aspect of the city.

Riverside's first initiative was to open its doors to technology professionals capable of spearheading a change of this magnitude. In 2004, the city partnered with the Dean of Economic Development for Riverside Community College District (RCCD) to assemble a high technology task force responsible for leading the charge (Awards 2012). This collaborative group of volunteers was comprised of a handful of technology professionals and business leaders from the private sector, all entrusted with the job of devising strategies to help Riverside become a hub of high technology. Their goal was to integrate innovation into the way the city worked and the services it provided.

Collaborative Technology and Partnerships

As part of these early transformation efforts, the task force pioneered the Riverside Technology CEO Forum, a platform for technology CEOs to collaborate and work on turning Riverside into a high technology capital (Awards 2012). Additionally, the city's first ever Chief Information Officer was hired to work with city departments to manage the use of technology as a means of improving internal processes and external services for citizens (Innovation and Technology 2012).

Through partnerships with private sector high-tech businesses, consulting with technology experts, and bringing technology professionals on staff, high-tech Riverside successfully fused innovation into the nucleus of its identity.

Today, Riverside has an entire division dedicated to technology and its use. A full staff of IT professionals and technology leaders collaborate with other internal departments and outside organizations to deliver innovative solutions to the city, improving the quality of governmental processes and public life in Riverside. Several high-level technology leaders guide the strategic use of the technology within the city, but the process is an enterprise-wide effort. A project management system connects different departments throughout the city and reveals smarter ways of working from the successes and failures of past initiatives, helping to direct current efforts (Innovation and Technology 2012).

Continued Advancement, Sustained Growth

Having branded the city as "The City of Arts and Innovation" in 2009, Riverside has more than made innovation a part of its title—it has lived it for nearly a decade (Innovation and Technology 2012). During this span, the city has demonstrated innovation by:

- giving rise to a digital inclusion program that provides free computers and technology education to families in need;
- kick-starting the development of a free city-wide Wi-Fi network to spread Internet access to residents throughout the city;
- drawing in 35 high-tech businesses to what was previously a market full of low-tech companies (Awards 2012);

- stimulating the formation and adoption of numerous e-government programs leading to better ways of meeting the public's needs;
- fostering the growth of 20 tech startups putting innovation at the forefront of Riverside's economy (Awards 2012).

As a result of these successes, the Intelligent Community Forum named Riverside the "Intelligent Community of the Year" in 2012, marking the first time an American city had won the award in ten years (Perry 2012). But the satisfaction of achieving this prestigious honor didn't curb the city's craving for innovation. Riverside continues to advance its current technologies and develop new initiatives aimed at enhancing the city's ability to work smarter internally and provide improved services for residents.

Armed with constant communication among city staff and outside partners and a dedication to new ways of thinking, Riverside is poised to adapt with the ever-evolving state of government well into the future—and its drive for innovation doesn't appear to be letting up anytime soon.

Discussion Questions

1. What are some examples of how the human factor in technology is changing the ways work gets done?
2. What are the functions of software specialists and data specialists in government IT departments?
3. What are some special considerations public sector organizations are facing when it comes to the recruitment and retention of IT specialists?
4. What is rapid iteration and what role does it play in the creation of useful and usable software?
5. What makes Digital Natives different from previous generations of workers?
6. How is technology enabling workers to simultaneously be more independent and more collaborative?
7. What is telework and why is the Telework Act of 2010 significant?
8. What are three best practices from the private sector that managers can modify to remove barriers preventing the adoption of new technologies in their organizations?
9. What strategies can you recommend that addresses the issue of employees who are uncomfortable with learning and adopting new technologies?
10. How do you keep up on new technology trends in business and government? What blogs do you subscribe to? What website or information services do you visit most often?
11. What concerns you the most about the fast-moving pace of new technologies?
12. Do you believe that our laws and administrative procedures are on par with technological progress? Can you cite an example?

References

Appirio, Inc. in partnership with the International Association for Human Rescource Information Management. 2013. "The Emerging Social Intranet." Accessed October 17, 2014. http://thecloud.appirio.com/rs/appirio/images/Appirio%20IHRIM%20Intranet%20Survey%20Report.pdf.

BLS.gov. (a). http://www.bls.gov/ooh/Computer-and-Information-Technology/Software-developers.htm.

———. (b). http://www.bls.gov/ooh/computer-and-information-technology/database-administrators.htm.

Crosby, Olivia. 2004. "How to Get a Job in the Federal Government." *Occupational Outlook Quarterly*. Vol. 48, No. 2. Accessed October 17, 2014. http://www.bls.gov/ooq/2004/summer/art01.pdf.

Ingraham, Patricia W., Sally C. Selden, and Donald P. Moynihan. 2000. "People and Performance: Challenges for the Future Public Service." *Public Administration Review*. Vol. 60, No. 1. Page 55. Accessed October 17, 2014. http://www.lafollette.wisc.edu/facultystaff/moynihan/par%20wye%20article.pdf.

Kash, Wyatt. 2009. "Kundra Pushes Case for Adopting Web 2.0." *GCN*. June 1. Accessed October 17, 2014. http://gcn.com/Articles/2009/06/01/Web-Kundra-pushes-Web-2.0-adoption.aspx?s=gcndaily_020609&Page=1.

Lathrop, Daniel and Laurel Ruma. 2010. *Open Government: Collaboration, Transparency and Participation in Practice*. O'Reilly Media, Inc, Sebastopol, CA. Page 2.

Lenhart, Amanda, Kristen Purcell, Aaron Smith, and Kathryn Zickuhr. 2010. *Pew Internet & American Life Project:* February, 3. Accessed October 17, 2014. http://pewinternet.org/Reports/2010/Social-Media-and-Young-Adults/Part-3/2-Adults-and-social-networks.aspx?r=1.

Mason, Robert M, Karine Barzilai-Nahon, and Nancy Lou. 2008. "Organizational Impact of Digital Natives: How Organizations are Responding to the Next Generation of Knowledge Workers." Proceedings of the 17th International Conference on Management of Technology, Dubai. Accessed October 17, 2014. http://faculty.washington.edu/rmmason/Publications/IAMOT_DN_2008.pdf.

Mastracci, Sharon H. 2009. "Evaluating HR Management Strategies for Recruiting and Retaining IT Professionals in the US Federal Government." *Public Personnel Management*. Vol. 38, No. 2. Accessed October 17, 2014. http://mba-studygroup.wikispaces.com/file/view/Evaluating+HR+Management+Strategies+for+Recruiting+and+IT+Professionals+in+the+US+Federal+Government_Mastracci.pdf.

Myers, Karen K. and Kamyab Sadaghiani. 2010. "Millennials in the Workplace: A Communication Perspective on Millennials' Organizational Relationships and Performance." *Journal of Business and Psychology*. Vol. 25, No. 2. Pages 225–38. Accessed October 17, 2014. http://www.ncbi.nlm.nih.gov/pmc/articles/PMC2868990/.

Prensky, Marc. 2001. "Digital Natives, Digital Immigrants." *On the Horizon* Vol. 9, No. 5. Page 1. Accessed October 17, 2014. http://www.marcprensky.com/writing/Prensky%20-%20Digital%20Natives,%20Digital%20Immigrants%20-%20Part1.pdf.

Public Law 111-292. 2010. *Telework Enhancement Act of 2010*. December 9. Accessed October 17, 2014. http://www.gpo.gov/fdsys/pkg/PLAW-111publ292/pdf/PLAW-111publ292.pdf.

Rogers, Paul. 2011. *United States Constitutional Law: An Introduction*. McFarland & Co., Jefferson, NC. Page 109.

Stone, Brad. 2010. "The Children of Cyberspace: Old Fogies by Their 20s." *The New York Times.* January 9. Accessed October 17, 2014. http://www.nytimes.com/2010/01/10/weekinreview/10stone.html?pagewanted=all).

Tapscott, Don. 1999. *Growing up Digital: The Rise of the Net Generation.* McGraw-Hill, New York.

Toossi, Mitra. 2012. "Labor Force Projections to 2020: A More Slowly Growing Workforce." *Monthly Labor Review,* January. Page 47.

Case Study Sources

Awards. 2012. "ICF Names Riverside, California, USA as its Intelligent Community of the Year 2012." Intelligent Community Forum, June 8. Accessed October 17, 2014. http://www.intelligentcommunity.org/index.php?src=news&refno=722&category=Awards.

Innovation and Technology. 2012. "Information Technology 2012-2014 Strategic Plan." City of Riverside. Accessed October 17, 2014. http://riversideca.gov/it/pdf/2012-ITStrategicPlan.pdf.

Perry, Cindie. 2012. "Riverside Named Most Intelligent City. . . In the World!" *PRWeb,* June 9. Accessed October 17, 2014. http://www.prweb.com/releases/2012/6/prweb9590304.htm.

Tillquist, John. 2004. "A Blueprint for High Technology in Riverside." City of Riverside, September. Accessed October 17, 2014. http://www.riversideca.gov/PDF/hitech-04-10-14-White-Paper.pdf.

Digital Destinations

Cisco White Paper. 2011. http://www.cisco.com/web/learning/employer_resources/pdfs/Workforce_2020_White_Paper.pdf

International Association for Human Resource Information Management (IHRIM). http://www.ihrim.org/About_Overview.html

Office of Personnel Management (OPM) Numerous studies and reports on technology and HR. www.opm.gov

Society for Human Resource Management. http://www.shrm.org/hrdisciplines/technology/pages/default.aspx

US Department of Labor. http://www.dol.gov/oasam/programs/history/herman/reports/futurework/report/chapter6/main.htm

——. http://www.dol.gov/oasam/programs/history/herman/reports/futurework/conference/trends/NewTrends_.htm#IVtechnology

US Government Policy and Resources regarding Telework. www.telework.gov

13 Digital Equity and Ethics

Ethics is a major component in most, if not all, public management and administration curricula across the nation. Digital ethics is simply a contemporary discussion of ethics—except it requires special attention given today's information technology environment.

In January 2010, President Obama's nominee to head the Transportation Security Administration (TSA) was forced to withdraw his nomination. The nominee was a highly regarded individual who had previously served as an FBI agent and homeland security specialist. Despite his stellar credentials, it was revealed by those opposed to his nomination, and reported by *The Washington Post*, that he had provided misleading information about incidents going back over twenty years when he inappropriately accessed a federal database to obtain information about his estranged wife's new boyfriend. While this may have constituted a violation against privacy laws, it would have been highly unlikely any such violation would have lead to any jail time (O'Harrow and O'Keefe 2010). Here is where ethics becomes somewhat tricky in that ethics violations carry different penalties. In some cases a person might indeed be sentenced to jail time, however, ethics violations more commonly lead to humiliation, damaged careers, position reassignments, and forced retirement.

In today's digital information age, almost nothing gets erased, and records that were once tucked away in paper file cabinets are now online for anyone to search and see. This is a result of archived newspaper stories and Freedom of Information Act requests (FOIA). In October 2010, the Federal Government's Deputy Chief Technology Officer was reprimanded for an ethics violation (Albanesius 2010). In this case, the former Google staffer was caught using a personal email account for official government business purposes. The goal here is not to render judgment regarding these two examples, but instead to point out how vulnerable we have all become in the digital information age. It appears there is always someone or group that is out to learn more about a corporate or public official background, beliefs, and more.

Public managers must be consistently aware and watchful of each of the five major categories regarding digital ethics.

Figure 13.1 Data protection must also include the protection of citizen privacy rights and freedoms

1. **The critical need to protect information and privacy.** Here, the temptations are great to take advantage of one's position and look at someone else's personal information without authorization or permission.
2. **Preserving and protecting data records in all mediums.** Similarly, one must be extremely prudent in what is written in an email, report, application, or even a resume in terms of openness and veracity. This caution also extends to postings on social media as well as pictures posted online. As but one example, one might be surprised to learn how many executives have embellished their resumes thinking no one would ever find out. Both the presidents of Radio Shack and Yahoo ultimately found themselves having to resign their positions after it was discovered they either greatly exaggerated or lied on their resumes (Giang and Lockhart 2012).
3. **The vast amounts of money spent on IT projects.** Because of the great sums of money spent on technology acquisitions and projects, there can be great temptation to steer a project to a favored vendor or to accept favors with the thought that no one would ever know. Newspapers across the country are filled with stories of people who should have known better being fired or sent to prison. In the City of Philadelphia an internal investigation found that the Deputy Chief Information

Officer for Communications and Operations and an Information System Operations Manager had accepted meals and gifts from vendors with city contracts, violating a mayoral executive order and provisions of the Philadelphia Home Rule Charter (Unknown 2011).

4. **The interaction between vendors and IT leadership.** It is human nature to build strong relationships between public managers and technology vendors. Even the appearance of having an authorized lunch or dinner can raise alarms among other public employees and quite possibly the press, which tends to have an obsession with such matters. Ethics in the public sector is not only about acceptable behavior—it is also about public perceptions.

5. **Technological complexity.** Many technology projects are highly complex, and, for non-technical managers, it is easy to look the other way, letting responsibility fall to the technology executives. As a result, when technical complexity is involved it is somewhat easier to hide unethical acts as compared to other government operations. The CIO of the City of Baltimore was forced to resign after it was found that he had violated ethical rules while serving as the Deputy Chief Information Officer for the Office for Technology, a New York State agency. The unethical violations stemming from his post in New York actually followed him to Baltimore and in the end cost him his job and reputation. The irony here is that he was looked upon as a true innovative leader in Baltimore until the disclosure of his previous misstep.

Accessing confidential information online is easy and tempting. Today, email exchanges document conversations where it once took recording devices to do the same. The digital world has made it easier to cross into the realm of unethical activity and at the same time it has created a landscape where unethical activity is easily recorded. Taking digital pictures and sending emails has become part of the daily activity of many citizens and government employees, so accidentally spying or leaking information is much easier to do. Ethical pitfalls exist everywhere in the modern, connected world.

> The digital world has made it easier to cross into the realm of unethical activity and at the same time it has created a landscape where unethical activity is easily recorded.

The world has changed in other ways that make unintentional ethics violations possible, too. The whole world is still not fully modern and connected, even within the borders of America's federal, state, and local governments. Instead of simply re-positioning notions of ethics into the context of the digital world, public administrators have a responsibility to extend notions of ethics and availability to include new contexts without fully abandoning the notions that have been held in the past. This is because the rise of connected devices has not been felt universally and equally across demographics. Mistakenly ignoring disconnected populations and other issues of digital accessibility can lead to unintentional discrimination among certain age groups, demographics, regions, and even ethnicities.

> Instead of simply re-positioning notions of ethics into the context of the digital world, public administrators have a responsibility to extend notions of ethics and availability to include new contexts without fully abandoning the notions that have been held in the past. This is because the rise of connected devices has not been felt universally and equally across demographics. Mistakenly ignoring disconnected populations and other issues of digital accessibility can lead to unintentional discrimination among certain age groups, demographics, regions and even ethnicities.

Ethics in Contemporary Government

In 2008, the nonprofit Ethics Resource Center released a study examining the ethics of the United States government at all three levels—federal, state, and local (Lee 2008). The study found that 57 percent of the government employees surveyed had "witnessed a violation of ethics standards, policy or the law in their workplace within the past year" (Ethics Resource Center 2008). Most workers at each level had personally witnessed unethical activities. Fifty-two percent of federal government workers, 57 percent of state government workers and 63 percent of local government workers had seen unethical activity in the last year (ibid.). Across government, some 24 percent of employees reported working in environments conducive to bad behavior (ibid.). At that time, 30 percent of the misconduct survey participants had witnessed in the past year had gone unreported.

Unethical activity is part of human behavior. People simply do not always do the right thing. It occurs across the private sector, as well. This is an ongoing issue in the pursuit of a better world. But more and more, tackling ethics issues in the contemporary world means tackling ethics on a new frontier—the digital frontier.

Ethics in the Digital Age

The Merriam-Webster dictionary defines the noun *Ethic* simply as "rules of behavior based on ideas about what is morally good and bad" (Merriam-Webster website). In government, ethics are the basis of public trust, an imperative for the survival of democracy. Without public trust, a system based on representation elected by the people would be in serious jeopardy. If the role of public administrators is to protect the public interest, then part of the way public administrators will be judged is by their ability to conform to ethical guidelines.

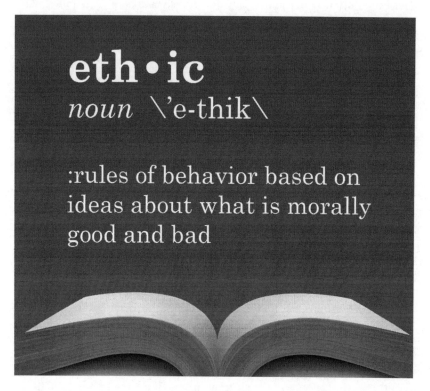

eth•ic
noun \'e-thik\

:rules of behavior based on
ideas about what is morally
good and bad

Figure 13.2 Digital ethics is a particular challenge for IT professionals

Even though efforts to fully smother the flames of ethical misconduct might never prove completely effective, efforts to tamp down on bad behavior will remain critical to the maintenance of public trust. Congress acknowledged this fact when it passed the Ethics in Government Act of 1978, establishing the US Office of Government Ethics (OGE), which has a mission to "foster high ethical standards for executive branch employees and strengthen the public's confidence that the government's business is conducted with impartiality and integrity" (OGE 2014b).

Interestingly, one of the roles of the OGE is to ensure that executive branch ethics programs comply with laws and regulations (ibid.). It's no secret that the sands of ethics are always shifting. Laws, too, change regularly. It's important to note that just because a behavior has been acceptable in the past does not mean it always will be. As laws and expectations shift, so must ethics. This means that even if something was acceptable or even encouraged in the past, it may be unethical, or even illegal, today. Given the rapid expansion of digital frontiers, especially where notions of privacy and ownership are concerned, it will remain critical for tomorrow's public administrators to pay attention to new ethical standards and laws.

> It's important to note that just because a behavior has been acceptable in the past does not mean it always will be. As laws and expectations shift, so must ethics.

In 1989, President George H. W. Bush issued an executive order to encourage the adoption of a formal set of fourteen core guiding principles designed to create a unified understanding of what it means to behave ethically in the executive branch (OGE 2014a). This came as the result of a recommendation from the President's Commission on Federal Ethics Law Reform that individual agency codes of conduct be replaced with a single regulation that applied to all executive branch employees (ibid.). The regulation was put into effect on February 3, 1993, and has been amended several times already as expectations and interpretations have shifted (ibid.).

The following is a summary of the ethical code of conduct promoted and enforced by the OGE and is included as an example of the kinds of core guidelines that have been adopted by government organizations at all levels across the United States.

A Summary of OGE Employee Standards of Conduct:

Subpart A: Establishes definitions and gives the rest of the document context.

Subpart B: Prohibits the receipt of gifts from prohibited sources or gifts received because of a person's station within their organization.

Subpart C: Prohibits gifts worth more than $10 from being exchanged between employees of the same agency, specifically gifts passing from subordinates to superiors.

Subpart D: Prohibits employees from participating in government work in which they have a financial interest and gives authority to agencies to prohibit employees from acquiring or retaining conflicting financial interests.

Subpart E: Prohibits conflicts of interest that may involve members of an employee's family or other people employees may have a specific relationship with, and is designed to prevent the perception of impartiality.

Subpart F: Prohibits government employees from participating in official activities that may have a direct impact on persons with whom they are "seeking employment."

Subpart G: Establishes a duty to protect government property and use it only for authorized purposes. Also prohibits activities that constitute misuse of an official position including using the office for personal gain, using nonpublic information to pursue financial gain or private interests, and using official time to perform unauthorized activities.

Subpart H: Prohibits participation in outside activities that may pose a conflict of interest.

Subpart I: Adds references to other statutes that direct employee conduct.

Of course, these guidelines and the other statutes set forth by the federal government as well as local and state governments are not fully comprehensive. Unlike in mathematics and physics, where theorems and laws can be established as near-certainties that can and will be relied upon to dictate the behavior of systems forever, ethics codes are the product of social mores and cultural standards. The same is true of laws, and the total set of ethical rules a public administrator must be aware of and follow is larger than but likely inclusive of all laws. Many ethical rules may seem gray. Some may apply in certain regions or among certain groups but not apply in others. This is not to say that establishing standards and formal codes of conduct is unproductive. On the contrary, the US legal system very clearly and deliberately tamps down on unethical behavior by citizens and the study referenced earlier in this chapter on the state of ethics in government demonstrated that, "When both a well-implemented ethics and compliance program and a strong ethical culture are in place within a government organization, misconduct drops by 60 percent, and reporting rises by 40 percent" (Ethics Resource Center 2008). Given the effectiveness of ethical codes in establishing and articulating what's right and wrong, it might benefit tomorrow's public administrators to consider codes of ethics established specifically to guide digital behaviors.

When both a well-implemented ethics and compliance program and a strong ethical culture are in place within a government organization, misconduct drops by 60 percent, and reporting rises by 40 percent.

Source: Ethics Resource Center 2008

Information Ethics and Cyber Ethics

There has been a great deal of thought put into notions of right and wrong regarding computers, information, and the web—these topics constitute the field of study called *Cyber Ethics*. The history of cyber ethics is not devoid of valuable contributions by government organizations either.

Back in 1973, the US Department of Health, Education, and Welfare (HEW) outlined an early set of guiding principles for *Information Ethics*, which is a field of ethical consideration that deals directly with issues of privacy, ownership, and the notion that information has appropriate and inappropriate uses (Electronic Privacy Information Center 1973). That set of guiding principles, known as "The Code of Fair Information Practices," was recommended by the HEW Secretary's Advisory Committee on Automated

Personal Data Systems, Records, Computers, and the Rights of Citizens (ibid.).

The Code of Fair Information Practices Established by the HEW

1. There must be no personal data record-keeping systems whose very existence is secret.
2. There must be a way for a person to find out what information about the person is in a record and how it is used.
3. There must be a way for a person to prevent information about the person that was obtained for one purpose from being used or made available for other purposes without the person's consent.
4. There must be a way for a person to correct or amend a record of identifiable information about the person.
5. Any organization creating, maintaining, using, or disseminating records of identifiable personal data must assure the reliability of the data for their intended use and must take precautions to prevent misuses of the data.

Of course, there have been many other codes of information ethics written, but the HEW's offers a good example of a code that is easy to understand and follow.

Information ethics fits within the larger notion of cyber ethics. But where information ethics tends to deal specifically with notions of right and wrong as they pertain to the appropriate use, storage, and dissemination of information, cyber ethics expands that conversation to include not just the information and data that exist on computers, but also the appropriate use of computer technologies as tools.

In 1992, the nonprofit Computer Ethics Institute proposed a set of principles called the "Ten Commandments of Computer Ethics" (CEI 1992). These were meant to describe the appropriate use of computers by human operators. Although computing technologies have changed dramatically in both form and function since these commandments were written, the rules still offer an excellent set of guidelines today.

The CEI's Ten Commandments of Computer Ethics

1. Thou shalt not use a computer to harm other people.
2. Thou shalt not interfere with other people's computer work.
3. Thou shalt not snoop around in other people's computer files.
4. Thou shalt not use a computer to steal.
5. Thou shalt not use a computer to bear false witness.
6. Thou shalt not copy or use proprietary software for which you have not paid.

7. Thou shalt not use other people's computer resources without authorization or proper compensation.
8. Thou shalt not appropriate other people's intellectual output.
9. Thou shalt think about the social consequences of the program you are writing or the system you are designing.
10. Thou shalt always use a computer in ways that ensure consideration and respect for your fellow humans.

The HEW's Code of Fair Information Practices and the CEI's Ten Commandments of Computer Ethics are both simple and yet far-reaching. Both decades old at the time of this writing, they still ring true as sound expressions of right and wrong. They are general enough to be valuable as the landscapes of information and cyber ethics evolve but specific enough to set clear guidelines. They are easy to recognize as guidelines and not so numerous to be difficult to remember. And they are both considerably comprehensive in their abilities to address the proper behavior of those they are meant to speak to. These are all common goals for any organization seeking to codify a system of ethics, and so they serve as sound examples.

Temptation, Ignorance, and the Gray Areas of Ethics

That neither of the two codes of ethics mentioned in the previous section is completely comprehensive is to be expected but imagine a full set of ethical rules as a continuum, much like the one in Figure 13.3. At one end of the spectrum are rules that are almost wholly universal in human society—rules articulating the wrongness of murder, theft, and other malicious activities. These are rules meant to prevent unethical activities that are premeditated and intentionally harm others. Unfortunately, the temptation to violate the clearest rules has perhaps never been greater for public administrators. Elected officials can often find themselves wielding unprecedented social and political power. And public administrators involved with technology projects are also often charged with operating massive financial budgets where those who don't adhere to ethical standards can easily find vast personal gain. You might never kill someone in

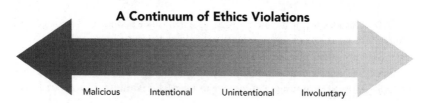

Figure 13.3 Continuum of ethics violations spectrum

cold blood, but malicious ethics violations for personal gain can often be as simple as a few keystrokes.

On the other end of the spectrum is a much fuzzier area, the spectrum of rules addressing unintentional or even involuntary ethical violations. Yes, even an ethics violation that a person is forced to do by his or her supervisor or someone else is still a wrongdoing. Here in the gray area of ethics rules, many pitfalls and snares await tomorrow's public administrators who will face public scrutiny that is more far-reaching than ever before. A simple copy-paste can do damage. A quick click of a button or tweak of a number can ruin a career. A well-intentioned meeting with a vendor over a cup of coffee that is photographed on someone's smartphone can sink the hopes of an entire political party. Information travels fast in the digital world and sometimes just the appearance of scandal is enough to ruin someone. Public administrators agree by virtue of their positions in government to uphold the ethical standards of citizens. Sometimes what a government employee sees as right might be wrong in the court of public opinion. This is one of the risks of public service.

> Sometimes what a government employee sees as right might be wrong in the court of public opinion.

Figure 13.4 Ethics is about societal norms regarding right and wrong

Ethics is often a gray area—subject to personal opinions and differing deeply held beliefs—both of which can shift dramatically over time. Look no further than the women's suffrage movement, the civil rights movement, or the more contemporary gay rights movement to see that ethical beliefs in America are a personal matter for everyone they touch. For this reason, the laws of the United States will likely never include or address every situation of ethical debate. That they seek to codify the national, state, and local values and morals held by the citizens therein—prioritizing the various kinds of rules in the spectrum on Figure 13.3—is both noble and problematic. As the number of laws that can be broken grows, the likelihood that those who break the law might not be aware they're doing so grows too. Ignorance about what constitutes an ethics violation is, unfortunately, all too common but it's no excuse for poor behavior.

Recognizing Ethical Dilemmas

Ethics violations can easily be obscured, and even intelligent individuals who intend to follow the rules and the law can wander into ethical mine fields. Like other human notions that mix logic and emotion—for example love or hope—notions of right and wrong can easily defy definition. Because they are subjective, it's impossible to clearly articulate what constitutes misconduct using a fully objective description or measure.

In the 1964 Supreme Court case Jacobellis v. Ohio, Justice Potter Stewart famously defined obscenity (in the context of pornography) by stating simply, "I know it when I see it." Stewart's assertion about the concept, which is admittedly difficult to define linguistically, was met with some criticism. His simple, candid words were certainly honest, but they subverted the impetus of the law to state itself clearly and plainly. Of course, Justice Potter's assertion was also easy to understand and identify with. Regardless of how one stands on whether pornography is right or wrong, most individuals would agree that they, too, know it when they see it. This is often the best litmus test for judging right from wrong when faced with an ethical dilemma.

As complex as ethics can seem in an academic setting, ultimately, most of tomorrow's public administrators will find it simple enough to trust their own moral compass to guide them. There are few hard and fast rules about ethics. Computers require precise instructions, which is part of the reason why the greatest computers in the world cannot fully simulate the human capacity for ethics (Somers 2013). Judging the difference between right and wrong may well be the single greatest barrier to the rise of an automaton class of androids and human-like computers. If a lack of self-awareness in societal contexts is what separates the smartest computers from humans today, then the path to furthering ethics in society and the public sector can likely be found in a deeper human introspection about self-awareness in the same contexts.

Computers require precise instructions, which is part of the reason why the greatest computers in the world cannot fully simulate the human capacity for ethics (Somers 2013). Judging the difference between right and wrong may well be the single greatest barrier to the rise of an automaton class of androids and human-like computers.

The Need for Self-Awareness

Ultimately, the ability to avoid a bad decision and the personal crisis that comes with it relies heavily on a person's capacity to recognize that a decision is, or might, be bad, and to realize that there could, or will, be consequences as a result. Unintentional ethics violations have simply become more possible in the digital world, as has the likelihood that someone will find or share proof of them after the fact. What follows is an anecdote that illustrates the nuance of misconduct gray areas faced by government workers. This example is not meant to argue for or against the innocence of those involved, but rather to demonstrate that notions of right and wrong are complicated in contemporary society, especially where public funds are concerned.

A Team Building Retreat to Catalyze Productivity or Taxpayer Dollars Squandered?

On April 2, 2012, less than two years after taking the position, General Services Administration (GSA) chief Martha N. Johnson was forced to resign amid scandal (Rein and Davidson 2012).

GSA's scope is massive. The organization manages a broad swath of activities for the federal government, providing procurement services to federal agencies, maintaining government buildings and properties, and managing contracts, among other things. In 1999, when she was GSA chief of staff, Johnson described GSA to the publication *Fast Company* as a combination of Office Depot, Home Depot, an airline, and a real-estate agency (Sittenfeld 1999).

Johnson had been an accomplished leader with a knack for building the kinds of strong public and private sector organizational cultures that get things done (Rothman 2008). A former senior vice president of culture at IT firm Computer Sciences Corporation, a major contractor for GSA, Johnson had also been the vice president of the Council for Excellence in Government, a nonprofit organization dedicated to improving the effectiveness of federal, state, and local governments (AllGov.com 2010). So when Johnson took the helm at GSA, which had been plagued by scandal, many expected major changes for the organization; there were high hopes for a dramatic turnaround (Weigelt 2009).

Johnson viewed her charge as a chance to change GSA so dramatically that it set new standards in government as well as the private sector (SOM.Yale.Edu 2011). About a year after her appointment, she told a group at the Yale School of Management, from which she held a degree, "This is a fabulous place to be right now as we get to play with executive management notions . . . We're carrying an agenda that the GSA has never had before." To enact the change she had been brought in to accomplish, Johnson and her staffers apparently put together a corporate team building and educational retreat in Las Vegas, Nevada. Although this kind of hands-on cultural alignment was common in the private sector, it became a fatal misstep for Johnson and her career at GSA.

At the time of her resignation, *The Washington Post* reported that the retreat had involved public funds spending that included, among other things, "$130,000 in travel expenses for six scouting trips . . . $6,325 [spent] on commemorative coins in velvet boxes to reward all participants for their hard work on stimulus projects," and a "$31,208 'networking' reception" featuring "$7,000 of sushi" (Rein and Davidson 2012). What's worse, Johnson was publically lambasted for failing to follow the same contractor regulations for the conference that GSA was charged with developing for federal agencies (ibid.).

Ultimately, Johnson released a book titled *On My Watch: Leadership, Innovation, and Personal Resilience* (Clark 2013). At the time of the release, Johnson was quoted as saying, "I was shocked and stunned and I felt as if things had gone haywire . . . I also felt that politics were stepping in and there is just no way around that at times and we can see how that slams into performance" (ibid.).

It seems clear that Johnson was trying to create the kind of change at GSA that she felt she was hired to deliver. She was stepping out of line from the status quo purposefully and also doing what she felt was right, too. However, the corporate event her team put together was expensive and the fact that it broke procurement rules was unacceptable. In the court of public opinion, and in the eyes of many in government, her activities were unethical. The story stands as a great example of how gray ethics can be in government.

Self-awareness doesn't always mean knowing something is clearly right or wrong, but rather recognizing where an activity or decision might *appear* unethical after the fact—even years later, as the previous example demonstrates the gray areas that public discourse about what's right and wrong can cross into. Tomorrow's public administrators need to stay current on contemporary ethics debates, including anecdotal ones debated in the press, in an effort to retain a sound perspective on what is expected of public sector employees.

Common Sources of Ethics Violations

After looking closely at this example of ethics violations with dire consequences, it might prove useful to consider a few of the most common, practical scenarios where tomorrow's public administrators should be on the lookout for potential ethics violations. These scenarios all exist at the edges of perception about what's right and wrong. In many cases, they may not *feel* wrong, but they certainly can be wrong enough to result in major consequences.

Common Scenarios Where Ethics Violations Occur

1. Placing self-interest above public need.
2. Abusing special privileges and access to information.
3. Alteration of documents or financial records.
4. Lying to citizens, co-workers, vendors, or the public.
5. Misreporting hours.
6. Misusing public funds or resources.

Common Language Surrounding Ethics Violations

Although situations that involve these scenarios might seem obvious, sometimes the true nature of events may be obscured by other facts and goals that feel unquestionably right-minded. To help tomorrow's public administrators be prepared for situations likely to involve ethical gray areas that could prove dangerous, the following list identifies common phrases that might emerge in conversations about potentially unethical activities.

Common Excuses for Ethics Violations

1. No one will ever know! (obfuscation)
2. Everyone does it! (common activity)
3. I've covered my tracks! (disguise)
4. Who cares? (indifference)
5. This is just how we do it! (group think)
6. This is how we've done it in the past! (past practices)
7. It might feel wrong, but we've been above board! (transparency)
8. It's already in the budget! (managerial approval)
9. We're supposed to shake things up! (change imperatives)
10. It's our job to manage this kind of thing! (responsibility confusion)

Common Results of Ethics Violations

It is ultimately the responsibility of every public sector employee to know the bounds of ethics as they pertain to his or her station in public service, and to be aware of the negative scenarios that can result from ethics violations. These range from smudged reputations to incarceration, and having a general awareness of them can help tomorrow's public administrators understand the seriousness of their decisions and actions.

Common Consequences for Ethics Violations

1. Loss of respect and trust.
2. Censure or reprimand.
3. Reduction in rank or position.
4. Personal penalty in the form of fines and other costs.
5. Expulsion or firing.
6. Being black-listed as an un-hirable public employee.
7. Incarceration in local, state, or federal correctional facilities.

Misconduct among public sector employees is taken seriously in the United States. Whether elected or appointed, public administrators are employed by the public to protect their interests and their funds. Overtly illegal and clearly unethical activities often carry the stiffest penalties because they stand in direct opposition to these responsibilities. On the other end of the spectrum, unintentional or even involuntary abuses of power and ethical missteps can also carry noteworthy penalties. Every person's reputation is a primary player in the legacy they leave behind. Once tarnished, a reputation can often never be repaired. But what about those people whose reputations become tarnished due to things they are completely blind to, even after the fact? How can these situations be spotted and prevented? These issues are often tied to themes of accessibility. The next section of this chapter touches on accessibility and takes a look at why and how it often hides in plain sight, playing a critical role in the unintentionally unethical realm of contemporary public ethics.

Accessibility in the Digital Age

The topic of accessibility has become a critical one in the digital age. This is because unintentional biases by government employees and organizations have become more likely in the digital world. It's simply too easy for public administrators to forget that nearly one-in-four of American citizens do not have the Internet at home and assume that a migration from paper processes to fully digital ones might be wholly positive where in fact it leaves many in critical need without access to government services (Pew Research 2013). This is the kind of scenario that the digital world has enabled—creating the risk for situations where unethical biases occur completely unintentionally, sometimes with dire consequences.

> Unintentional biases by government employees and organizations have become more likely in the digital world. It's simply too easy for public administrators to forget that nearly one-in-four of American citizens do not have the Internet at home and assume that a migration from paper processes to fully digital ones might be wholly positive where in fact it leaves many in critical need without access to government services.

Unintentional accessibility issues didn't arise with the advent of Internet technologies. In fact, biases happen in private sector technologies surprisingly frequently. For example, the Microsoft Kinect interactive gaming system, which relies on facial recognition, has historically had trouble recognizing dark-skinned users (Sinclair 2010). This is a product of the fact that many image-recognition technologies have trouble differentiating dark-skinned people because they rely on light (ibid.). The result, in the case of the Kinect, is that technological bias inherent in image-recognition technologies led to social bias on the part of the Kinect device (ibid.). Similarly, there's evidence to suggest that Apple's Siri voice recognition technology may have difficulty recognizing some accents because the technology was tested in settings where the software was never exposed to those accents (Zax 2011).

Unintentional accessibility issues in government are not a new phenomenon, either. For example, in the middle of the 1900s, urban planner Robert Moses influenced much urban design in and around New York City and the surrounding areas (Boyd 2014). When planning the parkways on Long Island, Moses designed overpasses and bridges that were too low to accommodate buses. Some have posited that the design limitations were intentional, while others have argued that they were accidental. Nonetheless, one thing is certain about Moses' design limitations regarding the parkways of Long Island—those who rely on public transportation in the form of buses were unable to benefit from the new parkways when they opened. Whether intentionally or unintentionally, as long as small groups of people make decisions in government that apply to much larger citizen bases, biases will continue to crop up. For this reason, avoiding unintentional ethics violations in the realm of access will continue to be an issue of awareness. Public administrators have an even greater responsibility than private companies to serve the widest set of users possible.

The Digital Divide

One arena where debates about accessibility and bias have unfolded involves the *Digital Divide*, a general notion dealing with the fact that, while some in society have access to a seemingly unending flow of information as a result of the Internet, many others do not have access to the Internet and therefore do not have access to the same mass of information. Study and analysis in this realm typically centers more broadly on information and communication technologies in general, though the Internet is certainly at the heart of the conversation.

Policy makers began considering inequality in access to the Internet as early as 1995, when only 3 percent of Americans had been exposed to the web (Neckerman 2004). The digital divide impacts public policy, because while more Americans are online and consuming vast amounts of information many still are not-which diminshes the many growing opportunities for those not online to participate in civic engagement (ibid.). Where policy-making has been concerned, one thing working against the notion of the digital divide is that the term itself implies a single widening gap, where, in fact, there are many different gaps at play, some of which work to compound one another while others work to treat the problems of accessibility caused by one another.

> Where policy-making has been concerned, one thing working against the notion of the digital divide is that the term itself implies a single widening gap, where, in fact, there are many different gaps at play, some of which work to compound one another while others work to treat the problems of accessibility caused by one another.

The digital divide is a complex set of forces. Systems of categorization for the "haves" and the "have-nots" have spanned individuals to subgroups to whole nations, with correlations also being drawn between different groups and specific characteristics, such as race, geography, and income (ibid.). Discussions about the digital divide have also addressed different definitions of access, spanning from occasional Internet availability to clear cut adoption of Internet technologies, while also considering the myriad types of Internet-related technology that individuals, groups, and subgroups have access to, from web-connected televisions to tablet computers to wearable devices like Google Glass (ibid.).

No matter how you slice or define it, there is clearly a broad landscape of Internet-related scenarios for individuals to exist in today. Some have access while others do not. However literacy is defined, it has become obvious that some are technologically literate while others are technologically illiterate. Of course many in the technologically illiterate community are disconnected due to poverty and other causes beyond their control. But the simple truth is that many of the technologically illiterate are so by choice, too. These facts are incredibly relevant to tomorrow's public administrators, as are the inevitable strata that are unfolding and that will continue to unfold in the landscape of Internet-related scenarios for individual citizens. In some cases, it may not be possible to fully replace seemingly antiquated processes with digital ones. Duplicative efforts may simply be unavoidable.

In all its complexity, a number of notions about the digital divide seem to have been debunked as oversimplification of a complex problem in the first decade-and-a-half of the 21st century. The following list is not comprehensive, but it is included to help understand the kinds of oversimplified ideas about digital divide that have been explored as this global conversation has emerged.

General Misconceptions about the Digital Divide

1. Closing the digital divide is about giving poor people access to computers.
2. Getting the private sector to profitably serve the poor at the bottom of the pyramid is the sole answer to the digital divide.

3. Creating "shared use" of ICT products in the rural American country-side is the sole solution to the digital divide.
4. Closing the digital divide requires setting up a "super fund" that supports ICT projects.
5. The sole solution to closing the digital divide is investment in literacy and education.
6. Social entrepreneurs with IT skills must become the prime movers for closing the digital divide since they are able to introduce "disruptive technologies" to serve those without access.
7. If governments only open up their telecom sectors to foreign competition, market forces all by themselves will cause the digital divide to close.

On a very high level, it seems evident that the digital divide is "widening," as more and more different individual possible scenarios for technological literacy arise with each new device and communication system. This is happening at an ever-increasing rate, and the division has historically correlated with socioeconomic dividing lines, but the division isn't drawn exclusively across clear demographic lines. For every rule about the digital divide, there are certainly exceptions. Even the most basic trends seem to be wrought with complexities.

Moreover, it seems clear that ignoring society's need to close the digital divide will result in inequality. Closing it by providing some level of base technological literacy to society may be the only way to make globalization work for the poor, though measuring technological literacy has proven difficult (Warschauer and Matuchniak 2010). Closing the digital divide is about empowerment and could be the only way to sustain the growth of world markets, because it would make the whole of the global economy a truly information-based economy.

> Closing the digital divide is about empowerment and could be the only way to sustain the growth of world markets, because it would make the whole of the global economy a truly information-based economy.

World leaders from every sector can benefit from closing the digital divide, yet no one sector has the incentives to fully lead the effort to close it. It seems likely that closing the digital divide requires building an "enterprise ecosystem," that offers "end to end" solutions for all people, but the practical application of this notion has proven evasive. Midlevel countries appear to be the best settings for experimentation, not the poorest countries, because extremely poor populations have more urgent needs—like health care, food, and shelter—although it seems possible that truly closing the digital divide could involve using new technologies to formalize the "informal economy," thereby bringing the poor into established markets. All this in mind, the notion that the digital divide will be closed still seems very much in question at the time of this writing—many uncertainties remain. Tomorrow's public administrators should take notice—the digital divide is something they are sure to confront.

The Future of Digital Ethics and Accessibility

Imagine a future in which the digital divide is closing but may never close entirely—after all, young children and the poorest citizens may always be technologically illiterate. New programs have reversed the widening gap(s), arising from a variety of public, private, and nonprofit sources. Like problems of illiteracy in the United States in past decades, technological illiteracy is an issue society as a whole is working together to cure.

Public administrators and their employees still bump into ethical dilemmas and the world still reacts similarly to them, but there's much greater awareness about them—more of the ethical issues in government are intentional than unintentional. Still, temptation has been alleviated through new regulation and a heightened sense of awareness about consequences. Humans are still humans but fewer stumbling blocks go altogether unseen by those who slip up. Occasionally, major ethical lapses still take place and land in the headlines, but these occur more on the frontiers and in the grayest of gray areas. Strong leaders with sound moral compasses are setting new standards for ethics in government.

This future may still be far away and the imperfection of the human race may never be fully "cured," but healthy public debates about notions of right and wrong are enabling progress already. Tomorrow's public administrators have an opportunity to carry that torch and use it to avoid personal career-landmines. In this realm, a perfect future may never be possible, but with clear eyes, full hearts, and heads brimming with awareness, tomorrow's public administrators are likely better prepared for success in ethics than any of their predecessors.

Discussion Questions

1. Why is ethical perfection in government likely an impossibility regardless of innovation and new technology?
2. How is technological advancement compounding the complexity of ethics for public administrators?
3. Why do codified rules for behavior like the OGE's Employee Standards of Conduct enable public employees to avoid ethical missteps?
4. Describe what the authors mean when they talk about "gray areas" in ethics.
5. Describe the continuum of ethics violations discussed in the chapter.
6. Describe the range of consequences that can result from ethics violations by public administrators.

7. What is the digital divide?
8. Why does oversimplification of the digital divide pose such a large risk to progress in this arena?

References

Albanesius, Chloe. 2010. "White House Deputy CTO Reprimanded for Ethics Violation." *PC Magazine,* May 8. Accessed October 17, 2014. http://www.pcmag.com/article2/0,2817,2363926,00.asp.

AllGov.com. 2010. "The Long Wait: Who is Obama GSA Nominee Martha Johnson." January 9. Accessed October 17, 2014. http://www.allgov.com/news/appointments-and-resignations/the-long-wait-who-is-obama-gsa-nominee-martha-johnson?news=840159.

Boyd, Danah. 2014. *It's Complicated.* Yale University Press, New Haven, CT. Page 157.

Clark, Charles S. 2013. "Ex-GSA Chief Releases Tell-all on Conference Spending Scandal." *Government Executive.* Accessed October 17, 2014. http://www.govexec.com/federal-news/fedblog/2013/10/ex-gsa-chief-releases-tell-all-conference-spending-scandal/72575/.

Computer Ethics Institute. 1992. "In Pursuit of a 'Ten Commandments' for Computer Ethics." Accessed October 17, 2014. http://computerethicsinstitute.org/barquinpursuit1992.html.

Electronic Privacy Information Center. 1973. *The Code of Fair Information Practices.* Accessed October 17, 2014. http://epic.org/privacy/consumer/code_fair_info.html.

Ethics Resource Center. 2008. "National Government Ethics Survey: An Inside View of Public Sector Ethics." Accessed October 17, 2014. http://www.ethics.org/files/u5/The_National_Government_Ethics_Survey.pdf.

Giang, Vivian and Jhaneel Lockhart. 2012. "Busted: This Is What Happened To 10 Executives Who Lied About Their Resumes." *Business Insider,* May 7. Accessed October 17, 2014. http://www.businessinsider.com/9-people-who-were-publicly-shamed-for-lying-on-their-resumes-2012-5?op=1.

Lee, Christopher. 2008. "Study Finds Government Ethics Lapses." *The Washington Post.* January 30. Accessed October 17, 2014. http://www.washingtonpost.com/wp-dyn/content/article/2008/01/29/AR2008012902908.html.

Neckerman, Kathryn. 2004. *Social Inequality.* Russell Sage Foundation, New York.

OGE. 2014a. *Employee Standards of Conduct.* Accessed October 17, 2014. http://www.oge.gov/Laws-and-Regulations/Employee-Standards-of-Conduct/Employee-Standards-of-Conduct/.

———. 2014b. *Mission & Responsibilities.* Accessed October 17, 2014. http://www.oge.gov/About/Mission-and-Responsibilities/Mission---Responsibilities/.

O'Harrow, Robert Jr. and Ed O'Keefe. 2010. "Erroll Southers, Obama's Choice to Head TSA, Withdraws Nomination." *The Washington Post.* January 21. Accessed October 17, 2014. http://www.washingtonpost.com/wp-dyn/content/article/2010/01/20/AR2010012001765.html.

Pew Research. 2013. "Who's Not Online and Why." Pew Research Internet Project. September 25. Accessed October 17, 2014. http://www.pewinternet.org/2013/09/25/whos-not-online-and-why/.

Rein, Lisa and Joe Davidson. 2012. "GSA Chief Resigns Amid Reports of Excessive Spending." *The Washington Post.* April 2. Accessed October 17, 2014. http://www.washingtonpost.com/politics/gsa-chief-resigns-amid-reports-of-excessive-spending/2012/04/02/gIQABLNNrS_story.html.

Rothman, David. 2008. "GSA: A Checkered Past." *SolomonScandals.com*. December 12. Accessed October 17, 2014. http://solomonscandals.com/gsa-a-checkered-past/.

Sinclair, Brendan. 2010. "Kinect Has Problems Recognizing Dark-skinned Users?" *Gamespot*. November 3. Accessed October 17, 2014. http://www.gamespot.com/articles/kinect-has-problems-recognizing-dark-skinned-users/1100-6283514/.

Sittenfeld, Curtis. 1999. "Here's How GSA Changed Its Ways." *Fast Company*, May 31. Accessed October 17, 2014. http://www.fastcompany.com/37247/heres-how-gsa-changed-its-ways.

SOM.Yale.Edu. 2011. "GSA head Martha Johnson Speaks about Driving Change in the Federal Government." *Yale School of Management*. February 18.

Somers, James. 2013. "The Man Who Would Teach Machines To Think." *The Atlantic*, October 23. Accessed October 17, 2014. http://www.theatlantic.com/magazine/archive/2013/11/the-man-who-would-teach-machines-to-think/309529/.

Unknown. 2011. "Division of Technology Deputy Fired for Exploiting City's Verizon Contract." Philadelphia Office of the Inspector General (blog), July 20. Accessed October 17, 2014. http://philadelphiainspectorgeneral.wordpress.com/2011/07/20/division-of-technology-deputy-fired-for-exploiting-citys-verizon-contract/.

Warschauer, Mark and Tina Matuchniak. 2010. "New Technology and Digital Worlds: Analyzing Evidence of Equity in Access, Use, and Outcomes." *Review of Research in Education*. Page 207. Accessed October 17, 2014. http://rre.sagepub.com/content/34/1/179.

Weigelt, Matthew. 2009. "Martha Johnson May Bring Old Era Back to GSA." *FCW*, April 6. Accessed October 17, 2014. http://fcw.com/Articles/2009/04/06/Web-Martha-Johnson-old-era.aspx.

Zax, David. 2011. "Siri, Why Can't You Understand Me?" *Fast Company*. October 18. Accessed October 17, 2014. http://www.fastcompany.com/1799374/siri-why-cant-you-understand-me.

Digital Destinations

Digital Divide Institute. http://www.digitaldivide.org

Digital Divide Network. http://orgs.tigweb.org/digital-divide-network

Federal Communications Commission. http://www.fcc.gov/document/fact-sheet-protecting-and-promoting-open-internet

———. http://www.fcc.gov/document/protecting-and-promoting-open-internet-nprm

———. http://transition.fcc.gov/national-broadband-plan/broadband-adoption-in-america-paper.pdf

———. http://transition.fcc.gov/national-broadband-plan/equal-access-to-broadband-paper.pdf

Merriam-Webster.com. http://www.merriam-webster.com/dictionary/ethic

Pew Research and Internet Project. http://www.pewinternet.org/search/digital+divide/

US Department of Energy (Ethics Example). http://energy.gov/hc/ethics-fourteen-principles-ethical-conduct-federal-employees

US Office of Government Ethics. http://www.oge.gov/

14 Nonprofit Technology Management

Nonprofit management has become an increasingly important and popular topic of interest in the public administration community. While shorter in length when compared to other chapters of this book, it is by no means any less important and is simply best treated as a stand-alone chapter. There are essentially two ways to discuss technology and nonprofit management, which is to better comprehend: (1) how the available technology solutions can assist management as never before, (2) how nonprofit associations play an important role in furthering knowledge, professional development, and sharing experiences amongst technology managers. Depending on the issue many associations respond to or introduce legislative and regulatory initiatives.

> There are essentially two ways to discuss technology and nonprofit management, which is to better comprehend; (1) how the available technology solutions can assist management as never before, (2) how nonprofit associations play an important role in furthering knowledge, professional development, and sharing experiences amongst technology managers.

How Technology is Shaping the Future of Nonprofit Management

We know that nonprofit institutions play a very important role in serving as an interface in various forms and fashion between citizens and government. It used to be that the three most common metrics for judging the effectiveness of an association were: (1) size of budget, (2) size of staff, and (3) number of members. Today, given the advances in technology these metrics have far less meaning. Instead of focusing on the size of an association's budget, one can measure how effective it is in managing its resources. Because of technology, much more can be done with less, at least in relative terms. Instead of focusing

Figure 14.1 Technology is increasingly playing a critical role in nonprofit management in every department

on the number of staff an association has, one needs to review how effectively the various tasks are being managed. And finally, instead of focusing on the number of members, it is as important to measure how successful an association is in terms of living up to its mission, its reach, success in influencing policy, and promoting its message. This means that an association with few staff, a small budget, and a relatively small membership can be highly effective with the appropriate use of technology. For example, some rather small associations with very limited resources can design and maintain a dazzling website with full functionality as if it had a large budget and staff. An association that once operated with at least 25 to 100 staff employees can now perform the exact same functions with two-thirds or less staff thanks to technology.

> Most issues regarding technology and nonprofit management are quite similar to government—except that they operate on a much smaller scale.

Most issues regarding technology and nonprofit management are quite similar to government—except that they operate on a much smaller scale. Nonprofit associations have some distinct advantages too, for example, they have the "luxury" of having a narrow focus, or its employees do not fall under any civil service or union rules, thus providing management with greater flexibility if and when required. Just like government, however, nonprofits are dealing with issues such as communicating with their various constituencies, exploring cloud-based solutions, managed services, cyber and network security, and database management. They must also embrace and master social media as a means of better connecting with their stakeholders (members) and creating a dynamic collaborative environment.

When looking at nonprofit organizations through the eyes of a technologist, one would quickly realize that every nonprofit management function has a set of technology solutions or applications at its disposal as never before. These applications can be internal or external—or both. Examples of internal applications might include any or all of the following:

1. **Payroll**: Today, there are many services that provide complete payroll processing that not only includes paper and direct deposit distribution, but filing local and multi-state and federal tax forms, vacation and leave tracking, etc. What used to be managed by internal staff can now be performed by an outside company under contract where services are often superior when compared with in-house staffing. The chief financial officer, while still very much in charge, can do more with less internal staff, and have more time to plan and manage.

2. **Human resources**: Like payroll operations, HR functionality can now benefit from automated systems that free up internal staff and still be responsive to employees regarding time-sheet tracking, benefit processing, and information, as well as providing employees with uniform online policy manuals. Forms that used to be primarily paper-based can now be downloaded in an instant anywhere, any time. Employee information can now be found online along with brief tutorials with answers to often asked questions. Here too, there are companies that specialize in managing routine forms and application processing.

3. **Internal communication**: For small nonprofits, simply circulating emails may suffice as the tool of choice regarding internal communications. Larger organizations generally use what is called an "Intranet." An Intranet is usually an internal facing (not open to the public) website that is designed to provide and share information as well as to serve as a place to store internal documents. Finally, an Intranet is designed primarily for greater collaboration among staff and association volunteer leaders. Less paper is circulated and finding information, especially reports and documents, can be made easier.

4. **Finance and accounting**: Not too long ago it was considered a best practice to have all financial information reside on a dedicated server (computer) located on premise. Today, there is a growing trend to utilize software as a solution or managed service where financial information is stored remotely and usually more securely than having it maintained on premise. This also allows for greater access to those authorized as long as they have good and secure access to the Internet.

5. **Membership and database management**: Every nonprofit association needs to know whom their members are, what category or classification

they are placed in, and their contact information as well as payment history information. A membership database can be used to query what activities members are involved in such as committees, task forces, speaking and writing expertise, and much more. While the need to know everything about its members and donors remains constant, many nonprofits find that having a database membership system maintained and serviced by an outside vendor can be cost-effective, and often more reliable than office systems. Whether an association chooses to maintain its own internal database system or turns to a managed out side the office system—today's contemporary association cannot exist without a solid member database system. Companies that specialize in developing and maintaining membership systems claim that they provide a more secure and feature-rich system where the costs are spread across a larger base of associations with associations paying only for what they need or use. Such outside companies have strong incentives to keep up with ongoing updates that include new innovations and upgrades, thus leaving association staff to be more productive performing more mission-critical tasks.

6. **Credit card processing**: Association staff taking credit card payments used to have to manually swipe credit cards or call in a number for processing. Today's technology allows for online payments, or if away from the office or at a meeting, one can swipe a card using a smartphone or tablet device and realize instant payment confirmation with an instant emailed receipt to the customer. The automation of credit processing saves both time and money and usually leads to greater member/stakeholder satisfaction.

7. **Email hosting**: Many associations still maintain email servers that require on premise technical staff to keep systems updated and running smoothly. There is now a growing recognition that it makes sense to consider having email services hosted (managed) by an outside provider. At least in the long-term, associations should be able to save money in several ways. First, savings can be realized when there is no longer a need to maintain equipment, back-up drives, and the need to update software that includes security. Second, savings can also be realized with a reduction in staff or perhaps the reassignment of staff.

Another aspect of email hosting is a term called "e-discovery." E-discovery is a legal requirement that falls under federal, state, and local laws that obligate a government to make available electronic records including emails and any other form of digital documentation that are often required in civil and criminal law proceedings as a means of evidence. Local governments, in particular, have spent millions of man-hours researching files and fielding e-discovery requests. Documents—including emails—that can go back a decade or more, are to be preserved, and goverments are required to do so, in a specified time frame. As you might have guessed a new outside service is emerging where high-tech search tools have been developed to allow associations to perform

Email Discovery Software

Email is the main data source targeted during the electronic discovery process. Organizations need email discovery software that helps them quickly cull irrelevant messages and identify those emails that are most critical to a given case or investigation. The Symantec eDiscovery Platform powered by Clearwell leverages a variety of valuable tools to make it a leader amongst other email discovery software programs.

Watch how eDiscovery Platform users can efficiently manage email discovery
Flash Demo ▣

The eDiscovery Platform delivers intelligent email discovery that helps reduce costs by culling and filtering data, providing insightful analytics, and helping to manage legal, regulatory, and investigative matters – all in a single application. Symantec's email discovery software offers enterprises, law firms, and government agencies the ability to:

- **Generate filters:** Prior to searching, this email discovery software allows users to automatically generate filters using parameters like sender/recipient name, sender/recipient domain, date range, and language.

- **Search Transparently:** Quickly ID emails that match specific search terms and variations, which cuts down on false positives and the amount of data searched, resulting in quicker and more cost-effective reviews.

eDiscovery Information Center

eDiscovery Definition & Process

What is eDiscovery?

Electronic Discovery Reference Model (EDRM)

Legal Hold

Electronically Stored Information (ESI)

Electronic Evidence Discovery

Email Discovery Software

Legal Electronic Discovery for Law Firms

eDiscovery Rules and Regulations

Federal Rules of Civil

Add ➕

Figure 14.2 Example of e-discovery software solution from Symantec.com

Source: http://www.symantec.com/page.jsp?id=eic-email-discovery-software

exhaustive searches through special software packages, or through contracting out the e-discovery process on a government agency's behalf. Having e-discovery tools or contracted services at one's disposal can save enormous amounts of staff time and resources.

8. **Website hosting**: Most associations no longer find it necessary to physically own and maintain their own website. Hosting is the term used to describe where the physical website and all its content reside. Associations have found it makes a great deal of sense to have an outside expert company host the website—usually in a more secure and maintenance-free environment.

9. **Technology support services**: Even the largest nonprofit associations turn to outside technology support services that can purchase equipment such as PCs, laptops, and tablets, and can also configure them. Technology support services include remote help desks and in many cases having a technician remotely gain access to a computer can solve problems. Associations large and small can benefit from having outside support services either as an augmentation to existing capabilities, or to serve as a full technology support function. The latter case can be especially attractive to small organizations that lack the resources to have their own dedicated technology staff. In this type of environment, associations pay for what they need and often find that they have access to a greater variety of experts than they could possibly afford on their own. Outside services can save associations time and money while functioning as if such services were handled by their own staff.

Each of these examples illustrates how nonprofit organizations are seeking and finding ways to become more efficient and effective—just as is found in the government environment.

In approaching any given nonprofit operation one should not begin with any pre-conceived notion without first doing a thorough needs assessment analysis followed by a careful competitive analysis. While good general examples have been offered, there are many cases when an in-house system makes more sense. The overall point here is that association managers simply have more options and tools at their disposal than ever before. When it comes to external nonprofit management applications, where members and donors see and interact with the applications, there are many great examples similar to that of internal applications which include:

1. **Website functionality**: Website functionality has evolved into becoming more "user (staff) friendly." Association staff are no longer dependent on having to turn to in-house web managers or IT staff to update every piece of information. With a little training, staff can carry out most routine functions by themselves. Of course, as with government, it's important to adhere to strict policies for access, content, and editorial controls. There are hundreds of companies that specialize in designing

and hosting websites specifically for the association management community. As websites become user-friendlier, many nonprofits are utilizing and including infographics, maps, pictures, and videos to help tell a "story" about their organization, mission, cause, or campaign.

2. **Social media**: Most of today's contemporary nonprofit organizations maintain at least one website. They must be able to communicate to their members and stakeholders alike and can no longer depend solely on email. Social media is becoming strongly embraced by nonprofit associations either as part of their own website operations or utilizing an outside service. Take for example, the American Society for Public Administration (ASPA) where they maintain a Facebook page as well as a Twitter account. Moreover, they also manage a special interest section on Linkedin where members can post comments or respond to others' questions or discussion.

   On most nonprofit homepages and email signatures, a "follow me" symbol appears directing a potential contact to visit one of the social media sites such as Twitter, Facebook, or others. Associations need to keep members informed as well as engaged and social media certainly helps in both instances. Furthermore, social media now includes greater opportunities for collaboration and sharing of information.

3. **Newsletters**: Nonprofits have always had a need to publish and broadcast information, traditionally through magazines and newsletters. The rising cost to print and mail publications has forced many organizations to reconsider their communication options. While many associations still maintain their print version magazines and journals, most have

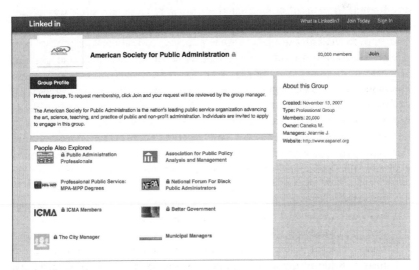

Figure 14.3 ASPA's Linkedin homepage

Source: http://www.linkedin.com/groups?gid=41639

Follow us on:

Figure 14.4 Today, every nonprofit webpage seeks member and donor engagement through social media

moved to (however reluctantly) digital formats. Companies now exist that basically produce a digital newsletter as if it came from the association itself. These specialized companies produce customized association newsletters either for a fee, or free if they are allowed to pursue advertisers. Editors are assigned to an association account and either collect content or add content that the association staff provides—or both. In 2014 there were two major companies that produced over 3,000 different association newsletters. Unlike paper versions, built-in social media tools provide invaluable data that goes far beyond who actually received a newsletter; it reports if and when it was opened, read, or not, and which stories received the most attention. This internal data certainly helps in attracting and maintaining advertisers and helps staff understand which issues and topics are of the greatest interest to their members.

4. **Research**: It used to be that the only way to do research was either by phone, mail-in surveys, or in-person interviews. Now with online research tools and services, attractive surveys can be sent out to members and non-members alike via email, with instant scoring, analysis, and graphical presentations of responses. E-surveys can be used to poll members' needs, interests, and opinions aimed at better aligning resources with member preferences. E-surveys can also serve as a valuable tool in demonstrating member preferences in regard to public policy formulation.

5. **Issue monitoring**: Programs and services exist as stand-alone applications aimed at monitoring preselected issues. Issue monitoring can be a function that is contracted out or special software is used to scour the Internet for action on a particular subject. An example of issue monitoring might be on a topic such as water or air quality related to proposed federal regulations or Congressional initiatives. Issue monitoring can help association staff remain on top of a single issue or multiple issues without having to rely solely on internal resources as most services are fully automated. Additionally, issue monitoring can be shared in real-time with members too as another inducement or reason to be a member. This latter service can be accessed either on an association's website or smart device app.

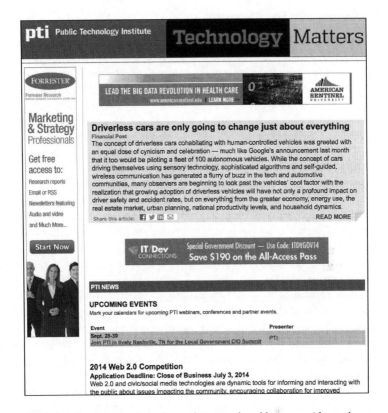

Figure 14.5 Sample of an association's newsletter produced by an outside vendor

Source: PTI.org

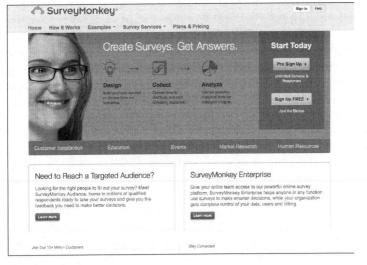

Figure 14.6 Example of a popular online survey company

Source: https://www.surveymonkey.com/

6. **Professional development, training, and education**: Many associa-tions provide some form of educational learning programs—be it profes-sional certifications, certificate programs, or issue development training. Many associations provide free or low-cost webinars that generally span an hour or less and focus on a particular topic of interest. Given the cost of time and money, associations now provide either or both online learning, self-paced programs, or live video programs. The technology behind today's learning platforms has become increasingly reasonable both in cost and functionality for even the smallest of associations.

7. **Meetings and exhibitions**: Few would disagree with having a strong preference for a face-to-face meeting; however, budget realities have cre-ated new opportunities for online video meetings, conferences, webi-nars, and even virtual trade shows. Some companies offer associations a highly visual online conference experience with avatars, virtual coffee stations that serve as a means of chatting with others, and/or virtual meeting rooms as well as interactive exhibits.

8. **Public relations**: Associations looking to issue a press release once had to rely on the US mail and messengers for immediate distribution. Today, nonprofit associations can choose among several different service pro-viders that offer writing, editing, and/or distribution of news releases. Outside public relation services also electronically distribute releases to thousands of contacts either selectively or en masse, and if required across the globe and in multiple languages. Another major benefit is that most newswire service providers also maintain and send out reports on each release showing who actually used the story and when.

9. **Job posting sites**: Associations have traditionally posted job listings that focus on their members or profession. It used to take a lot of staff time and resources in processing and finding job openings; however, today there are companies that will work with an association including the hosting and complete management of what appears to a member as the association's website. The company makes money directly through paid listings and advertisements, and the association receives a percentage and requires almost no association staff involvement.

There are many other web-based applications nonprofit associations have at their disposal, such as donor tracking, that tracks the amount a donor has given to a particular association or other organizations over a period of time. Having this information can help an association tailor targeted programs with the aim of further maximizing donations. The fact is that technology has forever altered the field of association management.

Today, even the smallest association can create amazing websites and leverage their message to millions of people from almost anywhere and be as effective as a larger association. While not every nonprofit organization can afford to have its own CIO, most have some designated person who is the go-to-technology staff person. In the case of the small association, the executive director

pti Public Technology Institute

PublicTechJobs.com

City and County Government Technology Jobs

JOB SEEKERS: Search career opportunities with local government-related employers. Post your resume anonymously if desired. Set up an alert so the newest openings are delivered straight to your inbox.

CITIES & COUNTIES: Advertise your open positions and browse our database of resumes. **PTI members receive a discount rate** when posting jobs. PTI continuously promotes these job listings across the Web.

Welcome to PublicTechJobs.com, the online career center of **Public Technology Institute** (PTI). This site connects local agencies with job seekers interested in technology related positions.

PublicTechJobs.com is intended for openings in IT and telecommunications, energy, environmental services, public safety and emergency management, public works and transportation, E-government and web services. For customer service, please contact our partner **JobTarget.**

Jobseekers

• Post an Anonymous Resume

Post your resume online today! Whether you're actively or passively seeking work, your online resume is your ticket to great job offers!

• View Jobs

Access the newest and freshest jobs available to professionals seeking employment.

• Personal Job Alert

Create Job Alerts and never let a matching job opportunity pass you by! New jobs that match your search criteria will be emailed directly to you.

• Create Jobseeker Account

Your personal jobseeker account will allow you to find jobs, manage your resumes,

Employers / Recruiters

• View the Resumes

Check out our resumes and only pay for the ones that interest you! We have access to some of the best professionals in the field.

• Post a Job

Reach the most qualified candidates by posting your job opening on our online Career Center.

• Products/Pricing

Regardless of your staffing needs or budget, we have a recruitment product that's right for your business.

• Create Employer Account

Quickly post job openings and manage your online recruiting efforts with ease by

Figure 14.7 Example of a vendor-provided job posting website

Source: http://www.publictechjobs.com/home/index.cfm?site_id=3710

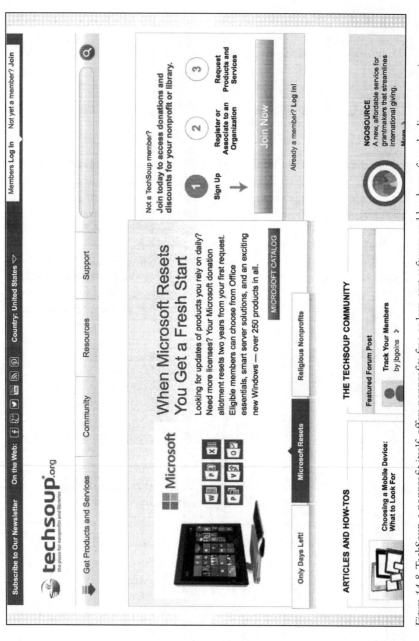

Figure 14.8 TechSoup, a nonprofit itself, offers nonprofits free or low-cost software and hardware from leading companies

Source: http://www.techsoup.org/

may perform the role of the CIO. However, it appears there is a growing trend to hire CIOs as part of the association management team in recognition of the importance technology plays in association management. Similar to government operations, information technology is growing in importance. The days when every department did its own thing independently are quickly disappearing only to be replaced by more comprehensive integrated technological systems that view the organization in its entirety.

Nonprofit Management and Technology Associations as a Service and Professional Development

As technology advancements have altered the nature of nonprofit management, so too have the many associations that have a stake in technology. There are hundreds if not thousands of organizations that represent certain segments of the information technology universe. Among this large number are companies and service providers that depend on the government markets, while others represent individuals who work in technology and more specifically federal, state, and local governments. Some are issue and policy-driven, while others are aimed at providing important information or promoting or helping individuals achieve greater skills or status. As this chapter is about technology and nonprofit management, it is important to have an appreciation of who and how associations are responding to and in some cases, shaping technology-related policies.

While not solely focused on government and technology, one of the oldest and largest professional technology associations is the Institute of Electrical and Electronics Engineers commonly referred to as IEEE (ieee.org). With its headquarters located in New Jersey, IEEE is the world's largest association for the advancement of technology. One does not need to be an engineer to benefit from being a member, and they have numerous government-facing communities and interest groups, and they develop important standards too.

Nonprofit Management Functions Having a Technology Component
(Either Software or Outside Service Provider)

• Seminars	• Training	• Community development
• Expos	• Professional development	• Education
• Research		• Recognition
• Information	• Public service	• Webinars
• Networking	• Fundraising	• Accreditation
• Advocacy	• Public policy	• Jobs listing and placement
• Services	• Lobbying	
• Certification	• Statistics	

Figure 14.9 Every nonprofit management function is supported by some form of technology

For those interested in what state CIOs are doing and the issues they are dealing with, the National Association of State Chief Information Officers would be the most likely and useful choice to visit (NASCIO.org). NACIO publishes useful reports and holds two major meetings each year. Likewise, for those interested in city and county technology developments, the Public Technology Institute (PTI) would be a good choice too (PTI.org). Both NASCIO and PTI have a strong history of working together and offer separate professional development programs and activities as well as publishing useful research and information. Another choice for local and state government might be the Government Management Information Systems Association (GMIS.org). While relying entirely on dedicated volunteers, GMIS has no professional staff of its own, but does have a strong presence via chapters in numerous states throughout the US.

There are numerous associations who focus on various portions of justice and public safety information systems as well as system interoperability such as the Institute for Justice Information Systems (IJIS.org). From police chiefs to fire chiefs, all have national associations that, among many pressing issues, examine and promote best practices when it comes to technology and innovation (IACP.org).

When it comes to transportation technology the Intelligent Transportation Society of America (ITS America) is the nation's largest organization dedicated to advancing the research, development, and deployment of Intelligent Transportation Systems (ITS) to improve the nation's surface transportation system (ITSA.org).

There are over fifty nonprofit associations, both trade and professional, that focus on broadband technology issues that are simply too numerous to list here, and there are several nonprofits that focus their efforts on cybersecurity too.

The American Council for Technology (ACT) provides a trusted forum where government employees (mostly federal) can enhance their organization and career. Its related partner, the Industry Advisory Council (IAC), promotes that fact and they fuse together to form ACT-IAC whose state purpose is to bring government and industry leaders together (actiac.org).

Often overlooked, a tremendous amount of professional development and networking occurs at the local level where there are nearly 100 local government technology associations. A sampling is as follows:

- **Colorado Government Association of Information Technology (CGAIT).** Its mission is to promote advances in information technology in order to facilitate networking, collaboration, cooperation, and education among government information technology leaders within Colorado, resulting in greater efficiencies and effectiveness for member organizations while enhancing services to Colorado communities and its citizens. This group is also very active in developing shared service among local governments too, see: http://www.colorado.gov/cs/Satellite/CGAIT2/CBON/1251580037933

- The **Florida Local Government Information Systems Association (FLGISA)** is very similar in mission and composition to NCLGISA and is also an organization for CIOs, IT Managers, and technology decision makers from the state's local government agencies, see: http://www.flgisa.org/
- The **Municipal Information Systems Association of California (MISAC)** is comprised of IT professionals working in cities and other local government agencies throughout California. It exists to promote understanding of the use and impact of information technology within local government agencies as a whole, and to strive for the advancement of information systems through professionalism and high ethical standards, see: http://www.misac.org/
- The **North Carolina Local Government Information Systems Association (NCLGISA)** is an organization for CIOs, IT managers, and technology decision makers from the state's local government agencies, whose purpose is to assist its members in sharing experiences and ideas and in undertaking cooperative efforts intended to achieve the association's goal of improving the effectiveness of local government information systems, see: http://www.nclgisa.org/
- The **Texas Association of Government Information Technology Managers (TAGITM)** began in 1978 as The Texas Association of Governmental Data Processing Managers (TAGDPM). It is a not-for-profit organization that provides information systems professionals a forum for generating ideas, sharing problems, and developing solutions. Its purpose is to enable the cities, counties, school districts, and appraisal districts within Texas to realize the full potential of automation benefits, see: http://www.tagitm.org/
- **State-wide Internet Portal Authority (SIPA).** The Statewide Internet Portal Authority (SIPA) was created in 2004 by an act of the Colorado State Legislature to provide efficient and effective e-government services for eligible governmental entities and citizens through the use of modern business practices and innovative technology solutions. Though not a nonprofit in the traditional sense, SIPA serves eligible governmental entities including state and local governments, school districts, and other eligible entities within the State of Colorado. SIPA provides among many services to local governments—PCI compliant credit card processing and clearing, website content management, application development and support—and signs master contracts on behalf of its members with companies such as Google Docs, and Salesforce.com, etc., see: http://www.colorado.gov

One of the more unusual technology focused associations is TechSoup. TechSoup is a nonprofit organization with a clear focus: connecting nonprofits, charities, foundations, or public libraries with discounted or donated technology products and services, plus the free learning resources staff need to make informed technology decisions and investments (TechSoup.org). Eligible nonprofits can receive special discounted rates (sometimes free) for popular software and hardware products and services.

In summary, nonprofit associations play an important role for government professionals, helping them to be better managers and leaders as well as stay abreast of new issues, polices, technologies, and innovations. Nonprofit associations have access to a wide variety of time and money-saving technologies that better enable them to leverage their meager resources and thus freeing up staff to become more effective and productive.

Discussion Questions

1. How many nonprofit associations do you belong to? Have you noticed any changes in the way the website functions or the way news and information is pushed to you?
2. What technology features do you value from a nonprofit you are familiar with? Why?
3. Assuming an interest in nonprofits, how might you apply some of the services mentioned in this chapter, why, and how?
4. As an individual or group project, research and identify at least one service provider company in both the internal as well as external applications.
5. Now that you have identified many good resources for enhancements for nonprofits, please list in order of importance which ones you believe are most significant, and briefly state why.

Further Reading

Cox, John ed. 2007. *Professional Practices in Association Management, Second Edition: The Essential Resource for Effective Management of Nonprofit Organizations,* ASAE, Washington, DC.

Hart, Ted, James M. Greenfield, Steve MacLaughlin, and Philip H. Geier Jr. 2010. *Internet Management for Nonprofits: Strategies, Tools and Trade Secrets.* John Wiley & Sons, Inc., Hoboken, NJ.

Kanter, Beth, Allison Fine, and Randi Zuckerberg. 2010. *The Networked Nonprofit: Connecting with Social Media to Drive Change.* Jossey-Bass, San Francisco, CA.

Ross, Holly, Katrin Verclas, and Alison Levine eds. 2009. *Managing Technology to Meet Your Mission: A Strategic Guide for Nonprofit Leaders.* Jossey-Bass, San Francisco, CA .

Digital Destinations

American Council for Technology-Industry Advisory Council (ACT-IAC). http://www.actiac.org

American Society of Association Executives (ASAE). http://www.asaecenter.org/Community/content.cfm?ItemNumber=15982

Colorado Government Association of Information Technology (CGAIT). http://www.colorado.gov/cs/Satellite/CGAIT2/CBON/1251580037933

Florida Local Government Information Systems Association (FLGISA). http://www.flgisa.org/

Government Management Information Systems Association (GMIS) http:// www.gmis.org

Institute for Justice Information Systems (IJIS). http://www.ijis.org
Institute of Electrical and Electronics Engineers (IEEE). http://www.ieee.org
Intelligent Transportation Society of America (ITS). http://www.itsa.org
International Association of Chiefs of Police (IACP). http://www.theiacp.org/ViewResult?SearchID=2361
International Association of Fire Chiefs (IAFC). http://www.iafc.org/Programs/content.cfm?ItemNumber=1425
Municipal Information Systems Association of California (MISAC). http://www.misac.org/
National Association for State Chief Information Officers (NASCIO). http://www.nacio.org
National Council of Nonprofits. http://www.councilofnonprofits.org/resources/resources-topic/technology
North Carolina Local Government Information Systems Association (NCLGISA). http://www.nclgisa.org/
Public Technology Institute (PTI). http://www.pti.org
State-wide Internet Portal Authority (SIPA). http://www.colorado.gov/cs/Satellite/SIPA-v2/SIPA2/1249666471452
Symantec Software. http://www.symantec.com/page.jsp?id=eic-email-discovery-software
TechSoup. http://www.techsoup.org
Texas Association of Government Information Technology Managers (TAGITM). http://www.tagitm.org/?page=TAGITM_History

15 Privacy, Trust, and Future Challenges

Welcome to the new digital world where nothing ever gets erased, being anonymous has largely disappeared, and privacy as we thought we knew it is being further eroded every single day. Machines read all of our emails and they know everything about us—where we live and with whom, what we purchase, where and how we travel, our habits both good and bad, our friends and our enemies, our expressions of love or anger, what we watch on TV, what kinds of movies we enjoy, what we like to read, what we eat and where we go out to eat, our political views, our pictures knowingly and unknowingly—and security cameras are everywhere. They can measure the intensity of our feelings through our Tweets and online chats/emails, they

Figure 15.1 The future of IT and government is limitless

know the medications we take, the cars we drive, the investments we make, the balance in our bank accounts, and outstanding loan balances. They know our credit scores, where and what time we were born, our unique fingerprints, the color of our eyes, the status of our relationships, our sexual orientation, and things about our personality that go way beyond any Myers-Briggs type personality test. They know what schools we attended, what courses we took (completed or not), what certifications and degrees we hold, and what grades were earned. They know about any awards and recognition we may have received, or disciplines we may have faced. Machines know who we call, and how often, they know who we email and what we are writing about. The machines can "listen" to our conversations. If we repeatedly say certain words we may be placed on special lists and get even greater scrutiny. Most troubling perhaps is the less known fact that much of what we see through browsing the Internet is never really erased, and for most people, merely pressing the delete button does not necessarily mean the message, photo, video, or document is really gone.

Yes, the "they" are largely machines that are programmed to know it all and mostly from the private sector with some government involvement. Most of this information is collected by banks, credit card companies, and marketing companies, which is perfectly legal, often with our permission. Most people ignore or agree to online terms of service agreements as well as "privacy statements" sent to us on a routine basis. For the most part, we blindly accept these "agreements" for fear of not having access to a particular product or service. Government agencies, in particular the federal government, enjoy rather broad legislative latitude regarding national security requirements with no required notice to citizens. Humans are just beginning to become aware of how far-reaching information technology has taken us—or away from us. Humans are beginning to recognize the connecting of some of the dots, understanding the patterns, connections, and so much more. In fact we largely are ignorant, not knowing what we do not know (Shark 2014).

Government agencies, in particular the federal government, enjoy rather broad legislative latitude regarding national security requirements with no required notice to citizens. Humans are just beginning to become aware of how far-reaching information technology has taken us—or away from us.

The future of information technology can be best described in terms of cumulative, if not explosive, growth; it has been evolutionary as opposed to revolutionary, but nevertheless dramatic and fast changing. The tools that public managers have available to them will only become smarter and more complex. There will undoubtedly be many dramatic changes in the way we manage technology and its impact on jobs and employment. However, with every technological advance there is a corresponding challenge. For example, larger more centralized systems will become an even bigger target for those who seek to do harm, and any intrusion can lead to greater harm as the larger and more complex the system, the more damage can be done. As governments place more technology infrastructure into cloud-based systems, there is the potential for disconnects and cyber issues that may be more difficult to detect. Information technology today has the ability to change how people and government communicate with one another and can provide a new paradigm for modern democracies—while at the same time challenging our system of representative government, as we know it.

Information technology today has the ability to change how people and government communicate with one another and can provide a new paradigm for modern democracies—while at the same time challenging our system of representative government, as we know it.

Figure 15.2 Governments and society are forever intertwined in cloud-based solutions

The famous psychiatrist Carl Jung is best known for his theory in which he describes the collective subconscious—where everyone is somehow connected through our subconsciousness. Similar to the collective subconscious, we now face the concept of the "collective digital conscious" (Shark 2014), better described as the "Internet of Things" (Pew Research 2014a) as well as the "Internet of Everything" (Cisco 2014), where everything is connected virtually in real-time through a multitude of digital platforms that include emails, social media, text messages, pictures, video, and even electronic signage. We are all connected directly and indirectly to a vast array of people, sensors, and machines. Public managers have their challenges trying to reach out to and connect with citizens who are bombarded with information overload from emails and other forms of digital communications. They are saturated with messages of all kinds— from friends, organizations, news outlets, commercial interests, all sending a message and seeking a response. To add to this dilemma, we can now receive messages from our home security systems, our cars, and refrigerators, with more to come.

Similar to the collective subconscious, we now face the concept of the "collective digital conscious" (Shark 2014), better described as the "Internet of Things" (Pew Research 2014a) as well as the "Internet of Everything" (Cisco 2014), where everything is connected virtually in real-time through a multitude of digital platforms that include emails, social media, text messages, pictures, video, and even electronic signage.

Technology and Representative Government

Today, information technology, and in particular, social media, present new challenges as well as opportunities regarding representative government. It used to be that the single most important function citizens could perform would be to elect leaders to represent them and their common collective interest. Newsletters would be sent on occasion to tell constituents what their representatives did for them. Aside from some localized town hall meetings, most people were asked to do one thing—and that was to vote. Today, with the growth of social media, there is hardly a politician without at least a Facebook presence and a Twitter account. Citizens are encouraged to contact and even send pictures to their elected representatives through social media and often they receive return messages that appear personalized.

This "instant" communication can unintentionally provide a false sense of personalized attention, and high expectations may turn into disappointment and disillusionment. For example, when emails are not responded to in a reasonable fashion, citizens may become dissatisfied. So the very promise of improved communications through technology can easily fall short of expectations if not implemented and maintained correctly. Citizens may have been given a false sense of "personalized" and immediate communication with their elected representatives. They may feel they have weighed in communicating directly to the President and perhaps prominent members of Congress who appear to be simply a click away; a rather false sense of exclusivity. In the end, with all the new technologies, citizens might begin to feel no one is listening to them. Because of instant communications and information found on the Internet and social media, some citizens are restless and want to do more than simply wait for the next election cycle to vote, they want to be become more actively engaged. Tools that can capture such citizen input are limited and are not commonly made available—just yet. We must also recognize that there is still a sizable portion (19 percent) of the US population that either does not have or does not want Internet connectivity (Pew Research 2014b).

> Information carried by the Internet can travel at just about the speed of light, and consequentially the speed of ignorance can travel just as fast which simply means that information and misinformation can travel at the same speed.

Information carried by the Internet can travel at just about the speed of light, and consequentially the speed of ignorance can travel just as fast which simply means that information and misinformation can travel at the same speed. There is also the issue of censorship that governments have attempted with varying success since the beginning of time. With the Internet, governments will face greater challenges when it comes to censorship (Schmidt and Cohen 2013). Take for example the 25th anniversary of what has been referred to as the Massacre at Tiananmen Square where hundreds (or more) of protestors were killed during protests in 1989 when the army marched in to stop a protest by unarmed civilians. Because no official records were kept, death toll estimates range from hundreds to thousands killed. In June 2014, China, a nation with a population of well over 1.3 billion, managed to censor and eliminate all information on the Internet regarding this event as if it never happened. Anyone in China searching for information about what happened in 1989 in Tiananmen Square would find absolutely nothing online, yet the rest of the world by comparison still had access to its complete history and related stories and information. Governments, especially totalitarian ones, will find it increasingly more difficult to repress, censor, or withhold data as the new information technologies, aided by the Internet, have evolved into a form of democratization of information that transcends government borders, both physical as well as digital (Schmidt and Cohen 2013).

Anonymity and Privacy as a Threat to Accountability and Democracy

When it comes to the Internet, it is still somewhat easy to remain anonymous thus leaving lots of room for mischief—either intentional or not. Our democracy was and is predicated on an educated citizenry and seeking the facts and truth online can be both frustrating and maddening. Perhaps the current federal trusted identity initiatives that are underway will develop in the way that they were set up to accomplish and that is to certify (verify) any sender of information through the Internet as a trusted source. This could open the door to greater online collaboration, research, and ultimately, online voting—and despite its many skeptics, it will surely happen at some point in time. With efforts underway to verify one's online identity, many citizens have a yearning to remain anonymous or want to maintain a greater sense of privacy than the new digital order provides.

For those who wish to do our country harm using technology to work against us, as was the case on September 11, 2001, we have awoken to the fact that cybersecurity has to be one of the nation's top and ongoing priorities. Cybersecurity must be a number one working priority at every level of government throughout the nation. However, in protecting our nation from cyber and network attacks, and preventing those who prey on innocent people while remaining anonymous, there are other consequences such as balancing the need for security with that of personal liberties that have been granted by tradition and law.

> In protecting our nation from cyber and network attacks, and preventing those who prey on innocent people while remaining anonymous, there are other consequences such as balancing the need for security with that of personal liberties that have been granted by tradition and law.

The concept of privacy has perhaps changed forever. Privacy has been regarded as a cherished American principal with protections found in the 4th Amendment that protect citizens from unreasonable searches. Remaining anonymous and maintaining privacy, as we knew it, will become increasingly difficult at best. However, the Internet, let alone electricity and broadband, did not exist when the Bill of Rights was passed, leaving much to our lawmakers and courts to decide how to apply both intent and context to our digital world. Today's enemies of the type of freedom that we cherish are far more sophisticated and dangerous.

Figure 15.3 Privacy and trust are becoming ever more important in a digital world

The nation's laws have been slow to catch up with the digital realities found in today's modern world. As an example, it is still unlawful to search someone's paper mail but this protection does not extend to email.

The nation's laws have been slow to catch up with the digital realities found in today's modern world. As an example, it is still unlawful to search someone's paper mail but this protection does not extend to email. Wiretap laws that pertain to calls made on landlines were extended to wireless devices, but with the passage of the Patriot Act in 2001, it is relatively easy for law enforcement agencies to obtain a warrant allowing them to eavesdrop on just about anyone *suspected* of being connected to a crime or possible terrorist activity. Mobile devices contain location-based information that makes tracking people as to their whereabouts relatively easy. Automatic license plate readers (ALPRs) can read, analyze, and store up to 2,000 license plates per hour thus allowing law enforcement officials to scan thousands of vehicles using license plates to seek out those with outstanding arrest warrants and tickets, and perhaps identifying suspicious behavior (see the ACLU website). Today 70 percent of law enforcement agencies are using ALPRs. People may be surprised to learn that such records were being stored as many as two or more years until this topic came to light mostly through the efforts of the American Civil Liberties Union, whose actions in turn caused public agencies to reconsider their data storage policies (see the ACLU website). Most troubling is the fact that license plate readers have been purchased by marketing companies that use this equipment to comb neighborhoods and shopping malls to seek out consumer patterns and behaviors. Video surveillance cameras are placed everywhere these days; some public and some private that remain largely unregulated. There are no uniform laws or regulations as to what can be shown, shared, or stored. The bold exception to this is child pornography where the laws are very strict with very stiff penalties.

Most citizens are largely unaware of just how much information they are yielding to others when they shop or browse online, post something on Facebook or YouTube, or simply upload or post a picture or video. Most Internet browsers, that serve as the gateway to the Internet, are constantly tracking us through a variety of sophisticated tracking cookies sending back useful and perhaps personal information to marketing companies. In many cases cookies are useful and enable us to return to websites that recognize us, display preferences that best match our interests, and in some cases bypass signing in, as they already know who we are. The problem is that some cookies can be associated with personally identifiable information (PII). Like a jigsaw puzzle, criminals, and digital stalkers and hackers alike can collect pieces of information from different places that when combined can reveal a larger picture of one's identity leading to someone's bank account and PII which could include an address, social security number, and health record information. One can easily be tracked with this information and one's identity could be stolen or one's house or office could be broken into. Imagine the true story of a person who posted their vacation travel itinerary online only to find upon their return their house was left nearly empty as thieves had plenty of time to take what they wanted without fear of being caught in the act. Of course technology makes it possible for ordinary citizens to install reasonably priced security cameras connected through the Internet that either record all the time or are activated by motion, and that someone could access remotely from almost any device while on vacation. Security systems are now offered that tie to our mobile smart devices providing real-time awareness of what is happening in one's home or office.

Government officials at all levels of government have many new tools at their disposal that enable them to collect an ever-growing amount of data aimed at providing better services to citizens, collecting better information leading to better performance and data-driven decisions, or preventing or solving crimes. It appears the growth of new technology products, many of which are available as consumer versions to the public, far outpaces the laws and regulations that normally have accompanied such offerings. Consumers can readily purchase tracking devices that, when placed

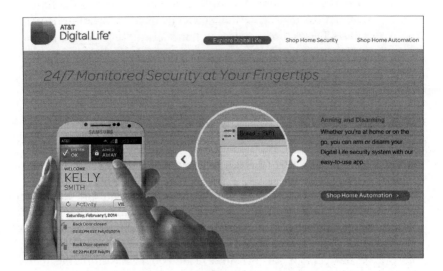

Figure 15.4 AT&T webpage for Digital Life app

Source: https://my-digitallife.att.com/content/learn/ExploreDigitalLife.html

in a vehicle, record the history of where a particular vehicle traveled. Or they can purchase devices that can track website searches, as well as see what someone was typing to someone else—or worse, capture someone's passwords and sign-in information. Miniature pen cameras equipped with a microphone that take pictures even in low light are on the market. Baby monitors have been replaced with sophisticated cameras that can remain hidden and are able to record events, including sound, when motion activates them—all of these products can be found online and some for even less than $200.

It appears the growth of new technology products, many of which are available as consumer versions to the public, far outpaces the laws and regulations that normally have accompanied such offerings.

Award-winning investigative reporter and author Julie Angwin writes about what she refers to as "America's surveillance economy" and provides a chilling and surprising account of her efforts to conceal her whereabouts and personal information and describes the great lengths she went to in order to conceal her identity, including spending patterns, etc. (All Tech Considered 2014). In the end she may have only been partially successful, but was it worth it? (Angwin 2014).

Public administrators will have a challenging time navigating the future as the temptations to exploit new technologies only increase with each new feature and advancement. Attention needs to be paid not only to the legal framework from which a particular technology operates, but also the requirement to balance the needs for information against the long-held values regarding privacy and protection.

Recognizing Recognition

One of the more powerful technologies to emerge can be found in the overall field of recognition. On the consumer front, we have no less than three speech recognition systems found in the most popular smartphone operating systems. Speech recognition gained much attention with the advent of Apple's Siri, one can request directions, make a reservation, or find out information such as the weather conditions, just by asking. This book was in part dictated using speech recognition software (that had amazing accuracy). It is not difficult to imagine how speech recognition might work with regard to other home or office appliances and equipment.

Facebook surprised its fans when they unveiled face recognition technology. In its current form, it has room for improvement, but it does a reasonable job recognizing faces. However, on the research front, Facebook's facial recognition research project named "DeepFace" claims to be as accurate as the human brain. DeepFace can look at two photos, and irrespective of lighting or angle, can say with 97.25 percent accuracy whether the photos contain the same face. Humans can perform the same task with 97.53 percent accuracy. DeepFace is currently just a research project, but in the future it will likely be used to help with facial recognition on Facebook's website (Simonite 2014). Facial recognition has its place in law enforcement too as the FBI has a billion dollar project underway called Next Generation Identification.

At this time the next-gen initiative only consists of pilot programs and is still in its early stages of development. When Google unveiled its Google Glass product, it was a beta test of a promising technology seeking practical applications and a new market to sell to. Yet, before formally becoming commercially available, many businesses had banned its use, fearful of its potential for spying or photographing in areas that are deemed off-limits. The glasses allow the wearer to see a small screen in the upper corner of the eye. By pressing small buttons, the user can bring up information, maps, and can accept incoming calls as well as view emails and text messages. Google Glass does not merely serve as a sleek information display, it is also a camera that can record everything that it "sees" and can store it on a mobile device. It doesn't take too much imagination to envision a policeman interviewing someone while at the same time a background search can be underway checking to see if there is any additional information on file.

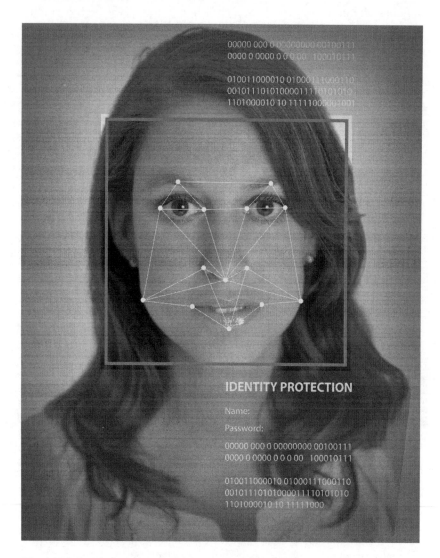

Figure 15.5 Facial recognition technologies will soon become an accepted form of identity verification

Perhaps a government worker in the field would benefit from having their hands free as they view records on their eyepiece while the system is feeding them real-time information that cannot be heard by anyone but the employee. Facial recognition could be used to bring up a person's record without a person having to log in or fill out an online form. This technology may be used someday to, at least in part, replace the need for passwords.

Today, so much is being recorded on video cameras in shopping centers, government buildings, traffic thoroughfares, and public places that it is only

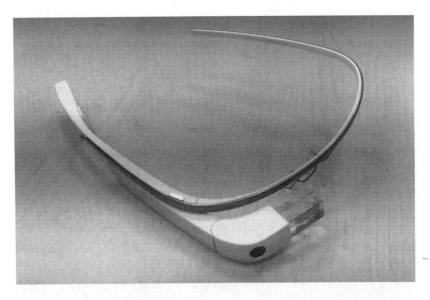

Figure 15.6 Google Glass wearable computer with optical head-mounted display

a matter of time before facial recognition will play a much greater role in public safety. After the bombing at the Boston Marathon in 2013, public safety officials reviewed hundreds of hours worth of video feeds—mostly from private security systems. While facial recognition did nothing to capture the culprits, the video footage they were able to obtain helped build the case against the perpetrators by providing visual evidence showing before and after pictures that placed the suspects at the scene of the bombings.

> Today, so much is being recorded on video cameras in shopping centers, government buildings, traffic thoroughfares, and public places that it is only a matter of time before facial recognition will play a much greater role in public safety.

In addition to facial recognition, and as mentioned earlier, 70 percent of local public safety agencies now utilize automatic license plate readers that can scan up to 2,000 plates per hour. The world of scanning and the world of recognition are converging and will provide new product and service offerings to both the general public as well as government agencies at all levels.

Perhaps the most dramatic example of recognition technology can be best illustrated by Amazon's announcement of its new smartphone that offers an innovative product search function called Firefly. Firefly contains the very

Figure 15.7 Video teaching is being deployed

latest in image, text, and audio-recognition technologies. With this technology, a user is able to scan and identify books, songs, movies, and TV programs in an instant, as well as make purchases by merely pointing a smart-phone camera on an item or its microphone to a piece of music. The most remarkable feature is that the system can presently scan and identify over 100 million items—and this is only a starting point.

Automation, Robotics, and Drones

The growth of automation in the workplace has caused many researchers and economists to be concerned about the number of jobs that are being eliminated due to automation. In the past, most agreed that while there has always been job displacement due to office automation, history has shown thus far that new businesses emerge as well as new jobs often requiring new skills that make up for the deficit (Atkinson 2014). Now, however, there is renewed concern that the speed of automation is occurring at a far greater rate, making it difficult at best to keep up job repleishment (Brynjolfsson, McAfee, Cummings 2014). Think what would happen to our society if by 2050 the unemployment rate were hovering at 50 percent? The new digital economy has become extremely efficient, shuttering retail storefronts or branch offices, where everything moves the consumer online. These

new digital companies enjoy a large and loyal customer base. H*
actual number of workers in 2014 employed by Amazon, G*
Facebook, and Netflix together is merely 177,740—these are major *
panies but they only employ a miniscule fraction of the current US workforce (Shark 2014).

Automation has moved into the area of robots and unmanned vehicles,
often referred to as drones. Robots can now be found in the classroom helping teachers and students alike (Online Degrees 2014).

Company	Employed in 2013
Amazon	88,400
Google	47,000
eBay	33,500
Facebook	6,818
Netflix	2,022
TOTAL	177,740

Figure 15.8 Number of employed by the five major digital companies in 2013

Source: Shark 2014

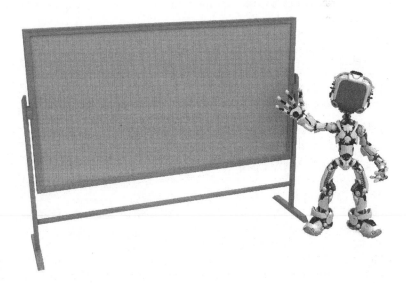

Figure 15.9 Robots are working their way into the classroom as a new tool for improved
teaching and learning

Robots are used to augment human teachers as well as challenge students to work on projects that actually create robots too. Robots assemble cars, pick inventory off shelves for delivery, and weld parts of airplanes. Robotics has become a growing field in most schools of engineering as the pursuit of efficiency and speed drives innovation faster and further. The most notable advances in robotics are occurring in the field of miniaturization and medicine where people can take a pill that is a highly sophisticated sensor system equipped with a camera. This micro-sized, camera provides a doctor with a unique internal, noninvasive view of exactly what is going on in someone's body firsthand, such as clogged arteries or a faulty heart valve. These new robotic miniature pills can also be used to inject a particular dose at the exact spot such as on-contact radiation or chemical treatment.

Robots are not typically thought of as unmanned vehicles to prowl the oceans or scan the skies. Congress has requested that the Federal Aviation Administration draw up regulations that govern unmanned flying vehicles or drones by 2015. With so much attention directed at our nation's war effort in using drones, there is a growing market for domestic applications and many are impatient and wanting to start deployment sooner than later. Imagine a farmer waking up and launching a drone to scour his field to check on the condition of his crops or his livestock. Traffic reporters can fly drones more cost effectively than having to maintain equipment and crew for helicopters or small planes. State police can fly drones to check on road conditions and report accidents. Realtors want to use drones for house inspections and home sales promotion adding aerial views to the mix, while Amazon has been experimenting with rural home delivery using drones. It may not be too far into the future that our pizza will be delivered

- Animal control
- Bomb site protection and removal
- Farming (checking crops, livestock, weather)
- Inspections
- Mapping
- Pest control
- Real-estate marketing promotion and inspections
- Situational awareness
- Surveying
- Transportation—(track and road conditions)
- Weather
- Other

- Border control
- Deliveries
- Hazardous and radio active monitoring and removal (hazmat)
- Land usage
- New reporting
- Public safety
- School safety (monitoring the perimeter)
- Sports coverage
- Traffic control and monitoring
- Utilities management
- Zoning

Figure 15.10 Unmanned vehicle usage examples

by drones too. In the hobby environment, a small remote controlled heli-copter with flashing lights may cost fifteen dollars while other more sophis-ticated machines could cost several hundred to several thousand dollars. Mounted with a small HD camera, drones have many incredible uses for hobbyists and commercial applications, as well as government operations.

Of course two major issues arise when it comes to civilian use of drones. First and foremost is the issue of safety. Since 2001 *The Washington Post* reported that there have been over 400 crashes of military drones, some occurring in the US (Whitlock 2014). Where will drones be allowed to take off and land, under what conditions, what will be the qualifications for those who fly them, what areas will be restricted, and how will unmanned and manned flight be coordinated? Finally, who will bear the liability if some-thing goes wrong? The second major issue will, of course, be privacy. What protections can one expect from unmanned vehicles with high definition cameras, some with microphones? Will drones be able to take pictures of one's house without permission, or take pictures of people in their private backyards? If cameras are in use, in the case of law enforcement, how long can pictures and videos be kept? Public managers have much to do by way of planning for what certainly will be an unstoppable technology and service. Finally, what will the regulatory environment look like? Besides the federal government, what will the role of state and local jurisdictions be in terms of regulations? In one small Colorado town, a law that would have allowed citi-zens to shoot down drones was defeated and this was not the first attempt or even the first city to try and do so. While encouraging the shooting down of drones sounds seems somewhat reckless and crazy, it underscores the frustra-tions of many people who view drones as simply further invasion of privacy (Oldham 2014).

Sensing Sensors

When discussing the Internet of Things, the focus has been on the non-people side where sensors will grow and be everywhere. Today, it is not uncommon to have traffic sensors that detect the speed and volume of traffic. In major cities censors are strategically placed that can sense a chemical or biological attack. Some cities deploy sensors to measure air or water samples. Sensors themselves are not new, but connecting them through the Internet is what makes sensors more interesting. As a result they can also serve in a two-way capacity, where we can remotely adjust our thermostats, water heaters, cooling and heating systems, lights, feed our pets, and allow for door access. We can record our favorite shows and movies without being home. New refrigerators are being equipped with sensors that can alert someone when they are low on certain types of food like milk or juice. Likewise, sensors can be deployed in inventory control systems alerting managers when the stock of any item runs low, or alert authorities of suspicious movement in a given area. Smart sensors are becoming part of our new digital ecosystem, thus providing enhancements to our original five senses, and operate continuously, even when we sleep or are away. But sensors can work against us when they are used to stalk, track, and invade our privacy. Sensors, while convenient and efficient, also provide new targets of opportunity to criminals and terrorists alike that can quite possibly turn our sensors against us. If in the wrong hands, sensors could possibly be taken over and provide false readings or cause a system to overheat or blow up or something worse. In the end, sensors require a great deal of scrutiny when connected to mission-critical systems and infrastructure and must be included in any active cybersecurity monitoring process.

> Smart sensors are becoming part of our new digital ecosystem, thus providing enhancements to our original five senses and operate continuously, even when we sleep or are away. But sensors can work against us when they are used to stalk, track, and invade our privacy.

Wearables

In many ways the future is truly now as we are dazzled every day with some new technological development. The concept of wearables will most likely continue to expand into watches and wristbands that measure our heart rate, blood pressure, glucose readings, and body temperature and that are displayed and stored on our smart devices. Some companies are experimenting with skin-applied patches that are designed to sense when a particular dosage should be dispensed directly through the skin. Biometrics, coupled with smaller and smaller sensors that communicate with our smart devices, will present both opportunities and challenges for public managers. First, who will pay for this new technology, and how do we protect those who can't afford it? Second, there will be a need to further protect citizen privacy and data wherever it is stored, which will require new safeguards.

Wearables have actually been around for over a decade but known by different names such as electronic bracelets/anklets that keep track of prisoners' whereabouts, or part of an at-home detention system that limits one's ability to leave a certain area. They have also taken the form of radio frequency information devices better known as RFID. RFID technology is used in many situations where tracking of an individual is important. This technology is also used in our modern passports or inventory control. When tied to a shoelace, runners crossing the finish line can be instantly identified with their names and time of completion at a running event or marathon.

Not counting Google Glass, wearable cameras have been a growing sensation among active sports crowd where they are widely used by surfers, bikers, mountain climbers, skiers, skydivers, and underwater divers. GoPro is the leading manufacturer in this growing market selling small, light, and high definition video cameras (Agrawal 2014).

3D Printers

Three-dimensional printers are gaining attention in the consumer environment with a few boutique demonstration stores in major cities that began opening in 2013. Customers can make a bracelet and a few other choice objects that demonstrate how the 3D printing process works. Office supply company Staples announced in 2014 that some of its stores would feature 3D printing. Unlike a traditional printer that uses ink, 3D printers are highly sophisticated machines that create an object by adding layers of a special resin that can turn into a bracelet or smartphone case, or to the more serious 3D produced weapon (gun) or a body part such as an ear. Someone designs the product online and the highly sophisticated software turns it into a 3D object. This emerging technology holds the potential to make critical machine parts in the field as well as making replacement body parts in remote locations where speed and access are critical. 3D printing can also be used to create lifelike 3D models that can be used in law enforcement situations as well as for urban planning. Like so many new technologies, public mangers and lawmakers are struggling to better understand the implications of this new technology as well as the need for a regulatory structure if necessary.

Figure 15.11 Architect using 3D printer in office

Intelligent Transportation

Many advances in technology and transportation will continue to develop. The State of California is poised to be the first state in the nation to adopt a law making self-driving cars possible. The idea behind self-driving cars is to prevent or reduce accidents. If self-driving cars become widespread, there may be less need for people to own their own vehicles as the expense of ownership may force people to reconsider owning versus the many new options that are either now available or will be. Ride sharing is becoming more popular in urban settings where you can set up an account in advance and look online for a car near you and reserve it—all online. In this scenario, after a reservation is made, one merely goes to the vehicle and uses a code to open the door and you pay for only the time needed.

On the state and local government side, police have been experimenting with wearable cameras that capture actions as seen by an officer and that can be very valuable in training and acquiring important evidence. Miniature cameras with microphones can be mounted as part of a pair of glasses or on a vest.

The same is true for bike sharing where many cities have allowed certain franchises to provide bike-sharing outlets through key areas of the city with renters going online and reserving and renting as needed.

Figure 15.12 Example of bike sharing

Cities and states are struggling to rewrite regulations governing traditional taxi car services. Companies like Uber and Lyft offer new and convenient ways to hail a ride by simply setting up an account in advance online and then using their free app to do the rest. The app allows the customer to set the pickup location and once the button is pressed, a driver is identified, along with the driver's picture and car description. The app also shows the route the car is taking in getting to the customer. When the trip is complete, there is no physical exchange of money as it is automatically paid by a credit card of choice on file (there can be more than one) and the customer receives a detailed receipt instantly. Finally, there is a rating system that both the driver and customer can use to rate and evaluate each other as a form of quality control.

As one can imagine the regular cab drivers have been strongly opposed to these online dispatching services claiming that these new entrants are not required to have the same insurance requirements and do not have to go through the same background checks. In 2014, the State of Virginia DMV issued a ban on Uber and Lyft claiming it needed time to review current rules and possibly change its regulations. Many cities have issued bans or moritoriums despite the fact that those who use these services have been very satisfied. This is a good example of how technology can often challenge administrative and regulatory structures where public managers have been totally unprepared.

Technology is also changing the cars we own and drive with new HD back-up cameras, lane change warning systems, self-parking car systems, and comprehensive accident avoidance systems. Our car and truck cabins are now equipped with sophisticated navigation and entertainment systems with hands-free and speech recognition capabilities. Luxury cars can sense an accident and automatically call for help.

All electric vehicles and hybrids are very much part of the intelligent transportation. While technology is certainly an important factor so is the need for new regulations and zoning. For example, as a market incentive, can or should hybrids and electric-only vehicles receive special treatment regarding local property taxes or receive special treatment on high occupancy (HOV) lanes? Will a city as well as private parking lots offer an incentive to provide special higher voltage charging stations in convenient locations?

> All electric vehicles and hybrids are very much part of the intelligent transportation market. While technology is certainly an important factor so is the need for new regulations and zoning.

Any discussion about the future needs to include a discussion about mass transit intelligent transportation systems.

In order to attract and keep customers, our buses and trains need to be looked at in a completely different way. Despite the many improvements to mass transit, there is no system in the US that can exist or operate without heavy government subsidies. If urban planners are truly committed to getting more cars off the streets and people into public transportation more has to be done, and technology can and will certainly play a strong role. We seem to know what people don't like about public transportation as seen in the following list, at least half of which being technology-related.

What We Dislike About Public Transportation

- Lack of reliable real-time schedule signage.
- Unreliable (or too complicated) real-time bus or train location apps.
- Bad schedules.
- Wrong stops.
- Dirty buses or trains.
- Complicated schedules requiring transfers.
- Complicated fare structures.
- Unpredictable lateness.
- Over crowdedness.
- Poor or no Wi-Fi.
- Unprotected stations and stops.
- Uncomfortable seats.
- Complicated maps.
- Poor lighting.
- Issues of safety.
- Other.

Urban planners and public works departments have many planning tools such as GIS mapping, automated vehicle location tracking and monitoring systems, real-time signage, and lane direction change systems as well as controlling traffic signals based on time of day and traffic conditions. Many road improvements have been paid in full or in part with federal funds which, aside from special earmarks and specialized legislation, come from the Highway Trust Fund with revenues coming largely from fuel taxes. As cars become even more fuel efficient or electric cars and hybrids become more popular the revenue base will most likely go down while the need for infrastructure continues to rise. One thing is clear, technology and transportation are inextricably intertwined when it comes to public management.

Future of Currency (Bitcoin)

The concept of money as a medium of exchange is undergoing a transformation. With credit card usage at all time historic highs, it would seem that little could change except the fees paid one way or another. However, with credit card theft on the rise, the US has been slow to convert its plastic (or metal in some cases) cards to include a security chip making theft more difficult. Europe and Asia began to adopt this new pin and chip card technology a number of years ago (Klernan 2014).

The Target store hack along with some other well-known thefts have caused US credit card companies to speed up the introduction of smarter and more secure credit and debit cards sooner. While many cards remain free to the consumer, merchants continue to pay a fee on every transaction. Escalating transaction fees, and the quest to remain anonymous, are contributing factors that led to the birth of Bitcoin. While many countries have discouraged or banned the use of Bitcoin as a form of payment, the US has been surprisingly adaptive.

Bitcoin began in 2009 with the creation of open source software. Payments travel to and from individuals without a central depository, relying instead on a complicated series of networks that track payments and update each of the participating systems (Wikipedia 2014). While it has its advantages, it also has its downsides. First, it remains unregulated which some might find as an advantage. This also means there are few protections for the consumer.

Figure 15.13 Digital currency is expanding and becoming more accepted

Second, Bitcoins are highly speculative for some hoping to make money on the exchange of Bitcoins. There have been a few high-profile arrests with people trying to hide assets or launder money. Third, Bitcoin is still in its infancy and despite some compelling advantages, its acceptance is still quite limited but growing (Chokun 2014). To date the following companies all accept Bitcoins– Overstock, Amazon, Target, CVS, and Zappos. The US Treasury and Internal Revenue Service Departments are now exploring how and under what circumstances Bitcoins may be accepted in the future.

Snowden, Privacy, and Trust

This brief journey in technology and public management concludes with the beginning topic of this chapter—privacy and trust. Society has the tools at its disposal to potentially erode civil liberties in the name of the common good and national security. The US has always stood out as a nation of laws that goes to great lengths to protect civil liberties—by ensuring a suspect is read his or her Miranda rights or considering a suspect innocent until proven guilty. Law enforcement officials are required to obtain a search warrant in order to search one's home or property.

Immediately following the terrorist attacks of September 11, 2001, the public was concerned about government's ability to protect the people and there was general consensus that the nation's surveillance needed to be reviewed and perhaps modified. This of course led to the passage of the Patriot Act that was signed into law in 2001 and was several hundred pages in length. The Patriot Act was passed with strong bipartisan support and with the goal of arming law enforcement with new tools to detect and prevent terrorism (see Justice.gov). The Act has been amended, modified, and updated to reflect new technologies and new types of threats. For example, the Act now allows victims of computer hacking to request law enforcement assistance in monitoring the "trespassers" on their computers. This change made the law technology-neutral; it placed electronic trespassers on the same footing as physical trespassers. Now, hacking victims can seek law enforcement assistance to combat hackers, just as burglary victims have been able to invite officers into their homes to catch burglars. While the Patriot Act is deemed somewhat controversial, its basic principles endure to this day.

The Foreign Intelligence Surveillance Act of 1976 (FISA) was passed to provide procedures for the physical and electronic surveillance and collection of "foreign intelligence information" between "foreign powers" and "agents of foreign powers" which may include American citizens and permanent residents suspected of espionage or terrorism. Since 9/11 the Act has been amended many times. This Act was hardly noticed until it was revealed that the Bush administration authorized warrantless domestic wiretapping in 2005 and perhaps earlier than that. The FISA Act also created the Foreign

Intelligence Surveillance Court (FISC), which is even less known and understood than the Act itself. Until June 2013, the National Security Agency was known to be a huge and extremely secret intelligence gathering body, which focuses on foreign intelligence gathering and terrorist monitoring and prevention.

In June 2013, a government contractor who once worked for the CIA and NSA named Edward Snowden, decided on his own to try and put a stop to what he believed was unlawful and unconstitutional use and abuse of the nation's intelligence gathering agency (NSA). He single-handedly stole thousands of top-secret documents that seem to prove his allegations. The actual number of documents stolen is still unclear and Snowden, a fugitive from the US legal system, at the time of this writing is in exile in Moscow. His disclosures, made public through a few select news gathering organizations, have been considered the most significant leak in US history. Since June 2013, the public has become aware of high-tech surveillance programs with names like Five Eyes, Boundless Informant, PRISM, XKeyscore to name just a few.

For the first time, it was brought to light that the federal government, with the best of intentions regarding safeguarding the nation, had undertaken massive surveillance of US citizens at home. It was also found to be both widespread and massive, often knowingly and unknowingly, tapping into the private sector's databases. Officials at NSA, however, point out that they are not listening to or recording phone conversations, but instead they are collecting metadata. In such programs, metadata is simply data about data which in this instance could be a collection of data that stores phone numbers, length of a call, the frequency of calls to a particular number, especially outside of the US, time of day calls are made, etc. Adding to the controversy, while some companies have cooperated with NSA, others did not and have consequently been hacked into by the US federal government. The controversy is far from over as in June 2014, the Foreign Intelligence Surveillance Court allowed the NSA to continue to collect phone records, mostly in the form of metadata of people in the US, while lawmakers consider new legislation that might block such action in the future.

Americans have always been wary of the concentration of power to any one branch of government, concerned about the limits of government, and interested in preserving liberty and privacy. At the heart of the on-going debate is the sanctity of trust in government. Whether one regards Snowden as a hero or a traitor (or both) the public trust in government has been seriously damaged. In the case of striving to fulfill a mandate to better protect citizens against terrorism and criminal activities, the technology to do so simply grew more sophisticated and perhaps took on a life of its own. As long as things were kept secret and out of the public view, no harm would be done. Hence, while the issues related to the Snowden disclosures are sorted out, the issues of internal security, whistle-blowing policies, ethics, administrative policy, and technology have been challenged as never before. Public managers to this day still do not feel as comfortable with technology or managing technology as they do with other forms of management areas. Regardless how one ultimately views Snowden's actions, what he did should serve as a strong warning regarding the dangers that exist when staff at any level dealing with sensitive information are allowed to operate with little to no oversight. How is it possible for one individual to have the capacity to cause so much damage to a country in order to prove a point? As a nation of laws, there must be a better way for self-expression balanced with the need for protecting a nation's intelligence gathering apparatus.

> Americans have always been wary of the concentration of power to any one branch of government, concerned about the limits of government, and interested in preserving liberty and privacy. At the heart of the on-going debate is the sanctity of trust in government.

Privacy, the Digital Age, and the Supreme Court

In late June 2014, the Supreme Court ruled that cell phones can no longer be searched without a warrant. As remarkable as the decision itself was, the fact is this, it was a rare ruling where the justices agreed unanimously that a person's cell phone conatins a wealth of personal information. Writing as the lead voice, Chief Justice Roberts stated,

> An Internet search and browsing history can be found on an Internet-enabled phone and could reveal an individual's private interests or concerns—perhaps a search for certain symptoms of disease, coupled with frequent visits to WebMD. Data on a cell phone can also reveal where a person has been. Historic location information is a standard feature on many smartphones and can reconstruct someone's specific movements down to the minute, not only around town but also within a particular building.

This ruling was seen as a first step in attempting to create laws that recognize the new digital world in which we all reside and in particular a true victory for citizens and privacy.

Trust and the Cost and Return of Technology in Public Management

Trust is also about what we spend and how we spend money on information technology. Federal, state, and local IT spending is over $140 billion dollars per year—not counting the military. Over the past dozen years there have been many notable and colossal failures of mostly federal systems that either cost far more than planned or had to be scrapped or completely restarted because they never worked as they should. It appears that while each case is unique, there are some common threads which include: overly ambitious goals and objectives, poor upfront planning and follow-through, lack of project management discipline, poor oversight and reporting, lack of strong overall leadership at all levels, poor communication, and dealing with the politics of government budgeting. One can only hope that with improved measurement and planning tools, as well as executive training and development, future projects will achieve a better track record for success. Many government workers who are retiring or nearing retirement were thrust into the world of information technology with little or no training. Government workers merely adjusted to the new realities of IT and did a remarkable job considering the lack of precedence. The hope is that new public managers fill in the gaps and bring their more natural proclivities to technology, resulting in a vast improvement in technology and public management as they become better digital mechanics and architects.

Most federal government agencies have suffered through many years of technology mismanagement as well as severe budget cuts making it very difficult to catch up let alone innovate. The Social Security Administration might have improved their public-facing online presence, but in the background there are thousands of computers that rely on an ancient programming language that is becoming extinct. IRS Comissioner John Koskinen, testifying at a politically-charged Congressional hearing in June 2014, stated "I fondly refer to our IT system as a Model T with a very nice GPS system and a sound system and a redone engine, but it's still a Model T" (Carroll 2014). The agency claims it needs $400 to $500 million for IT modernization.

> The Social Security Administration might have improved their public-facing online presence, but in the background there are thousands of computers that rely on an ancient programming language that is becoming extinct.

Not all federal agencies are dealing with information technology in the same fashion. In a small town in Pennsylvania, 230 feet below the surface, approximately 600 government workers who work for the Office of Personel Management carry out their tasks each day in an old limestone mine. Apparently the government has taken advantage of caves where the internal atmosphere is conducive to preserving paper files along with their file cabinets.

Despite the Paperwork Reduction Act, paper files still exist across the nation (Fahrenthold 2014). Another example is the Veterans Administration where, for all the modernization of its health records system, it still has an alarming time-consuming backlog of paper files. In at least one location, the paper files were so heavy it led to a warning that the weight of the paper files created a safety hazard as the load exceeded the building's capacity (Tobia 2013).

The GSA has been critical when it comes to IT spending and security and all of this leads to the reduction of public worker morale, and a public who is beginning to think that government can't ever get it right. In looking ahead to the future, one can only hope that greater emphasis is placed on all public managers to better manage and maintain information technology systems. There is a need for better and more frequent staff training and development at all levels, and there is the need for vastly improved performance measurement of IT. Finally, there is a great need for improved technology leadership at all levels of government.

Discussion Questions

1. To what extent is privacy in the new digital age important to you? Please explain.
2. Is government doing enough to protect privacy and if not what more can and should, in your opinion, be done?
3. Have you or your organization been victimized by a security breach or hack? If yes, what have you learned from the experience?
4. What does the concept of Internet of Things mean to you personally and to your organization?
5. Do you agree that technology has or can change representative government? Please explain and what do you see as the advantages and disadvantages?
6. Do you currently use any wearables? If not, might you in the near future? What would you be looking for in terms of functionality?
7. What do you see as the role of government in better managing public transportation?
8. Are you generally optimistic or pessimistic about the growth of information technology and public management?
9. Can you list the top five challenges that public managers will face in the next five years or more?
10. What area of technology and public management interested you the most, why?
11. Given what you know and understand, do you regard Edward Snowden as a hero or a traitor? Why?
12. What can government agencies do in order to better protect against either disgruntled employees or those who wish to take matters into their own hands?

References

Agrawal, Tanya. 2014. "Action Camera-maker GoPro Makes Picture-perfect Debut." *Chicago Tribune*. Accessed October 17, 2014. http://www.chicagotribune.com/business/sns-rt-us-gopro-ipo-20140625,0,3121592.story.

All Tech Considered. 2014. "If You Think You're Anonymous Online, Think Again." Accessed October 17, 2014. http://www.npr.org/blogs/alltechconsidered/2014/02/24/282061990/if-you-think-youre-anonymous-online-think-again.

Angwin, Julia. 2014. *Dragnet Nation*. Macmillan Publishers, New York.

Atkinson, Robert D. 2014. *Choosing A Future: "The Second Machine Age" Review*. Accessed October 17, 2014. ITIF, Washington, DC. http://www.itif.org/publications/choosing-future-second-machine-age-review.

Brynjolfsson, Erik, Andrew McAfee, and Jeff Cummings. 2014. *The Second Machine Age*. W.W. Norton & Company, New York.

Carroll, Rebecca. 2014. "IRS Chief Compares Agency's IT System to a Model T." Nextgov. Accessed October 17, 2014. http://www.nextgov.com/cio-briefing/2014/06/irs-chief-compares-agencys-it-system-model-t/86932/?oref=nextgov_today_nl.

Chokun, Jonas. 2014. "Who Accepts Bitcoins As Payment? List of Companies, Stores, Shops." BitcoinValues.net. Accessed October 17, 2014. http://www.bitcoinvalues.net/who-accepts-bitcoins-payment-companies-stores-take-bitcoins.html.

Cisco. 2014. *The Internet of Everything*. Accessed October 17, 2014. http://www.cisco.com/web/about/ac79/innov/IoE.html.

Fahrenthold, David. 2014. "Sinkhole of Bureaucracy." *The Washington Post*. Accessed October 17, 2014. http://www.washingtonpost.com/sf/national/2014/03/22/sinkhole-of-bureaucracy/.

Klernan, John. 2014. "Chip-and-PIN vs. Chip-and-Signature." CarHub. Accessed October 17, 2014. http://www.cardhub.com/edu/chip-and-pin-vs-chip-and-signature/.

Oldham, Jennifer. 2014. "Colorado Town Rejects Plan to Let Residents Shoot Drones." *Bloomberg News*. Accessed October 17, 2014. http://www.bloomberg.com/news/2014-04-02/colorado-town-rejects-plan-to-let-residents-shoot-drones.html.

Online Degrees. 2014. "The RUBI Project: Preschoolers and Autistic Children Benefit from Teacher Robots." Accessed October 17, 2014. http://www.onlinedegrees.org/the-rubi-project-preschoolers-and-autistic-children-benefit-from-teacher-robots/.

Pew Research Internet Project. 2014a. "The Internet of Things Will Thrive by 2025." Accessed October 17, 2014. http://www.pewinternet.org/2014/05/14/internet-of-things/.

Pew Research Internet Project. 2014b. "Internet Use Over Time." Accessed October 17, 2014. http://www.pewinternet.org/data-trend/internet-use/internet-use-over-time/.

Schmidt, Eric and Jared Cohen. 2013. *The New Digital Age: Reshaping the Future of People, Nations and Business*. Vintage, New York.

Shark, Alan R. 2014. From class lecture, Rutgers University. March–April.

Simonite, Tom. 2014. "Facebook Creates Software That Matches Faces Almost as Well as You Do." Accessed October 17, 2014. http://www.technologyreview.com/news/525586/facebook-creates-software-that-matches-faces-almost-as-well-as-you-do/.

Tobia, P.J. 2013. "Veterans Affairs Backlog Files Stacked So High, They Posed Safety Risk to Staff." *PBS Newshour* (blog), April 2. Accessed October 17, 2014. http://www.pbs.org/newshour/rundown/veterans-affairs-backlog-files-were-stacked-so-high-they-posed-a-safety-risk-to-va-staff-1/.

Whitlock, Craig. 2014. "When Drones Fall From The Sky." *The Washington Post.* Accessed October 17, 2014. http://www.washingtonpost.com/sf/investigative/2014/06/20/when-drones-fall-from-the-sky/.

Wikipedia. 2014. "Bitcoin." Last modified June 30. http://en.wikipedia.org/wiki/Bitcoin.

Further Reading

Greenwald, Glenn. 2014. *No Place to Hide: Edward Snowden, the NSA, and the US Surveillance State.* Metropolitan Books, New York.

Kellmereit, Daniel and Daniel Obodovski. 2013. *The Silent Intelligence: The Internet of Things.* DND Ventures LLC, San Francisco, CA.

Pew Research Center. 2014. *The Web at 25 in the US.* Accessed October 17, 2014. http://www.pewinternet.org/files/2014/02/PIP_25th-anniversary-of-the-Web_0227141.pdf.

Scoble, Robert and Shel Israel. 2014. *Age of Context: Mobile, Sensors, Data and the Future of Privacy.* CreateSpace, Charleston, SC.

Shark, Alan R., Sylviane Toporkoff, and Sebastien Levy. 2014. *Smart Cities for a Bright Sustainable Future—A Global Perspective.* Public Technologies Institute and ITEMS International, Alexandria, VA.

Townsend, Anthony M. 2013. *Smart Cities: Big Data, Civic Hackers, and the Quest for a New Utopia.* W.W. Norton & Company, New York.

Digital Destinations

American Civil Liberties Union (ACLU). https://www.aclu.org/alpr
———. https://www.aclu.org/protecting-civil-liberties-digital-age
American Council for Technology-Industry Advisory Council (ACT-IAC). http://www.actiac.org
Forbes Future Tech. http://www.forbes.com/intelligent-technology/
Future Technology. http://itechfuture.com/
Justice.gov. http://www.justice.gov/archive/ll/highlights.htm
National Assciation of State Chief Information Officers (NASCIO). www.nascio.org
Pew Research Internet Project http://www.pewinternet.org/2014/04/17/us-views-of-technology-and-the-future/
Public Technology Institute (PTI). www.pti.org
White House. http://www.whitehouse.gov/blog/2014/01/23/big-data-and-future-privacy
http://www.whitehouse.gov/administration/eop/ostp
———. http://www.whitehouse.gov/issues/technology/

Index

Page numbers in *italics* refer to figures.